D0340670

Withdrawn

12/8/10
$28.00
B+T

☆5
14 day

12/10

WILL EISNER

BY THE SAME AUTHOR

Reasons to Believe: New Voices in American Fiction

Creative Conversations: The Writer's Complete Guide to Conducting Interviews

Dharma Lion: A Critical Biography of Allen Ginsberg

Crossroads: The Life and Music of Eric Clapton

There but for Fortune: The Life of Phil Ochs

Francis Ford Coppola: A Filmmaker's Life

Family Business: Selected Letters Between a Father and Son,
by Allen and Louis Ginsberg (editor)

Mighty Fitz: The Sinking of the Edmund Fitzgerald

Mr. Basketball: George Mikan, the Minneapolis Lakers,
and the Birth of the NBA

Wreck of the Carl D.: *A True Story of Loss, Survival, and Rescue at Sea*

WILL EISNER

A Dreamer's Life in Comics

Michael Schumacher

BLOOMSBURY

NEW YORK • BERLIN • LONDON

Copyright © 2010 by Michael Schumacher

All rights reserved. No part of this book may be used or reproduced in any
manner whatsoever without written permission from the publisher except in the
case of brief quotations embodied in critical articles or reviews. For information
address Bloomsbury USA, 175 Fifth Avenue, New York, NY 10010.

Published by Bloomsbury USA, New York

All papers used by Bloomsbury USA are natural, recyclable products made from
wood grown in well-managed forests. The manufacturing processes conform to
the environmental regulations of the country of origin.

Library of Congress Cataloging-in-Publication Data

Schumacher, Michael.
Will Eisner : a dreamer's life in comics / Michael Schumacher.
p.   cm.
Includes bibliographical references and index.
ISBN 978-1-60819-013-3
1. Eisner, Will.   2. Cartoonists—United States—Biography.   I. Title.
PN6727.E4Z78 2010
741.5'6973—dc22
[B]
2010011283

First U.S. Edition 2010

1   3   5   7   9   10   8   6   4   2

Typeset by Westchester Book Group
Printed in the United States of America by Worldcolor Fairfield

To Ivy and Dylan
whose dreams I can't remember or imagine

I wasn't aware that I was making a revolution. I knew what I was doing was different because I meant it to be different, and I was talking to a totally different reader.

—Will Eisner

We used to feel very much like a Mama Rabbit and a Daddy Rabbit, who were running around, being chased by a bunch of dogs. They dove into a hole and the Mama Rabbit is quivering. She's saying, "Oh, this is terrible. We're doomed." The Daddy Rabbit says, "No, don't worry about it. We'll stay here, and in a half an hour, we'll outnumber them." I always think of that when people ask me how I felt about all those years of so-called struggle.

—Will Eisner

CONTENTS

Loveland Public Library
Loveland, Colo. 80537

chapter one

THE DEPRESSION'S LESSONS

*I carry with me a cargo of memories, some painful and some pleasant,
which have remained locked in the hold of my mind. I have an ancient
mariner's need to share my accumulation of experience and observations.
Call me, if you will, a graphic witness reporting on life, death,
heartbreak and the never-ending struggle to prevail . . .
or at least to survive.*

Will Eisner boasted that he could draw the New York City of his childhood from memory, that he didn't have to consult old photographs or
conduct research to conjure up images of towering tenement buildings with their wrought-iron fire escapes and broken front stoops, of
clothes hanging on lines cast between buildings, of fire hydrants and subway grates, of endless rows of grimy windows, of kids playing stickball in
the street and their parents engaged in the mighty struggle of stretching
a few last dollars from Tuesday to Friday, hollering their frustrations at
one another or, if the moment was right and the shades were drawn, slipping into tenderness offering reassurance, if not promise. To the New
Yorker growing up in Depression-era Bronx or Brooklyn, as Eisner did,
the neighborhoods, packed tight with immigrants and buildings and
shifty politics, were places to survive until hope began to make sense.
Eisner's graphic novels caught all this and more, often in tenement buildings on the fictitious Dropsie Avenue, where Eisner's memories gathered
and, in the solitude of a drawing board, took flight.

"The city, to me, is a big theater," he once said. "It's a never-ending
source of story, largely because there's a concentration of human beings
who are impacting on each other. And each human carries with him, or
her, a whole story. It's a struggle for existence."

Eisner was always the outsider. His family moved frequently, usually as the result of his father's inability to pay rent and make ends meet, so as the perpetual new kid on the block, he was continually the observer, again and again learning the lay of the land, guarding his younger brother and sister, dealing with these lower-middle-class neighborhoods' anti-Semitism, finding a way to fit in—surviving. And, too soon, at an age when other boys were trying out the fit of adolescence, he became the unofficial head of the household, the provider. His childhood was over and his city shrank.

Born on March 6, 1886, Shmuel (Samuel) Eisner, Will Eisner's father, was an old world artist and intellectual who learned, during the bleak days of the Depression, that neither art nor intellectualism could buy you a half a loaf of bread or a few eggs at the corner store. Sam Eisner's perfect world was Viennese café society: fine art painting, intelligent conversation, literature, friends, and endless cups of strong coffee. And, yes, watching his children grow into healthy, happy adults. Life was enrichment of the mind, and joy was finding a creative way to express that enrichment.

His real world bore little resemblance to this. He was born in Austria, in Kollmei, a village not far from Vienna. His father, a laborer—"a kerosene miner or something like that," as Will Eisner would recall—had all he could handle in feeding his wife and eleven children.

Although he never formally studied art, Sam was a natural painter, gifted with backgrounds and landscapes, enough so that when he moved to Vienna as a teenager, he was able to find a job as a muralist's apprentice. Wealthy patrons hired him to paint scenes on the walls of their homes, or more often Sam would find himself decorating the walls and ceilings of Vienna's Roman Catholic churches. This irony, of a thirteen- or fourteen-year-old Jewish boy painting blue skies and fluffy clouds and rosy-faced singing cherubim in a Catholic church, would amuse his son for his entire adult life.

One by one, Sam's brothers and sisters moved away, some to other cities in Europe, others overseas to America, where they established residence, found work, and sent for other siblings. Rather than face enlistment in the army, Sam left Vienna for the United States, arriving in New York just before the outbreak of World War I. If he envisioned America as a land brimming with opportunity and potential wealth, that notion was quickly put to rest. Sam knew how to speak German and Yiddish, but not English, and he learned early on that job hunting was going to be challenging: there was very little demand for alfresco painters in New York City. He eventually landed a job as a background painter for stages in Yiddish and vaudeville theaters—a far cry from the kind of art he aspired to create and earning him barely enough to get by. Like many immigrants, he attended night school to learn English, but it was tedious and the language came slowly to him.* Fortunately, though, he was gregarious and charming by nature, and he made friends easily.

Perhaps it was this charm, and particularly his ability to tell a good story, that attracted Fannie Ingber to him, for it is otherwise difficult to imagine what brought together this most unlikely couple. Fannie, a Romanian, had been born on April 25, 1891, on a ship bound for America. Her father, Isaac, seventy at the time of her birth, had been married to Fannie's mother's older sister, and when she died of influenza, he'd returned to his homeland for another wife. Fannie's mother, a sickly woman, died on Fannie's tenth birthday, and Isaac Ingber died later that same year, leaving Fannie in the custody of an older stepsister, Rose, who treated her more like a slave than family. Besides being overloaded with household chores, Fannie helped Rose do piecework for a garment factory and looked after her younger brother and sister. She found very little time or use for enjoying friends, hobbies, or the big city around her. When she grew older, she dated a few young men, but none of them met with the approval of her stepsister, who in all likelihood was more concerned about losing a servant than gaining a brother-in-law.

Fannie dreamed of saving enough money to open her own business, preferably a bakery, but by the time she had met, courted, and married Sam Eisner, she was hard-bitten and realistic enough to know that dreams were meant for people with better backgrounds than hers. She had worked while others had attended school; she knew English, but she couldn't read or write it—a fact that she went to great lengths to hide from her children. Factory work, at which she had excelled, had prepared her for a life of repetition. To Fannie, life was something to endure.

According to Will Eisner, his parents were distantly related, maybe second or third cousins, and they had been introduced by family. They had absolutely nothing in common, other than they were single, had ties

---

* One of Sam Eisner's prized possessions was a book about Julius Caesar, given to him by a teacher upon his completion of his English class. Sam eventually gave the book to his son Billy, who, in one of his earliest artistic exercises, drew illustrations based on the text.

to Europe, had a few nearby relatives they weren't especially close to, and possessed limited marketable job skills. They did have each other, but, as Will Eisner showed in his autobiographical work, *To the Heart of the Storm*, that offered little cause for celebration. Fannie wept when she accepted Sam Eisner's marriage proposal. The only thing that frightened her more than the prospect of marriage was the possibility of growing old alone.

William Erwin Eisner, the first of his parents' three children, was born in New York City on March 6, 1917, the same month and day as his father. As time would show, he was an almost perfect combination of his parents' strongest traits: artistic dreamer and steely realist. A brother, Julian, followed four years later, on February 3, 1921, and a sister, Rhoda, was born on November 2, 1929.

Called Billy or Willie by his parents, Eisner claimed that, as a boy, he never fully realized how impoverished his family was. His father was always working at some type of job, normally a low-paying one, and his family lived in modest but not run-down apartments. If his parents were

Billy Eisner, at age one. (Will Eisner Collection, the Ohio State University
Billy Ireland Cartoon Library & Museum)

ill suited for each other, at least it wasn't open warfare all the time. Fannie Eisner would berate her husband, often in front of the children, for his failure to earn a decent living and for the way he always seemed to be borrowing money or relying on other assistance from his older brother Simon, but Sam seemed willing to shrug off the barbs rather than allow them to escalate into serious altercations.

Billy saw enough hardship in his friends' families to lead him to believe that tensions over money were normal. When the sniping began, Billy would turn his attention to a book, close himself off in his room, or head outside, to a cacophony of noise that obliterated the angry sounds within his apartment, unaware that someday his graphic novels would bear the fruits of this distraction.

Fannie Eisner suffered from debilitating headaches, which she attributed to her difficult life. Sam, she claimed, was killing her with his job problems. She would have preferred that he just take a job painting houses, a practical enough solution to their money woes. But he would hear none of it. He was smarter than the common laborer, and he would find a way of using his talents to succeed.

Unfortunately, even though his labor wasn't common, it was sporadic, and success eluded Sam Eisner. Opportunities for scene painting dried up as time went on, with vaudeville slowing down and movies picking up in popularity. At Fannie's urging, Sam left that work for a more promising— and far less interesting—job painting finish on metal beds, making the beds look as if they had been constructed of mahogany or walnut. But the benzine and turpentine used in the process made him ill, and after consulting with a doctor, he had to quit. Then he tried his hand at opening a secondhand furniture store, but it lasted barely a year. Sam reasoned that new furniture was being produced and sold so cheaply that he couldn't compete. After the furniture store debacle, Sam, bankrolled by his brother Simon, opened a fur-coat-manufacturing factory. This, too, spiraled to disaster, and after four years of lousy sales, largely because Sam couldn't spot the trends in the business, Simon and a couple of other investors pulled the plug on the venture.

For the Eisner family, these different jobs meant a lot of moving around—or at least that's the story Sam preferred to tell them. More likely it was a matter of moving before the family faced eviction. It was getting tougher and tougher to make rent, and the moves were to cheaper places. The bed-painting job found the Eisners relocating to New Jersey, only to head to Brooklyn for the furniture store. Then it was off to the Bronx. Staying hopeful wasn't easy for the normally upbeat Sam Eisner, not when

Mother and son, in an undated photo. (Will Eisner Collection, the Ohio State University
Billy Ireland Cartoon Library & Museum)

Billy Eisner, age three, with his parents, Sam and Fannie Eisner. (Will Eisner Collection,
the Ohio State University Billy Ireland Cartoon Library & Museum)

he was being badgered by an increasingly impatient wife and when he saw
the difficulties the moves placed on his kids, particularly his oldest son.

Each new neighborhood meant establishing a presence, making friends,
fending off threats, and meeting new schoolmates and teachers. The neighborhoods were occupied by Irish and Italians with appalling anti-Semitic
attitudes, and young Billy Eisner, not the most patient person to begin
with, wasn't inclined to take a lot of crap. He'd use his fists whenever he
felt it necessary, despite his father's counsel that brainpower would beat
brutishness. Sam Eisner had faced such anti-Semitism in Europe, and for
him, the United States was just more of the same. Billy would come
home with cuts and scrapes and black eyes, still seething in anger from
the latest string of slurs flung in his face, only to have his father advise

him that bigotry, sadly enough, was an element of living in a city where different kinds of people gathered. At one time, Sam explained, the Italians and Irish picking on Billy had been victimized by prejudice themselves.

One incident, when Eisner was nine or ten years old, stayed with him his entire life. He'd talk about it in interviews and depicted it in *To the Heart of the Storm*. Sam Eisner had just started up his fur business and had relocated his family to a tough neighborhood in the Bronx. One day shortly after the move, Billy was taking his younger brother for a walk when they ran into several neighborhood bullies who asked Eisner for his name and demanded to know if he was a Jew. When Eisner told them that he was, they announced that they were Catholics and didn't want any Jews around them. Eisner replied that there was nothing he could do about it, that his family had just moved into the neighborhood. The kids then asked about the little boy clutching Billy Eisner's hand. What was his name?

"Julian," Eisner responded.

The kids laughed. "Jew-leen," they taunted. "A sissy name."

Eisner launched himself, fists flying, into the group. The fight, of course, was entirely one-sided. Billy came away with torn clothing, cuts and bruises, and a black eye. He took little solace from his father's usual suggestion that he use his head rather than his fists to deal with these kids.

Later that day, he took his father's advice in a way that would permanently change Julian's life. If Julian's name sounded Jewish to the kids on the street, Billy reasoned, maybe it would be safer for all concerned if he had another name.

"From now on," Billy told his younger brother, "your name is *Pete*."

The name stuck.

Eventually, Will Eisner would be recognized for the way he addressed his Jewish heritage and the anti-Semitism he and others endured in his graphic novels, but his feelings on the subject were more complex and, at times, ambivalent than he let on. He never changed his name, as did many Jewish comic book writers and artists, and he never backed away from the pride he felt in his heritage or the anger he felt toward the slights he witnessed on a daily basis.

The religious elements of his Judaism were another matter.

The Eisner family was far from Orthodox, regardless of whether that meant kosher cooking or attendance at the local synagogue. The family went to temple sporadically, usually on the High Holy Days, and both Eisner boys were bar mitzvahed, but practicing religion was never a high priority in their household. This might have been simply a matter of convenience for Sam and Fannie Eisner, but it was a far more calculated decision on Will's part.

It was one of their observances of the High Holy Days that set off his strong feelings on organized religion. As Eisner told the story, his father had taken his family to the synagogue for one of the holy days—he couldn't remember which one—and as they attempted to enter the temple, Sam was mortified to learn that he didn't have enough money for admission. As a result, he and his family were forced to sit on the steps leading to the synagogue and listen to the services. Billy stewed throughout the ordeal. It was one thing, he reasoned, to live at the edges of poverty and watch the effects *that* had on his father; but to see him denied his spirituality over a buck was more than he could take.

Eisner would never forgive or forget it.

One thing Billy Eisner's parents could agree on was pulp fiction. The pulp magazines, they felt, were trash—cheap entertainment aimed at lower-class working people who couldn't read more challenging literature. Billy read everything he could get his hands on, from Chekhov to Chandler, and he wasn't discriminating about where his reading material came from. One of the tenants in his building read *Black Mask Detective* magazine, and he would slip Billy the latest issue as soon as he was finished with it. The young Eisner would read it on the sly, in his room with the door closed, and he hid it from his parents' view, much the way teenagers would stash their girlie magazines several decades later. Pulp characters such as the Phantom and the Shadow not only kept him turning the pages, they had a tremendous influence on his creation of the Spirit, his best-known comic book character.

Billy's parents were at least partially correct in their assessment of the pulps: the magazines *were* cheap entertainment. They were printed on wood pulp paper, cost a dime each at a time when magazines printed on slick paper were running a quarter, and had a way of falling apart almost as soon as they were read. Most ran about 128 pages and were genre based. There were detective pulps, science fiction and fantasy pulps, horror pulps, romance pulps, men's adventure pulps—all sparsely illustrated, sensational, and filled with as many short stories as they could squeeze into an issue. Some serialized novels assured a continuing readership—assuming, of course, that the novels had any merit. The more popular ones sold in excess of a million copies per issue.

Billy Eisner loved the short story form. They didn't take long to read, were filled with action and suspense, and often had surprise endings that

Eisner would favor later when he was writing his own comics. "From those pulps, I learned how to write short story material," he'd say. "I learned how to compress and structure a story. To this day, I choose the ending and write from the beginning to the end."

The budding artist in him also appreciated the pulps' cover artwork. Lurid, full-color paintings—done by some of the best illustrators in the business and rivaling the best B-movie posters, depicting damsels in distress barely contained in ripped dresses or handsome heroes, muscles bursting out of their shirts—all but leapt out at you from the newsstand racks. Pulp magazines paid more for the art, which sold the magazine, than they paid for their stories, and competition for these jobs was fierce. For a young, talented artist with no hope of breaking into slick magazine illustration, these covers promised a future.

Billy absorbed all this—and more. On those rare occasions when he had loose change in his pockets, he'd head to the movie theaters, where, like most boys his age, he reveled in the exploits of the heroes of the day. But for Billy Eisner, like other comic book artists of the future, movies were more than just entertainment: they served as informal templates for the medium, offering an education about ways to structure and pace narratives, develop character, and stage action sequences; equally important, they provided invaluable tutorials on how to use camera angles to heighten suspense and create mood—skills that would eventually distinguish Will Eisner as a leader in the field.

"I grew up on the movies—that was my thing, that's what I lived on," Eisner told comics journalist John Benson, speaking of an interest that began in his boyhood, when he watched the popular action feature of the day, and extended to his late teens and early adulthood, when he screened more mature, artsy productions, which left their own lasting impressions.

> The movies always influenced me . . . The early Man Ray films interested me tremendously. I used to go down to the New School and spend hours looking at these old Man Ray experimental films; and it gradually dawned on me that these films were nothing but frames on a piece of celluloid, which is really no different than frames on a piece of paper. Pretty soon it became to me film on paper, and so obviously the influence was there. But timing, sequences—I think I was influenced by almost any film.

Young Billy, of course, wasn't aware of how movies would influence him while he was sitting in a darkened theater and watching action stories of the Wild West or swashbuckling tales of pirates on the high seas, but readers would see evidence of his interests in his early work, just as journalists would later remark on the heavy influence of Orson Welles's *Citizen Kane* on Eisner's *Spirit* adventures. Billy only knew that he favored the stories, much the way he liked the ways stories were told in the pulp magazines. This interest in story would ultimately set him apart from most of his contemporaries when, as a young adult, he picked up a pen and brush and successfully found a way to work his narratives on paper.

Stickball was the popular street game in Billy's neighborhood, and Eisner might have made friends more easily if he'd been any good it. He was a big kid, tall for his age and sturdily built, but he was a poor athlete, the kind of boy picked last when sides were chosen. His athletic prowess wasn't going to make him a neighborhood hero. Instead, he relied on one skill that his schoolmates and the kids in the neighborhood envied: he could draw. He could take a stick of chalk and in no time make beautiful sketches on the sidewalk or in the street. Airplanes were his specialty. Charles Lindbergh was a national hero at the time, and Billy Eisner was able to draw a convincing likeness of the famous aviator's *Spirit of St. Louis*, impressing his friends and making his life in the neighborhood easier.

Eisner had been exposed to art for as long as he could remember. Sam Eisner had artwork all over their many apartments, and as a very young boy, Billy occasionally accompanied him to work. Sam Eisner, self-taught and with no formal training in figure study, couldn't paint people, but he could do just about anything else. Billy idolized his father, and it was only natural that he would try to emulate him, much to his mother's mounting disapproval. Fannie Eisner had seen how little money an artist could earn and wasn't about to stand by and watch one of her children take her husband's wayward path. Sam, on the other hand, was pleased by Billy's apparent talent, and he gave him art supplies and encouraged him to continue. Billy, at least early on, wasn't thinking about a future career. He simply loved to draw, and he loved the attention that his artwork gained him.

Sam Eisner's money woes were worse than ever by the time Billy was finishing his elementary school education. He held a series of odd jobs, including housepainting; each evaporated, for one reason or another, until Sam became a fixture around the Eisner apartment, spending more time looking for employment than actually working. The Eisners cut corners to hang on to what little money they had. They bought day-old bread and milk on the margins of spoiling. Billy wore clothes handed down from an older cousin. Even with these economies, what little Sam Eisner had left disappeared when the stock market crashed, banks failed, and the Depression rolled in, uncompromising and by all appearances indefinite.

Billy Eisner was old enough to appreciate the gravity of his father's plight. He would vividly remember the drama of the Depression, played out on the streets of his city, in the hallways of the tenements buildings, in his own living room—as clear as newspaper clippings saved for future reference.

"As always, my father seemed to be right in the eye of the disaster," he'd say. "I recall a very sad scene at home one evening when he announced that he had just come from the bank, there was a big line, they had shut the doors, nobody could go in and get their money, and we were dead broke. Zero."

Ever an observer of the city, Eisner took note of the desperation around him, amazed by how the fight for survival could destroy the old sense of order and dignity and replace it with something else, something more modest.

Later, he described it: "Seeing people in chesterfield coats with velvet collars and a nice bowler hat, good shoes, standing in Wall Street with an orange box selling apples at five cents each. These were weird, almost theatrical scenes. People who had a car in the yard, a very good car, which they couldn't drive because they didn't have the money for gasoline. They couldn't sell it. And anyway they didn't want to give it up. Some kind of times. They helped shape your outlook."

A new work ethic took shape in America during the Depression years, forged by the loss of faith that the economy was strong enough to adapt; by the necessity of forced sacrifice; by the belief that in the years ahead, one could never take one's status, however modest, for granted. Boys watched their fathers, out of work and on the prowl for any means of earning money, and they vowed that when they were grown and supporting a family, they would never take work for granted; if they had to be workaholics to eke out peace of mind, so be it.

Stan Lee, a comics creator, writer, editor, and figurehead at Marvel Comics, and a contemporary of Eisner's who worked well into his eighties, maintaining a schedule that would have exhausted people half his age, traced his attitudes and work ethic back to the Depression years and his family's grim circumstances.

"He had been a dress-cutter, and it was almost impossible for him to find work," Lee said of his father. "My earliest memories were of him sitting in our tiny apartment, reading the want ads with great frustration, running out and trying to get something, and then coming back empty-handed. I felt that it must be the most awful thing in the world to be a man and not have a job, and not feel that you're needed. I think it was the Depression and seeing my father that made me want to have a job and keep it. If I had a steady job, I was the success that I always wanted to be. My only thought, my only objective, was to have a steady job."

Billy saw the same thing in his own household—the way the lack of work, coupled with his mother's criticism, had become that "most awful thing in the world" for his father. It was an awkward position for someone like Billy, as he grew into his high school years, only a handful of years away from manhood himself. He needed the strength that a son hopes to gain from his father's example; but to gain his own strength, he had to move beyond the pity felt for the man.

Whatever Billy's conflicted feelings, all were set aside when he was approached by his mother and told that he had to find a way to contribute to the family's income.

"Your father isn't making a living," she told him. "You're the man of the house."

It was 1930. Billy Eisner was all of thirteen years old.

To earn money, Billy sold newspapers in lower Manhattan, his favorite spot being a place in front of a building at 37 Wall Street. Years later, he would occupy an office in that very same building.

"I got there at three in the afternoon, every day, winter and summer," he said. "I could then see daily the fire hydrant, which stuck out of the side of the building where I'd sit in cold weather. On those days, I hugged that hydrant so tight you could almost read its embossed lettering on the seat of my pants. Those little things are always an influence on you. I'd recall *The Little Match Girl* at times like that."

The newspaper job gave Eisner his first lessons in business. There was an all-out competition for the prime selling locations, and the person who won a good spot was usually the biggest and strongest competitor. Billy would set up his stand, only to be chased away by a kid capable of beating the bejabbers out of him. Billy would move to another location until another big kid came around. Eventually, he found a place where he wouldn't be challenged, a place where by process of elimination he was the biggest kid in the area.

Linoleum block illustration for the *Medallion*, a politically charged
high school magazine. (© Will Eisner Studios, Inc., courtesy of Denis Kitchen)

Billy wasn't happy about having to work every day, but he didn't resent it much, either. He could dismiss any feelings of resentment with the
knowledge that his family needed the money. Besides, New York had a
lot of newspapers at the time, and all but the *New York Times* published
comics, which Billy would read religiously whenever he found some
downtime. He'd been reading comic strips for years, but now, with far
greater supply, he began to study them more seriously. His favorites included E. C. Segar's *Thimble Theatre*, George Herriman's *Krazy Kat*, Alex
Raymond's *Flash Gordon*, and Milton Caniff's *Terry and the Pirates*. He studied the comics, trying to dissect each artist's methods. Later, at home, he
would try to imitate the style of each in his own sketches, based on what
he had learned.

Art was becoming the big priority in Eisner's life. Using a makeshift
drawing table fashioned out of a board angled against a small stack of
books, Billy (with plenty of encouragement from Sam Eisner) would
draw whatever captured his fancy. There was no doubting his talent or
enthusiasm. On occasion, father and son would head to a park and sketch
landscapes or take the train to Manhattan and visit the Metropolitan
Museum of Art, where they would study the classical painters or, if they
managed to eke out the fee, take advantage of the Met's policy of allowing artists the opportunity to copy the classics in their own sketchbooks
or paint them on their own canvases.

Comics artist Nick Cardy, although a few years younger than Eisner,
grew up during the Depression years, and he too learned many of his basic
sketching and painting skills from sessions at New York's famous art

High school study: "Man in Russian Cap." (Will Eisner Collection, the Ohio State
University Billy Ireland Cartoon Library & Museum)

museum. "We couldn't afford my going to art school," he recalled. "What
I used to do is go to the library and look at the art books. Then I started
walking to the Metropolitan Museum of Art. I'd go there at certain
times of day and they'd put their easels out and paint. I used to look at the
paintings. I'd look at the painting at the weakest part of the painting, to
see what he painted over. I'd be about a half inch away, trying to find out
what the undertone was, of what he did on that. People thought I was
crazy."

Like Cardy, Eisner was either too young or too poor for the better art
schools. In a scene depicted in *To the Heart of the Storm*, Sam Eisner scraped
together enough money to enroll Billy in a cut-rate art school, located in
a run-down old building and hosted by an eccentric teacher who used a
strange contraption to teach students to draw. The machine had two arms,
one attached to the teacher and the other to the student, and art would be
"taught" when the teacher drew: the student had no choice but to let his
arm and hand be guided in whatever direction the teacher chose. The
teacher promised to make Billy an artist in three weeks; Billy fled the
school after one session.

Fannie Eisner watched her son's growing interest in art with skepticism
at first, and later, when his talent was apparent, with increasing alarm.
Her husband hadn't been able to parlay his talents into a decent living, but
here he was now, with a nation mired in economic crisis, encouraging his
oldest son to chase a dream. And that, to a practical woman like Fannie
Eisner, was all that art was: a dream pursued by talented people doomed
to fail. Some of the greatest musicians and painters and writers in history
had created immortal work and died in poverty. While he was painting

scenery for the Yiddish theater, Sam had met such actors as Emanuel Goldenberg and Meshilem Meier Weisenfreund, who would change their names to Edward G. Robinson and Paul Muni, respectively, and achieve stardom in the movies. But their successes were rare exceptions. Most of the actors in the theater moved on to other careers or, if they persisted, toiled in anonymity and poverty their entire lives. Fannie firmly believed that Billy would suffer the same fate if he insisted on continuing in art. He'd be much better off financially if he studied to be, say, a teacher. There was always a demand for a teacher's services.

Billy had no recourse but to hear out everything his parents said—to him or to each other. His mother, he knew, was utterly correct in her pleas for practicality; Billy *was* selling newspapers because his father couldn't find work as an artist. On the other hand, his father loved his art, and he presented a compelling case for the argument that life, when the final ledger was tallied, was defined more by joy and experience than by numbers in a bankbook or material possessions.

Both arguments made sense. Billy hated to disappoint either of his parents, so he listened again and again to his parents' ideological tug-of-war, unaware that in less than a decade he'd be having it both ways—the aesthetic and the practical, the seemingly incompatible pair, married into a career that would set him apart from all of his contemporaries and establish him as a model for artists in the future.

Billy's choice of high schools wound up being a good one. DeWitt Clinton High School, an all-boys' school located nearby in the Bronx, would become, over time, an incubator for great achievers. Its alumni would include an incredible range of talent: James Baldwin, Arthur Gelb, Paddy Chayefsky, Ralph Lauren, Richard Rodgers, George Cukor, Fats Waller, Burt Lancaster, Avery Fisher, Martin Balsam, Neil Simon, and A. M. Rosenthal focused on the arts; basketball Hall of Famers Dolph Schayes and Tiny Archibald starred on the school's team; and comics artists Stan Lee, Bob Kane, Bill Finger, and Irwin Hasen walked the school's halls. And this is only a partial list. Stan Lee would one day joke about how film and television creator, producer, and director Garry Marshall would beam every time he met someone who'd attended his alma mater. "Garry is so proud of the fact that he went to DeWitt Clinton that it's like the biggest thing in his life," Lee quipped.

Eisner, now calling himself "Bill"—or, if he was feeling really formal, "Will"—wasted little time in establishing a reputation at the school. Although only a marginal student, he was an excellent artist and writer, much

"Peddling at the Wrong Door": This one-panel cartoon was published in the *Clintonian*,
Eisner's high school newspaper. (Will Eisner Collection, the Ohio State University
Billy Ireland Cartoon Library & Museum)

more advanced than his classmates, and he signed on to work on the *Clinto-nian*, the school's student paper, for which he did illustrations and a regular comic strip. His first published art for the paper, an illustration for an article entitled "Bronx's 'Forgotten' Ghetto Revealed; 'Is School for Crime,' Doctor States," a drawing of Bronx street vendors operating out of carts and entitled "At the 'Forgotten' Ghetto," appeared on December 8, 1933.

Over the course of the next three years, his work seemed to be every-where. He worked on set designs for Clinton's "Class-Nite" variety show, designed posters for the school, appeared in *Magpie*, Clinton's literary maga-zine, and, with classmate Ken Ginniger, started an independent literary magazine, the *Hound and the Horn*. When Ginniger ran for class president, Eisner designed his campaign posters. The workload wasn't just a matter of beginning a portfolio; each assignment or activity exposed him to new ar-eas of art, from cartooning to art deco to commercial design, giving him remarkable range for someone so young. Clinton couldn't afford expensive metal plates for its publications' illustrations, so Eisner learned to make cut-

"Clinton Commerce": A woodcut appearing in the November 9, 1934 issue
of the *Clintonian*. (Will Eisner Collection, the Ohio State University
Billy Ireland Cartoon Library & Museum)

tings out of wood and linoleum. Later, while still in high school, he took a
job at a Manhattan printing company, where he learned the ins and outs of
printing presses.

Even as a high school student, Eisner was extremely curious, with a
capability of seeing, grasping, and retaining large volumes of information. He aspired to be a syndicated cartoonist—"[it] represented a way
out of the ghetto," he'd explain later, adding that this was his "primary
motivation"—but after working on the drama projects, including the variety show, which was written by fellow student Adolph "Singin' in the
Rain" Green, Eisner seriously contemplated following in his father's foot-
steps and working as a stage designer. As Eisner would recall, George
Dunkel, a fellow student and the son of the designer of the Metropolitan
Opera's scenery, mentioned that he could find them work with his father
on road productions—a proposal that Eisner found enticing. Predictably,
Fannie Eisner opposed the job, which would have taken her son away
from home for extended periods and exposed him to all the wrong types
of people.

"She had an aunt or a sister who was a showgirl," Eisner remarked, "and
this would lead to all kinds of terrible things for her boy. And, not only
that, but I had to stay around and make some money. So that fell apart."

"My mother stepped in and put a stop to it," he said on another occasion, "because, she said, 'that kind of life, actors were nothing but bums
and the women were trash, and if you get involved in that, you're going to
be ruined.' She would hope I'd get a nice, honest job."

This setback was nothing in comparison with the clash that Eisner had
with his mother when, while still a high school student, he attended classes

at the prestigious Art Students League of New York—an institution that gave starts to such artists as Georgia O'Keeffe, Roy Lichtenstein, and Jackson Pollock. The school boasted a supremely gifted staff, and Eisner studied under George Bridgman and Robert Brackman, two of the finest teaching artists of their day.

Fannie Eisner wasn't impressed by the artists or the school's credentials. Instead, she was mortified when her son showed her his paintings of live models.

"She was extremely shocked when I went to art school and came home with a painting of a nude woman," Eisner told interviewer Jon B. Cooke in 2002. "She couldn't understand how they would allow 16-year-old boys to 'watch naked women,' which is how she said it. And Father, he tried patiently to explain to her that this was the way art schools worked."

Ironically, as Eisner told biographer Bob Andelman, the nude studies marked the first time he felt like a professional. He had an adolescent's interest in sexuality and nudity—he lost his virginity to one of the school's young models in a brief after-school encounter—but he was more interested in how the studies affected his future as an artist.

Eisner's growth as an artist accelerated under Bridgman and Brackman's tutelage. Bridgman had an *artiste*'s ego and temperament, but his lessons in anatomy impressed Eisner to such an extent that he eventually incorporated many of them into his own textbook *Expressive Anatomy*. Eisner was also taken by the fact that both these men were *working* artists, more than willing to set aside their more highbrow tendencies if a decent commission was involved. Art and commerce were more compatible than Eisner had believed.

There were other classes as well, federally funded by Roosevelt's Depression-era Works Progress Administration programs, all free to students. Eisner took as many as he could, absorbing every tidbit of information as if his life depended upon it. He knew, even at that point, that it did.

Sam Eisner's cousin Lou Stillman owned one of the city's best training facilities for boxers, and through Stillman, Bill Eisner met two of the premier comics artists of the day. Ham Fisher, creator of *Joe Palooka*, hung out at the gym, and Stillman, learning that he was looking for an assistant, arranged a meeting between Fisher and Bill Eisner at the Parc Vendôme, the upscale Manhattan complex where Fisher lived. Eisner gathered samples of his best work, packed them into a portfolio, and turned up at Fisher's place at the appointed hour.

Fisher was nowhere to be found. The cartoonist, one of his assistants informed Eisner, was in an apartment on another floor. Eisner took down the number and headed up. His knock was answered not by Fisher, but by James Montgomery Flagg, the renowned artist famous for his World War I Uncle Sam "I Want YOU for U.S. Army" poster. Flagg was the spitting image of Uncle Sam.

"I almost fainted," Eisner recalled. "I was speechless with awe."

Flagg invited him in, but Eisner stood frozen in the hall, fumbling for something to say to the artist. He avoided the "I admire your work" cliché but could think of nothing else to say. Finally, in desperation, he managed, "What kind of pen do you use?"

"After a few minutes," Eisner remembered, "out comes Ham Fisher, a pudgy, balding little man, and he was in a blind rage about something. He looked at me and said, 'Oh yeah, you're Lou's cousin's kid,' and I said I was. Then he told me I was a day late to get a job and that he had just fired this young cartoonist who had betrayed him and stolen his ideas, and the more he talked, the more neurotic I could see he was."

The fired cartoonist, it turned out, was Al Caplin, who as Al Capp would go on to create *Li'l Abner* and become one of the business's most highly regarded daily cartoon strip artists. Eisner didn't know it at the time, but he had just witnessed the beginning of one of the most infamous feuds in comics history.

Eisner's high school social life was a mixed bag. He was popular around the Clinton campus because of his gregarious nature and the attention he received for his art, but his duties to his family and his job, along with his devotion to art, kept him from having more than a handful of close friends. He tended to be shy around girls, at least when it came to dating. He enjoyed double dating, where he could be loose and entertaining without the pressure of having to hold up 50 percent of the conversation.

One of his favorite double-dating partners was a tall, thin, good-looking classmate named Bob Kahn, who always knew an attractive young girl looking to go out dancing. Kahn also liked to draw, and though he wasn't nearly as skilled Eisner, he was adept at self-promotion. His chatter drove Eisner to distraction, but Eisner tolerated it, mainly because Kahn was constantly fixing him up with dates. Kahn would eventually change his name to Kane, and he would go on to create Batman and, as far as Eisner was concerned, earn more money than his talents warranted.

For all that he learned at DeWitt Clinton, Eisner walked away from the school without a diploma—a secret he managed to keep until late in his life. He had failed geometry, a required course, and he didn't bother to take a makeup class. He was getting a practical education elsewhere, on his job and in the art classes he attended in the evenings. Long after he'd achieved his acclaim as a cartoonist, he would admit that he might have been an entirely different artist and person if he'd graduated from high school and had a college education. At age eighteen, however, it didn't matter. He was itching to apply his artistic talents to some kind of work, and with all that DeWitt Clinton had given him, Eisner was ready to move ahead.

The nation's slow recovery from the Depression spelled trouble for Bill Eisner and his efforts to find a job. Good commercial art and magazine illustration work, extremely competitive to begin with, was closed to someone with Eisner's lack of experience. The fact that he was Jewish didn't help, either. As Eisner would discover, many Jewish artists wound up going into comics because of anti-Semitism in the ad agencies. Eisner lugged his portfolio from place to place, he sat around in the waiting rooms with other hopefuls, he showed his work to editors and art directors, and then he'd walk away, defeated. A lot of potential employers did little more than give his art a cursory glance. One outfit, a Mob-controlled company producing pornographic comic books, offered him steady work, but Eisner rejected the opportunity. He might have been desperate for work and money, but there were limits to what he would do.

These experiences taught Eisner invaluable, if painful, lessons.

"One of the difficulties of this business is that you have to learn to deal with rejection," he said. "Every kid coming out of school, sooner or later, will walk into an art director's office or a publisher's office and the editor will look at his work and say, 'now don't take this personally . . . but this is the stupidest, crappiest work I've ever seen.'

"It happened to me," he continued. "I remember, as a young kid, I showed my work to a magazine and the editor looked at this work and laughed and said, 'These are the stupidest faces I have ever seen.' And I walked out of there very dejected. And sitting out in the waiting room, waiting to see this editor next after me, was Ludwig Bemelmans, the famous illustrator [of *Madeline*]. A foreigner. And he said to me in broken English, 'Don't vorry, boy, somebody vill like your vork.'"

Later in his career, Eisner illustrated this encounter in a four-page story commissioned for a compilation of stories entitled *Autobiographix*, a collection devoted to personal narratives capturing important moments in the contributors' lives. Eisner entitled his piece "The Day I Became a Professional."

Eisner eventually scored a job in the advertising department of the *New York American*, working the graveyard shift and drawing illustrations for the paper's "pimple ads"—the tiny ads that ran along the paper's borders. Eisner divided his paycheck between his family and himself. Lunch was his favorite time of the day. At midnight, he'd head up to the roof of the *American*'s building, where he watched New York's nightlife and, he'd say later, picked up the nuances of the way shadows played on the street scenes, lessons he would use to great effect in his graphic novels and *Spirit* stories.

The pay at the *American* was lousy, and Eisner tried doing freelance work on the side to supplement his income, but with little success. The advertising work posed no creative challenge, and Eisner yearned for something else, if not in comics, then in commercial art. When he heard that a new magazine called *Eve*, geared toward young Jewish women, was looking for an art director, he applied for the job, even though he knew almost nothing about what young Jewish women wanted in a magazine. He got the job, most likely because he would work for little money, and he set out to provide the magazine with illustrations of all kinds, publishing under the name "Julian Willi," which was a combination of his brother's name and his nickname. Neither the magazine nor Eisner lasted long. Eisner was fired when it became evident to the editors that he had very little knowledge of the magazine's target audience and that readers would have little interest in illustrations of, say, women with firearms. The magazine folded a few months later.

A chance encounter with Bob Kahn set Eisner's career in another direction. Kahn had been hustling his work all over town, occasionally selling single-panel cartoon jokes. He told Eisner of a periodical called *Wow, What a Magazine!*, which published cartoons and illustrated stories for boys.

"They buy from everybody," Kahn assured Eisner. "Go up there and see."

Eisner packed his portfolio and headed downtown to the magazine's offices.

chapter two

A BUSINESS FOR THIRTY BUCKS

*You stop anybody on the street and ask him, "What is art?" They'll
say, "Well, an oil painting—that's art. And an etching—that's art."
But how about a series of pictures in sequence with words and text
over it. He'll say, "Oh, that's not art. That's comics."*

When Bill Eisner first set foot in the *Wow, What a Magazine!* offices, he
was not stepping into the nerve center of a modern publishing mag-
nate. The magazine, like so many comics magazines of the time,
operated on an extremely limited budget, with the understanding that
the current issue could very well be its last. The magazine's editor, Samuel
Maxwell Iger, who preferred to be called "Jerry," was, to be charitable, a
dynamic presence, a one-man show who sold ads, worked as the magazine's
distribution director, hired freelancers, edited copy, dealt with printers,
and, when necessity dictated, did artwork.

The *Wow* offices reflected the magazine's borderline existence. Located on Fourth Avenue in Manhattan's garment district, the offices were
little more than a shoebox. John Henle, the magazine's owner, wanted to
be a publisher; he had enough business acumen to know that shirts were
a safer bet. Henle gave Iger control over the magazine, but he made it clear
that there was only so much money he could sink into it.

Iger was the kind of man who desperately wanted to be everything he
wasn't. He would have liked to be six or so inches taller, better looking,
wealthy, and much less harried. He would have liked to be a better draftsman, when in fact his lettering was only passable and his cartooning was
embarrassingly rudimentary. He was broke, overworked, and in the process of divorcing his second wife. Yet his bluster could take paint off a
wall.

He got by—partly on his exceptional salesmanship, partly on unadulterated chutzpah. He had a way of balancing his personal books by living over his head by night and pinching pennies by day. He liked to be seen at the right places, with a beautiful woman or two (often prostitutes) at his side, and he talked as if he owned a sizable chunk of Manhattan. People would see through it, but that didn't prevent Iger from carrying on.

Nick Cardy, who worked for both Eisner and for Iger in his early years in comics, recalled a time when he was asked to deliver drawings to Iger's apartment, only to get a firsthand look at the way Iger tried to impress people in ridiculous ways.

"I went up to this little apartment—it must have been eight by ten—and this fella opened the door. He was the *butler*! I mean, how would you use a butler in an eight-by-ten room? He said, 'I'll see if he's in, sir.'"

If not for Eisner's persistence, his initial meeting with Jerry Iger would have fallen through. Eisner had just begun showing his portfolio when Iger picked up the phone and learned that he had still another crisis on his hands. There was a problem at the engraving plant requiring Iger's immediate attention.

"I don't have time to talk to you now," he told Eisner. "I've got a serious problem. Come back another day."

Eisner knew better than to go along with that. It was tough enough to get an editor to glance at your work; there were no guarantees that Iger would see him at another time, let alone remember talking to him. As the two took the elevator down to the lobby, Eisner suggested that he might show Iger his portfolio while they walked to the engraving plant. Iger reluctantly agreed. Eisner presented his work as well as he could while they walked briskly down the sidewalk, but Iger's attention was elsewhere.

At the engraver's shop, they found several men standing at a huge stone table in the center of the room. The engravers used the table to inspect the plates when they came out of the acid bath. The problem here was that the plates were punching holes in the mattes used in the reproduction process, and the men were at a loss as to how they might correct the problem.

Eisner listened to the discussion before clearing his throat and addressing the group.

"Excuse me," he said. "Does anyone have a burnishing tool?"

"I had been working for years in a print shop on Varick Street, and I'd seen this before," Eisner told the *Comics Journal* in 2002. "What happens is when the etching is complete, it frequently left burrs along the indentations, and these burrs were what was making holes in the mattes. They handed me a burnishing tool, and I rubbed the burrs off the edge of the plate."

The men standing around the table couldn't believe what they'd just seen.

"Who is this kid?" they asked Jerry Iger.

Iger responded without missing a beat.

"He's my new production man."

Eisner, of course, had no interest in the production end of the business. He and Iger talked all the way back to the *Wow* offices, where Iger took a closer look at Eisner's portfolio. He liked what he saw and asked what Eisner might be able to do for his magazine. Eisner proposed doing an adventure series modeled after the kind of story that H. Rider Haggard wrote for the pulps. Iger gave him the go-ahead. The piece would appear in *Wow*'s August 1936 issue. More significant, Eisner would get a crack at illustrating that same issue's cover.

Energized by this unexpected success, Eisner responded with a story about a heroic character named Scott Dalton, a sort of precursor to Indiana Jones. Eisner hoped the feature would be a regular installment in the magazine. His cover painting, also of Dalton, depicted a handsome, blond-haired hero, his shirt open to the waist and a holster at his side, waving a smoking pistol in the air. Eisner also revived a couple of characters he'd created while still at Clinton High—*Harry Karry* (then called *Harry Carey*), a detective strip that he'd originally hoped would work for the syndicate, and *The Flame*, a buccaneer adventure strip heavily influenced by Milton Caniff. Eisner would always be known as an artist with more ideas and energy than time, and as a nineteen-year-old looking at a future that had been a dream only a couple of years ago, he was ready to prove to the world that a new, formidable comics artist had arrived.

The euphoria was short-lived. After failing to make a dent in what was proving to be a rapidly growing and saturated market, *Wow* suspended publication following its fourth issue. A depressed Bill Eisner returned to the Bronx and considered his next move.

In the beginning, comics weren't intended to be highbrow entertainment. They'd started in the late 1800s and early 1900s as strips or single-panel newspaper entries and, over the course of the next three decades, entertained newspaper readers while businessmen schemed over how to make them more profitable. The comic book itself was a happy accident, its appearance the result of a happenstance. In *Men of Tomorrow: Geeks, Gangsters, and the Birth of the Comic Book*, Gerard Jones described the setting in which the comic book was born as "counter-cultural, lowbrow, idealistic, prurient, pretentious, mercenary, forward-looking, and ephemeral, all in the same instant."

When Joseph Pulitzer began publishing *Hogan's Alley*, generally regarded as America's first comic strip, in the *New York World* in 1895, the strip was strictly populist fare, a circulation booster aimed at the masses at a time when the circulation wars among the New York newspapers were fought with no holds barred. The comic's central character, an unnamed boy known by readers as "the Yellow Kid" (for the yellow nightshirt-type garb that he wore every day), was a kind of street urchin capable of getting into all kinds of mischief, with or without the help of his ragtag bunch of friends. Kids and adults could laugh at him, not so much because he was innately funny or clever, but because no matter where they hailed from, he was everything they were not. Heavy immigration had divided New York's neighborhoods, and to readers, the Yellow Kid, although never identified as being from any particular European background, was the kid who lived two blocks away—backward, uneducated, from some other country, capable of only poor or broken English, a little dirty (and possibly smelly), always in some kind of trouble, and facing a future you wouldn't wish on your own kids. Subtle social commentary ran like an undercurrent in his daily travails.

The Yellow Kid was a huge hit, so much so that William Randolph Hearst, after buying the *New York Journal*, made certain, when raiding Pulitzer's staff, that he managed to secure the *Hogan's Alley* strip and the services of its creator, Richard Felton Outcault. A lot of screaming, finger-pointing, and litigation followed, with Pulitzer even going so far as to publish his own Yellow Kid feature, written and drawn by another cartoonist. But by this point there were enough dopey kids, foggy-minded immigrants, stump-jumping hillbillies, stereotyped African-Americans, and confused souls to go around. Such comic strips as *Happy Hooligan, Katzenjammer Kids, Hairbreadth Harry, Skippy, Barney Google and Snuffy Smith, Bringing Up Father, Mutt & Jeff*, and a host of others captured the fancies of New York readers and, with the development of the newspaper syndicates, the rest of the country. Soon, *Little Orphan Annie, Krazy Kat*, and *Thimble Theatre*, all heavy influences on Will Eisner, elevated the comic strip to a higher artistic level. Newspapers ran as many of these black-and-white comic strips as they could squeeze in on weekdays, but the comics' strongest appeal fell on Sundays, when color versions of these same strips ran in separate sections of the newspapers. The humorous content of most of these comics sections led people to label them "the funny papers," later shortened to "the funnies."

But it wasn't all jokes, slapstick, and lowbrow humor. Beginning with Winsor McCay's *Little Nemo in Slumberland* in 1905, comics combined classic storytelling with realistic—even surrealistic—artwork, and with stories continuing from day to day, these comic strips played a significant role in their newspapers' circulations. These strips were filled with action, adventure, danger, romance, flights of imagination, and, in the cases of *Buck Rogers* and *Flash Gordon*, speculation on the future. The popularity of Edgar Rice Burroughs's *Tarzan* novels led to a comic strip adaptation. Chester Gould's *Dick Tracy* introduced crime and detective stories, later to become a comic book staple, to the newspaper strip. Young Bill Eisner followed these and other strips and saw the potential for making comics creative outlets for serious stories. He drew a connection between the prose he read in pulp magazines and sequential art, rendered in the supreme draftsmanship of such artists as Milton Caniff and Alex Raymond.

The comic book as we know it today didn't exist in America until 1929, when George Delacorte issued the *Funnies*, a weekly tabloid publishing comic strips that hadn't made the grade with the newspapers. It featured all original material but failed to catch on with readers. Prior to that, comic books were strictly reprint vehicles, packaging previously published newspaper strips such as *Little Nemo in Slumberland*, *Mutt & Jeff*, or *Buster Brown* into cheaply produced magazines meant to compete with pulp magazines on newsstands. Retailers found uses for comic books as well, reprinting newspaper strips into small booklets and handing them out as promotional giveaways. Publishers of pulp and girlie magazines, clawing away at one another for every dime they could wrestle from consumers, couldn't help but notice the upswing in these books' popularity at a time when their publications were in a downturn.

Enter Major Malcolm Wheeler-Nicholson, a character so colorful that he might have sprung from the pulps themselves—or, to go further back in time, the dimestore novels. A master of self-promotion and tall tales, Wheeler-Nicholson was in his mid-forties by the time he made his presence known on the comics scene in 1934—and with his Panama hats, cigarette holder, fashionable suits, and cane, he was quite the presence. According to the legend—and one could never be certain what was fact and what was fiction with the Major—Wheeler-Nicholson had fought Pancho Villa in Mexico before earning his rank while serving in the cavalry during World War I. He'd gone on to fight the Bolsheviks in Russia, married a Swedish countess, and survived an assassination attempt, during which he was shot in the head. He'd also survived a court-martial, which he instigated when he complained to the wrong people, including President Warren Harding, about practices in the military. Back in the States, he published a book and scads of magazine and newspaper articles about his adventures, then decided to try his luck at publishing comics. Problem was, he was a poor businessman and often had very little money—an issue that would plague him throughout his spotty business career. He always found a way to get by—but barely.

Still, his contribution to comics was noteworthy. His comic book, *New Fun*, a thirty-six-page magazine featuring all new material, initially appeared in 1934 and ran for six issues until a lack of interest forced it out of existence. Wheeler-Nicholson wasn't concerned with the comic book's value as a periodical; instead, he hoped that the syndicates would look at his books' contents and sign the comics they liked for regular inclusion in newspapers. It wasn't a bad idea, and it might have worked if he'd had quality work to offer. As it was, he operated on a shoestring budget, picking up newspaper strips that nobody wanted and advertising for submissions from up-and-comers looking for a chance to break into comics and willing to take next to nothing to do so. Aesthetically, the books weren't much—the Major couldn't afford color except for the covers, and the contributions tended to be amateurish—but *New Fun* served as a marker, evidence of the possibilities for a well-financed publisher willing to take a chance on original material. Wheeler-Nicholson lost two editors because he couldn't afford to pay them, but he was just sly and charming enough to talk his creditors and contributors into floating him long enough for another issue.

The challenge with comic books, as with all other forms of publication, was in the printing and distribution. Wheeler-Nicholson had connections with *McCall's* magazine until his luck and money disappeared. Other comic book producers boasted of connections that reduced financial risk. Maxwell C. Gaines, a salesman for the Eastern Color Printing Company and, later, founder of the formidable EC Comics company, and Eastern's sales manager, Harry Wildenberg, had teamed up in 1933 to publish *Funnies on Parade*, a collection of reprints designed as radio show giveaways for such sponsors as Wheatena and Canada Dry. Their access to Eastern's printing press during the third shift, when the presses were quiet, made publication possible. The comic books were free to customers until the two decided to test a paying market by affixing a ten-cent price sticker on the cover and selling them on newsstands. To their surprise, a lot of people were willing to pay for reprints of comics they'd already read.

New titles, produced by both big companies like Dell and fly-by-night operators, surfaced in the wake of Wheeler-Nicholson's *New Fun*. Sales figures, although not overwhelming, moved upward, to the quarter-of-a-million-copy range—enough to encourage aspiring publishers like John Henle to take a flier on issuing a magazine like the ill-fated *Wow*.

Bill Eisner had watched the birth and growth of the comic book business, and as he sat up in the Bronx, pondering what he would do after the failure of *Wow, What a Magazine!*, he reasoned that there had to be a way for him to capitalize on the popularity of this new entertainment medium. He was confident of his ability, which, he judged correctly, was equal to or better than what he was seeing on the newsstands. All he had to do was find the proper entrée into the business.

And that realization—that it *was* a business—provided his answer. For years, he'd listened to his mother harp about how *art* never paid off and how he needed to pursue a career with a need for his services; he'd worked hard at developing as an artist, with the hope that somebody out there would appreciate his talent and reward it with steady work. But artists could be found anywhere and everywhere, so to be needed, Eisner suddenly concluded, he'd have to become a businessman. He would provide a service the comic book publishers badly needed.

And the need, he saw, was right in front of him. With the increasingly large number of comic books hitting the newsstands every month, publishers were bound to discover a shortage of material to reprint. There would be an urgent call for new comics to fill the books, and this was something Eisner could provide. What would happen if he wrote and illustrated camera-ready stories for the publishers? He would be his own company, beholden to no individual publisher, and if he could drum up enough accounts, he could make a serious go of it in the field. As a packager, he wouldn't have to worry about how to get his material printed or distributed; that would be up to his customers.

The problem, he realized, was in his business connections: he had none. He needed an aggressive salesman to contact companies and push his art, somebody with connections and experience in the business, somebody who could do the legwork and leave him with the time to create comics. That person would have to be available immediately, and he would have to be willing to work with a young, relatively inexperienced artist. Eisner knew of only one such person: Jerry Iger.

Eisner gave it some more thought, conducted additional research and developed his plan, talked it over with his parents, and finally, despite reservations about working with a man who on even his best days could be difficult to deal with, he gave Iger a call.

Since the demise of *Wow*, Iger had been doing nothing but watch his money disappear. He had appreciated Eisner's enthusiasm when they'd worked together, but he'd knocked around enough to know that he was in a really bad spot. With a pending divorce, he was looking at losing a sizable chunk of his money and possessions, and losing both a wife and a job in short order had left his motivation at a low ebb. When Eisner called and suggested that they get together for lunch, he wasn't optimistic about anything productive coming out of the meeting.

The two met at a little hole-in-the-wall restaurant on Forty-third Street, across the street from the *New York Daily News* press shop. Eisner would eventually depict the meeting in *The Dreamer*, his roman à clef graphic novella about his early days in comics, as well as in numerous interviews. As he recalled, both of them were unbelievably broke, yet even after listening to Eisner's plans, Iger was hesitant about entering into a business partnership. He wasn't sure he wanted to be involved in the kind of company Eisner was proposing, but even if he was interested, he had nothing to contribute in seed money. That was no problem, Eisner countered: he had $15 he'd earned from a freelance advertising job he'd done for Gre-Solvent, a grease-cutting soap, and he could borrow an equal amount from his father. The thirty bucks would get him a couple months' rent in a small room in an old office building on Madison Avenue and Forty-third Street. The place was a popular spot for bookies needing only enough room for a desk, chair, and telephone; and the room Eisner was looking at, about ten by ten, wasn't going to give its two occupants more than enough space to shoehorn in a desk, drawing board, and maybe a filing cabinet and coat-rack. Still, it was a place to start.

The firm, Eisner & Iger, Ltd.—"my name was first because I was the big money man," Eisner quipped later—was born. It would be a fifty-fifty partnership, with no outside owners or stockholders—not that anyone at that point would have been crazy enough to invest in the company.

Feeling every bit the hotshot, Eisner insisted on paying for lunch. The bill came to $1.90, a nickel less than what Eisner had in his pocket, leaving him with just enough to catch a subway back to the Bronx, but not enough to avoid admonishment from his new business partner.

"Y'know, Billy, that wasn't nice," Iger said as the two were leaving the restaurant. "You didn't leave a tip."

Eisner shrugged him off, claiming he'd forgotten. He had other things holding his attention. For one, before formal business papers were drawn up, he'd have to come up with a way to tell Iger that he'd lied about his age when the two of them first met. He wasn't twenty-five, as he'd claimed

The fifteen dollars earned from this ad, Eisner's first paying job, along with a small loan from his father, financed the opening of the Eisner & Iger Studio. (Will Eisner Collection, the Ohio State University Billy Ireland Cartoon Library & Museum)

then; at nineteen, he was barely old enough to hang out and drink in one of Iger's favorite watering holes.

Eisner's idea of starting a comics packaging company was not original, nor was the Eisner & Iger shop the first of its kind. Harry "A" Chesler Jr., a short, stocky, transplanted Chicago advertising salesman, already ran a shop at 276 Fifth Avenue. Called "the Chiseler" by some of the artists working for him, Chesler was one of the more colorful characters populating a business known for its colorful characters. No one knew what the "A" stood for—he said it meant "anything"—or why he chose to bracket his middle initial in quotation marks, but, like the "Jr." tacked on at the end of his name (he wasn't one), these were suitably quirky ornaments, as inextricable from the man as the cheap cigars he was constantly smoking or the derby that he perched on the back of his head and refused to remove, even indoors. He stationed his desk at the front of the studio, near the elevator and stairway, so no one could enter or leave without walking past him.

Chesler had tried his luck at comic book publishing with very little success. Under the name Chesler Publications, Inc., he had published *Star Comics* and, in a new twist in the business, *Star Ranger*, a book devoted entirely to westerns. Both fizzled at the newsstands. Part of his problem could have been format—the entries were very brief, only a page or two, more in the style of newspaper strips than the fully developed stories that Eisner would favor—but whatever the reason, Chesler dumped the titles and concentrated on his shop. As comics historian Ron Goulart would note, "Chesler never did manage to produce a really successful comic book of his own, [but] his various shops developed and trained a great many artists who became successful after they left the field."

Depending upon the person you were talking to, Chesler was either a no-nonsense taskmaster demanding maximum effort for minimum pay or a tough but reasonable patrician who, on occasion, could display a heart of gold.

Joe Kubert would remember Chesler—and Will Eisner, for that matter—as being open to letting a young kid hang around the shop and learn the craft by watching the other artists at work.

"Harry was extremely kind to me," Kubert said. "When I first started out as a kid, I learned all the addresses of the publishers in New York. I attended the High School of Music and Art, which was up on 135th Street and Compton Avenue in Manhattan. And Norman Maurer, a buddy attending school with me, who was later my partner, and I would make the rounds from place to place. One of the places we stopped off at was Harry Chesler's. I went up there with my work, not knowing what the hell was happening or what was being done there, with the hope that I might get something to do.

"Harry allowed me to come into his place after school, on my way home to Brooklyn. I would stop off there and stay until maybe five, five thirty, and I would do an old script or something that he would put me on. He would tell the other guys, 'Keep an eye on the kid and help him along.' It was terrific. It was one of the first situations I found myself in where I was actually sitting next to professional people. This was a non-paying job, but eventually he gave me five dollars a week for doing nothing. He'd say, 'Here, kid, buy yourself a couple of hotdogs or something.' Five dollars a week was a lot of money at that time."

Carmine Infantino, another artist who would rise to the top of the comics business, had similarly positive memories of dealing with Chesler when he was learning the ropes.

"I loved Harry," he said. "He had this broken-down studio. You'd take an old-fashioned elevator up to the third or fourth floor, and when you'd get to that floor and the door opened, there, sitting in front of you, was Harry, in front of an old beat-up desk, with a soiled derby on. He gave me money to come up there and sit and watch artists work, which I thought was terrific. It was the Depression, and this guy couldn't afford it, but he did it. Harry gave me a great break, meeting these interesting artists. I hear all kinds of terrible stories about him, but this was not the man I knew."

Irwin Hasen, who created single-page sports cartoons for Chesler, experienced one of those terrible stories. "Just don't work for him," Hasen said, laughing, when asked about Chesler. Hasen worked in the bullpen with such notables as Mort Meskin, Jack Cole, and Charlie Biro, and while he admitted that Chesler was a "nice guy and a worker," he bristled when the topic of payment was raised.

"At the end of the week, you'd go up to him and he was like a teacher at a desk," Hasen recalled. "He would say, 'How little do you need to live on?' I swear to God."

Rather than pay his artists by the page, as was the custom of the day, Chesler paid a flat rate, usually $20 a week, in exchange for all the rights and original artwork produced by his staff. The studio consisted of a large, wide room, with the artists' and writers' desks lined up in rows, not unlike a classroom. Pages would be roughed out, penciled, and inked by different workers, assembly-line style, with the pages passed around under Chesler's watchful eye. Workers were expected to report to work on time and could be docked a day's pay if they showed up even a few minutes late. For all his reservations about Chesler's methods of payment, Irwin Hasen conceded that Chesler's English schoolmaster approach to running a shop was probably necessary. "You needed a guy like that around," he said, "because he had all these guys working with him and for him."

Eisner adopted a similar approach to running a shop when Eisner & Iger had expanded to such an extent that he could no longer produce the artwork by himself. He initially brought in his high school buddy Bob Kahn, now going by Bob Kane, to work as freelance on an animal feature called *Peter Pupp*, a Disney cartoon knockoff he'd been developing in his days of freelancing for *Wow*. He brought in writer/artists Gill Fox and Dick Briefer as well. Others, most notably a young artist named Jacob Kurtzberg, came later. Eisner would state, half-seriously, that he ran his shop "pretty much the way a Roman galley operates. I sat at the end of a row of sweating artists."

Eisner treated his work very seriously, as if comics were a sacred vocation, but he never fooled himself into believing that those working under him felt the same passion for their work. A good number of them, like those toiling for Chesler, aspired to move into commercial art, and for these men, comics represented a steady paycheck, a means of treading water until the effects of the Depression passed and better opportunities opened up. In fact, many of the artists were ashamed of their jobs. You could have studied with the most respected teachers in New York's finest art schools and be producing work that stood up against the best being rendered by gallery or commercial artists, but when the sun went down and you pulled off your shoes for the night, you still had to live with the knowledge that you were creating something designed, as the disparaging saying went, for "ten-year-old cretins from Kansas City."

"It was the bottom of the barrel," remembered Bob Fujitani, who spent time at the Eisner & Iger shop. "All of the comics artists wanted to be an illustrator, another Norman Rockwell or [J. C.] Leyendecker—the top illustrators of that time. That's what we all wanted to be, but very few guys made it."

Stan Lee agreed. "Comic book writing was considered the lowest thing you could do in the creative field. Nobody had any respect for comics—even the person I worked for. My publisher felt they were only read by very little children or semiliterate adults. There was no point in trying to make the stories literate, or worry about character development or anything: 'Just give them a lot of action and don't use too many words.' That was his philosophy."

Nick Cardy, who aspired to be an illustrator before earning his reputation in comics, recalled a conversation he had with fellow artist Jim Mooney about how comics was a dirty word. "He said, 'You know, if my mother had ever found out I was doing comics, I don't know what would have happened. I would have gotten along if I said I was a pimp.'"

In his 1947 landmark study, *The Comics*, British cartoonist Coulton Waugh sneered at comic books as an important but appalling descendant of the newspaper strip. "It doesn't seem possible that anything so raw, so purely ugly, should be important," he wrote. "Comic books *are* ugly; it is hard to find anything to admire about their appearance." Waugh, who spent a decade to working on the comic strip *Dickie Dare* after the departure of Milton Caniff, reflected the elitist attitudes of the newspaper artists of the time when he critiqued comic books. He was totally put off by the paper used in comic books, the colorization, by the "soulless emptiness" and "outrageous vulgarity" that he saw in the little newsstand magazines. "It is quite clear that you can laugh at the comic books but you can't laugh them off," he said. "They are a startling addition to both children's and grownups' reading matter with which we all might become better acquainted—if only to understand what our children are looking at."

Eisner confessed to being embarrassed about being a comics artist when he first started out, not because he felt that his work was inferior, but because of the reputation attached to anyone working in the medium, the low self-esteem he witnessed around him, the "comic book ghetto" in which comic book artists felt trapped. It was especially galling to Eisner that the syndicated daily newspaper strip artists disregarded the comic book artists as inferior. "We were living in an environment that led us to believe that we were subhuman," he said.

One of his favorite anecdotes from those early days, repeated frequently over the years, involved a cocktail party he attended on Madison Avenue. He had established his reputation as one of the best in the business, and he felt honored to be invited to such a highbrow affair.

"There were a lot of artists there," he recalled. "I was standing against a wall, holding a drink, and a lady came by with long black hair, bangs, a long cigarette, and holding a drink, and she said to me, 'What do you do?'

"And I said, 'I'm a comic book artist.'

"And with a very large balloon with very tiny letters, she said, 'Oh, how nice.'"

Over the passing years, Eisner learned to joke about the incident. It wasn't funny at the time.

Eisner's business instincts were on the money. Iger looked up his old contacts, and Eisner & Iger's client list took off, netting Eisner as much work as he could handle. He'd go into work early and leave late in the evening, usually long after Jerry Iger had gone home. Eisner's social life, not much to begin with, ceased to exist. He had work and he had sleep, with an occasional time-out for a hurried meal. One publisher, needing a lot of material produced on strict deadlines, asked Iger about his staff. Was it big enough to handle the workload? Eisner instructed Iger to tell the publisher that Eisner & Iger employed a staff of five artists; they certainly could handle the publisher's needs. Iger landed the account, and Eisner would maintain the ruse by writing five different features in five different styles, signing each with a different name—his own and four pseudonyms.

"One was Willis R. Rensie—that's 'Eisner' backward," he explained. "Another was W. Morgan Thomas, another Spencer Steele. That's a marvelous name, isn't it. I always wanted to be named Spencer Steele." The fifth name, William Erwin, was simply Eisner's first and middle name.

Eisner & Iger established a reputation of producing high-quality work on deadline—a high recommendation in a business not known for its artists' sense of responsibility. Freelancers could be quirky or temperamental, many were known to drink too much, and most missed deadlines. Eisner, perhaps because of his youthful experience of supporting his family, quickly established a professional standard that he would follow throughout his life. He was creative enough to move easily from genre to genre, from fantasy to detective stories to westerns to jungle stories. Just as important, he worked quickly. After spending decades in the business, he'd boast that he never missed a deadline—a claim that may or may not have been true; in any event, a blown Eisner deadline was so rare that neither he nor his clients nor fellow artists could remember one.

The key, Eisner would respond whenever asked about the secret to his success, was in the *story*. His voracious youthful reading, from pulps to the classics to newspaper comic strips, along with all the movies he'd seen, had taught him well. He knew the components of a good story, including characterization, point of view, plot, and action; he knew how to frame and construct a story in just a few pages. If he had a weakness early in his career, it was in writing dialogue: he had a strong feeling for vernacular and the rhythms of speech, but he could be too wordy, resulting in the disruption of a story's pacing.

But comics, despite his protestations to the contrary, were not a literary medium—not in the early days, at least. In their advent, comic books were read by all ages, but an overwhelmingly high percentage of readers were adolescent, particularly boys, who expected a lot of action, in as exotic a setting as the writer could drum up, in very few pages. Eisner ground his teeth but followed industry dictates, but even that wasn't enough for Jerry Iger, who'd impatiently chide Eisner for working too carefully on his art rather than churning out more pages. "The trouble with you is that you want to win an art director's award," he'd complain, "but we're turning out frankfurters here."

Iger had reason to push. Through hard work and hustle, the shop had connected with some impressive clients, including Editors Press Service, which gave Eisner & Iger its first international exposure. Iger knew Editors Press Service founder Joshua B. Powers from his *Wow, What a Magazine!* days, when Powers was trying to sell some of *Wow*'s material to magazines in the United Kingdom, Australia, and New Zealand. Powers, supposedly a former undercover agent in South America, possibly with the CIA, had concocted a moneymaking scheme that he hoped would see him through his retirement. He bought comics from the United States for foreign clients, who paid him in advertising space in their publications. Powers would then sell the space at a hefty profit to U.S. companies looking for an inexpensive way to advertise overseas. Some of the comics that Powers purchased were reprints, like the *Dick Tracy* and *Mutt & Jeff* dailies, but he was also interested in the kind of original work that Eisner & Iger could provide.

One of the Editors Press clients, a magazine called *Wags*, a weekly tabloid distributed in England and Australia, became one of Eisner & Iger's top publishers, leading to two of Eisner's more sophisticated features: a reprise of his *Flame* cartoon, renamed *The Hawk* and, after several appearances under that title, renamed again as *Hawks of the Sea*; and *Yarko the Great*, a detective series featuring a magician crime solver. These entries—*Hawks of the Sea* in particular—gave Eisner room to develop characters and plot, which he relished. There was still plenty of action in the swashbuckling *Hawks of the Sea* to keep young readers glued to the pages, yet each installment found Eisner, writing as Willis R. Rensie, sneaking in more mature approaches to subject matter and dialogue and even experimenting with the "camera angles" in some of the frames.

"There was a great deal of freedom for development," he said of those early days of working on *Hawks*, speaking in 1986 to his longtime editor, Dave Schreiner. "With an illustrative style, you can really move along and see yourself getting better . . . The things I used were, of course, sometimes beyond my capacity at the time. I think back to what a hell of a nerve I had trying some of the shots in this thing.

"But *Hawks* was my first attempt to run the mile. It was the first chance I had to go full out. There was no precedent and there were no restrictions. It was an ideal setup for me. I probably did it at the rate of a page a day, doing everything but the lettering."

The Eisner & Iger company had been around only a few months when the two partners, buoyed by the early response to the company, decided to create their own comics syndicate. Universal Phoenix Features Syndicate, initially designed to handle foreign clients, rose from a Joshua Powers split with his English partner, which left Eisner & Iger with the potential loss of *Wags*. The syndicate quickly found a market in the United States as well, largely due to the knowledge that Eisner & Iger had acquired from dealing with Joshua Powers. Small newspapers, they learned, wanted to publish comic strips, but their options were sharply limited because of territorial restrictions imposed by the big syndicates.

Popular features could appear in only one newspaper in any given region, which left a shortage of comics available to the smaller papers. Eisner & Iger filled that need in an ingenious way that worked beautifully for a while but eventually became an accounting nightmare. The setup was simple. Eisner & Iger hired two salesmen to travel all over the East Coast and sell comics to newspapers. Each of the five-panel comics, written and illustrated by Eisner, included a blank panel at the end of the strip, which would be filled by a local advertiser—in theory giving the newspaper the strip for free. The salesmen would initially sell the ads and collect the money on a onetime basis; after that, the newspapers were on their own.

All kinds of confusion followed. The salesmen pocketed the money, wires were crossed between the newspapers and advertisers about whom the advertisers had to pay, and Eisner & Iger was caught in the middle, producing weekly strips but not knowing when—or if—the company would be paid. Frustrated newspapers canceled their subscriptions.

Fortunately for Eisner and Iger, their workload at the comic book end of their company had increased to such a degree that their attention was focused elsewhere. Other large clients were entering the picture. There was plenty of reason to train their eyes on the future.

chapter three

SUPERMEN IN A WORLD OF MORTALS

Basic business acumen comes from hunger. That also goes for ideas,
I suspect. Many years ago, when I was giving a talk,
somebody asked me what prompted my ideas, and all
I could tell them . . . it was malnutrition.

Over the years, Will Eisner would point out that success in the comic book business in general, and at Eisner & Iger in particular, was difficult to gauge when it was actually happening. By the late 1930s, comic books were sprouting everywhere. Some lasted only a few issues and went under, only to reappear later under different titles but using the same characters and, in some instances, essentially the same stories. Strips could be cut up and rearranged, given new dialogue and plots, and recycled in different markets. The industry's growth was steady enough to convince entrepreneurs that there was probably a future in the business, but when that future might arrive, and what form it would take, was anyone's guess.

Two teenagers in Cleveland would be answering these questions in very short order.

But in the meantime, producing comics was a scattershot enterprise, dependent upon the whims and moods of very fickle readers. For his part, Eisner found himself working overtime to produce every type of comic imaginable, from continuing multipanel adventure strips to single-panel sports features; from westerns to science fiction and fantasy. He'd vary his styles to meet a publisher's demands, hit his deadline, and head to the next assignment. The pulp magazines, virtually dead in the water, had moved on, with some of their publishers going into comics. When they did, Eisner was there to work for them.

Fiction House was one such pulp publisher looking to change direction. With such titles as *Wings*, *Planet Stories*, *Fight Stories*, and *Jungle Stories*, Fiction House had seen its popularity slipping. After consulting with Eisner & Iger, publisher Thurman T. Scott decided to try to alter his fortunes with a comic book, and his first effort, *Jumbo Comics*, was a formidable entry into the field. With its oversize tabloid format, sixty-four pages of content, black-and-white entries printed on pastel-colored pages, and a cover that screamed, BIG PAGES—BIG PICTURES—BIG TYPE—EASY TO READ, *Jumbo* offered plenty of promise.

Eisner & Iger supplied the entire content for the book's first issue. Eisner had no trouble scaring up ideas for *Jumbo*'s contents, but he could no longer consider shouldering the shop's workload by himself. He'd already been using the work of Dick Briefer, an older artist who was more of a painter than inker and colorist, and Jacob Kurtzberg, a diminutive, scrappy young artist now calling himself Jack Curtiss, on other endeavors, and for *Jumbo #1* he assigned Curtiss the task of adapting *The Count of Monte Cristo* to sequential art form, while Briefer did the same with *The Hunchback of Notre Dame*. Eisner contributions included a recycled *Hawks of the Seas* and, to assure an issue packed with action and adventure, a new feature called *Sheena, Queen of the Jungle*, a *Tarzan* knockoff written under the nom de plume W. Morgan Thomas and illustrated by new staff artist Mort Meskin.

Sheena would last long after Eisner had abandoned the feature and left Eisner & Iger. Will Eisner and Jerry Iger would both stake claims to having created *Sheena*, though the feature's development and continuity were clearly Eisner's and Meskin's. In the shop environment, the creation of a comic could be a group effort, with ideas being bandied about at a dizzying pace and work on a project being rendered by several people. Eisner would become known for generating an idea, providing sketches of the principal characters, and even coming up with plots for the stories. He would then assign the feature to another artist (or artists), who would do the breakdowns, pencils, inking, lettering, and (if the comic was in color) coloring. Eisner usually handled the cover art. Each artist's contribution was vital to the success of the feature, though usually only one name—Eisner's or one of his pseudonyms—was placed under the title.

Sheena came about as the result of the enormous popularity of Edgar Rice Burroughs's *Tarzan* books and as a natural extension of the type of

material published in Fiction House's *Jungle Stories*. As scantily clad as her
male counterpart, Sheena took on man and beast in a series of entertaining but preposterous adventures. This was the stuff of dreams for teenage
boys, a combination of adolescent pinup and action story, and it didn't
seem to matter that this young woman, born in deepest Africa, always had
perfectly cut and brushed blond hair, spoke textbook English, and wore
outfits, albeit leopardskin ones, that seemed to be designed by a Hollywood tailor. *Sheena* was a creation on demand and definitely not the type of
character Eisner would have preferred to deal with, but he wasn't about to
turn down work, either.

By 1938, Eisner & Iger had developed into a full-blown comics studio,
employing an expanding roster of writers and artists and supplying material to nearly every comic book company in the business. Eisner re-
cruited his staff by placing an ad in the *New York Times* and carefully
reviewing each respondent's portfolio, his final decisions based on both
talent and the way an applicant might fulfill the stylistic needs of Eisner &
Iger's clients. Eisner was no older than most of the people he hired, yet
his ability and accumulated experience in the business gave him an authority that belied his years.

Working on *The Spirit* with Nick Cardy (with pipe) and Bob Powell. (Will Eisner Collection,
the Ohio State University Billy Ireland Cartoon Library & Museum)

In terms of comics history, the artists and writers passing through the Eisner & Iger shop between 1937 and 1939 is a staggering list of some of the most respected names in early comics history. Lou Fine, Bob Powell, Bernard Baily, Mort Meskin, Bob Kane, George Tuska, Klaus Nordling, Gill Fox, Reed Crandall, Nick Cardy, Vern Henkel, Chuck Mazoujian, and Jack Kirby—all logged time at the shop as employees or freelancers. With the arrival of new help, Eisner & Iger moved to a bigger place on Madison Avenue and Fortieth Street, with a large room to accommodate the bullpen and a small room, located in the front, for Jerry Iger's office. Eisner sat at a desk at the head of the big room, facing the artists like a teacher in front of his students.

The star of the group, beyond question, was Lou Fine, a thin, red-headed twenty-three-year-old former student at the Grand Central Art School and Pratt Institute. A childhood bout of polio had left Fine with a badly weakened left leg and noticeable limp, and from the long recovery period away from school, he developed a quiet, almost withdrawn personality. He'd begun drawing during his long hours alone. As good as, if not better than, Eisner as a draftsman, Fine was a point-and-direct kind of artist with no inclination to write his own material. Fine preferred to go off on his own, in a private office if possible, and work in his slow, tediously methodical fashion, treating each panel as if, upon delivery, it was going to be shipped to an art museum and viewed in perpetuity. He liked to work with a mechanical pencil, though he was gifted enough to ink directly onto the page with no pencils acting as a guide. When he submitted one of his completed pages, the other artists gathered around to admire the kind of exquisite work they could only dream of accomplishing.

Joe Kubert was one of those artists. "When his work came out every month," Kubert said, "every artist I knew wanted to get his hands on the stuff he was doing, just to look at it. It was like magic. I don't think it was so much that they wanted to work *like* him, but he was a kind of beacon: that's where you could go, the direction you could take, if you pushed yourself. You could accomplish what this guy was accomplishing—the way *you* wanted to do it."

According to several of the Eisner & Iger shop artists, Eisner envied Lou Fine's abilities, though he was frustrated by his unwillingness to handle other chores.

"Lou had never had any interest in the writing end of the business," Eisner recalled. "He had a brilliant technique, the best of anyone working then, and when I did the writing he was free to spend his time rendering a magnificent piece of art. There are writers who are capable of inspiring an artist, bringing things out of him that he might not have known were there. There has to be a kind of emotional welding between the two where trust takes place. That's why we worked so well together."

Bob Powell was Eisner's kind of man, at least in terms of what he did around the shop. Loud, abrasive, opinionated, and aggressive, with a streak of open anti-Semitism that irked Eisner no end, Powell could do anything that needed doing at Eisner & Iger. Powell worked quickly in any genre and required no supervision—the kind of pro's pro Eisner could appreciate. Born Stanislav (Stanley) Pawlowski in 1916 in Buffalo, New York, Powell moved to Manhattan and studied at the Pratt Institute before latching on to Eisner & Iger. Eisner appreciated his leadership skills enough to make him shop foreman, but his style, the polar opposite of Eisner's laid-back but hands-on way of treating employees, grated on those working under him.

Bob Fujitani, who worked with Eisner later, after Eisner and Iger had parted ways, remembered Powell as the kind of guy who let the power of his position go to his head. "When Eisner would leave, Powell would take over. He was the boss then. And immediately, as soon as Eisner was out the door, it would be, 'All right, you guys, let's hear those pencils sing.' I never liked him."

"He was a hell of a nice guy, but he was very brusque," allowed Nick Cardy, who joined the Eisner & Iger staff when he was very young and still going by the name Nicholas Viscardi. Powell looked out for him and helped him with his art. But even Cardy could be put off by Powell's bluster. "Every time I think of Powell," he said, "I think, 'full of sound and fury, signifying nothing.'"

One Eisner & Iger employee, artist George Tuska, took great exception to Powell's bluster. Muscular and blond, Tuska looked like one of the superhero characters the shop might draw. When he started at the shop in 1939, he instantly developed a huge crush on Toni Blum, a staff writer and the only woman working in the studio. Tuska was painfully shy, however, and he never approached Blum, even though his feelings were known by everybody in the bullpen. One day, Powell was shooting off his mouth about Blum, about how he could sleep with her anytime he wanted. Without uttering a word, Tuska carefully and deliberately cleaned off his brush, put it down, walked over to where Powell was holding court, and decked him with one punch. "You shouldn't have said that, Bob," was all he had to say.

Of all the writers and artists logging in time at the Eisner & Iger shop, none would achieve the acclaim and influence of Jack Kirby—the former Jacob Kurtzberg, Jack Kurtzberg, Jack Curtiss, et al., who with Joe Simon would create *Captain America* and, after a noteworthy partnership with Simon, go on to co-create, with Stan Lee, such Marvel Comics mainstays as *The Fantastic Four*, *The X-Men*, *The Silver Surfer*, and *The Hulk*. Only nineteen when he began working for Eisner & Iger, Kirby had obvious talent but was still learning the ropes, penciling and inking whatever he was assigned. He legally changed his name to Jack Kirby after he'd put in his short stint with Eisner. In time, his nickname would be "King," as in "the King of Comics."

One of his most memorable moments in the shop, recounted in Eisner's *The Dreamer*, involved Kirby saving Eisner's hide during a brief but intense visit from a Mafia thug sent to the Eisner & Iger studio to strong-arm Eisner in a dispute that would have been funny had it not been so serious. The misunderstanding began shortly after Eisner & Iger had moved to a new location. Eisner, disappointed with the building's towel service, had contacted the towel firm and inferred that he was thinking of switching to a better, cheaper service. As Eisner told the story, he was unaware at the time that the Mob controlled the business—thus the visit from the huge, imposing, walking stereotype dressed in a black shirt, black suit, and white tie, complete with a broken nose and shoulders that looked to be about two ax handles wide.

The strong-arm took what he considered to be a reasonable approach at the beginning of his conversation with Bill Eisner and Jerry Iger.

"Look, we don't want to have no trouble with you," he told them. "We want everything to go nice, see? You tell me what your problem is, and we'll try to fix it."

Eisner responded by saying that he wanted another service, that there were other places to call.

Negotiations broke down; some shouting ensued. The visitor insisted that his boss controlled the building's services and that was all there was to it.

Jack Kirby, sitting at his drawing table and listening in on the dispute, had heard enough. He stormed up to the front of the room and confronted the thug, even though he was a foot shorter than the other guy.

"Look, we don't want any crap from you," he shouted. "We don't like your goddamned towel service. Now get the hell out of here."

For Kirby, this wasn't a show. The short, stocky artist was a wrecking ball with attitude. He'd been raised in a rugged neighborhood on New York's Lower East Side, where aggression was the preemptive strike you took against the guy capable of beating the hell out of you and discretion was a word used by kids attending the private schools. Kirby loved movies, especially action pictures, and even his first cartoon job, working as an animator on the *Popeye* cartoons produced by Max Fleischer, was all about the little guy gaining justice by standing up to the big brute. Kirby might not have been big, but he was legitimately tough. He wasn't about to sit by and watch his bosses be intimidated by some Mafia muscle.

The thug left without further incident.

"He comes back again, call me," Kirby instructed Eisner. "I'll take care of him."

Years later, Eisner could see the humor in the incident and in the way Kirby had taken on the thug in his own David and Goliath scenario. "Jack was a little fellow," Eisner said. "He thought he was John Garfield the actor! Very, very tough."

In changing his name, Jack Kirby was in no way unusual in the comic book business. Like Hollywood actors, comic book artists changed their names to mask their ethnic or Jewish backgrounds. If comics were a ghetto, as Eisner repeatedly suggested throughout his career, its artists were perfect inhabitants. Many, like Eisner, had come from European stock, lived impoverished childhoods in tough neighborhoods, barely survived the Depression, and studiously worked on their art, only to discover that the better-paying jobs were closed to people with their backgrounds. In addition, names like Powell and Kirby were easier to sign on artwork than Pawlowski or Kurtzberg. Eli Katz became Gil Kane, Bob Kahn became Bob Kane, and Alfred Caplin became Al Capp.

Stan Lee, born Stanley Lieber, said he changed his name because he wanted to reserve his given name for the novels he hoped to write. "I was kind of embarrassed to be writing comics," he admitted, "so I didn't want to use my real name. I was saving that for the *good* stuff I would someday write."

Nicholas Viscardi changed his name to Nick Cardy after becoming fed up with the ribbing he took about the Mob, his Italian heritage, and, during World War II, the idea that Italians were the enemy. When he was doing freelance work, he even heard from a boss who, thinking he was being funny, signed Viscardi's check with a "P" rather than a "V." The next month, his last name began with a "B."

Viscardi was rightfully offended. He'd been raised in a lower-class, ethnically diverse neighborhood, where this type of xenophobia was foreign. As a boy, he'd come home from school and, while waiting for his mother to return home from work, sit on the front stoop of his apartment building and talk to a rabbi from the same building. He hated the anti-Italian jokes he heard, but he needed the job. "I was upset," he remembered, "but I was young at the time and I was trying to make a living. So I changed it. I just put in the last part of the name."

Cardy didn't abandon his name entirely—at least not right away. When working on *Lady Luck* for Eisner, he used the house name "Ford Davis" when he signed the feature, but he always found a way to disguise his initials, "NV," in the artwork.

In the early comic book days, artists were fortunate to find any permutation of their names attached to their work. Publishers and shops, including Eisner & Iger, preferred to use house names. They'd assign a generic name to a feature, which would always be used regardless of the artist doing it. Using a house name was insurance for publishers, protection from lawsuits that might arise if an artist walked away from a firm but still wanted to use a character he'd created. Artists didn't own their creations in any event, but to a a publisher, owning a feature *and* using a house name was failsafe protection.

Eisner had written under so many names that he would have been forgiven if he lost count. He could shrug it off as part of the business, and he expected the others working for him to see it the same way. "We had a whole bunch of phony names," he explained, adding with a laugh, "We just handed them out with the salary."

Sometime in early 1938, the Eisner & Iger studio received an unsolicited package in the mail, postmarked Cleveland and containing a cover letter and two complete comic stories, one a spy thriller, the other an adventure about a costumed hero with superhuman strength and an unexplained need to rectify the injustice he saw in the world around him. Eisner rejected both as substandard. Iger didn't like them, either. The two men were accustomed to hearing from young artists looking for a way to enter into comics, and as far as Eisner (then only twenty-one himself) could tell, this was another one of those cases. The writer and artist, Jerry Siegel and Joe Shuster, respectively, needed more time in art school to hone their craft if they expected to meet market and audience demands.

"I wrote them a long letter and told them they weren't ready to come to New York," Eisner recalled. "It was a tough town and their style wasn't professional yet."

Eisner had a personal aversion to superhero stories—to costumed heroes, as they called them in those days. Each passing month in the business left him all the more convinced that he was destined to do more mature material. He loved to write and he loved to draw, but he had concluded back in his Clinton High days that he wasn't gifted enough as either to make an impact in the adult world of serious literature or gallery art. He could, however, thrive in comics, and if he worked hard and long enough at it, he might be able to move his material into avenues geared toward adult readers. In Eisner's mind, this Superman idea, featuring a character who switched from a business suit to tights and a cape, was strictly kid stuff. It required a suspension of belief that dipped into the realm of bad science fiction or fantasy, as well as a format that demanded more action, less story. Eisner was spoiled by the quality of art and writing coming out of his shop, including the work aimed at younger readers. These Siegel and Shuster kids had a long way to go before they matched the work he was seeing on a daily basis.

So in one of the few giant missteps in a career characterized by strong instincts and judgment, Bill Eisner shot down *Superman*.

Not that he was alone. *Superman* had visited the surface of nearly every comics editor's desk in New York and elsewhere, always with the same results. In reflecting back on it, Eisner thought that the reluctance to accept *Superman* might have risen out of the ugliness of the times and the strong feelings generated by Hitler's rise to power.

"We were all concerned with the Nazi shtick, the Nazi concepts," he explained. "*Mein Kampf* was published here around 1935, and there was a lot of talk on the subject of *supermen*. The psychological impact of these ideas on the imaginative fantasy creators was immense."

In his book *Disguised as Clark Kent: Jews, Comics, and the Creation of the Superhero*, comics historian, editor, and former comics writer Danny Fingeroth, while not disagreeing with Eisner's assessment, wrote that Superman and other superheroes to follow had deep roots in the response to Hitler and Nazism. The predominance of Jews in comics, he felt, was a huge contributing factor:

The creation of a legion of special beings, self-appointed to protect the weak, innocent, and victimized at a time when fascism was dominating the European continent from which the creators of the heroes hailed, seems like a task that Jews were uniquely positioned to take on. One might say they were cornered into it. The fantasy of godlike beings who could solve our problems was a cry of hope as well as of despair, as the Jews were the canaries in the coal mine of hate that was Nazism, sounding a simultaneous cry for help and a warning that *you could be next.*

Only a strange, unpredictable turn of events saved *Superman* from the trash bin. At the beginning of 1938, Major Malcolm Wheeler-Nicholson was reaching the end of the line in his involvement with National Comics. He had managed to stay in the business through IOUs, the goodwill and generosity of some of his creditors, and low payment (sometimes nonpayment) to his contributors. *Detective Comics*, a new title that he'd hoped would pull him out of the doldrums, slogged along unimpressively. Drowning in debt, Wheeler-Nicholson began work on a new title, a comic book called *Action Comics*. If he could successfully launch the book, he might be able to buy a little more time.

Why he believed this is hard to figure. *Action Comics*, as concocted by Wheeler-Nicholson, was just another hodgepodge of the type of material he'd been foisting on the public from the get-go—forgettable stuff now rotting on newsstands. He might have been able to purchase mediocre work for less than premium prices, but the cover price for his books was the same as it was for some of the better titles on the market, and readers wanted more bang for their dimes.

Desperate for a new, first-rate feature to anchor his book, Wheeler-Nicholson called his business contacts and asked if they had anything lying around. Somehow, a much-handled copy of *Superman*, languishing on Maxwell C. Gaines's slush pile at *All-American Comics*, found its way into his office. Wheeler-Nicholson knew Jerry Siegel and Joe Shuster from past business dealings; they had been regular contributors to his comics for more than a year. This *Superman* idea, although designed originally as a newspaper strip, required work before it would be self-contained enough for a comic book, but it was better than the other material Wheeler-Nicholson had earmarked for *Action*.

His plans for *Action Comics* never reached fruition. Harry Donenfeld, partner in the firm that printed Wheeler-Nicholson's comics and publisher of girlie pulp magazines with such imaginative titles as *Juicy Tales* and *Hot Tales*, pulled the plug on Wheeler-Nicholson's company early in 1938. In the past, Donenfeld had been willing to accept a small percentage of Wheeler-Nicholson's enterprises in exchange for debt; this time around, he wasn't looking for a piece of the business. In what was designed to look like a generous gesture, Donenfeld sent Wheeler-Nicholson and his wife on a cruise to Cuba, supposedly to give the Major the chance to come up with fresh ideas. But when Wheeler-Nicholson returned, things had changed. The locks on his office had been changed and Doneneld had filed a suit against him for nonpayment of bills. Facing a disastrous court ruling, Wheeler-Nicholson accepted a mediocre buyout offer from Donenfeld and disappeared from comics.

Neither Donenfeld nor his right-hand man, Jack Liebowitz, had any concept of what they had on their hands, or that *Superman* would turn into the publishing and marketing phenomenon that it eventually became. The comic's creators had no idea, either. They saw it as just another job and assigned no special significance to the character, even as they signed away the rights to *Superman* when they endorsed their $130 paycheck for the feature.

Action Comics didn't just do well at the newsstands; it exploded into existence, starting strong and, over the next few months, snowballing until it had become the industry standard for a burgeoning superhero comics market. Donenfeld's company became very wealthy. Donenfeld would label *Superman* "a fluke," and Liebowitz would call it "pure luck"—which, in fact, it was.

And Bill Eisner walked away with the anecdote of a lifetime.

Actually, the success of *Superman* had a much greater effect on Eisner than he ever could have anticipated. For starters, *Superman*'s popularity kicked the comics industry to a new level. Sales jumped for other books; every publisher clamored for a costumed hero with an exotic background, some kind of superpower, and a nose for truth and justice, if not the American way. Eisner & Iger, as suppliers to comic book publishers, followed the trend, producing work as fast as the studio artists could crank it out. Once again Eisner sent out a call for more writers and artists, and once again he was rewarded with employees capable of staying on pace.

Two of his more recent hires, an artist named Alex Blum and his writer/daughter, Audrey (nicknamed Toni), added not only badly needed help to the studio, but, in the case of Toni Blum, a touch of romance that Eisner, had he been thinking about it, might have anticipated. Aside from taking jobs as secretaries, women were extremely rare in the early days of comics. Studios, like baseball clubhouses, were men-only environments inhabited by adults working in a children's game. The bad behavior, language, practical jokes, off-color humor, drinking after hours, and in some cases fooling around were all practiced freely, without concern for disapproving female perspectives. It was the same in the chain of command: Bill Eisner and Jerry Iger, like baseball managers and front office personnel, maintained a division between themselves and their employees, fraternizing with them only occasionally, which led some of their workers to think they were standoffish.

Toni Blum, an aspiring playwright, turned heads—literally and figuratively—from her first day at the studio. She was young, attractive, intelligent, and, as the men around her learned, very good at her job. Jerry Iger's earlier quip about the shop's grinding out frankfurters was now a reality, with two new, influential companies—Quality Comics, run by Everett 'Busy" Arnold, and Fox Publications, operated by Victor Fox— pushing hard for an increasing volume of material. Eisner worked closely with Toni Blum, coming up with new ideas every day and delivering them to his new writer, who would type out scripts for the pencilers to break down into comic panels. Eisner, so cloistered at work that he had no social life to speak of, took notice of Toni Blum.

The attraction was mutual, though nothing serious ever developed. Eisner was too busy, too devoted to advancing his career and the fortunes of Eisner & Iger, to commit to a relationship. They dated briefly, but Eisner broke it off before things advanced. He would depict the fling in *The Dreamer.* "I've got dreams," he tells Toni, renamed Andrea in the book. "Do they include romance?" she asks. "I guess that will come with success," he answers. Hurt by the response, she asks him, "Oh? . . . Is that all?" "What else is there?" he wonders, oblivious to the notion that as an aspiring playwright biding time at Eisner & Iger until one of her scripts was discovered, Toni Blum might have been offended by the comment.

Eisner's obsession with work—at the cost of close friendships or relationships with women—became legendary at the shop, so much so that Jerry Iger himself tried to intervene by setting him up for an evening with one of his acquaintances. Eisner wined and dined her, then took her to bed, and the next time he saw Iger, he thanked him for arranging the date. Iger, thunderstruck by Eisner's naïveté, informed him that his date had been a prostitute. Eisner, he pointed out, should have paid her, not fallen in love with her.

Comic books' accelerating sales figures attracted a strange gallery of wacky characters, lowlifes, talent-free wannabes, rogues, and shifty businessmen, all eager to pick up a fast buck before the fad died out. Art, to those educated enough to know how to spell, was a three-letter word attached in some vague way to the colors in these skinny, pulpy magazines; fine work was a bonus, not a requirement. To those creating the comics, from the individual artists to shops like Eisner & Iger, the line of demarcation dividing the good guys from the bad guys could be thin, almost indefinable. But in the aftermath of the Depression and a global conflict darkening the future, nothing much mattered as long as the product was being served and the bills paid.

Fox Publications was a case in point. The company's founder, Victor Fox, a short, stout, balding, cigar-chomping, fast-talking former accountant, could come across as a real low-rent operator, but in his brief history in comics, he'd held on to just enough credibility to keep the worst suspicions at bay. He'd been counting beans for Harry Donenfeld at National when *Action Comics* and Superman broke through, and he knew enough about Donenfeld and his cronies to recognize that these people, while not stupid by any means, had essentially backed into a fortune. Reasoning that he had enough business sense to put together his own company and wait for luck to traipse through his doorway, Fox quit National and formed Fox Publications. Eisner & Iger supplied him with the bulk of his material.

Eisner tolerated Fox, but he had little use for him. "Fox was like an Edward G. Robinson kind of guy," he'd recall. "He ran around the shop and he had delusions of grandeur. He went bankrupt four times. He once said to me, 'Kid, if you go bankrupt, go big!' And he did! He went bankrupt once for $400,000, most of it owed to the paper house. It was so much money that the paper house financed him to get him back in business so they could recover the $400,000 he owed!"

Golden Age comics legend Joe Simon served as Fox's editor in chief in one of his very first jobs. As he described him, Fox was "a Wall Street hustler" who "didn't have the slightest idea of how to put a comic book together, but that didn't prohibit [him] from setting up a palatial office and announcing to anyone within earshot, 'I'm the king of the comics.'" The way Simon remembered it, Fox might have been the king of marketing schemes, a guy who would use his comic books as a means of promoting the questionable products he concocted.

"Kooba Cola was the most bizarre," Simon wrote in his memoirs, *The Comic Book Makers.*

In 1940, inspired by the popularity of Coca-Cola, the inside covers of his comics heralded the arrival of "the world's newest and best-tasting soft drink, delightfully refreshing and fortified with 35 USP units of vitamin B_1 (for the sake of health and nutrition)." The slogan, "Each bottle has enough for two," was accompanied by a picture of a pretty girl or a couple of typical young Americans sipping contentedly on a bottle of giant sized Kooba Cola.

Later the ads featured coupons offering a bottle of Kooba Cola free of charge. Coupon redemption as well as distribution of the soft drink was to be handled by newsstand and magazine distributors. In addition, there were the premium refund offers. The reader could save and redeem Kooba Cola bottle caps for toys such as baseball bats—and for 250 bottle caps, a Buck Rogers pop-pop pistol. A kid would have rotted every tooth in his head before he could ever earn enough points to win these prizes. Luckily, no evidence of any Kooba Cola has ever come to light. Certainly, we who worked for the company never saw one single bottle.

Fox always owed Eisner & Iger a healthy sum for their work, but never enough to be cut off. The shop was now charging $10 a page, which translated into a handsome profit if someone like Fox came around and needed enough material to fill a sixty-four-page comic book. Eisner had heard the rumors about Fox, and despite his reservations about a man he would describe as "a thief in the real, true sense," he could do business with the man as long as he played aboveboard and sent some money Eisner & Iger's way.

Then Fox came in with a demand that Eisner found hard to digest: He wanted Eisner to create a character that was more than just a Superman knockoff; he wanted a character that was virtually identical to the Siegel and Shuster creation, a man of unparalleled strength, clad in tights and a skintight shirt emblazoned with a large "W"—for Wonder Man. This character would be big enough to merit his own book—*Wonder Comics*—and the sooner Eisner & Iger could put it together the better.

This knockoff of the new, immensely popular *Superman*, created to order for Victor Fox, nearly cost Eisner his studio. (Courtesy of Will Eisner Studios, Inc.)

Eisner struggled with the order from the moment Fox delivered it. He wasn't experienced enough to know much about copyright laws and their enforcement, but he suspected that the similarities might be enough to land the shop in some trouble. *Action Comics* had touched off a slew of Superman-like characters in the business, but so far they had been different enough from the Man of Steel to avoid legal problems. Victor Fox's history with Donenfeld wasn't going to help matters, either.

Eisner consulted with Jerry Iger, who, not surprisingly, looked at it from a business angle. Eisner & Iger, although reaching the peak of the company's success, had huge bills to pay, from payroll for their large bullpen to general overhead. Bill Eisner and Jerry Iger were compensating themselves well for their efforts, further eroding the shop's profit margin. If Eisner refused to create the *Wonder Man* comic and Victor Fox moved his business elsewhere, Eisner & Iger stood to take a tremendous loss. "It's his magazine and he's asking for this," Iger concluded, "[so] we'll do it for him."

Fox had given Eisner a written memo with directions for what he expected for *Wonder Man*, and Eisner followed it to the letter. The result was a comic book that, from cover to content, resembled *Superman* to a shocking degree. Eisner had worked in some differences to disguise the similarities—Wonder Man, for instance was blond, whereas Superman had dark hair; Wonder Man's costume was red and yellow, and Superman's was red, blue, and yellow; Wonder Man received his superhero powers from a magic ring rather than from the sun of an alien planet—but the characters were essentially the same. Even the covers were strikingly similar: in *Action Comics #1*, Superman is seen holding an automobile aloft while the bad guys scatter; on the cover of *Wonder Comics #1*, Wonder Man is taking on an airplane.

Wonder Comics hit the streets, and Harry Donenfeld reacted as Eisner feared he would, suing Fox Publications for copyright infringement. As Wonder Man's writer and artist, Eisner was subpoenaed to testify in court as a material witness. Shortly before the case finally went before a judge, Fox met with Eisner and attempted to coach him on the proper way to testify.

"I want you to tell them there was no intent to copy," Fox said.

"As far as I'm personally concerned, I had no intent to copy," Eisner averred. "I was following your instructions."

Fox had anticipated this answer from someone as young and idealistic as Eisner. Ideals—and the truth—were for dreamers; it was time to speak in terms that Eisner was more likely to understand. Fox reminded Eisner, as if it were necessary, that he owed Eisner & Iger $3,000—an enormous sum in those days and enough to jeopardize the shop's future—and if Eisner failed to testify as directed, Fox would withhold the entire amount.

Once again, Eisner consulted with Jerry Iger, and as before, Iger took a business perspective: telling the truth presented too great a risk.

At least this was Eisner's story. There are two versions of what happened in the courtroom hearings. Eisner claimed, in interviews and in his depiction of the legal proceedings in his graphic novel *The Dreamer*, that he stood his ground, told the truth, and faced the consequences for his youthful idealism. "I suppose when you're young it is easier to adhere to principles," he told an interviewer more than three decades after he testified.

A transcript of his testimony in a November 1939 appellate court hearing, published by comics journalist Ken Quattro in July 2010, tells an entirely different story. The transcript shows Eisner capitulating in every sense to the demands of Victor Fox and Jerry Iger. He denied reading *Action Comics* or knowing much of anything about Superman until after he created Wonder Man. Wonder Man, Eisner claimed, was based more on the Phantom than on any other character. He denied plagiarism, even though a comparison of a number of panels in *Action Comics* and *Wonder Man* showed incontestable similarities in the art and writing.

Despite a major (and, fortunately for Eisner, posthumous) hit on his carefully maintained public image, the later revelations about Eisner's perjury didn't affect history. Fox lost the case and delivered on his promise. He never paid Eisner & Iger a cent.

Although he never formally addressed the issue for the record, the Wonder Man episode must have truly frosted Bill Eisner. He never cared much for Jerry Iger—"Don't pay any attention to him; he's here because he's a good businessman," he'd instruct shop workers disgusted with Iger—and the Wonder Man affair effectively fractured what little was left of their mutual trust. To make matters worse, Wonder Man was precisely the type of costumed superhero that Eisner despised. To have been forced to create the character and then deal with it in court couldn't have done much to improve his disposition about the types of comics that by 1939 were the rage of the industry.

To top this off, Bob Kane, Eisner's old high school chum and former Eisner & Iger freelance contributor, had teamed up with a gifted writer/artist named Bill Finger to create a costumed character that was about to become the next big thing. As a character, Bat-Man, as he was initially called (the hyphen would later disappear), was more complex and fully realized than Superman. He was a human with no superpowers, reliant on his wits and gadgets he stored in a utility belt, and while Superman's heroics were witnessed in broad daylight by throngs of adoring citizens, Bat-Man was more a creature of the night, a loner, part detective and part vigilante. Unlike Superman, he didn't have to find ways to duck away from his day job to go out and save the world; under the dark cowl hiding his true identity, Bat-Man was a wealthy, mansion-dwelling socialite, totally self-sufficient and capable of heading out on a moment's notice.

Bat-Man made his debut in *Detective Comics #27*, and readers responded favorably—not in the frenzy that built so quickly with Superman, but enough to salt away Bob Kane's legacy in comics.

Will Eisner was nothing but gracious when discussing Kane's success, but those closest to him knew Eisner to be extremely competitive and, on occasion, envious of others' good fortune. He never hid his opinion that Kane, as an artist and creative individual, was vastly inferior to others working in comics; on a personal level, he could take Kane only in limited doses. In Eisner's view, Kane was far too loud for his talent.

There was no debating that Bat-Man, coupled with the overwhelming popularity of Superman, had changed the direction of comics while making National the top comic book publisher in the business. Eisner & Iger continued to produce huge volumes of material for Fiction House and other publishers, but as 1939 drew to a close, Eisner was aching for a change of direction, for something that would advance him beyond the juvenile audience that restricted his talents and vision. He believed to his core that this could be accomplished in comics, but he was stumped by how that might happen.

The solution was nearby, and for one of the few times in his life, Eisner didn't have to invent it himself.

chapter four

A SPIRIT FOR ALL AGES

*I guess I'm like a guy with a mission who believes that what he's doing
is right. I felt, not immortal, but I felt like a guy who is going into
combat, believing the bullets won't hit him.*

In late fall 1939, shortly before Christmas, Eisner heard from Everett
"Busy" Arnold, publisher and editor of Quality Comics, one of the
leading comics producers in the business. Arnold, who couldn't stand
Jerry Iger and wanted no part of him, wanted to meet Eisner alone.

Eisner and Arnold had known each other for more than a year. Arnold
had been tossing the Eisner & Iger shop a fair amount of work, even
though he had his own staff of artists. Eisner liked Arnold, who was a ge-
nial presence in a business of loudmouths and posers, and Quality Comics
was an enterprise that lived up to its name. Arnold cared about the material
he published.

Born in Rhode Island in 1899, Arnold took an interesting path to his
position in the comic book business. According to Dick Arnold, Busy's
son, the family lineage could be traced back to Benedict Arnold. Accounts of how Everett M. Arnold earned his moniker vary: perhaps he
was tagged "Busy" because he was always on the go as a child, or perhaps
he was such a chatterbox that he was called a busybody. In any event, the
nickname fit a boy who was active, intelligent, and very athletic.

After graduating from Brown University with a history degree in
1921, Arnold moved to New York and took a job with the press manu-
facturer R. Hoe and Company; a short time later, he became a sales representative for the Goss Printing Company. He relocated to Connecticut,
where one of his biggest clients, Eastern Color Printing, had its offices
and where his interest in comics began. He'd always loved the color

comics section in the Sunday newspapers, and the nearby Greater Buffalo Press printed these sections for most of the major newspapers east of the Mississippi. Arnold wound up taking a job with the company, rising to the position of vice president. He'd hoped that he and company president Walter Koessler, another comics fan, might partner on a comic book venture similar to *Famous Funnies*, published by Eastern Color, but Arnold and Koessler had a falling-out and it never happened. Arnold quit the Greater Buffalo Press and created his own comic book, *Feature Funnies*, in New York, debuting in 1937. Like *Famous Funnies*, Arnold's comic relied mainly on reprints of newspaper strips.

Busy Arnold connected with Eisner & Iger a year later. He was aiming to fit original material into *Feature Funnies* and, if possible, create new titles. Eisner liked working for Quality Comics Group, as Arnold called his company. He admired Arnold's business panache and his insistence on high-quality work, even if he wasn't an artist and could only judge art instinctively.

Eisner also appreciated the fact that Arnold was willing to pay for good work. "Busy Arnold was an astute buyer of comic features," he pointed out. "When all the other publishers believed in buying on the cheap, Arnold's theory was to pay well. He knew he could get better talent by paying well."

When Arnold contacted Eisner about a private meeting, he'd hatched a plan that even Eisner, a master of creative thinking, had to stand back and admire—a plan combining the current interest in original comic books—Eisner's forte—with the traditional popularity of the Sunday newspaper strips. Eisner's career was about to take a dramatic turn.

Comics sold newspapers, regardless of what their critics had to say about their cultural value. Newspapers nationwide, from large circulation to small, used their colorful wraparound comic sections to entice newsstand buyers, and by 1940, families all across America shared a common ritual of spreading the Sunday funnies section across kitchen tables or on living room floors, where kids would wander from panel to panel as they saw their favorite characters in full color for the only time that week.

The significant uptick in comic books' popularity worried newspaper publishers. Comic books offered benefits that newspapers couldn't touch. They had a shelf life, unlike the disposable daily papers; they could be collected and passed around. Their bigger format allowed them to present longer, more detailed stories. Newspapers couldn't compete with their eye-popping covers. If comic book sales continued on the upswing, newspaper sales figures were bound to suffer. Publishers felt certain of that.

Busy Arnold had been pondering this, and when he met with Eisner for lunch, he had a powerful newspaperman named Henry Martin with him. Arnold had been introduced to Martin back in his days at the Greater Buffalo Press, when the press was printing the Sunday comic sections for newspapers and Martin was an up-and-coming sales representative for the Des Moines Register & Tribune Syndicate. Martin had come up with the idea of creating a weekly comic book supplement—a sixteen-page comic book featuring all new material—to be inserted into Sunday newspapers, much the way weekly magazines and television supplements would be inserted in papers in years to come. He'd discussed the prospects with Busy Arnold, who had experience with both comics and printing, whereas Martin had all kinds of connections on the distribution end. Eisner, the two offered, could be the one producing this weekly comic.

Eisner liked the idea. With the right contract provisions, he'd have complete editorial and artistic control over his work—within reason, of course—and if Martin was capable at all, the comic book would be reaching millions of readers of all ages. The big challenge would be the weekly deadline: in the newspaper world, there was no margin of error, no acceptable excuse. You had to bring in the comic book's camera-ready pages by a very specific time, week after week, month after month. Henry Martin had seen *Hawks of the Seas* and needed no further convincing of Eisner's talent. What he needed was absolute assurance that this talented artist (who at twenty-two was barely more than a kid) was up to the grind ahead. Busy Arnold assured Martin that Eisner was as reliable as they got.

Negotiations—Eisner's favorite part of business, then and always—commenced. The agreement would be an equal two-way partnership between Arnold and Eisner. Besides producing the weekly newspaper supplement, Arnold required Eisner to contribute the entire contents for two new, as yet to be determined comic books for newsstand sales. For the weekly comic, Arnold and Martin wanted costumed heroes, the type that had come into favor with Superman and Bat-Man. These serial characters would provide continuity in pulling readers from issue to issue. Eisner would have to find a way to accomplish all this without the services of the Eisner & Iger shop—or at least without it as it was currently structured. Arnold and Martin both loathed Jerry Iger, so he was out. Eisner would have to either buy Iger out or sever ties with his company.

Eisner agreed to these provisions, although, ever his practical mother's son, he winced at the thought of totally abandoning the security of an established, successful company for the uncertainty of a project that had never been attempted.

The negotiations hit a snag when Eisner insisted on keeping the copyrights to the characters and content of his work in his name—a demand that the other two flatly rejected. By industry standards, the publisher or syndicate held the copyrights. The practice had been established to protect publishers from greedy or temperamental artists who might be inclined to pack up and leave if, say, they wanted more pay or had other serious issues with an editor or publisher or if they proved to be unreliable and publishers wanted to replace them.

Eisner refused to budge. The practice may have been the industry standard, but he couldn't abide them, as an artist or businessman. Many of the artists working in comics didn't mind the work-for-hire method of operations; they were content to turn in their work and pick up their payment. Every time they endorsed a paycheck, they were reminded, by agreements stamped on the back of their checks, that their signatures constituted a contractual agreement granting all rights to the publisher. To artists who viewed comics as hackwork, signing away rights was no big deal. But to Eisner and other artists who took pride in their work in comics, it was a very big deal indeed.

"That kind of rubbed me the wrong way," said Al Jaffee, who worked for Eisner before eventually moving on to make his name at *Mad* magazine. "Bill Gaines had a contract on the back of every check. I wouldn't have minded if he came to me and said, 'Well, you have to sign a contract if you want to work for me, and I got all the rights.' I would think about it and then I'd say, 'Okay, I'll sign the contract because I want to work.' But I've already done the job and I've got a check in my hand, and the check says I have to sell all my rights. What am I going to do, tear the check up? I've done the work. So, you know, you're caught between a rock and a hard place."

Eisner the artist bristled at the idea of anyone claiming ownership of his creative work—as far as he was concerned, publishers were paying him for permission to print it—but Eisner the businessman hated the arrangement even more. He'd watched how National Comics, now calling itself DC Comics, had raked in a fortune on Superman, with no end in sight. The way it was set up, the publisher could—and, in the case of DC, eventually did—cut creators such as Jerry Siegel and Joe Shuster out of the action. As owners of the characters, the publisher could assign them to other artists or, in the case of a character as popular as Superman, use the character for other lucrative marketing adventures, from movies to toys, without having to give the creators a fair cut of the profits.

Young as he was, Eisner never deluded himself about the nature of the business he was conducting with Busy Arnold and Henry Martin. He later joked in interviews that he would have loved to believe, as he sat across the table from Arnold and Martin, that they were interested in him because he was the best artist in the comic book business; in fact, he knew that they sought his services because he was a dependable commodity. "To the syndicate, [the supplement] was merchandise, and I was always conscious of that," he said. "I wasn't flattering myself into thinking that they saw it as anything but something their salesmen could use to sell more newspapers, and that didn't bother me."

The men argued at length, and for a while it looked as if they'd be breaking off the meeting without reaching an agreement. Then Eisner came up with a creative solution. The partnership contract would stipulate that the supplement would be copyrighted in Busy Arnold's name, with the written agreement that all rights to character and content would revert to Eisner if the partnership dissolved. As Eisner recalled, Arnold was particularly concerned about what would happen to the character if Eisner was drafted—a likely enough scenario given the escalation of the war in Europe—and if something happened to him while he was in the service.

"We agreed that the stories would carry his copyright," Eisner said, "and that at any time I returned, I would get the copyright back." Arnold proved to be good to his word. "When I got back I went to him and told him I wanted to disassociate him from *The Spirit*, and he signed an agreement in which he gave the rights back to me."

Arnold and Martin could live with this. The three men shook on the deal, and when Eisner got up to leave, he was convinced that he was now involved in something important, something career changing. Arnold and Martin hoped to launch the comic as soon as Eisner could put it all together—a tall order, considering they hadn't discussed any specifics about the characters that Eisner would be presenting. In fact, Eisner himself had no idea what he'd be doing. His future, like a blank page on his drawing board, was all potential.

Jerry Iger thought his partner had lost his mind when Eisner explained the new project to him. He was undoubtedly hurt and angered by the prospect of his main creative force leaving him on his own, but beyond that, for all of Eisner's explaining, Iger could see no good reason for his leaving the company at the height of its success. A war, he told Eisner, was on the horizon, already being waged in Europe, and there was no telling what would happen to Eisner's comic strip if the United States became involved and Eisner was called into the service. There was a tremendous risk in leaving a proven success like Eisner & Iger for something that had never been attempted before. "Your dream could go up in smoke," Iger cautioned his partner.

At Fiction House, Eisner & Iger's biggest client, publisher Thurman T. Scott was also upset, but for a different reason. His business with the shop was based largely on his cordial relationship with Eisner, and he didn't want to deal with Jerry Iger. A southerner, with all the traditional gentility that implied, Scott found Iger's aggressive personality intolerable—to such an extent that he offered to lend Eisner any money he might need to buy Iger out if that meant Eisner would continue to supply Fiction House with comics. Eisner politely declined.

What neither man understood was the extent of Eisner's need to break away. Both understood that newspaper comic strip artists were highly regarded and well compensated for their work—much more so than the comic book artists—but for Eisner this was only part of the attraction. He was already well compensated for his efforts at Eisner & Iger; he lived well, and he felt secure enough to move his parents, brother, and sister to an apartment on Manhattan's Morningside Drive. At twenty-two he was already able, in essence, to support a family of five. Money wasn't an issue.

What working for newspapers offered Eisner was an opportunity he would never have as long as he continued to work in the Eisner & Iger vein of producing comics. With newspapers, he could write and illustrate stories for adults as well as young readers. He might not have known, while he explained the deal to Iger, exactly what kind of character he would be creating for the newspaper supplement, but he was certain that despite Arnold and Martin's desires, it wouldn't be a guy from another planet, somebody wearing a costume like a strongman in the circus, someone who could fly, or someone who'd battle weird mutants from outer space. Whatever he decided to do, it would be entertaining but story driven and would stay as far from gimmicks as possible.

When they had formed their company, Bill Eisner and Jerry Iger had a formal buyout provision written into their partnership agreement. According to the contract, if one partner wished to opt out of the company, he was required to offer his partner the chance to buy him out at an agreed-upon price. Eisner and Iger talked it over and decided that Iger would keep the company at a $20,000 purchase price—a decent return on Eisner's original investment by anyone's standards. In addition, Eisner relinquished ownership of all the characters he had created at Eisner & Iger, including Sheena and the cast of *Hawks of the Seas*. When he left Eisner & Iger, he would truly be starting from scratch.

At first glance, it might appear that Eisner, who prided himself on his business acumen, might have been taken on the deal—and Iger would present it that way when he talked about the breakup in the future. The buyout price that Eisner received was undoubtedly lower than the company's market value, and Iger now controlled all the characters that Eisner had created during his time with the company. Eisner, however, walked away with three invaluable assets when Jerry Iger agreed to let him take Lou Fine, Bob Powell, and Chuck Mazoujian with him. In effect, Eisner had raided the shop for its best artists.

It hadn't been easy. Iger had an eye for talent, and at a time when comic book companies, shops and publishers alike, were making sport out of raiding each other's bullpens, Iger was sensitive about losing his staff to Eisner or anyone else. When word spread about his leaving, Eisner was approached by most of the artists working for him, all wishing to be part of the new enterprise. Knowing that he'd be permitted to take only a few men with him, Eisner held hushed, confidential meetings with the ones he hoped to employ.

"There were a few tight-lipped moments then, because talent was very precious," Eisner said. "Bodies were being traded back and forth. Some people wanted to go with me, but I had to say, 'You can't come with me because Iger will be mad.'"

Eisner moved quickly in setting up his new shop. He found a two-room, fifth-floor apartment at 5 Tudor City on Manhattan's East Side and installed his bullpen in its large living room. He used the bedroom for his office. Quarters were tight, especially when Eisner began hiring other artists to complement the staff he'd brought over from Eisner & Iger, but nowhere near as cramped as the conditions when he and Jerry Iger had opened their first shop in what was little more than a large closet.

Eisner's ideas for the Sunday comic book were starting to take shape. The format had already been determined in his earlier conversation with Busy Arnold and Henry Martin. The book would be sixteen pages long and have a self-contained cover. There would be three weekly features; Eisner figured the main story, which he would handle himself, would run eight pages, with the two other features sharing the remaining eight.

At the drawing board in his Tudor City studio. (Will Eisner Collection,
the Ohio State University Billy Ireland Cartoon Library & Museum)

All three entries would be detective stories, in one form or another, that would be appealing to both young and adult readers. Bob Powell and Chuck Mazoujian would handle the other two installments, while Lou Fine and the rest of the staff worked on the other books for Quality Comics.

The character anchoring the comic book took months to develop, mainly because Eisner set the bar so high when he mapped out his goals for the feature. In his main character, he was trying to accommodate two conflicting ideas: since he wanted to concentrate on story rather than character, his hero should be able to blend almost unnoticed into each week's story line, yet at the same time, that central figure had to be strong enough to make readers return week after week. He wanted an entirely human character, a hero operating without superpowers or even a weapon, a detective fallible enough to make mistakes and take a licking as he worked on solving a case. He would live outside the law, as adventurers often do, but honor it enough to devote his life to maintaining justice and order.

"When I decided upon [the character], I worked from the inside out, you might say," Eisner explained. "That is, I thought first of his personality—the kind of man he was to be, how he would look at problems, how he would feel about life, the sort of mind he would have. When that was worked out, I didn't have to imagine him as a person. I began to see him. Handsome, obviously, and powerfully built, but not one of those impossibly big, thick-legged brutes. He was to be the kind of man a child could conceive of seeing on the street."

The character's name—Denny Colt—was easy to come up with. It was an easy name to remember, and it had an All-American sports hero ring to it. To give him a personality, Eisner returned to the characters he enjoyed in his boyhood reading and to Hollywood leading men. In Sherlock Holmes, for example, Sir Arthur Conan Doyle had created just the type of character that Eisner had in mind.

"You read Sherlock Holmes stories for the stories," he explained years later. "The stories endure, not the idea of a super-detective."

Holmes, however, was a little too stodgy, a little too invincible in his powers of deduction and detective work, to be the only basis for Eisner's new hero. He hoped to inject a healthy dose of humor into his feature, an element so clearly absent in the superhero comics that Eisner saw every month on the stands.

"I didn't want him to be a conventional hero," he would insist. "I wanted him to be like James Garner in *Maverick*, which came much later. I wanted [Denny Colt] to have the appearance of a character who was strong and capable and yet very vulnerable, and even a little clownish."

Cary Grant, who was rising in popularity with such movies as *Topper*, *Bringing Up Baby*, *Holiday*, and *Only Angels Have Wings*, seemed to be an ideal model for the combination of humor and drama that Eisner was seeking.

"I like using what I consider to be a Cary Grant type of humor, where the big, strong, masculine guy is clowning around," he explained. "At the same time, he never lost a bit of his heroism. One of the wonderful things about doing [the book] is that I never had to say to myself, 'Well, he really wouldn't do this,' because I know the only thing he wouldn't do is take himself seriously."

Eisner was pleased with the way his character was developing. Unfortunately, his partners were not. This was not the type of character they bargained for when they'd met for lunch. Denny Colt didn't at all resemble the comic book heroes taking the country by storm. Where, for instance, was his costume?

Eisner promised to work on it, but he'd reached a dead end. He'd come up with costumed—or, at least, exotically dressed—characters for the supplement's other features: *Mr. Mystic*, little more than a knockoff of Eisner's earlier *Yarko the Great*, and *Lady Luck*, a blond female answer to Denny Colt. Lady Luck wore a cursory costume (featuring an oversize green hat), had no superpowers, and seemed to stumble onto her adventures as much by accident as by design. The character's looks, Chuck Mazoujian would remember, were "patterned after [his] wife."

But Denny Colt, Eisner had to admit, was missing something. There was nothing unusual about him. As things stood, he was just another detective, which might have been great for the types of stories Eisner wanted to tell, but he also failed to distinguish himself from the pulp or comic characters of the past—characters that had made their run and disappeared. Eisner, unaccustomed to having to strain to come up with usable ideas, was stumped.

Busy Arnold's calls to Eisner became increasingly concerned, but he didn't offer any sage suggestions, either, until he called Eisner in the wee hours of one morning after a night in a bar.

"He suggested a kind of ghost or some kind of metaphysical character," Eisner recalled. "He said, 'How about a thing called The Ghost?' and I said, 'Naw, that's not any good,' and he said, 'Well then call it The Spirit; there's nothing like that around.' I said, 'Well, I don't know what you mean,' and he said, 'Well, you can figure that out—I just like the words, 'The Spirit.'"

Then, during another late night call, he inquired about the character's costume. Eisner had been avoiding the topic whenever he discussed the feature with Arnold, but now he felt trapped into an answer. Fortunately, he was sitting at his drawing board when Arnold called, and he improvised while they talked.

"He's got a mask," he told Arnold, drawing a mask on the character's face.

"That's good." Was there anything else?

"He's got gloves and a blue suit."

Eisner hated the idea even as he mentioned it to Busy Arnold. He didn't want to create a character like Batman or Superman—a superhero with a secret identity—because the dual identities would shift the focus from story back to character. The Spirit's dual lives would need to be explained. On top of that, there were bound to be credibility problems if the Spirit was seen only in his mask, as Eisner favored. "When you draw a character walking down the subway wearing a mask and a blue suit, and he's being ignored or accepted by the people in the subway—that's a little far-fetched."

In the end, the Spirit's origins, as Eisner presented them in his first installment, were more than a little far-fetched. Denny Colt, a detective friend of Police Commissioner Eustace Dolan, is seriously injured while battling Dr. Cobra, a demented scientist who's designed a secret formula that he intends to use to poison New York's water supply. During a struggle in Dr. Cobra's lair, Colt is doused with the formula, which leaves him in a state of suspended animation. Everyone, including the coroner, mistakes him for dead. He's interred in a vault in the Wildwood Cemetery on the outskirts of town. On the night after his burial, he awakens and somehow manages to dig himself out of his grave. He builds a secret underground hideout beneath his burial vault, devises his disguise, and pays Dolan a visit at the police station. Dolan sees through the disguise—for some reason, he's the only person capable of doing so—and Colt tells him that as the Spirit, he will be able to work outside the law in his efforts to fight the bad guys.

The mysterious and unlikely origins, the mask, the very public crime fighter walking down the streets of New York, night and day, always in costume, unnoticed—all demanded a suspension of belief that worked against Eisner's goal of writing for adults, who would have demanded something plausible. But somehow, despite his worries, he got away with it.

"It's an interesting point to make about the medium," he allowed. "Had this been done in film, there would have been hooting and hollering from the audience. There would be laughter. But through all the years, no one ever called me on it. No one ever wrote me a letter saying, 'You expect me to believe this guy would do this wearing a mask?'"

Readers, Eisner learned, were not unlike audiences at a magic show: they would overlook sleight of hand if the trick was good enough. Readers were willing to suspend belief if they cared enough about the characters and the stories were strong. After a slow start, in which characters and stories weren't that different from the others, Eisner began to build his readers' trust. Commissioner Dolan, the father figure, was stern but fair, a man totally dedicated to the law but in need of help in maintaining it, a man who on occasion could get in the Spirit's way and on other occasions became a strong ally. Dolan's daughter, Ellen, a beautiful blond "girl next door," became the Spirit's love interest, but for Eisner she was a continual work in progress, intelligent enough to eventually run for mayor of Central City, flawed enough to find herself in trouble and in need of rescue. Ebony White, the Spirit's African-American sidekick, started out as a bit player, a cabdriver who showed up to give the Spirit a ride; but Eisner developed him to the point of his becoming the Spirit's most trusted assistant, an essential ingredient to many stories—and, in fact, the central character in a handful of them. All three characters began as little more than stereotypes, as figures that needed to be kept simple in order for readers to learn what they needed to know about the Spirit, but all evolved significantly during the Spirit's newspaper run.

Setting became a vital component to the storytelling. Eisner devoted great care in setting his stories in an environment that his readers could identify with. There was standing water in the streets, paper and other refuse on the sidewalks, elevated tracks and subway cars that represented the constant motion of the city, and people everywhere, all looking as if their biggest accomplishment might be surviving from one day to the next. This was *Eisner's* city, the city he had grown up in as well as the city he created for his stories, but it was also the city of his readers, whether they resided in Baltimore, Philadelphia, New York, or Chicago. Astonishing events could occur at any time, day or night, but readers knew to expect the unlikely in their cities. Since this was their reality, why wouldn't they accept a masked hero coming to their aid?

The *Weekly Comic Book*, offering the exploits of the Spirit, Lady Luck, and Mr. Mystic, made its debut on Sunday, June 2, 1940, appearing in only five newspapers, but with a circulation of a million and a half readers. Eisner celebrated the occasion by going to Philadelphia and attending a party hosted by the *Philadelphia Record*, the first paper to pick up the comic book. It might not have been *Superman*, but in the months ahead, other newspapers, aware of the way the comic book bolstered sales for papers including it, decided to carry the supplement, giving Eisner the largest readership he had ever imagined.

As for the costume, Eisner exacted a small measure of revenge on the man who insisted upon the Spirit's having one: besides the blue suit, blue gloves, and ever-present mask, the Spirit wore a fedora exactly like the one worn by Busy Arnold. This became a big inside joke around the Tudor City studio. Arnold never noticed.

No one, including Eisner himself, could ever date the exact moment he ceased being "Bill" Eisner and became "Will" Eisner. Nothing in his life—professional or personal—precipitated the change. In all likelihood, the name change became permanent with the arrival of *The Spirit* or when Eisner entered the service. He'd been called Willie at times as a child, so becoming Will wasn't a radical departure. As Eisner explained it, the new name sounded more professional.

"It was just an attempt to be arty," he said. "It's like using a circle for a dot in the 'i' [in Eisner's signature]. 'Will' just sounded better to me."

Eisner was hitting another creative peak. With no romantic relationships or other time-consuming endeavors to take him from his work, Eisner had no constraints on his time beyond the actual number of hours in a day. He was free to work as he pleased.

The Tudor City studio, although it employed as many artists at any one time as Eisner & Iger did, enjoyed a very productive period. Over the next

year and a half, between the opening of the studio and the beginning of
the United States' involvement in World War II Eisner brought in another
group of gifted draftsmen to complement the artists he'd brought over
from Eisner & Iger, all providing him with high-quality work. Lou Fine,
Chuck Mazoujian, Bob Powell, Nick Cardy, Klaus Nordling, Joe Kubert,
George Tuska, Tex Blaisdell, Alex Kotzky, Dave Berg, Al Jaffee—this
partial list comprised an impressive slice of early comics history's most
noteworthy contributors, all making their chops as budding young artists,
all developing at a time when comic books were a wide-open field, receptive to new ideas and experimentation. These artists made up the rules as
they went along.

They came from all over New York, from all backgrounds. They'd
arrive in answer to a newspaper ad or when they were recommended by
other Eisner employees. Dick French, brought in to beef up the writing
staff, particularly on *Lady Luck*, was Tex Blaisdell's brother-in-law. Klaus
Nordling, who had worked briefly at Eisner & Iger, wrote plays for New
York's Finnish theater. Nick Cardy took a circuitous route, working for
Jerry Iger at Eisner's recommendation before catching on later with Eisner, after the departure of Chuck Mazoujian. Joe Kubert, just a teenage
kid, turned up off the street, an aspiring artist looking for something to
do. Eisner gave him a job sweeping and cleaning the place, but after seeing some of his sketches (and perhaps remembering his own days as a high
school upstart), he had some of the staff, mainly Tex Blaisdell, coach him
on his art.

Kubert would always look back fondly at the Tudor City bullpen and
his on-the-job training.

"I was just starting out in high school," he said. "I was just erasing the
other artists' work and sweeping out the place. Those guys were extremely
kind to me. These were older people. I was just an obnoxious kid coming
up there, trying to find out what the hell was going on, and these guys
extended themselves in every way. They had the patience of several saints
to correct my work, tell me about the materials, and help me along.

"The room was comparably small, maybe fifteen by twenty, and it was
very quiet, as I recollect. The guys who did the work all sat in the same
room. Will had a separate office. It was very, very businesslike. There was
no nonsense going on. The guys had fun, but it was not a noisy place. I
was a kid dealing with adults, and they dealt with me as an adult. I talked
to them on an equal level. During lunchtime, Tex Blaisdell and I used to
play handball downstairs, in the handball court across the street."

Al Jaffee was just out of high school himself when he visited the Tudor City studio, looking for work. His sense of humor (which later became legendary through his work with *Mad*) won him a job.

"I had to create an idea," he recalled, "and I didn't have an idea except a silly drawing of a character called Inferior Man. He was bald and had a little mustache and looked like a pipsqueak. By day he was a little accountant, and then by night he would put on a cape and, for some reason, I had him flying. I don't know where he got the power to fly, but he did. I took this up to Will and he said, 'Great. Your drawings are funny. I have a drawing table here, right behind Dave Berg. I'll pay you ten dollars a week and you can just draw this thing as a filler for *Military Comics*.'"

Inferior Man wasn't long for the world, but Jaffee's association with Dave Berg would be very fruitful in later years, when both contributed significantly to *Mad*.

To Eisner, shop chemistry and the ability to produce quickly weighed as heavily as artistic ability in his personnel decisions. Eisner's ability to spot talent was almost unparalleled in the industry, but as he would joke long after he'd quit running a shop, the real key to running a successful studio involved his having one foot under the drawing table and one under the desk. Finding individual artists was relatively easy; assembling a team that worked well together, with a collective eye on churning out quality material on tight deadlines, required an instinctive understanding of human nature.

"I hired guys based not so much on their portfolios, but on their personalities," he said. "I would interview a guy before I even looked at his portfolio. One of the things that you learn over the years is that you can hire a guy based on his portfolio, but that doesn't mean that, when he works in your shop, he can deliver the same quality of work. He might have taken ten hours to do one piece, and in a shop you can't spend ten hours on one piece."

In a shop boasting this kind of talent, holding egos in check and avoiding flare-ups and hard feelings could be a challenge. Eisner ran his shops the way Walt Disney ran his animation studio: even though you employed talents with disparate styles, you aimed for a studio *look*, a sense of singular vision.

"Everything had his name; he was the brand," noted David Hajdu, author of *The Ten-Cent Plague: The Great Comic-Book Scare and How It Changed America*. "He ran this shop on the production model. He ran this little art-making factory—it was a factory, but what it made was art, and

Eisner took special pride in his ability to write as well as illustrate
his comics stories. (© Will Eisner Studios, Inc., courtesy of Denis Kitchen)

it was important to Will that the product be art. The best way to really
understand Will is to apply the matrix of the Duke Ellington Orchestra,
because Will was to comics what Duke Ellington was to jazz. Will has
created in this factory a laboratory and a hot house that gave opportunities for people not only to work, but to achieve a kind of greatness in a
place where greatness mattered, where they would be rewarded for being
great. This was largely in part to make money and to gratify Will's ego,
which was insatiable. You could not have enough talent in that room.
They could not do enough great work on a high enough level to satisfy
him. That stimulated people. They're playing off each other, they're
learning from each other. He's empowering individuals who might not
have been empowered in other ways, not just to do Will Eisner work but
to contribute in a creative way, and to bring their own styles and voices
and sensibilities to work, to serve this larger whole. This kind of system
is a complicated way of making art. The standard perception of the creative process is that art is the expression of an individual communing

with the Muses. Will represented something a lot more complicated: a kind of a collaborative, a communal way of making art, the coming together of art and commerce in a way that doesn't negate the value of either one, or doesn't corrupt either one."

Eisner was actively involved in all aspects of the art being produced in his studio. He'd wander up and down the aisles, glancing at pages over the artists' shoulders, offering advice that he hoped was more coaching than criticism. "Since the comments were not personal, no one registered annoyance over a suggested change," he explained. Eisner liked to believe that the easygoing yet professional work setting could be attributed to a young, talented staff "open to criticism, unafraid of competition, and in a work environment that respected them."

Yes, Eisner liked to believe that, but it wasn't the whole story. On a day-to-day basis, his staff *did* respect him as a boss, and they worked well together as a team. There was a sense of camaraderie that extended after hours, when some of the guys would get together and wind down at a bar or restaurant. But Eisner's managerial acumen wasn't infallible. There were times, as there are in any shop setting, when members squabbled among themselves, complained about the long hours and low pay, or mumbled under their breath about Eisner's demands. It was no secret that Chuck Mazoujian and Lou Fine had their sights set on leaving comics and going into commercial illustration, or that Chuck Cuidera, whom Eisner regarded as a shop leader, actually disliked Eisner intensely, or that some of the artists would happily take their talents elsewhere if someone offered them a better deal.

Busy Arnold, of all people, tried to entice Bob Powell and Lou Fine into leaving Eisner and coming to work for him directly at his Quality Comics studio in Connecticut. Both would have gone if Eisner hadn't raised hell about it. Eisner's working relationship with Arnold had cooled considerably after their partnership agreement—largely, Eisner felt, because of a difference in the way they perceived each other. Despite their agreement, Eisner complained, Arnold still saw and treated him like an employee, not a partner.

Arnold's thinking, Eisner concluded, stemmed from the fact that, aside from their partnership, Arnold had his own publishing company— one that Eisner & Iger had worked for—and now, with the dissolution of Eisner & Iger and the formation of a new Eisner company, they were competitors as publishers, even as they worked as collaborators on *The Spirit* and two other books.

This misunderstanding boiled over when Arnold tried to hire Powell.

"He offered Bob Powell an increase on what I was paying him for working on *The Spirit* section," Eisner recalled. "Bob came to me and said, 'I can make more with your partners.' I called up Arnold and said, 'You want a lawsuit?' Arnold apologized, but Powell got very angry, and he said, 'You ruined my career! You cut me off!' I said, 'Well, you want to quit me and go down the street and work for someone else . . . well, all right. But you're not going to work for my partner while I'm around.'"

It was the kind of double standard that could set off grumbling around the studio. Eisner might have taken Powell from his earlier partnership with Iger, but he wasn't going to let Arnold do the same.

Chuck Cuidera's problems with Eisner ran much deeper—more than Eisner ever realized. Cuidera, who had graduated from the Pratt Institute with Bob Powell and had taken a job with Eisner at Powell's urging, disliked Eisner from the beginning. "I didn't like the way he handled people," he said, admitting that he admired Eisner as a writer and artist but had great issues with him personally. "There was no way I was ever going to get along with him."

Eisner wouldn't have been the only name on Cuidera's list. A man of emotional extremes, Cuidera could be fiercely combative or unbelievably loyal, generous with his praise or scathing with his criticism, and hyperbolic in stating his opinions. One of his problems with Eisner, he intimated, originated with Eisner's refusal to allow Lou Fine to leave for Quality Comics, just as he had Powell. Cuidera was very close to Fine, and he seethed when he learned of Eisner's actions. "I wanted to knock Eisner on his butt like you wouldn't believe," he said.

Cuidera was directly involved in the lengthiest, most storied feud of Eisner's career, one that puts Eisner's earlier fight for control over his creations in a new light. Early in his career, while working at Victor Fox's shop and, eventually, Eisner's Tudor City studio, Cuidera contributed extensively to two popular features, *The Blue Beetle* and *Blackhawk*. Cuidera believed that he'd created both of the long-running features, and he was infuriated later on when historians credited Eisner with creating *Blackhawk*—a claim Eisner didn't publicly contest. Cuidera stewed over being denied that piece of comics history.

These kinds of disputes weren't rare. The shop system, with the open exchange of ideas and the practice of having several people working on a single feature (often under one name, no matter who came up with the work's ideas), invited such disagreements. As head of his studio and its main idea generator, Eisner would usually dream up a basic idea, do rough pencil sketches of the new feature's main characters, discuss it with several artists in the shop, and, if he didn't want to develop the feature himself, assign it to another artist. Cuidera did more work on *Blackhawk* than Eisner, and he felt cheated when he didn't get the acknowledgment he felt he deserved for his contributions. As the years passed and Eisner's fame grew, Cuidera became more insistent and louder about his claims that Eisner had stolen credit for Cuidera's own creation.

Eisner refused to be pulled into the dispute. He remembered the ugly, drawn-out war between the paranoid Ham Fisher and his onetime assistant Al Capp, in which Fisher accused Capp of lifting some of his characters for his *Li'l Abner* strip while Capp worked for Fisher. The fight had severely damaged Fisher's standing as a cartoonist. Eisner had nothing to gain by tangling with Cuidera, but after hearing some of the things Cuidera was saying about him and his shop, he wasn't inclined to be generous in his assessment of the situation, either.

Their public tangle lasted for nearly six decades after *Blackhawk* made its first appearance on the stands. Finally, in 1999, Eisner and Cuidera sat together on a panel conceived and hosted by comics writer and historian Mark Evanier at the San Diego Comic-Con. Evanier, well versed on the history of the feud, had hoped that the panel would settle the issue once and for all.

"It always struck me that Will's wording, whenever he talked about it, was ambiguous," Evanier explained. "He never said he did; he never said he didn't. On the panel I asked him four different times who created *Blackhawk*, and I never got an answer. Will was not going to say the words *Chuck created it*, nor was he going to say the words *I created it*. He chose to keep it ambiguous, to protect his future options, which I thought was a very savvy thing to do."

The dispute appeared to be settled when Cuidera, seated next to Eisner and apparently in a conciliatory mood, said, point-blank to those attending the panel session: "He's the guy who started it all, the guy next to me. Believe me."

Eisner, who might have been forgiven if he'd chosen to bypass the convention panel in the first place, was relieved. "After the panel, Will came up to me and thanked me for organizing it," Evanier recalled. "He felt he had some unresolved problems with Chuck, and he was very happy to have dealt with them.

"There is no universally accepted definition of the word *creator* in comics, and there are arguable claims, especially in cases where guys were working in a shop arrangement. What I think happened here was Chuck made a massive contribution which you could argue was creation, and Will made a massive contribution that you could argue was creation. If Will was not willing to concede the word *creator* to Chuck, I wasn't going to drag it out of him. I thought Will was very smart about the way he handled it. He wasn't endorsing what Chuck did. He praised Chuck and talked about how great he was, and he gave Chuck his dignity, because Chuck was a celebrity at the convention because of his association with Will. I was happy with how it came out."

Despite the outward appearance of a reconciliation, Cuidera remained bitter for the rest of his life. Two days before his death in 2001, in an *Alter Ego* magazine interview with comics historian Jim Amash, Cuidera was still taking the offensive, attacking Eisner and holding firm to his previous statements about his role in comics history.

"I created *Blackhawk* before I met Will Eisner," he declared. "Eisner had nothing to do with creating *Blackhawk*. When Bob Powell got me to come over to Eisner, I had already started creating *Blackhawk*. I finished creating it when Will Eisner was down South hunting With the second or third *Blackhawk* story, the feature took off and even outsold *Batman*."

Blackhawk was but one of many new titles issued from Eisner's shop. *Doll Man, Uncle Sam, The Ray, Black Condor*—in almost every case, Eisner came up with the idea, sketched out characters, wrote the first episode or two, and even did early covers. Tacked on to his duties on *The Spirit*, which required him to produce more than a page of new material per day, plan new episodes, and oversee the work on the weekly comic book's other two stories, the workload drained him of his prodigious energy and pulled his creative mind in every imaginable direction. Producing a weekly sixteen-page comic book and a couple of monthly newsstand books might have seemed well within reach when an ambitious young Will Eisner formed his partnership with Busy Arnold, but after trying to hold up under the continual production demands, he was so overwhelmed that by late 1940, he actually started rerouting work to Jerry Iger's shop.

But there was always more. *Superman* had been so successful as a monthly entry in *Action Comics* (and, not long thereafter, in its own self-titled book as well) that it was now appearing as a daily newspaper strip. When presented with the same opportunity for *The Spirit*, Eisner jumped at the chance. In hindsight, it proved to be a questionable decision. The weekly newspaper installments required a short story writer's thought process; each eight-page story had a beginning, middle, and end, with an entirely different type of pacing from that which Eisner faced with a daily strip. Eisner, quite naturally, coveted the respect garnered the daily newspaper comic strip artists, but as soon as his first *Spirit* daily started up on Monday, October 13, 1941, he began second-guessing himself.

"I wasn't ready to do dailies, because I had never done a big-time daily before," he recalled. "To me it's like trying to conduct an orchestra in a telephone booth." The syndicate, he explained, believed that the daily strip would be a natural extension of the Sunday comic, but the experimentation Eisner was attempting on Sunday didn't translate well into the daily installments. "The dailies weren't doing all that well, because I was trying all these weird ideas, like a whole daily strip with nothing but footprints in the snow and so forth."

Eisner also learned that the daily strip left him little room to develop his characters. *The Spirit* had been a work in progress all along, with Eisner tinkering with his title character and supporting cast on a week-to-week basis, fine-tuning as he learned more about them. Daily strips discouraged this. Readers demanded consistency.

"I discovered that daily strips would not allow the artist to experiment and grow, necessarily," Eisner told Danny Fingeroth in 2003 when reflecting on the daily. "If you look at the daily strips over the years, the ones that have survived for 50 years, they're pretty much the same as they were when they started."

In the beginning, the daily strip needed a promotional boost, and Eisner often found himself on the road with a salesman, hawking the merits of the new feature. As Eisner later recalled, the salesman valued his presence during meetings with an editor.

"It gave him something to pitch—he could have a dog-and-pony act," Eisner said. "Salesmen would use something like that as a way to see the editors who might not want to see a salesman, but might want to meet an artist."

The ploy backfired on at least one occasion, when Eisner and a salesman were visiting the editor of a New Jersey newspaper. The editor looked at a sample of the daily strip, listened to the salesman's pitch, and agreed that it would be a suitable feature for his paper.

The editor opened up the paper to his comics page, looked down at it, then looked at the salesman and me, and said, "Well, which one should I drop? I've got to drop one to carry *The Spirit*." The salesman and the editor both looked at me and said, "What do you think?" I was dismayed, thinking, "My God, they've asking me to stab another cartoonist in the back." Here I am, a kid of 23 with all these ideals, and I'm being introduced to the harsh realities of the world. It never occurred to me that to take my strip he'd have to sink another strip. I shifted from foot to foot, and finally my eye lit on *Buck Rogers*, which, as far as I was concerned, was an old strip, so I pointed it out and said, "Here's a strip that's old hat. The idea of science fiction is kind of passé now, because we're in the '40s and there's a war on."

The editor said, "Yeah! That space-travel business is for yesterday. Let's drop that and put *The Spirit* in." I've always felt guilty about doing that to *Buck Rogers*, but that was my introduction into the business world of comics.

The daily strip's appearance gave Eisner his first big splash of publicity when one of the subscribing newspapers, the *Philadelphia Record*, published a full-page profile that ran the opening day of the strip. Eisner traveled to Philadelphia for the interview and to pose for photographs, including a photo of him sitting at a drawing board, inking a large head shot of the Spirit, and another with Eisner, one of the *Record*'s editors, and Busy Arnold, also in the city for the unveiling of the strip, in which Eisner is seated at a drawing board and the editor stands behind him, threatening to smack him with a yardstick, while Arnold stands by in bemusement. The profile, standard fare for newspapers, was exceptional in one respect: Eisner became perhaps the first comics artist to publicly state (although he was not quoted directly) that he thought comics could be more than just entertainment.

The comic strip, [Eisner] explains, is no longer a comic strip but, in reality, an illustrated novel. It is new and raw in form just now, but material for limitless intelligent development. And eventually and inevitably it will be a legitimate medium for the best of writers and artists.

"There was no precedent for that interview with the *Philadelphia Record*," David Hajdu remarked more than a half century later, long after Eisner's words proved to be prophetic. "He not only believed in comics as a legitimate art form as early as the 1940s, but he had the guts, the *chutzpah*, to say so publicly, in print, on the record. He was utterly unique in his eagerness to champion this art in public."

Eisner's statements would have been bold predictions for a well-established comic book artist with clout in the industry, but coming from a twenty-four-year-old, virtually unknown to anyone but his peers in the business, they came across as brash and a tad highbrow. Rube Goldberg would confront Eisner at a National Cartoonists Society meeting in

New York, dismissing Eisner's beliefs in the literary potential of comics as so much hogwash. "We're vaudevillians," Goldberg admonished Eisner. "Never forget that. We tell jokes!"

As Eisner recalled, his colleagues found the statements funny: "I got back into New York and the kids in the shops kept laughing and saying, 'We read that, are you trying to be uppity?' Nobody really believed that this was what it later on seemed to prove itself to be, which is a true means of expression, story, and idea."

He would never waver from these beliefs.

Eisner's relationship with Busy Arnold deteriorated in the wake of the Bob Powell dustup. The two remained cordial, but Eisner found Arnold's meddling almost intolerable. A day didn't pass without the arrival of a piece of mail, a memo, or a call from Arnold's office in Stamford. Eisner had no choice but to take whatever Arnold dished out when he complained about misspellings and typos and inconsistencies in the comics—and there were enough of these to raise the hackles of the most even-tempered editor.

"Here is a terrible example of the terrible work your staff is doing," Arnold scolded in his usual overstated style. "In one panel of 'Lady Luck,' Lady Luck and another man are in a rowboat. In the next panel, there are two men in the boat with Lady Luck. How about checking more carefully?"

Six days later, Arnold was on Eisner again, this time for the sloppy proofreading in the first issue of *Uncle Sam*: "There are at least 200 mistakes in spelling in the entire book and the same applies to *Doll Man Quarterly*. In this book your boys didn't even spell a word the same way twice in a row."

How much of this is true and how much exaggerated is impossible to tell, since the original art no longer exists. In interviews, Eisner acknowledged that such problems did occur and that he had no choice but to hear out Arnold's criticism and pass it along to the responsible parties. Arnold, he'd concede, was the first to hear from disgruntled newspaper editors who in less than subtle terms pointed out problems that could have easily been avoided.

"Whenever anyone complained about *The Spirit*," Eisner said, "Busy took the brunt of the criticism and then he passed it along to me. It was his idea to 'shake Bill up,' as he put it. He was like the fight manager and I was his boxer, his creation. That's what it was like."

Eisner was less agreeable when Arnold attacked the artwork in the different publications. He wasn't happy to hear Arnold's familiar complaints about less than perfect borders—one of Arnold's pet peeves—but statements such as "I can get good second- and third-rate independent artists who are superior to the ones you hired," or "Nick [Cardy] has too many far shots and not enough close-ups," or on a more personal level, "The last eight pages of *The Spirit* looked like they had been hammered out in no time and the job looked second-rate," did nothing to improve Eisner's disregard for Arnold's lack of knowledge of comics art. He respected Arnold's business experience, as he had Jerry Iger's, but, as he liked to point out, Arnold's appreciation of art was linked directly to how much it sold.

Arnold also felt compelled to forward all complaints about *The Spirit*. Eisner openly admitted that *The Spirit* was a work in progress, a continually developing feature that in the beginning was hit or miss. (Ironically, *The Spirit*'s first two years, in retrospect, were tame in comparison with Eisner's later work on the feature.) Arnold, worried that a paper might decide to cancel the supplement, constantly cautioned Eisner against using material that might frighten or disturb young readers, especially violence, blood and gore, or spooky facial expressions. When critical letters arrived at Arnold's—or Henry Martin's—office, Eisner was certain to hear about it. Arnold would attempt to mollify an unhappy editor, and then he'd confront Eisner, who was learning on an alarmingly regular basis that his hopes of writing for an adult audience were being undermined by editors who still regarded comics as the domain of children.

Fortunately for Eisner, Arnold rarely looked at *The Spirit* until after it had been published, and newspaper editors, although unhappy with some of the content, made no attempts to censor it. But when calls or letters from angry readers came in, the complaints were passed along, often with not-so-veiled threats of cancellations. One early *Spirit* entry—a two-part episode, "Orang the Ape-Man," involving a talking ape that falls in love with young women, including Police Commissioner Dolan's daughter, Ellen—brought in a flood of angry responses; another, in which an undercover Adolf Hitler visits the United States, did the same. At a moment in history when America was precariously close to entering World War II, hypersensitive editors objected to any name (such as "Kurt") that might indicate German heritage.

Eisner continued to experiment with *The Spirit*, regardless of the uproar from Busy Arnold, Henry Martin, and the newspapers subscribing to the comic book insert. He toyed with unusual panel shapes and sizes, camera angles, and the use of shadows and black ink. Eisner would eventually deem these innovations a response to necessity, to an attempt to solve problems. His experimentation with panel sizes and shapes, he said, could be traced back to his days of working on *Hawks of the Seas*, when the feature was being marketed to different-sized publications; he'd had to cut and rearrange the panels to fit the smaller-sized formats, and from this he had learned how to compress story and action as well as create a visually appealing style. His interest in movies, dating from his childhood in the Bronx, also contributed to *The Spirit*'s cinematic feel. Finally, there was Eisner's hyperactive creative mind: never content to stay put, he was constantly on the lookout for something new.

The Spirit's splash page, to the exasperation of the Register & Tribune Syndicate, became Eisner's most creative and enduring innovation. In the beginning, *The Spirit* opened like a traditional newspaper comic strip—an opening panel plunging readers into the story—but after a few weeks, Eisner tried a single-page opening that served several functions. First and foremost, it acted as a cover for *The Weekly Comic Book*, giving the insert the feeling of a magazine independent of the other sections of the Sunday paper. In addition, it cast a mood to the story and gave readers an indication of what to expect. Finally, Eisner used the splash page as a clever, creative means of placing his comic's title in front of readers.

"I knew if I didn't get the reader's attention as he flipped through the Sunday newspaper, I might lose him," Eisner said of his splash pages. "So I began to innovate on the covers. Also, I had only eight pages—seven pages, later on—to tell the story, so I had to bring the reader in very quickly, set the scene very quickly."

Newspaper marketing analysts, their eyes set to increasing circulation numbers, weren't impressed with Eisner's unusual approach. *Superman*, they argued, had a standard, eye-catching logo that readers could immediately spot on the page. Newspapers carrying the comic could plaster the logo on the sides of their delivery vans, and in an extremely competitive market that found newspapers trying to find ways to bump up their readerships, advertising a popular comic strip could goose newsstand sales. The way Eisner designed his splash page, the words *The Spirit* seemed to be intentionally hidden on the page. They might be part of a building or a portion of a page designed to look like the front page of a newspaper; readers, Eisner's critics complained, would find this confusing.

Eisner strongly disagreed. Rather than turn away from the feature, readers would look forward to each new way he'd spell out *The Spirit* on the splash page. This opening page would become the feature's identity and its strongest selling-tool.

"My audience was transitory," he countered. "I had to catch people on

The Spirit's unique splash pages, such as this opening page for the December 8, 1940 entry, established Eisner's reputation for being one of the most innovative comics artists of his time. (© Will Eisner Studios, Inc., courtesy of Denis Kitchen)

the fly, so to speak. So I began to design the front cover, the first page, as dramatically as I could, and in a way that would intrigue people into the story, and tell a little bit of the story to begin with. I would tell them the kind of story they were getting."

Eisner bore up under the criticism from Arnold and the papers, but he didn't have an impenetrable shell. The artists in his shop watched for the telltale signs of Eisner's mounting anger—he'd speak very softly, his pipe clenched in his teeth, then he'd speak even more softly—and the studio would lie low until it passed. He was far too busy to brood for too long.

On the morning of Sunday, December 7, 1941, Will Eisner was in his Tudor City studio, munching on a sandwich and listening to an opera on the radio, when an announcer broke into the broadcast with the news that Japan had attacked the Pearl Harbor naval base. That the United States was now entering its second global conflict in a quarter century (something Jerry Iger had foreseen two years earlier) came as no surprise. Servicemen and civilians alike had been gearing up for it for a long time. Like all men eligible for the draft, Eisner knew that it would be only a matter of time before he was called into the service.

"I was ambivalent," he confessed when asked to recall his feelings about being drafted. "Everybody was very in favor of the war, particularly because of the Nazis and because of the fact that the country seemed to be in danger. So I was kind of eager to be part of it. I felt that I'd want to be a part of the war effort. On the other hand, this was a year after I had started *The Spirit*, which represented a whole new career for me. And I knew that if I went into the Army the whole thing would kind of fall apart on me."

Prior to his being drafted into the service, Eisner had been trying to find a way to get a deferment from the military, mainly on the grounds that without him an entire business would be in jeopardy. He had been interviewed by the draft board back on July 29, and he'd shown authorities samples of his work and explained his case. The draft board demanded more—proof that without Eisner, the *Spirit* newspaper section might not survive and that a large number of people would lose their jobs if the newspaper section fell through. Busy Arnold and the Des Moines Register & Tribune Syndicate had pleaded Eisner's case as well, and Eisner had been left alone until the United States officially entered the war.

With the declaration of war, Eisner was called up, and he was operating on borrowed time, having been granted time to make arrangements for others to cover for him while he was away. All during this period, Eisner struggled with his emotions. As a Jew, he felt strongly about Hitler and his murder of European Jews; had they not emigrated, his parents—and he himself—could have been these very people. As an American—and an artist involved with such projects as *Uncle Sam Quarterly* and *Military Comics*—he was caught up in the national furor of patriotism that immediately followed America's entry into the war. Still, he couldn't help wondering what would become of him and all he had worked so hard to achieve if the war dragged on for a lengthy period of time. Would he even have a career when he returned?

chapter five

A PRIVATE NAMED JOE DOPE

*Comics—sequential art—is my medium. I regard it as much
my singular medium as a writer who writes only words or the
motion-picture man who writes only in movies. This is a definable,
singular medium: it has perimeters and it has parameters;
it has grammar; it has distinct rules; it has limitations; and it has
possibilities which have not really been touched.*

Prior to his induction into the army in May 1942, Will Eisner had been living, in essence, the life of a hermit in the largest city in the United States. He went from home to office to home again, with very little time for play or socializing. He had few friends away from the office and no serious romantic involvements. His family's money woes had robbed him of much of his adolescence, and now his young adulthood was disappearing under the avalanche of work. When he reported for processing at Fort Dix in New Jersey, he was about as far from home as he'd ever ventured. He was more mature and advanced in his adult career than most of his fellow inductees, yet at the same time far less worldly on a social level. The army gave Eisner his first real taste of freedom.

Not that the army removed him from *The Spirit* and other work demands. Before leaving for basic training, Eisner visited Busy Arnold at his Quality Comics offices in Connecticut, and the two discussed the best way to continue while Eisner was away.

"[I] talked to him about the problem of going into the army, and he said, 'Well, we'd better move the studio up here to Stamford, to the Gurley Building,'" Eisner recalled. "So we took space right next door to Busy's office on the same floor and began moving the shop. As a matter

Eisner's official army portrait. (Will Eisner Collection, the Ohio State University Billy Ireland Cartoon Library & Museum)

of fact, I remember we set up a fund to help the artists who wanted to move up there, to pay a down payment on mortgages for houses."

Not surprisingly, Eisner wanted to maintain some measure of control over *The Spirit*—or at the very least the Sunday installments—while he was away. He reasoned that he could write the episodes and leave the penciling and inking to others. Eisner favored Lou Fine for *The Spirit's* artwork, and he helped Fine and his wife find a house in Stamford.

After checking in for a brief period at Fort Dix, Eisner was assigned to Aberdeeen Proving Ground near Baltimore, where he was pleased to discover that he enjoyed some celebrity status. The *Baltimore Sun* carried *The Spirit*, which impressed his fellow recruits but left his drill sergeant sour. Eisner, the sergeant scoffed, didn't look anything at all like the Spirit, nor was he anything like his creation. "The Spirit was a heroic character and I looked a little less than that," Eisner cracked.

Eisner remained conflicted about the war. In the months leading up to his being drafted, he and Busy Arnold had tried to find a way to get him classified as a journalist in lieu of active combat. When that failed, Arnold contacted influential connections to see if they might place Eisner in a war-time job in the States. Time changed Eisner's thinking. He'd been through basic training, befriended other inductees, and decided that he really did want to go to Europe and fight. An office job, he decided, wouldn't do.

His reputation and abilities scotched his chances of shipping overseas, however. He hadn't been at Aberdeen for long before he was visited by two editors of the *Flaming Bomb*, the base newspaper. The paper needed a cartoonist, and the job was Eisner's if he wanted it. Beginning on July

Rather than send Eisner overseas during World War II, the army had him working on such
publications as the *Flaming Bomb*. (Will Eisner Collection, the Ohio State University
Billy Ireland Cartoon Library & Museum)

4, 1942, Eisner produced a weekly strip, *Private Dogtag*, a jokey throw-
away bit that followed the exploits of Otis Dogtag, a dim-witted, buck-
toothed private incapable of doing much of anything correctly. Set in
Aberdeen Proving Ground, *Private Dogtag* included characters based on
real soldiers, including Eisner himself and his editor, Sergeant Bob La-
mar, with references to actual events in the camp. In addition to the
weekly strip, Eisner illustrated column headings and advertisements and
contributed occasional single-panel editorial cartoons, all at a time when
he was still hanging on to his chores with *The Spirit*.

Other opportunities rolled in. The base was developing a "preventive
maintenance" program, which was really nothing more than trying to
convince the GIs to take care of their weapons and equipment. Maintaining equipment prevented unnecessary breakdowns, malfunctions, and
waste. It was that simple. The trick was to persuade the men to do it voluntarily. The U.S. Army Ordnance Corps, looking for an artist to design
posters promoting the practice, hosted a contest and Eisner won the job.

After talking to his newspaper editors over the months and seeing the

way things were handled (or mishandled) by the army, Eisner had become convinced that comics could be used as an educational tool for his
fellow soldiers. Part of his reasoning involved literacy, part a natural reluctance to learn something new: maintenance manuals were written
in such technical language that less educated soldiers couldn't understand
them; and even if they did, they needed a *reason* to follow the directions
they were given. Comics could be informal, entertaining, and easy to
follow while still being educational. They could also speak the language
of the soldier.

Eisner explained this line of thinking to his commanding officer, a
lieutenant colonel who also oversaw the production of the *Flaming Bomb*.
The lieutenant colonel liked the idea enough that, unbeknownst to Eisner, he pitched it at a meeting of higher-ups. They too responded enthusiastically, and before he knew what was happening, Eisner was being
transferred to Holabird Ordnance Motor Base in Baltimore, where he was
expected to develop his idea for the maintenance engineering unit.

Juggling his duties in the army and his work on *The Spirit* turned out to
be a much more daunting task than Eisner had anticipated. He was still
able to come up with new stories each week, but, as he'd concede later,
they weren't up to the standards he'd set back when he was working at
Tudor City. As a character, the Spirit was too complex to entrust to just
anyone. Eisner's style of illustration could be imitated by several of the
shop's artists, most notably Lou Fine, but his stories were another matter.
Eisner hung on to the scriptwriting and breakdowns for as long as he
could, entrusting the penciling and other duties to Fine, but by November
1942, the weekly grind of writing scripts and sneaking them off to the
post office had become too much. He had no alternative but to relinquish
his involvement and watch Fine and the Quality Comics staff take over.

The daily *Spirit* was in even worse shape, which is difficult to imagine,
given the talents working on it: Lou Fine handled the art, while Jack Cole
took over the writing and, later, the art. Cole, a holdover from the Eisner &
Iger shop, was a brilliant yet troubled and eccentric draftsman, perhaps as
imaginative as anyone Eisner had ever worked with, possessing a powerful
eye for detail and an impeccable sense of action. In his character India
Rubber Man—eventually called Plastic Man—Cole had created the kind
of superhero Eisner could appreciate—powerful and fluid, offbeat, humorous, and dedicated to his mission in life. Cole, a native Pennsylvanian, had
moved with his wife to Manhattan, connected with Eisner and Busy Arnold, and divided his time freelancing for both.

Ironically, shortly after Eisner was drafted but before he reported for duty, Busy Arnold had pulled Cole aside and asked him to create a *Spirit* knockoff. Eisner, of course, owned the Spirit name and character, but Arnold was concerned about what he would do if something happened to Eisner. Cole's creation—a detective named Midnight—would be his insurance. Midnight, who made his first appearance in *Smash Comics* in January 1941, was indistinguishable from the Spirit, from the blue mask and hat to the rumpled suit. Cole, however, was unhappy. Troubled by the thought of ripping off somebody he admired and respected, Cole met Eisner over dinner and explained his dilemma.

"I feel it's not morally right," he told Eisner.

"Well, Jack," Eisner responded, "I can't tell you not to do it because it's your livelihood and, frankly, I don't think I can sue Busy over a thing like this. He has a right to create characters for his magazines, if he wants to."

As Eisner told it later, the two discussed Cole's predicament for a while before coming up with an alternative. "I don't know if it was Jack or me who got the brilliant idea to make him a funny character," Eisner said. "That way, Jack could satisfy Busy Arnold and it'd be a totally different character. And from there, he went on to create 'Plastic Man.'"

When it came time to find a writer/artist to work on the daily *Spirit*, Cole seemed like the perfect fit. He could write—something Lou Fine could not do—and he was very familiar with the character. It didn't work out, however, for reasons that no one was quite able to pinpoint. In all likelihood, it was a case of vision: Cole's Spirit was more of an action figure, whereas Eisner preferred to use the more subtle sides of the character, including humor, to add dimension to his version. That, along with the usual issues of pacing, created problems that Cole and Fine couldn't overcome.

The daily strip dragged on until March 11, 1944, when it was mercifully put to rest. By his own admission, Eisner never felt a strong connection to it—or to the Sunday *Spirit* series that appeared during his absence.

"Except for the ownership of the concept, I felt *The Spirit* had ceased to be mine while I was away," he said.

Will Eisner was by no means the only comic book artist to find a way to apply his talents to the war effort. The army bestowed a respect on comic book artists in the military that they hadn't enjoyed as civilians, and rather than hand these artists a weapon and send them to the Atlantic or Pacific theaters, the army found uses for them stateside. Stan Lee designed posters, including the famous "VD? Not Me." Nick Cardy, before seeing action that earned him two Purple Hearts, designed the patch worn by the Sixty-sixth Infantry Division. In some cases, an artist's talents helped earn him a promotion. Eisner was promoted to the rank of corporal at the end of 1942, and just before leaving for Holabird, he tested for an administrative officer position—warrant officer, second grade. He eventually wound up a chief warrant officer.

At Holabird, Eisner was put to work on *Army Motors*, a mimeographed publication devoted to equipment maintenance. As soon as he saw a copy of the sheet, he began listing ways to improve it. To begin with, it needed to look more professional. As it stood, *Army Motors* looked as though it had been produced in a high school principal's office; it was bound to be taken less seriously than a professionally designed publication that was well written and illustrated. *Army Motors* was the kind of product that was foisted on indifferent readers. It needed an identity, a reason for someone to pick it up and glance at its contents.

Private Joe Dope, the most inept soldier ever to pass through the United States Army, rose out of this line of thinking. Although Joe Dope and Eisner's earlier Otis Dogtag were virtually the same character, Dogtag's domain had been a single army base; Joe Dope would belong to everyone in the army, regardless of where he was stationed. Joe Dope would become a sort of brand name, seen on posters and in other instructional materials, as well as in *Army Motors*. For Joe Dope to work as designed, a GI had to take one look at the character and understand that this was a soldier bound for a disaster that could have been easily prevented—if, that is, he hadn't been such a dope.

"What arguments do you use in the quest for voluntary cooperation?" Eisner asked rhetorically when trying to explain how he developed Joe Dope to fit the army's new preventive maintenance program. "Well, you use the threat of death. Death or physical harm. You say to a guy, 'If you don't put air in your tires, one of these days you'll be in combat and you'll get a flat tire and you won't be able to escape—and it'll be your ass, buddy!' That was the first step. Then, if you carry it on, you can create another image that people don't want to face, another threat, and that is looking like a fool among their peers. That is how Joe Dope was created, on those grounds."

Eisner concocted other characters to complement Joe Dope in the strip and in other sections of the magazine: Sergeant Half-Mast, a mechanic nearly as inept as Joe Dope, who also had an advice column; Private Fosgnoff, Dope's closest buddy; and Connie Rodd, a shapely, irresistible mechanic who had her own column, "Connie's Bulletin Board," devoted to keeping readers informed on equipment changes and upgrades. The characters, although clever and serving specific functions, had to walk a tight line between being entertaining and informative. The army frowned upon material that made it look as if it couldn't train its personnel, and it strictly forbade anything that ridiculed its policies or officers. The characters' foibles had to be individual flaws that even the army, at its very best, couldn't overcome.

Readers responded favorably to Eisner's early efforts in *Army Motors*, and Eisner had barely settled in at Holabird before he was on the move again, this time to Washington D.C., to work under General Levin H. Campbell, the army's chief of ordnance. Eisner had clearly impressed the army's top brass: he was headed to the Pentagon.

The popularity of comic books reached an all-time high during the war years. They no longer appealed only to the adenoidal cretins of Kansas City; they also belonged to those kids' older brothers or cousins or uncles, the ones donning uniforms and trying to win a war that, by the beginning of 1943, had no end in sight. GIs came from all over the United States, from different backgrounds and educational levels, and they loved comics—so much so that by the end of 1942, three out of every ten pieces of mail shipped overseas to soldiers were comics. Eisner guessed correctly when he predicted, during his discussions with his editors at *Army Motors*, that servicemen would connect to comics.

The producers of comics, on the lookout for new readers, adapted to this new, more mature readership. Bundles of superhero comics still rolled off the presses every month, but new comic books featuring solders, detectives, and, more popular yet, sexy, barely clothed women appeared almost overnight, hitting readers on a more visceral level. Competition among publishers was greater than ever. Genre comics featuring tales from outer space, shoot-outs in the Old West, accounts of gangsters and the men who hunted them—the direct descendants of the pulp magazines, now aimed at young people flooding the movie theaters and listening to radio serials—continued to turn up and, in most cases, just as quickly disappear. With the government rationing paper and zinc (used in making printing plates), publishers could ill afford to wait for readers to catch on to their latest offerings. Comic book publishers, like book publishers, preferred to shepherd their resources into surefire titles rather than risk limited supplies on experiments. As a result, the actual number of available monthly titles decreased over the war years, even though the overall number of printed comic books increased.

One new detective title, *Crime Does Not Pay*, a true-crime entry with more sex, violence, gore, and mayhem than ever seen in a comic book, made a huge splash during the war years. That America loved crime stories was hardly a revelation; the obsession with crime and punishment dated back to the Wild West and never abated. The country was fascinated by, and even glamorized, its outlaws, from Billy the Kid and the James brothers to Al Capone and Pretty Boy Floyd. That fascination had been exploited to great success in the cinema, through characters portrayed by Edward G. Robinson, James Cagney, and others, and in books and pulp magazines. Comics, including *The Spirit*, had presented a wide range of stories not involving superheroes, but since the target audience of these comic books was the young reader, publishers and editors self-regulated their books' content. It was permissible to have beginning-to-end, panel-to-panel, sock-'em-up action, and people (usually the bad guys) could die over the course of all the violence; but there were limits to blood and gore, depictions of shootings and stabbings, and close-ups of fallen bodies. Sex, of course, was strictly off-limits, and artists could strip down their characters only so far, usually to what amounted to little more than their underwear, but it had better stop at that point. Artists were always happy to push their limits, but they knew when they literally had to draw the line.

Crime Does Not Pay went beyond those customary boundaries. Characters were sprayed by machine-gun fire at point-blank range; the pools of blood looked like small lakes. The more realistic and detailed the better. The comic's first cover depicted, in extreme close-up and full color, a knife blade driven through a hand, pinning it to a table. Only two rules seemed to apply: The stories had to be true, or at least within screaming distance of it; and the criminals had to be punished, by prison or death, by the end of the stories. But between the beginning and retribution, it was anything goes.

Crime, it turned out, paid by the boatload. *Crime Does Not Pay* flew off the newsstands and drugstore shelves, with a huge percentage of sales going to soldiers overseas. Over the next decade, imitators would pop up everywhere, and they, along with a line of horror comics offering increasingly gruesome tales, would lead to a showdown between publishers and citizen groups, church organizations, and lawmakers, with predictable but disturbing results

The war provided an ideal link among comic book readers of all ages and backgrounds. Patriotism—and the deep hatred for Germany and Japan—swept over the country, creating an urgent *need*—a need for involvement, a need for bravery, a need for victory over the forces of evil—and who better to offer a temporary gleam of security than heroic figures in comic books? Comic book publishers understood this, and before the war was over, it seemed as if every superhero in the business had brushed up against the enemy. New heroes with such names as Mr. Liberty, the Defender, the Liberator, the American Crusader, and the Fightin' Yank sprang up.

Few characters—or names, for that matter—pounced on the patriotic fervor like Captain America, the red-white-and-blue-clad superhero created by Jack Kirby and Joe Simon. *Captain America Comics*, issued by Timely, turned up in early 1941, before Pearl Harbor but at a time when frustrated Americans were impatiently awaiting their country's inevitable entry into the war.

"Captain America was created for a time that needed noble figures," Kirby explained. "We weren't at war yet, but everyone knew it was coming. That's why Captain America was born; America needed a super-patriot." The costume, Kirby went on, was carefully designed to plug into the patriotism. "Drape the flag on anything, and it looks great," he said. "We gave him a chain mail shirt and shield, like a modern-day crusader. The wings on his helmet were from Mercury . . . He symbolized the American dream."

Captain America could sock Hitler in the jaw or take on a platoon of Nazis and escape unscathed; in short, he was the fulfillment of many Americans' aching fantasies.

"Here was the arch villain of all time," Simon wrote of Hitler in his autobiography, *The Comic Book Makers*.

Adolf Hitler and his Gestapo bully-boys were real. There never had been a truly believable villain in comics. But Adolf was live, hated by more than half the world. What a natural foil he was, with his comical moustache, the ridiculous cowlick, his swaggering goose-stepping minions eager to jump off a plane if their mad little leader ordered it . . . I could smell a winner.

Unbeknownst to the producers of superhero comics, interest in the costumed crusaders had reached its peak and was about to decline. Older readers—the targets of this brand of comics only a few years earlier—were losing interest in muscle-bound men in tights, capes, masks and secret identities. Their fantasies were turning elsewhere, to more grown-up faire. Watching a grown man and his teenage sidekick wasn't nearly as compelling as following the stories of well-proportioned young women squeezed into skimpy outfits and placed in harm's way. It was a no-lose scenario: if the woman was strong and capable of taking care of herself, it tripped fantasy triggers everywhere; if the woman was a traditional damsel in distress, in need of a brave young man to save her and, ultimately, claim his reward . . . well, that was good, too. You didn't have to hold a degree in psychology to figure this out or to appreciate how a reader, now in his early twenties, might find it a little unrealistic to see a virile young man so immersed in saving the world that he fails to notice (or at least interact seriously with) a world of beautiful young women surrounding him.

It was, in fact, a Harvard-educated, middle-aged pop psychologist who created Wonder Woman, the most enduring female superheroine to rise out of comics' Golden Age. Dr. William Moulton Marston, an eccentric pop psychologist and author, collected credentials the way others collected stamps or coins, and he was just marginally good enough at each of them to have credibility. He'd been instrumental in the development of the polygraph machine, and using his background in psychology, he'd written for *Family Circle* and sat on DC's advisory board. Now, writing under the name of Charles Moulton, he joined with abandon a medium that, in the not-too-distant past, he himself had criticized as being too darkly violent. His Wonder Woman, who made her debut in DC's *All Star Comics* in 1941, was as much dominatrix as superhero, using a golden lasso and bracelets of submission in her battle with evildoers while oozing a sensuality that appealed to teenagers and young adult readers alike. An Amazon of incredible strength and agility, Wonder Woman was also erotic and vulnerable. Her adventures, filled with tools of bondage ranging from her golden lasso to whips, chains, and ropes, bore a not-so-subtle S&M underpinning designed to hold older readers' interest and had enough uncovered skin to keep young boys turning the pages as well. You could have your heroine and those closest to her bound and beaten, tortured and berated, you could open an industrial-sized can of heavy-duty whup-ass on her, and all was well if, by the final panel, the forces of good came away victorious. Or as Marston would have you believe, there was a lesson buried somewhere in all that mayhem that males of the species would do well to hold close to their hearts: "Only when the control of self by others is more pleasant than the unbound assertion of self in human relationships can we hope for a stable, peaceful human society."

If Marston and DC believed they were issuing a superhero comic book geared to older male readers who might pick up this strange message, or to young female readers looking for an alternative to the male superheroes, they learned otherwise very quickly. According to the market numbers, nine out of ten buyers of comic books containing Wonder Woman stories were teenage boys.

Girls apparently wanted something more wholesome, featuring characters they could identify with rather than fantasize about, and they were rewarded with two such characters at almost the precise moment Wonder Woman was taking off. The two girls, named Betty and Veronica, while attractive enough, looked and dressed a lot like typical high schoolers, dealt with teenage problems like parents, teachers, and dating, and wouldn't have known what to do with superpowers if they had them. The girls were the brainchild of cartoonist Bob Montana, who cast them as competing love interests for his main character, Archie Andrews, a redheaded teen who took his first comic book bow in December 1941 in MLJ's *Pep Comics*. Archie, Betty, Veronica, and Archie's bumbling friend, Jughead, caught on as soon as they were introduced to readers, and by the end of the war, Archie had his own eponymous comic book. If Robin, Bucky, and other teenage sidekicks to superheroes were the good-looking, athletically built, street-savvy teenagers that kids wished they could be, Archie and company were the teenagers they already *were*— and, increasingly, they were the success that some superhero comics wished they could be, too.

Will Eisner tracked these developments from his Washington, D.C., office. Even though he was nose down at work, producing a mass of material for the army, he made a point of checking out the daily strips and monthly comic books, watching for trends, trying to calculate the next big thing. This would become a personal trademark, a practice he would employ well into his eighties. While colleagues might be content to complete an assignment and move on to the next one, or stick with one character or style for decades, Eisner wanted to be nothing less than part of the cutting edge defining the direction of comics. His colleagues had laughed at him when he insisted that comics could serve a higher purpose than mere entertainment, that they could be a new form of literature, and he was determined to prove them wrong. To do this, he had to fully grasp both art and market, and the war couldn't be a deterrent to his education. He'd be going home someday, and he wanted to be ready.

His work in *Army Motors* and, in Washington, D.C., *Firepower* (a publication used to boost morale, issued by a citizen group, Army Ordnance Associates) prepared him for his return to civilian life in ways he never could have predicted. Before the war, from his experiences as a businessman, Eisner had learned how to work with customers with whom he didn't always agree, with know-it-alls who knew very little about art but pretended they did. In civilian life, strangely enough, the chain of command was clearly defined, and Eisner worked well in it. The army was different. Personal ambition and politics could make dealing with different offices a challenge. No one knew a lick about art—or even wanted to know about art—but that didn't prevent an officer from weighing in on how a new type of art—comics—could be applied to a new type of policy: preventive maintenance.

"During the war, I had continually been in a battle with the adjutant general who was in charge of all technical manuals," Eisner would remember. "He regarded me as creating a kind of blasphemy because I was introducing comics into what he regarded as a very stabilized form of technical manual. Every time they tested what I produced, however, we came out way ahead of what they would produce.'

The testing was an important victory, affirming Eisner's faith in comics as an educational tool. The adjutant general had sent copies of the standard technical manuals and of Eisner's new versions to the University of Chicago, to be assessed by a group of actual readers. Eisner's manuals, the study concluded, were easier to read, to understand, and, perhaps most important, to remember.

As rewarding as this victory was to Eisner personally, he still might not have pulled it off if he hadn't used the diplomacy he'd learned in business. "I had to assure the adjutant general that what we were doing would not replace these technical manuals, only supplement and enhance them," he said.

Eisner discovered that he enjoyed dividing his creative energy among the different kinds of duties and publications assigned him by the army, whether they involved designing a poster for general distribution, a *Joe Dope* strip for *Army Motors*, a technical manual for the U.S. Army Ordnance Corps, or illustrations for articles in *Firepower*. He easily adjusted to the requirements and demands of the different types of work, and the variety added depth to his art. Up until his entry into the service, in all the years he'd devoted to producing commercial comic book material, Eisner had been anchored to an assembly-line style of planning and production and to a broad target audience ranging in age from adolescent to adult, and despite his many innovations, this limited the range of his art; most notably, before the army he was responsible only for entertaining. His work in the army extended his range of style, point of view, and narrative—all of which served him well when he returned to commercial comics after the war and, later, when he worked extensively in educational comics.

But perhaps more significant than its broadening of his talent, Eisner's time in the army broadened his life beyond comics. It was a badly needed escape from New York, his family, and his very limited social life. He still kept in close contact with his family—especially when his brother, Pete, was drafted and he tried to use his connections at the Pentagon to keep Pete out of harm's way, or when a financial crisis demanded his help with the bills—but his physical removal from New York gave him room to grow. He had his own apartment, a new set of friends, and, toward the end of the war, his first serious relationship with a woman.

The woman's name was Leona, and not surprisingly, Eisner met her through work. *Army Motors* had moved its offices to Detroit, ostensibly to be closer to the companies manufacturing the trucks, tanks, and other vehicles used in the war effort, and Eisner often traveled to Detroit to work on assignments or deliver artwork for the magazine. Leona worked as a staff writer for *Army Motors*, and she immediately caught Eisner's eye because, as Eisner explained to biographer Bob Andelman, she was not only "blonde, slim, and attractive, a gung-ho girl," she was also strong, independent, and intelligent. "She caught my eye because she was one of the staff writers who would go out to the testing field and drive two-ton trucks around."

Like so many wartime romances, this one was doomed by time and geography. The two saw each other whenever Eisner was in Detroit, which was often enough, and while they fell in love and even spoke of marriage, both understood the reality of their situation: he was a Jewish comic book artist from New York, she a Gentile writer from Detroit, and the war was going to end sooner or later. It wasn't going anywhere. But while they waited for the war to end, they went ballroom dancing and enjoyed going nowhere, together.

chapter six

FLIGHT

*I want to get my reader by his lapels, and I want to make him think
and I want to make him cry because of what I'm telling him.*

The war *did* end, and Eisner was discharged from the army. He had reason to be both relieved and optimistic about the days ahead. His fears
about the fate of his career had been unfounded, and *The Spirit*, in a
holding pattern while he was away, awaited his attention.

Eisner had a new perspective that he was prepared to apply to *The
Spirit*, and it was evident in the feature. Later, much would be made about
the dramatic difference between the prewar and postwar *Spirits*. Eisner
felt, as did most critics and comics historians, that the postwar *Spirit* was
more mature and experimental, better executed, and ultimately more fully
realized, with stronger supporting characters and stories, than the work
he'd done on the series before the war. The Spirit remained the same character that Eisner envisioned in the early months of 1940; it was Eisner who
had changed.

"When I came out," he explained, "I had seen the elephant and talked
to the owl. I had my own life experience and I began to apply it to what
I was doing. I was dealing with more realism after the war than I had
dealt with before."

But there was more—more than Eisner would care to admit. His drill
sergeant might not have seen much of Denny Colt or the Spirit in the
young draftee who stood in front of him in those dreary days of boot
camp and practice on the firing range, but Eisner's connection to his creation was intense. Indeed, there was no physical resemblance, but the two
were identical in their point of view, outlook on their world, and sense of
place in it—before and after the war. The prewar Spirit, like Eisner, saw

the world in dualistic, black-and-white terms; a lot of gray had been added between Eisner's bus trip to Fort Dix and his return to New York. If asked, Eisner would admit that there were many autobiographical touches to *The Spirit*. The Spirit's mask, he'd state, had actually served as a buffer between the creator and his creation.

"Those who are working in the medium with superheroes and so forth—we always hide behind the costume," Eisner told an interviewer long after he'd quit working on *The Spirit*. "I was hiding behind the Spirit's mask all those years. I was always saying, 'Well, this isn't me—it's him!'"

For Eisner, regaining control of *The Spirit* was nothing less than a reclaiming of his own identity as a civilian, businessman, and commercial cartoonist. His break with these identities during World War II had been a clean one: when he returned to New York, he had no office, none of the familiar artists working under him, and only vestiges of the character he'd created half a decade ago for the Register & Tribune Syndicate. It was just as well. Eisner needed to rebuild *The Spirit*, and to accomplish this, he needed new people with new ideas around him.

His first order of business was finding a place to work, and the office that he leased at 37 Wall Street had a special feeling of familiarity. Just over a decade earlier, when he was trying to help pay bills Sam Eisner couldn't cover, he had sold newspapers outside this very building. It was here that he'd begun seriously to study comics; now he was creating them in the very same place.

The Spirit weekly section, as written by Bill Woolfolk and penciled and inked by Lou Fine in Eisner's absence, was still being produced in Connecticut at the Quality Comics offices, and it continued that way while Eisner settled into his new office and hired a skeleton staff capable of assisting him with the feature. Martin DeMuth, who had been lettering *The Spirit* since December 1942, was retained in the same capacity; but Lou Fine, who wanted to go into commercial art, was out. He was replaced by John Spranger, who penciled over Eisner's layouts and rough pencils while Eisner himself did most of the inking and coloring. Compared with the staff Eisner had been working with at his old Tudor City studio, this was a small group, but Eisner was comfortable with it— enough so that he'd never again employ so large a staff to work on *The Spirit* section.

His first postwar *Spirit* entry appeared in the papers on December 23, 1945—a Christmas entry that continued a *Spirit* tradition that Eisner had begun before the war but had been discontinued while he was in the service. When asked how he, as a Jew, felt about writing his annual Christmas installments, Eisner answered that he had no problem with it, that it wasn't as much a business decision based on catering to a largely Christian readership as it was a matter of taking advantage of the goodwill generated during the season to deliver his own message.

"For some reason or another, that long-elusive aspiration for human goodness, which we share in all cultures, is present during the Christmas holidays," he explained. "It's not the kind of thing you discuss in a pool hall, but I really believe—at the risk of being laughed at—that there really is, deep in the psyches of all human beings, a desire to be—and I put this in italics—*good*."

That goodness, Eisner went on, was part of the phenomenon of gift giving and goodwill so prevalent during the holiday season, and that informed his annual feel-good *Spirit* stories more than the Christians' celebration of the birth of Christ.

"As far as I'm concerned, any celebration of Christmas on my part is not a celebration of Christ, or even a discussion of whether it happened. Rather, it's a celebration of a cultural phenomenon, if you will, that is unique and deserves support. That's why I, as a Jew, have no trouble with, in effect, celebrating Christmas."

Eisner plunged into his *Spirit* stories with a newfound vigor. After reintroducing readers to the Spirit's origins in a January 13, 1946, entry entitled "Dolan's Origin of the Spirit," Eisner took readers down a new path, adding new villains and revisiting some of the old ones, establishing a continuity from week to week that had been absent during the war years, refining and strengthening the character of Ebony, and turning in some of the best stories he'd ever written for the feature. Early in 1946, he hired a secretary, Marilyn Mercer, who turned out to be something of a scriptwriter herself. She couldn't draw, but some of her suggestions found their way into *Spirit* stories.

Comics had changed since Eisner left for the war. Comic book circulation was better than ever—about forty million per month in 1946—but interests were shifting as publishers pushed to satisfy all age groups on the market. The mid- to late forties saw not only a glut of new titles, but also a shift in the type of material being picked up by consumers. Interest in superheroes had declined, but detective and true-crime comic sales were jumping. *Classics Illustrated*, a new line of comics adapting classic literature to this new, easy-to-read, highly visual medium, took off. Joe Simon and Jack Kirby, whose macho *Captain America* had been fueled by patriotism during the war, created *Young Romance*, a new genre aimed at women, a previously untapped audience.

The Spirit waded through this building surf of new titles and comic book options, impervious to the changes and new interests. Eisner, while keeping his eye on the horizon for changes that might affect his work, never faltered in his belief that story, first and foremost, would direct his success. He saw signs of trouble ahead, from church and educational leaders who were beginning to complain that comics were corrupting the minds of young readers, protesting that the violence in comics had to be curtailed. But these issues didn't yet affect *The Spirit*, which was still good family reading. For the time being, Eisner and his creation were safe.

One rainy afternoon in early 1946, a teenage kid named Jules Feiffer, carrying a portfolio of his work, arrived in Will Eisner's office. The kid was thin, with a thick head of hair and glasses, and was barely out of high school. He'd looked up Eisner's Wall Street studio address in the telephone book, and fearful that he might be rejected if he tried to make an appointment over the phone, he'd headed down to the studio without calling ahead. He wanted a job—*any* job.

Eisner, who'd been in a similar position a decade earlier, was sympathetic.

"I said, 'What can you do?'" he recalled. "And he said, 'I'll do anything. I'll do coloring, or clean-up, or anything, and I'd like to work for nothing.'"

This was an idea that Eisner, notorious for his frugality, could appreciate. Problem was, the kid wasn't any good. He couldn't draw; his lettering was poor. For the life of him, Eisner couldn't think of anything he could do around the studio.

Eisner, in Feiffer's words, was "quite casually and disarmingly frank. He told me I had no talent and that my work just stank. I found this to be an unacceptable way of leaving the artist I greatly admired, so I began to improvise. I started to talk to him, and if I couldn't discuss *my* work in which he had no interest at all, I'd talk to him about *his* work. So Eisner found out, within thirty seconds, that I knew more about him than anybody who had ever lived."

Now Eisner had two reasons to hire the kid: He would work for free, and he was Eisner's biggest fan.

"He had no choice but to hire me as a groupie," Feiffer cracked, "and that was my first job: to hang around the office."

The law wouldn't permit him to hire Feiffer for nothing, so Eisner paid him a pittance—between ten and twenty bucks a week, as Eisner remembered—to function as an office gofer, number pages, ink in blacks, and, every so often, attempt backgrounds. The results were a testament to Eisner's patience.

As Feiffer recalled, "Every time they put a pen or brush in my hand, I screwed up, so they quickly learned not to do that, but I was useful as a loudmouth and cheerleader for the work, and as a kind of unofficial archivist and historian, because I knew everything about the art form."

Eisner agreed with Feiffer's assessment of his early contributions to the studio. Feiffer, he remembered, might have been a mediocre artist, but he liked the kid's spunk, the "intensity" that he brought to his studio. Although they were nearly twelve years apart in age, they had come from the same background, the same part of the city, the same kinds of experiences. Feiffer's father, like Eisner's, had struggled to support the family, and his mother, like Eisner's, was a strong figure, a pragmatist, the person who somehow managed to hold things together when the Depression threatened to yank everything in all directions. Feiffer grew up reading the comics, from Caniff and Segar to, later, Eisner and *The Spirit*, and in his youthful arrogance, he believed that he would grow up to be an important comics artist, even if he showed no evidence of artistic talent. He had a hunger for comics that Eisner rarely saw in the artists passing through his studio, and Eisner decided that there was something to this wisecracking kid.

Feiffer improved, and over the ensuing months, Eisner entrusted Feiffer with more work on *The Spirit*, including the coloring. Feiffer grew very comfortable talking to Eisner about his work, especially the writing end of it. In Feiffer's opinion, Eisner's best writing on *The Spirit* had occurred shortly after he began the feature in 1940. Feiffer preferred the art in the postwar *Spirit* issues, but he didn't think all that much of the writing.

"If you think you can do better, write a story yourself," Eisner challenged his young critic.

Feiffer did just that, and both came away surprised by the results, Eisner because the kid could really write, Feiffer because Eisner then gave him more story work. The resulting collaboration, the most productive during Eisner's years of working on *The Spirit*, was one of those instances of two very different talents coming together at just the right time and producing work that neither could have accomplished as well individually.

The two worked well together, batting around ideas and editing each other to the benefit of *The Spirit* in general and their individual careers in particular. Eisner trusted Feiffer's judgment. Feiffer had an uncanny knack for capturing the way people talked, and he had no patience for anything that seemed contrived. "He had a real ear for writing characters that lived and breathed," Eisner said. "Jules was always attentive to nuances, such as sounds and expressions, that he could work into a story to make it seem more real," he said.

But there were sore points and disagreements as well. Eisner, who liked to compare his shop style with that of a chef in charge of a kitchen—"I can't keep my hands out of the pot"—could irritate Feiffer with some of his meddling on stories that Feiffer had written, and as Feiffer's confidence grew, the mentor/protégé relationship, so strong in the beginning, began to erode. For all their teamwork on *The Spirit*, the feature still belonged to Eisner. Feiffer would go along with Eisner's bottom-line decisions on the stories and the direction *The Spirit* was taking, but he didn't always approve of them. Eisner was aware of this, of course, which led to a humorous *Spirit* entry, a parody written by Feiffer and published in 1950, in which both Eisner and Feiffer became characters in the story. The Eisner character is blocked and can't meet a New Year's deadline. The Feiffer character sneaks up behind him, shoots him at his drawing board, and substitutes one of his characters—a real-life Feiffer creation, a little boy named Clifford—for the Spirit.

"It made for an unusual story, and I was always after the unusual, anyway," Eisner said of the entry, noting that the story had roots in an actual deadline problem.

When reflecting on the story nearly a quarter century after its appearance, Feiffer couldn't remember whose idea it was to have a Feiffer lookalike shooting an Eisner look-alike. "Maybe I had me shooting Eisner, but my guess is I just had a guy shooting him, and Eisner turned it into me when he drew it. Or maybe I did have me killing him . . .

"We weren't getting along very well with each other at the time," he shrugged.

For all their bickering about politics, art, or anything else that came to the forefront in their discussions, Feiffer and Eisner never reached a point where their differences interfered with their work—or, for that matter, their friendship. "Our fights were always collegial," Feiffer recalled. "Never once did he pull rank on me. I was always amazed by what he let me get away with. It shows how close and tight the relationship was, that he let me do that parody. He had great generosity of soul."

Feiffer was absent from Eisner's studio for much of 1947 while he attended the Pratt Institute. He loved the storytelling aspects of the comic book trade, but his struggles with comic book art convinced him that with

With Jules Feiffer in 1988. Eisner gave Feiffer his first illustration work when Feiffer was still a teenager, and then watched him blossom into a Pulitzer Prize–winning cartoonist. (Courtesy of Denis Kitchen)

formal training, he might be better suited to a career in advertising art. Fortunately for those who eventually enjoyed his Pulitzer Prize–winning cartoons, children's books, plays, and films made from his screenplays, this didn't turn out to be the case.

By mid-1947, Eisner's creativity was reaching another high-water mark. Much of his success could be credited to his small but supremely talented shop. Eisner had worked with gifted artists over the years, but the studio contributing to *The Spirit* from 1947 to 1949 was far and away his best group yet. When reflecting on the *Spirit* issues published during this period, Eisner reserved for these artists some of the highest praise he would ever bestow on collaborators. All were specialists in areas that Eisner wanted to improve.

Abe Kanegson, a Bronx native who attended the same high school as Jules Feiffer, did *The Spirit*'s lettering, as well as some backgrounds, from 1947 to 1950. A large, burly Russian Jew, Kanegson was, as Feiffer remembered, "the left intellectual of the office," an opinionated presence with a heavy stutter that made his proclamations painfully slow to process. Eisner maintained that of all the letterers he employed over the years, Kanegson was one of the few who understood the nuances of lettering and who treated lettering as more than just a job. "Kanegson was brilliant," Eisner said. "He added a dimension of quality that typesetting could never get. His lettering is clear and legible, and in addition it lends warmth to the visuals."

Eisner used lettering to set tone or establish mood, and Kanegson's range allowed him to use types of lettering not often seen in comics, like blackletter, to great effect. "To me, lettering contributes as much in the storytelling as the art itself," he explained. "To my mind, there is no real border between the lettering and the artwork."

André LeBlanc, who would go on to work on such features as *The Phantom* and *Rex Morgan, M.D.*, was skilled at drawing animals—something Eisner could not do well and a deficiency in the studio since Bob Powell's departure. One of the period's memorable stories, "Cromlech Was a Nature Boy," in which Ebony befriends a boy capable of communicating with animals, would never have happened without LeBlanc's contributions.

"There's always been between André and myself a really good rapport creatively," Eisner noted. "That's strange, because his stuff does not concentrate on action. His work concentrates largely on strong draftsmanship and a warm quality of art. His animal drawings are marvelous, as are his depictions of children."

The Cromlech story grew out of Eisner's observations of a street poet and musician known as Moondog—"the first visible hippie," as Eisner would describe him. Eisner would see him hanging around Forty-second and Broadway, selling a paper called the *Hobo News*, and from there he let his imagination roam. He penciled a rough splash page and showed it to LeBlanc.

"I said, 'Let's do a Nature Boy story,' because there was a Nature Boy song that was built around Moondog," Eisner said. "I roughed out the story idea and André took over . . . We passed it back and forth."

Eisner's willingness to let others tinker with his ideas—another personal trademark—led to some of his most extraordinary work during the 1947–1948 period, including adaptations of two stories Eisner had enjoyed in his youth: Ambrose Bierce's 1894 horror story, "The Damned Thing," and Edgar Allan Poe's 1839 classic, "The Fall of the House of Usher." Eisner's love of adaptations dated back to his Fiction House days, although, ironically, he usually assigned adaptations to others. In his first studio, Jack Kirby had drawn *The Count of Monte Cristo*, and Dick Briefer had handled *The Hunchback of Notre Dame*. Eisner had adapted "Cinderella" and "Hansel and Gretel" in recent *Spirit* entries, with only marginal success. He assigned these two more recent adaptations to Jerry Grandenetti, a relatively new hire at the shop who'd expressed interest in doing a *Spirit* on his own.

"I was always faced with hiring somebody almost brand new in the field, who had basically good talents, but who was inexperienced," Eisner said. "The assistant would go along working in the shop, and then very suddenly, he blossomed into a man of his own.

"Typically, the assistant began to make more demands, which is normal, which is acceptable. The assistant was working on my feature, but he wanted to stretch out, to break out of the so-called enslavement that he perceived working in my shop."

Eisner had discovered Grandenetti while searching for a background man for *The Spirit*'s cityscapes. Grandenetti, ten years Eisner's junior, was then working as a draftsman with a landscape architectural firm, but he wasn't happy with the job. He wanted out, but he wasn't sure if he wanted to go into comics, which appealed to him, or become an illustrator for a magazine such as the *Saturday Evening Post* or *Cosmopolitan*, which promised to be much more lucrative but was also cutthroat. He decided to give comics a try. He packed a portfolio with samples and headed up to Quality Comics, but instead of landing a job with Busy Arnold, he was referred to Eisner. He felt blessed to have been hired by someone of Eisner's reputation and even more fortunate to be given a lot of freedom to learn on the job.

"I don't think Bill ever pushed anybody," he said, remembering the shop as being quiet and professional but easygoing. "He would let us do our thing, which was a tremendous break for me. I was dumped into the world of comics from the world of architecture, and here I was, trying to figure out how to do that. Bill wouldn't tell me; I *did* it. Bill would literally write the story right onto the page itself, and then we'd take it from there."

The two adaptations were almost entirely Grandenetti's. Eisner, as always, supplied the direction, penciling and inking the splash page for "The Fall of the House of Usher," which marked the Spirit's sole appearance in the entry, and then laying out the rest of the story with rough penciling. The rest, with the exception of the Abe Kanegson's lettering, was Grandenetti's. The resulting story looked nothing like the typical Eisner *Spirit*, though his influence is felt throughout, especially in the camera angles.

The shop worked so efficiently that, in time, Eisner couldn't remember the exact contribution each artist made to a given *Spirit* entry. This was especially true of his collaborations with Feiffer, which led to some interesting and occasionally testy discussions in later years, after Feiffer had established his reputation and interviewers asked about his work on *The Spirit*. One particular story, a 1949 *Spirit* classic called "Ten Minutes," brought out the possessiveness that each man felt about his own finer work.

The clever conceit of "Ten Minutes" was to tell a story in real time. "It will take you ten minutes to read this story," a voice-over narrator informs the reader at the onset of "Ten Minutes." "But these ten minutes that you will spend here are an eternity for one man. For they are the last ten minutes in Freddy's life."

Giving away a story's ending up front takes a lot of moxie, but doing so before a seven-page comic book story posed the challenge of making a reader care about a character in very short order. To give the reader a sense of the passing time, Eisner placed a clock in the opening panel of each new page. In a more subtle move, the reader also sees two little girls playing a game with a ball on the sidewalk outside Freddy's tenement building. The girls are running through the alphabet. The story opens with the letter "A," and by the fifth page—six minutes into the story— they have reached the letter "R."

The Spirit plays a marginal but important role in the story, appearing in the last minute of Freddy's life. The rest is about a down-on-his-luck gambler trying desperately to find a way out of his dead-end life. In holding up a candy store run by a kindly neighborhood icon and unintentionally killing him, Freddy sets in motion the last few minutes of his life. By this point, the reader sees Freddy as an unlucky loser but not evil, and his violent end is both poignant and sad, underscoring how a very brief period of time can change the direction of a person's life.

"That was mine," Feiffer said of the story. "That was simply an autobiographical fantasy based on my Bronx upbringing. And the fat candy store man was based on a candy man that I remembered from my childhood.

> I suppose what so interested me in that kind of approach was that I was living that sort of life in the East Bronx: painfully dull and painfully dismal, and painfully poor. Lower middle class; not poverty, but poor in spirit, certainly. And that one could take off from that vantage point and enter into all sorts of danger, which was fascinating.

Eisner, as Feiffer remembered, wrote Freddy's death scene in the subway, but the rest was his creation.

Eisner, of course, had a different memory.

"The philosophy [of "Ten Minutes"] is essentially mine," Eisner maintained, "as differentiated from Feiffer.

> Feiffer to this day doesn't think in terms of that kind of philosophical concept, like the ten minutes in a man's life. You look at my body of work, you'll see I always seem to build on that theme. On the other hand my dialogue isn't as crisp and as sharp and sometimes as incisive as Feiffer's is. Feiffer has—he always did have—an incredible ear for dialogue and in the way people talk, particularly. Now in the matter of this little girl bouncing a ball . . . Remember, too, that Feiffer and I have the same background, ten years apart. We both lived in the same area so we both came up and lived the same kind of childhood, except, perhaps, that his parents were half notch or a notch higher on the social scale than mine. So we would tend to say—probably, I might have said, "Hey, remember 'A, my name is Alice; B, my name is—'" "Oh yeah," he said, "I'll do that." He later included it in *Clifford* and so forth. But that doesn't mean I should get credit for it.

According to Eisner, he generally came up for an idea for a story during his more reflective moments, such as when he was deep in thought while taking the train home from work, and he would then discuss the idea with Feiffer and the others working at the shop. Producing the story became a cooperative effort, from Eisner's rough penciling to Feiffer's dialogue balloons to Abe Kanegson's lettering. The popularity of "Ten Minutes"—it became one of *The Spirit*'s most frequently reprinted stories— probably had more to do with the disagreement over authorship than anything.

In his memoir, *Backing into Forward*, Feiffer admitted that he intentionally mimicked Eisner when writing the Spirit stories and that "Ten Minutes," like the others that he ghostwrote for the feature, was "really a Spirit story that was really a Jules story in Eisner drag.

> While I was the writer on *The Spirit*, I was by no means its auteur. That was Eisner. Every scene I conceived, no matter how it turned out, started out as if I were he. Later, when I was throwing in more and more pieces of myself, nothing went in that didn't exist comfortably with Eisner's sensibility.
>
> He and I would first talk story. I'd do a layout of story line that was broken down into panels and dialogue. He'd okay it with changes, and I'd write in the copy. Next, I'd sketch a crude layout

on sheets of Bristol board that, when completed, would be the final art. Before the lettering was inked in, Will went over and revised, rewrote, and sometimes reconceived as he saw fit, seldom without discussion, sometimes even argument.

"It goes like this a lot with us," Eisner said in 1988. "Sometimes he always thought I wrote a particular story and I thought he did it. I guess we may never know for sure."

Whenever possible, Eisner injected humor into *The Spirit*, which humanized his characters and took the edge off some of the stories' violence. Every so often, as a change of pace, he'd present a story that was almost entirely humorous, and he'd even dabble with parody. This was the case when he published "Li'l Adam," a send-up of Al Capp's *Li'l Abner* that in time Eisner would call his "baptism of reality in the comic book world."

It started innocently enough, with a phone call from Capp, who proposed that he and Eisner stage a feud through their respective work. The loud, blustery Capp, one of the most popular daily comic strip artists in the business, had become famous for his feuds, real or fictitious, which, after the first one with Ham Fisher, he used for publicity.

"We'll have a little running feud," he suggested to Eisner. "I think that would be good for us."

Eisner, by his own admission, was starstruck.

"I thought it was great," he said of the proposed feud. "We would take potshots at each other's characters."

Eisner might have known better; his previous encounters with Capp had been less than stellar. They'd met briefly at a function when Eisner was in the army and working at the Pentagon. Capp had invited Eisner to one of his exhibitions in Boston, supposedly to get together and tour the city, but he was a no-show when Eisner flew up for the meeting. They crossed paths again a couple of years later, shortly after the end of the war, at a meeting of the National Cartoonists Society. Milton Caniff had invited Eisner to the gathering—a true honor for Eisner, since comic book artists, considered inferior by the daily strip artists, were excluded from the society.

As Eisner recalled, Capp approached him and, in his booming voice, made a big production of their meeting:

"I *caught* your *stuff* in the Philadelphia papers," he said. "It's really good stuff. You're quite talented." Of course, I was impressed.

"But," he said, "you'll never make it in this business." Inside, I collapsed, and said, "How come?"

He said, "You're too goddamn normal!" Then he threw his head back and gave a bellowing laugh.

Rather than being put off by Capp's showboating, Eisner felt anointed. As he viewed it, "any attention on his part was kind of an admission into the hierarchy of comic book artists."

The feud turned out to be nothing but a setup. Eisner held up his end of the deal, producing "Li'l Adam" for the Sunday *Spirit*. The following week, he heard from a *Newsweek* reporter interested in the feud. The reporter, Eisner surmised, had been contacted by Capp, who had a wealth of media connections. Eisner gave him a brief telephone interview. The interview appeared in the newsmagazine, and then . . . nothing. Capp never produced his parody of *The Spirit* and never addressed the feud, which effectively left Eisner looking like a young, envious artist taking cheap shots at a popular, established colleague.

Three and a half decades afterward, Eisner still fumed about what he felt was nothing less than a betrayal on Capp's part.

"I always harbored a kind of anger at him for doing something like that," he said. "It seems that all the contacts I had with him ended short of fruition. He was always offering something interesting that never materialized."

In March 1948, *Collier's* magazine published "Horror in the Nursery," an article profiling Dr. Fredric Wertham and his theories connecting comics and juvenile delinquency. The article, accompanied by lavishly staged photographs of a young girl, bound and gagged, and of a young boy being stabbed in the arm by a fountain pen, provided Wertham with a national audience while stoking the fires of an already mounting crusade against comic books. Waving around Wertham's credentials as a clinical psychiatrist, Judith Crist, the article's author, sounded an alarm that couldn't be ignored: comic books, which Wertham estimated were being read by nine out of ten kids, led to juvenile delinquency. This was an all-out parental alert, voiced by an indisputable authority who claimed that, through countless encounters with teenage kids, he had seen comic books' harmful effects on impressionable minds. According to Wertham, the mass market was flooded with comic books—up to sixty million sales per month—all unregulated by the government and publishers, all capable of flipping an unstable mind toward frightening behavior. "We found that comic book reading was a distinct influencing factor in the case of every single delinquent and disturbed child we studied," Wertham stated, concluding that "the time has come to legislate these books off the newsstands and out of candy-stores."

Wertham was no fool. He'd come to the magazine interview armed with statistics, anecdotes from his clinical research, open contempt for colleagues who didn't fall in lockstep with his thinking, a crusader's sense of self-righteousness, and a skill for using hot-button words and phrases guaranteed to seize attention. Wertham's arrogance bubbled like lava near the surface of every statement he issued in the article: *he* was the authority, *he* knew what was best, and if parents allowed their kids to read comic books, they should be prepared to face the consequences. After all, they'd been warned.

One look at Wertham made you believe that you were dealing with a *serious* man. He rarely smiled for photographs, and as a result, he came across like the neighbor who frightened you for reasons you couldn't quite pinpoint or the high school principal who kept a perpetual eye on you because, while he had no proof, he was certain you were up to no good. He had a long, narrow head, with pinched features capped by a receding hairline, glasses perched on a slender nose, and a chin that narrowed to an almost perfect point. Worry and scowl lines made him look older than his fifty-three years.

Wertham, whose name would become synonymous with the crusade against comics, defied simple definition. Shrewd enough to cultivate the kind of favorable public image beneficial to his almost unquenchable thirst for publicity, Wertham was a mass of contradictions. No one seemed to notice—until, that is, he had insinuated himself into the public consciousness in so many ways that it was all but impossible to stage a meaningful offensive against him.

Born Frederic Wertheimer in Munich in 1895, Wertham spent the early portion of his life racking up impressive credentials in psychiatry. He earned a medical degree at the University of Würzburg and studied in Paris and London before moving to the United States in 1922 and taking a job at the Phipps Psychiatric Clinic at Johns Hopkins University. Five years later, he legally changed his last name. (The alteration of his first name came later.)

While at Johns Hopkins, he built an impeccable reputation as a clinician, teacher, and scholar. After eight years, he left Johns Hopkins for New York City, where he conducted psychiatric evaluations of convicted

felons for the New York Court of General Sessions and later worked for
Bellevue Hospital, a facility known for its psychiatic treatment of pa-
tients. While at Johns Hopkins, he had worked for Dr. Adolf Meyer,
who strongly believed in a correlation between environment and mental
disorders, and in New York, while working with criminal and troubled
juveniles, Wertham began to apply Meyer's beliefs to his own theories.
In 1946, he opened the Lafargue Clinic in Harlem, a facility offering free
or low-cost psychiatric services to the neighborhood's poor, non-white
residents.

He also learned how to gain the spotlight in the country's largest
city. His courtroom testimony, offered as an expert witness, made
headlines; the press knew he was always good for a quote or two. His
fluid writing style, found in his 1941 book, *Dark Legend* (an account of
a seventeen-year-old's murder of his mother that was later made into a
Broadway play), garnered him writing assignments for newspapers and
magazines.

In his landmark book, *The Ten-Cent Plague: The Great Comic-Book
Scare and How It Changed America*, David Hajdu might have offered the
best capsule characterization of Wertham to date:

> Wertham was a nest of contradictions—intelligent and contempla-
> tive, yet susceptible to illogic, conjecture, and peculiar leaps of
> reasoning; temperate in appearance and manner, yet inclined to
> extravagant, attention-grabbing pontification. He abhorred comics,
> which were born of the immigrant experience, while he was deeply
> empathetic to the Negro condition . . .

The *Collier's* article added an air of legitimacy to anti-comics rumblings
heard since the end of the war. Local church, education, and civic groups
around the country were making noises about what they considered to be
inappropriate material in comics, especially the most mature material
aimed at soldiers returning home from the war—young men no longer as
captivated by superheroes as they might have been at one time but now
definitely interested in true-crime and detective stories. The anti-comics
crusade followed a tried-and-true method of attacking almost anything in
popular culture: first, intellectuals (critics, writers, teachers) vilified, ridiculed, and cast doubts on the value of the target; if that failed, there were
attacks on the local level, where greater degrees of success might be expected than on a national scale; if that failed, you brought out the big
guns—the national press and authorities. The key was to be relentless.

The same month in which the *Collier's* article appeared, ABC radio broadcast a panel discussion, "What's Wrong with the Comics?" on its *America's Town Meeting of the Air* program. John Mason Brown, drama critic for the *Saturday Review*, and novelist Maryn Mannes, author of "Junior Was a Craving," an article in the February 1948 issue of *New Republic*, took the anti-comics side; Al Capp and George Hecht, publisher of *Parents* magazine, spoke in defense of comics. The overheated rhetoric hinted of the days ahead, when an all-out assault on comics would prompt Senate hearings. Brown, taking the lead from Mannes's *New Republic* piece, in which she labeled comics "the greatest intellectual narcotic on the market," called comics "the marijuana of the nursery; the bane of the bassinet; the horror of the house; the curse of the kids; and a threat to the future." Capp, known for his quick wit and biting sarcasm, must have wondered what gods he might have offended to find himself trapped in a radio booth with the hyperbolic Brown.

If nothing else, 1948 saw the gathering of thunderheads in the distance. Comic book burnings, organized by schools and churches, flared up across the American landscape; concerned parents threatened to boycott drugstores and other outlets stocking titles deemed to be offensive. Newspaper and magazine editors, noticing the trend, ran articles in their publications. To hear their opponents talk, comic books derailed the mind, created juvenile delinquents whose disrespect for authorities would eventually devolve into a life of crime, festered communism, and usurped the roles of both God and country.

Wertham, for his part, was just beginning. His article "The Comics . . . Very Funny," published in the May 29, 1948, issue of the *Saturday Review of Books* and later reprinted in the August *Reader's Digest*, reiterated his earlier statements from *Collier's* while pushing his case even further. Comics, he suggested, didn't affect only those predisposed to bad behavior; they affected everybody, including, he insinuated, your previously well-mannered children. The article's illustrations, offered for maximum shock value, included a comic panel from the 1947 *True Crime #2*, drawn by Jack Cole, depicting a close-up of a hypodermic needle about to be shoved into someone's eye. The magazine's offices were flooded with letters.

Wertham's genuine concern for the welfare of youthful readers, though it never wholly disappeared, was now crowded out by the attention he was receiving. The comic book controversy was seductive. It offered the promise of advancing his career by anointing him the authority for a cause he truly believed in and, in the process, bringing him the kind of publicity that he could parlay into book contracts, public appearances, and positions on important government or educational boards.

To begin with, those creating and publishing comic books paid little heed. As long as sales continued to rise—or at least hold steady—there was no cause for alarm. A handful of publishers and distributors, in an effort to calm the critics and, in the best-case scenario, slow down the actions against the industry, banded together and formed the Association of Comics Magazine Publishers (ACMP), which in July 1948 adopted a formal code to address content, artwork, language, and attitudes in comic books of the future. The ACMP would act as the industry's self-policing agency, offering assurance to the public that ultraviolence, obscenity, and profanity would be absent in their code-approved books and that figures of authority, honored civic and religious groups, and racial and ethnic groups would not be ridiculed or improperly portrayed. Henry E. Schultz, a highly regarded attorney and academician, was installed as the ACMP's first executive director.

Will Eisner felt he had no reason to worry. *The Spirit*, in comparison with other available features, was tame stuff. Violence was carefully depicted; huge pools of blood were nonexistent. From the beginning of his career, Eisner had self-censored more cautiously than anything proposed by the Chicken Littles presently condemning comics, and even if he had been inclined to present material that some might find objectionable, newspapers (more prudish than those who stocked the drugstore racks) would never have stood for it.

This self-assurance led him to take a swipe at comics' early critics. In "The Spirit's Favorite Fairy Tales for Juvenile Delinquents: Hänzel und Gretel," Eisner included a pointed, satirical notice. "This is a public service feature and is based upon the requests of public-minded citizens who feel that juvenile crime is largely a result of deficiency in the wholesome literature we used to enjoy," Eisner wrote. "The author (who believes 'tis better late than never) is glad to cooperate. He hopes to 'reach' those strayed little lambs and perhaps fill a gap in their twisted lives."

When discussing the story in 1986, Eisner explained that the note not only addressed efforts to censor comics, it also commented on his long-standing disgust at the general perception of comics being for kids only.

"This was before the Comics Code, but there already was a big flap about comics being bad and naughty, destructive psychologically," he said. "The critics were talking about comics in general. This was still a time when comics were regarded strictly as children's literature. Comics

At a time when crime comics such as *Crime Does Not Pay* were reaching a height in
popularity but were being scrutinized for their violent content, Eisner proved to be a master
of combining action and violence without depicting the bloodshed. The opening page
of this January 5, 1947 *Spirit*, which includes an Eisner quip about the mounting criticism
of such comics, is an example. (© Will Eisner Studios, Inc., courtesy of Denis Kitchen)

are still regarded that way when you see them discussed in newspapers,
but the idea that only children read comics was more prevalent than it is
today."

But in the end, Eisner's work wasn't immune from criticism, nor did it
escape the notice of a would-be censor's watchful eye. In his ceaseless attempts to present stories that would appeal to older readers, he'd test the
boundaries of the day's standards, risking an editor's ire, pulling back if
necessary, and starting over again. Any suggestion of sex, of course, was
adult content, and Eisner had to be careful when dealing with the Spirit's
relationships with women. The Spirit was handsome, single, virile, athletic, intelligent, mysterious, and sexy—the type of man who just might
turn a woman's head. In the Spirit, Eisner had created a character who
was constantly attracted to beautiful women, and as with James Bond

Rather than use a standard logo for his *Spirit* entries, Eisner preferred to work the title into a story's artwork. This splash page from a June 26, 1949 story is one of Eisner's most memorable. (© Will Eisner Studios, Inc., courtesy of Denis Kitchen)

two decades later, that attraction could be dangerous. His relationship with Ellen Dolan, everybody's favorite girl next door, was chaste and playful—although in one story he did give her a spanking that raised a few eyebrows—but in his villainous femmes fatales, he was dealing with something entirely different.

Eisner had introduced these intriguing foils early in *The Spirit*'s history. They had catchy names—Black Queen, Sand Saref, Skinny Bones, Thorne Strand, Flaxen Weaver, Powder Pouf, Silk Satin, and, best known of the group, the indomitable P'Gell—and they had curvaceous forms, sharp minds, and past lives as mysterious as the Spirit's. They were strongly independent and seductive. They traveled internationally, giving Eisner occasion to place his stories in exotic locations. Most important of all, they were the Spirit's equals, capable of exposing his weaknesses and matching him in a battle of wits. In every respect, these women were more fully realized as characters than their male counterparts.

His femmes fatales, Eisner confessed, were precisely the kinds of women he himself found attractive.

"Every man who works in this field—whether he's writing short stories or novels, working in this medium or doing paintings—responds to his personal ideal of what is an attractive woman," he said. "I'm generally turned on by a very intelligent, self-contained, confident woman whose seduction represents a substantial action. As one writer once said, 'To seduce the maid is not great trouble. But to seduce the duchess—that's an accomplishment!' "

Each of these women attracted the Spirit in a different way. Sand Saref and Denny Colt had been childhood friends, and it's clear that they would have been adult lovers if Colt's uncle, a thief, hadn't been unjustly accused of killing Saref's father, a police officer pursuing him.

"I walked a tightrope with her," Eisner said of Saref, who originally was cast in a *John Law* story, only to be recycled in a two-part *Spirit* episode when the proposed *John Law* comic book fell through. "I wanted her to be in command, tough and independent, yet I tried to get the reader to feel compassion for her, to hope that she might turn away from crime." Happy endings, however, weren't in the cards for her. "That wouldn't have been true to Sand's character. She's too strong a character to change her life in an instant."

The other femmes fatales were similarly strong characters. Silk Satin, a Katharine Hepburn look-alike, is also a reluctant criminal, a woman trapped by circumstance, deeply in love with the Spirit, and under other conditions, she might have wound up with him. Skinny Bones, a Lauren

Eisner's femmes fatales, one of his trademark *Spirit* features, were beautiful, intelligent, sexy—and potentially lethal. This January 23, 1949 splash page is an example of how Eisner tried to work humor into his story. (© Will Eisner Studios, Inc., courtesy of Denis Kitchen)

Bacall knockoff, works for the Mob, while Black Queen, the first of Eisner's femmes fatales, *is* the Mob.

None, however, compared with P'Gell, the often married (and widowed), well-traveled villainess who appeared in more *Spirit* stories—seventeen in all—than any of these dangerous women. The ultimate foe, partly good but mostly naughty, P'Gell proved irresistible to the Spirit, who's drawn to her repeatedly, only to barely escape with his life with each encounter.

"The stories with her were always special ones," Eisner admitted. "I especially enjoyed these because it was always The Spirit's wits against hers, and that's an aspect of The Spirit that I've always enjoyed exploring—the way he can think his way through a situation."

These seductive, pinup-perfect characters, more than any of their male counterparts, helped propel *The Spirit* into the adult market. Male villains such as the Octopus, Dr. Cobra, Mr. Carrion, and the Squid seemed as familiar and packaged as the villains in the superhero comics and required action, more than thought, for the Spirit to defeat them. Eisner not only recognized as much he enjoyed poking fun at men's mistaken belief that they were the stronger sex. "The thing about women," the Spirit says to Commissioner Dolan in a splash page for a Thorne Strand episode, "is y'gotta outthink them . . . Keep a firm grip on your emotions and keep your brain clear."

The Spirit and Dolan's perch? The palm of Thorne Strand's hand.

On September 5, 1948, Eisner published a *Spirit* episode entitled "The Story of Gerhard Shnobble," a seven-page story that, in time, would prove to be his most critically acclaimed and frequently reprinted work from the series. The story featured Eisner's trademarks—a strong narrative, a memorable character, experimentation in form, interesting camera angles, and a powerful ending—and managed to do so with the Spirit being only an incidental presence in the story.

Of all his *Spirit* stories, this became Eisner's personal favorite.

"When I did 'Gerhard Shnobble,'" he told interviewer Tom Heintjes, "I found that I could take a simple theme and use it as a way of dealing with a philosophical point. The theme I was working with is that everyone, no matter how small they seem, has a moment of glory. I'm fascinated by the fact that the world has billions of people, each of whom does small things. And I'm convinced that small acts can have huge ramifications. I just can't get out of my mind the belief that our existence is part of a larger scheme."

Eisner would repeatedly return to this theme and expand upon it in his graphic novels, but "Gerhard Shnobble" stood out because of its combined intensity and brevity. This was clearly not kids' play. In the past, Eisner had been able to disguise his own feelings in his characters, but as he admitted later, he put himself on the line in this fable about a little nebbish with the ability to fly.

"It was the first time that I was truly aware that I could do a story that I had great personal feelings about," he said of the piece. "It proved to me that I could write something with a little more depth to it. Most of the stories I did up to this time were not as consciously personal as this."

In the story, the title character discovers on his eighth birthday that he has the ability to fly—if he *believes* he can. His parents, through scolding and beatings, discourage him from ever showing the ability to others, and he literally blots it out of his mind. He proceeds through a terminally ordinary life as a figure on the fringes of failure, an invisible nerd barely scraping by, whose greatest achievement is a promotion to night watchman at a bank. The bank is burglarized and Shnobble is fired, reinforcing his feelings of isolation and uselessness. Thoroughly defeated, he walks the streets of New York until, through the wall of his depression, he remembers his unique ability. Determined to prove to the world that he is indeed special, he takes an elevator to the rooftop of a skyscraper, from which he proposes to drop and then soar over the people on the street below. Instead, he becomes the ultimate person at the wrong place at the wrong time: the bank robbers have been trapped on the roof of the same building, and the Spirit, called to the scene to apprehend them, winds up battling them just as Shnobble steps off the building and begins his flight. Shnobble is hit by stray gunfire, and rather than wow the crowd with his ability to fly, he falls to earth, another victim of senseless crime. In the story's concluding panel, a narrator drives home Eisner's point: "Do not weep for Shnobble . . . Rather shed a tear for all mankind . . . For not one person in the entire crowd that watched his body being carted away . . . knew or even suspected that on this day Gerhard Shnobble had flown."

For all its fantastic drama, this Everyman's fable was deeply personal for Eisner, traipsing back to the tenements of the Bronx, to Sam Eisner's need (and failure) to prove his own artistic talent, to Will Eisner's discouragement and eventual faith in his ability, to his inextricable obsession with struggle and with spiritual and physical triumph. The ghosts of the past hovered over this tale and informed it in subtle but important ways.

To add realism to his sequential art, Eisner inserted actual photographs

AND SO... LIFELESS...
GERHARD SHNOBBLE FLUTTERED
EARTHWARD.

BUT DO NOT WEEP
FOR SHNOBBLE...

RATHER SHED A TEAR
FOR ALL MANKIND...

FOR NOT ONE PERSON IN THE
ENTIRE CROWD THAT WATCHED
HIS BODY BEING CARTED AWAY...KNEW
OR EVEN SUSPECTED THAT
ON THIS DAY GERHARD SHNOBBLE
HAD **FLOWN**.

The final page of "The Story of Gerhard Shnobble," Eisner's favorite *Spirit* story.
(© Will Eisner Studios, Inc., courtesy of Denis Kitchen)

of New York's cityscape as backgrounds in two of the panels—a bold, experimental move that had engravers screaming and Eisner's readers applauding. Once again, solving a problem had led to a memorable innovation.

"I had been wanting to do something like that for a long time," he said. "I wanted action against a real landscape, and this was a splendid opportunity for it because I needed city buildings. I simply got the photos from a file somewhere and put a screen on them, and just inserted them in the story."

Eisner was especially pleased that he'd been able to tell the story with only minimal involvement of the Spirit. This was the type of story that had enthralled him as a boy, when he'd steal away and read pulp magazines on the sly or study the short stories of O. Henry, Ring Lardner, or Ambrose Bierce and marvel at how much could be said, in such an entertaining way, in so little space. The Spirit's appearance in the story was only to satisfy the Sunday comics readers. "You didn't need The Spirit there," Eisner said of his presence in "Gerhard Shnobble." "It could have been somebody else."

Eisner could make light of the idea of his reducing his main character's role to that of a walk-on in "Gerhard Shnobble" and other *Spirit* stories.

"I guess I could be classified as having created the world's first useless hero."

Never content to settle in with a single feature in the late forties, Eisner began to look for other comics options to explore. He was creatively restless, ready to pounce on the next idea. *The Spirit* had its own boundaries and audience, which was fine on a week-to-week basis; the fast pace of producing new episodes satisfied both the feature's readers and its artists' creative drives. But it wasn't enough. Eisner stayed busy developing new projects and pitching ideas, most not advancing beyond the preliminaries of an idea and some rough pencils. Eisner pitched a few of these, such as *Sears, Roebuck Comics* and *Trade Name Comics*, books designed as giveaway promotional items for retail stores, but they never reached fruition. The businessman in Eisner told him that he had the ideas and staff to handle a wider variety of comics, ranging from kids' stories to work directed toward specialized audiences. His experience with *Army Motors* had convinced him that there was a large, untapped market for comics that did more than entertain.

All this led to the 1948 founding of American Visuals, a company that would put out a line of Eisner's own comics and explore other commercial and educational comics possibilities. Planned titles for the comic book line included *Baseball Comics, Kewpies, The Adventures of Nubbin the Shoeshine Boy*, and *John Law*. Not one of them enjoyed even a hint of success.

You didn't have to search far for answers for why these comics didn't work. *Kewpies*, the comic book adventures of characters based on the famous Rosie O'Neill characters, was too attached to a fad—and geared to consumers not inclined to buy comic books—to stand a chance on the market. Eisner undoubtedly hoped they would appeal to the same readership that followed the Walt Disney cartoon characters, and to simulate this, Eisner hired former Disney artist Lee J. Ames to do the art. One issue of the comic came out, did poorly at the marketplace, and *Kewpies* disappeared.

Baseball Comics suffered a similar single-issue fate. Written by Jules Feiffer, with artwork by Eisner and Tex Blaisdell, *Baseball Comics* followed the exploits of Rube Rooky, a talented but naive baseball phenom that Eisner hoped would catch the public's fancy similar to the way Ham Fisher's *Joe Palooka* had reached a large readership twenty years earlier. It didn't. The first issue bombed on the newsstand, and the title was discontinued. A second issue had been planned, written, and drawn, but it wasn't published until 1991, when Kitchen Sink Press resurrected the two books as part of its reprint operations. More than four decades after publishing the first issue, Eisner still seemed befuddled about the comic book's failure.

"*Baseball Comics* was a specialized comic book, a book devoted to one topic," he told Kitchen Sink editor Dave Schreiner. "Such books sold well in the pulp magazine field, and I didn't think there was any reason it couldn't work in comics."

The *Nubbin* and *John Law* comics, inextricably connected from the onset, had a longer history. Originally conceived to be a daily comic strip, *Nubbin* went nowhere. Eisner then thought he might be able to create another ready-print, Sunday newspaper insert similar to *The Spirit*, with *Nubbin* as the feature story every week and the *John Law* story to be included, much the way *Lady Luck* and *Mr. Mystic* had rounded out the original *Spirit* comic book supplement. Newspapers weren't interested in Nubbin, an orphaned shoeshine boy in the tradition of *Little Orphan Annie*, or John Law, a pipe-smoking, eye-patch-wearing detective with an unmistakable resemblance to the Spirit. Finally, Eisner considered just converting the insert idea into a monthly comic book before ultimately deciding to give each character his own book. Neither got off the ground. Eisner eventually converted the *John Law* stories into *Spirit* entries, though this was more a matter of his hating to see work go to waste than any great value they held.

Eisner lost a bundle producing his own line of comics, although American Visuals enjoyed success in other endeavors, as when the company produced one-off public service titles such as *The Sad Case of Waiting-Room Willie* and *A Medal for Bowzer*, with Eisner writing the scripts and doing the covers and Klaus Nordling, one of his shop's old standbys, taking the interior art. These books, though nothing special in terms of art or story, would serve as templates for a career waiting around the corner. Eisner, tiring of *The Spirit* even as the feature was reaching its zenith, had found his new direction, one that would take him away from entertainment and into instruction, giving him the opportunity to pioneer an entirely different brand of comics.

chapter seven

ANN

He said, "She's a very nice girl." I said, "My mother likes
nice girls. I don't like nice girls."

As restless as he could be creatively, Will Eisner preferred rock-solid stability in his life away from the office. To say that he didn't change readily would be an understatement. On the day he celebrated his thirty-second birthday, he was still living with his parents, brother, and sister, his daily routine alternating between work and family, just as it had been before the war. He still contributed to his family's financial welfare, assisting whenever necessary with the rent and bills. He'd even helped with his sister Rhoda's college tuition, assuring that she would obtain the degree he'd never have. He wasn't wealthy, but he was very comfortable. Ever the child of the Depression, he guarded his money carefully, always aware that in his line of work prosperity could disappear very quickly and with no warning. His social life had slowed to a crawl shortly after the war, when his relationship with the young woman from Detroit had fallen apart, victim of distance and Fannie Eisner's disapproval of her son's dating a Gentile. As far as Eisner was concerned, this was okay: American Visuals was progressing steadily, and *The Spirit*, although not as compelling to Eisner as it had once been, remained a steady, reassuring presence. Eisner's priorities, like those of any serious artist, began with his work.

Eisner looked forward to spending the extended 1949 Labor Day weekend on a brief vacation in Maine. He and a friend, Arthur Strassburger, made arrangements to drive to Camp Mingo in Kezar Falls, where they planned to relax, enjoy a few drinks, and, in Eisner's case, maybe pick up a local woman for a holiday fling. Eisner looked forward to his time away from the city.

Their plans changed abruptly when Strassburger called Eisner and asked if he'd be willing to give a young woman named Ann Weingarten a lift to another town in Maine. Eisner was immediately suspicious. The town wasn't anywhere near their destination, and from what he could surmise from this and subsequent calls, Strassburger's request was a formality; his friend had already consented to giving the woman a ride.

"Did you promise her?" Eisner pressed.

"Sort of," Strassburger answered sheepishly.

It turned out that Strassburger was interested in Ann Weingarten's younger sister, Jane, and his invitation to take Ann to Maine was spur-of-the-moment. Arthur and Jane had been sitting on a couch in the living room one day when Ann walked in and mentioned that she was hoping to visit her older sister, Susan, and her two young boys, Allan and Carl, aged five and two, respectively. Susan, seven and a half years older than Ann, had been widowed very young when her husband had a heart attack, and she and her sons were spending the summer in Maine. "Susan and I were very close," Ann would remember. "We were much more alike in tastes and things like that than Jane and I.

"Anyway, Jane was sitting in the living room with Arthur, and I happened to walk in. We started to talk and I said, 'I'd love to go up and see Susan over Labor Day.' Arthur said, 'Oh, this friend and I are going to Maine, and we'll be glad to give you a lift.' Arthur then called Will and said, 'You want to give some girl a lift up to Maine?' and Will said, 'No, I don't want to give some girl a lift up to Maine.' Arthur kept calling him and pushing him, and Will finally said, 'Okay, okay.' He was a good friend."

None of this appealed to Eisner, who suddenly saw his boys' weekend out turning into something much more tame and domesticated than he'd bargained for. He tried unsuccessfully to pawn her off on a friend, Jerry Gropper, who didn't know her any better than he did but who was driving up that same weekend. Gropper turned him down, using the transparently lame excuse that he didn't want to drive his new car over 35 mph until he'd broken it in properly. Eisner was stuck.

The trip went much better than either Will or Ann could have predicted. After a rocky start that found Eisner silent and sulky, Eisner's mood lightened considerably and he regaled his two passengers with stories and jokes. He was still in a rush to reach Holyoke, Massachusetts, where they planned to spend the night at the Roger Smith Hotel, a YMCA-like facility, before completing their trip the next day. They didn't stop for anything to eat, and by the time they reached the hotel, Ann, who had gone straight from work to Eisner's, was famished.

She also found herself attracted to Eisner. He was six years her senior and very unlike the young men she was accustomed to dating. He was sophisticated, not stuck on himself, good-looking, mature—and funny. As she would remember, she laughed heartily throughout the drive, and this, in turn, loosened him up and ultimately made him notice her. "I was having a marvelous time, and Will said that's what did it: I laughed at all of his jokes."

When they arrived in Holyoke, Arthur ran ahead and, for the sake of appearances, made certain that Ann had a room on a separate floor. The three then went their separate ways, Ann figuring that she wouldn't see either of the two men before the following morning, when they started out for the remainder of their trip to Maine. Although she was still hungry, Ann intended to clean up and turn in for the night.

"I was hot and tired," she recalled, "and I was starting to get undressed, and the phone rang. It was Arthur. He said, 'Will and I are downstairs in the bar, having a drink. Would you like to join us?' I got dressed very fast and came down, and we had a very good time. By the time we got to my sister's place, the boys had had a good time, too, and they stayed overnight there before they went on."

Eisner rarely spoke in detail about meeting his future wife, so it's impossible to say if he was trying to attract her attention with all his stories and jokes, first on the drive and later at Ann's sister place, where, as Ann remembered, he was also the life of the party. It must have been obvious that he was interested, because he instigated Arthur's call to Ann and the invitation for drinks. At one point Arthur asked him, "You like her, don't you?"

Eisner answered coyly, "She's okay."

Ann, on the other hand, wasn't about to let this one get away without at least one formal date. When she returned to New York, she called Arthur, and under the guise of wanting to call and thank Eisner for the ride, she asked for Eisner's number. She also learned from Arthur that they had taken a young woman named Margot back to New York when they returned.

"When I got him on the phone, I said, 'Hi, Will, this is Margot,'" Ann recalled with a laugh. "But Arthur had forgotten to tell me that Margot had a German accent. Will played along, and he finally said, 'Ann, what are you doing Saturday night?' And that was the beginning."

To that point, Eisner had said very little about what he did for a living. As Ann would learn, this was not at all unusual. Decades later, after her husband's death, Ann hosted a special screening of a documentary on Eisner at an auditorium on the grounds where she and her husband lived, and many of their acquaintances were startled by the extent of Eisner's fame. "We knew what he did," they told Ann, "but he never talked about it. We never knew he was famous. He never talked about his acclaim and how he had an award named after him."

"He just didn't talk about it," she said.

Not that it would have mattered in those early days. Ann couldn't draw and she had no interest in comics. In fact, she didn't even see Will's studio until after they were married, and she wouldn't read one of his *Spirit* stories until they had been married for more than twenty years. They connected through their interest in other arts. Both enjoyed music, ballet, movies, and theater, and their dates almost always began with dinner, which, Ann recalled, was something she wasn't accustomed to. They spent a lot of time just talking, learning more about each other.

Their backgrounds couldn't have differed more. Ann's father, Melville D. Weingarten, was a successful stockbroker with a Manhattan firm on Fifth Avenue and a branch office in Fordham. His first wife, Susan's mother, died in 1918 in the flu epidemic, and he remarried Ann and Jane's mother, Nanette, a couple of years later. Ann, along with her parents and sisters, lived what Ann described as a "Park Avenue lifestyle," very social, wanting for very little, with the girls attending the right schools. Ann wasn't impressed by it. By her own admission, she was a bookish tomboy, upsetting her mother because she wasn't the little girl of her times, playing with dolls and dressing in frilly clothing. She attended several different schools, including a boarding school, but the best of her education came from her own explorations in the books she read and the museums she visited. She balked when her father enrolled her at Barnard, where she managed to make it through a year before refusing to go back. She then attended secretarial school, more to satisfy her frustrated father than out of any real interest, but it proved to be more beneficial than she could have guessed: she found a job as a secretary, which put her in touch with much less privileged people than she'd grown up around—co-workers with whom she soon became friends.

"I saw a different part of life," she said. "These were different kinds of people, different than the people I had come in contact with through my family. I became friendly with them. I remember being friendly with a girl from a very large Irish Catholic family. We would go to the cafeteria there in the building where we worked, and she would be very careful to spend only fifteen cents—three nickels—in the Automat. She had to give money from her job to help support her family, and this was an eye-opener for me. I became very conscious of never spending more than fifteen cents, because I didn't want her to think anything."

Shortly before meeting Eisner, she had taken a job as an administrative assistant in Paramount's New York offices, working in the advertising department for the film company, doing everything from writing business letters to running errands. The job led to a *Spirit* episode that might have tested another relationship. Paramount had just released *Samson and Delilah*, a film greeted by critical derision. Will and Ann had attended a private Paramount screening of the movie, and Eisner hadn't thought much of the film, either. His *Spirit* story "Sammy and Delilah," a send-up of the movie, was unappreciated by the Paramount publicists. Fortunately for Ann, who was still relatively new on the job, her relationship with Eisner was unknown to her co-workers.

She was in her office the day after the *Spirit* story appeared in the papers when she heard a disruption in another office. "I was sitting at my desk and I heard screaming between the head of the department and my boss," she said. "They're screaming, 'We'll sue the son of a bitch.' They said something about Will Eisner, and of course my ears perked up." When she realized what all the shouting was about, she stole away to a phone booth, where she could talk without being overheard. "I got on the phone and called Will. 'They're going to sue you,' I said. He said, 'That's good.'"

As Eisner saw it, the publicity generated by a Paramount Pictures lawsuit could only work in his favor.

"They claimed we defamed the movie," he said. "I was rubbing my hands, saying it was great news. Ann said, 'What do you mean, great news?' I said, 'Just think if they sue me—think of all the publicity I'll get.' I was sure I'd win.

"During the two or three weeks that followed, Ann and I were brought closer together. I kept hoping they would sue. I kept telling the syndicate to get ready for a big burst of publicity, but ultimately, they didn't sue. They came to their senses. But this story has always been regarded by Ann and me as a very significant one because the incident occurred during our romance. I guess I was a little overwhelmed by her concern for me."

Their relationship moved along quickly. Eisner proposed by the end of the year, only a few months after their Labor Day introduction. Ann's parents, the Weingartens, liked their daughter's future husband, although both had reservations about his background and intentions. They had little use for Sam and Fannie Eisner, who seemed like peasants compared with the people with whom they usually associated; and although Eisner may have made a success of his career given *The Spirit*'s syndication in all those newspapers, the livelihood it afforded him was small-time next to the kind of money earned by a stockbroker. Ann's mother, who'd spent years dealing with her daughter's rebellious streak, decided that Eisner was acceptable if it meant getting Ann out of the house.

It was different with Ann's father.

"At first, my father was suspicious that Will was after my money—which I didn't have," Ann remembered, "and he wasn't going to give us any, either. We found out later that my father had Will investigated. One of his customers was in the magazine or newspaper business, and my father had him look Will up. Was he a reputable person? Did he steal? Whatever you looked into. I was furious when I found out, but Will said, 'Why not? Let him look me up. I haven't done anything bad.'

"After we got married, my father went to Will's office one day and said, 'This is what you do?' He was very gruff. Will showed him around the office. My father said, 'Don't you want to be in a gentleman's business?' And Will said, 'No, I'm happy. If I'm going to lose money, I'm going to lose it my way.' When Will came home and related this to me, I said, 'If you had said yes, I think we would have had a divorce immediately.'"

The were married on June 15, 1950, at the Temple Immanuel in New York City, with a reception at the Harmony Club attended by three hundred people. Ann had wanted a much smaller affair, but her father

The Eisners—Fannie, Sam, Will, Rhoda, and Pete—pose for a family photo at Will's wedding. (Courtesy of Ann Eisner)

Will and Ann Eisner dance at their wedding reception. (Courtesy of Ann Eisner)

wouldn't hear of it. He was going to send his daughter off properly, with his most highly regarded clients in attendance. There was great food, spirits, music, and dancing. Neither bride nor groom could dance three good steps—each accused the other of having no rhythm—but that didn't matter. They had a good time.

And they never looked back.

Leaving their wedding, June 15, 1950. (Courtesy of Ann Eisner)

Eisner's daily routine, sedate to begin with, became utterly domesticated. Weekdays could be long and grueling, but Ann insisted, then and always, that he reserve weekends for her. There would be an occasional exception, but Eisner made a point of trying to honor the arrangement.

The marriage—and, later, the arrivals of their two children—also appears to have had a subtle yet powerful effect on Eisner's work. By the time of his wedding in mid-1950, Eisner was losing interest in *The Spirit*. The weekly installments were still creatively strong, but Eisner's passion had been redirected to American Visuals and the prospects of discovering new venues for educational comics. The novelty of the newspaper comic book insert had worn off for Eisner, his newspaper clients, and readers. Eisner, who hoped to move out of his New York apartment and into a house, raise a family, and in general enjoy the rewards of all the hard work of his youth, was convinced that American Visuals, more than *The Spirit*, would take him down that path.

"I felt there was a whole new world to conquer," he said later. "*The Spirit* was nice and safe, but at that point there was nowhere to go with it. I wanted to leave while the show was still a success."

The project with the greatest potential for long-term business turned up unexpectedly when Eisner heard from Norman Colton, an old contact from his *Army Motors* days. Colton, along with another civilian named Bernard Miller, had worked on the publication from its early days as a mimeographed sheet, through its growing pains with Eisner, and on through its expansion in Detroit. *Army Motors* had ceased publication at the end of World War II, but with the United States becoming involved in a growing conflict in Korea, the army had approached Colton to edit a bigger, better preventive maintenance publication. Colton immediately thought of Eisner as the best choice to take charge of the new magazine's artwork.

Eisner liked the idea. A long-running government contract could provide a solid annual base income for American Visuals, plus it would give him the opportunity to further extend his interests in educational comics.

"It was a very, very important adjunct to my business," Eisner said, "because it made it possible to accumulate a fairly large staff of people, plus the fact that it allowed me to expand the operation into other areas of using comics as a teaching tool. [It] actually helped me build an enterprise, which is the way it often happens with companies that get military contracts . . . We began doing comics-related work at a rapidly growing rate."

Eisner took charge of the project's development as soon as he heard from Colton. He worked up a dummy copy of his proposed magazine, which brought back some of the popular characters from the old *Army Motors*. Remembering his previous problems with the adjutant general, who felt that *Army Motors* undermined the work in other instructional publications, Eisner named his magazine *P★S: The Preventive Maintenance Monthly*, intending it to be a postscript to existing army publications.

The army field-tested the dummy magazine that Eisner submitted, and it received positive feedback. Eisner's first *P★S* contract called for six issues, after which there might or might not be a renewal. The arrangement might have had more to do with the army's feelings about the Korean War than its confidence in the magazine: at the onset of the war, the military minds believed that it was going to be a brief conflict, perhaps measured in weeks or months. The United States would show its might, North Korea would capitulate, and that would be that. If that was the case, there would be no further need for *P★S*.

Paul E. Fitzgerald, who became the magazine's first managing editor in 1953, attested to the urgent need for the publication in his book *Will Eisner and PS Magazine*:

> Army personnel from privates to generals described the equipment used in the Korean War as "either too old or too new." Anything left over from World War II was at least five years old, perhaps marginally maintained in the intervening years, and frequently outdated by advancing technology. When development and production schedules were accelerated in response to combat needs, the resulting products often were not totally de-bugged and sometimes arrived without normal accompanying items—manuals, special tools, and stocks of replacement parts.

From his experiences with *Army Motors*, Eisner knew something of the difficulties of working for the military, where the individual agenda sometimes overshadowed that of the whole; where interoffice bickering, all conducted in overly formal military lingo, could make an editor or artist feel as if he were trapped in an inescapable crossfire; where every higher-up seemed to demand a voice in the magazine's content and the direction it was taking. During the war, Eisner had no choice but to deal as well as he could with the insanity. He was in the service, and even though he was a celebrity to some of the officers around him, he couldn't have walked away from *Army Motors* if he'd been inclined to do so. It was different for Eisner the civilian. He was trying to follow his standards for art and commerce while dealing with people who had little regard for either. As Eisner later told Fitzgerald, "He felt as if he were in a cage, with his hands tied, surrounded by hungry tigers and suicidal maniacs."

Eisner might have anticipated some of the problems. Once again, he found himself at the mercy of the Adjutant General's Office, which controlled all publications issued by the army and was definitely not a member of the Will Eisner Admiration Society. The office's opinion on using comics for instruction hadn't changed since Eisner's battles with the adjutant general during World War II, when he had reluctantly gone along with *Army Motors*. That magazine's success had loosened the negativity somewhat, but Henry Aldridge, the office's executive secretary, disliked the entire idea of *P★S* magazine. Comics, he felt, were inappropriate for the army; such Eisner characters as Joe Dope and Pvt. Fosgnoff came dangerously close to ridiculing the military. He wasn't happy about the approval of the magazine, but the secretary of the army and the army's chief of staff were among its fans, so the office had little choice but to go along with it. Still, he intended to keep an eye on Eisner.

Norman Colton, the magazine's single-minded editor, also presented a hurdle to contend with. Short, neatly groomed, and impeccably dressed, with a calm exterior that belied a scrappy personality, Colton could be a handful. He and Eisner had worked reasonably well together during the *Army Motors* days, first in Holabird, where Eisner saw him on an almost daily basis, and later, after Colton transferred to Detroit, when their working relationship was long-distance. Colton, Eisner determined, was a wheeler-dealer, capable of working all angles and, often enough, pitting one office against another. *Army Motors* had been Colton's baby, and he wanted a better cut of *P★S* than just a position and salary. As it was set up, Eisner controlled the magazine's cover art, the content in the middle of each issue, and other incidental art; Colton was responsible for the written material. Eisner got most of the attention and glory. Colton, for all his contributions, got very little.

Eisner didn't trust him. As a civilian, Colton worked outside the military, and Eisner suspected that he had his own agenda, which turned out to be true enough when Colton approached Eisner and demanded part ownership in the magazine. A bitter debate ensued. *P★S*, Eisner pointed out, belonged to the army and wasn't his to sell. Colton countered that Eisner could have set up an arrangement allowing him to hold stock in the publication, even though that wasn't Eisner's to sell, either. Colton insisted; Eisner refused. Finally, acting on his lawyer's counsel, Eisner flatly refused to discuss it with him.

There were matters other than internal politics. Since the magazine was publicly funded, Eisner had to keep a close watch on a restricted budget— not the easiest task when you're trying to print a color cover and a four-color, eight-page interior spread, which could be expensive. Any staff would have to be paid as well. Eisner, of course, was familiar with all this from his days of running a shop, but with so many people watching and demanding a say in the magazine's production, he felt as if he were always under surveillance, with each issue being an audition for the magazine's renewal.

Fortunately, he enjoyed a challenge.

Eisner's private life was changing as well. He and Ann had a son, John, in April 1952; a daughter, Alice, was born a year and a half later, in October 1953. Ann Eisner would remember her husband as being a doting father— an easygoing, benevolent figure around the house, inclined to go along with his children's wishes and leave the discipline to his wife. His work schedule, still very intense from Monday through Friday, kept him away from home much more than he would have liked, especially when he and Ann moved to suburban Westchester County, north of the city, first to a rented house in Harrison and then, a short time after John's birth, to a large house that they bought at 8 Burling Avenue in White Plains. Eisner commuted to the city every day and often didn't return home until late in the evening. Time with his children was precious.

It's not coincidental that *The Spirit* was reaching its end during the period when Eisner was starting up *P*S* magazine, moving out of New York City, buying a house, and starting a family. His work for American Visuals had reached the point where he was delegating more of his *Spirit* duties to others, and it was beginning to show, not so much in the quality of stories and art as in the continuity of the feature. Eisner still had top-notch co-workers contributing to *The Spirit*, but the character seemed to be drifting away from the kind of development Eisner had given him in the early days. The stories seemed familiar—and, in some cases, for good reason: Eisner would rework old stories, reasoning that enough time had passed since their original appearances for readers to notice. He still took an active role in the weekly installments, doing the stories' breakdowns and drawing the main characters' heads, but he left almost everything else to others.

The market itself affected the stories. The cost of newsprint had risen substantially, which forced the comic book section to shrink to eight pages, with talk of reducing it to four. Newspapers were dropping the section, but when Eisner talked about abandoning the feature, editors asked him to reconsider. Eisner agonized over whether he should continue. *The Spirit* had been a part of his creative life for a long time, and even with papers dropping it, it still generated considerable income. As Eisner told Tom Heintjes, "It was a dilemma I often found myself in when I became a businessman and an artist."

Subscribing newspapers complained about the falloff in quality. The art, they said, didn't look like the Eisner style that readers were familiar with. Eisner had to agree. He felt that the scripts, largely written by Jules Feiffer, were still strong, but with his attention divided, Eisner found himself relying on artists unable to imitate his style. "The obvious was staring me in the face," he wrote later. "Rather than allow the quality to disintegrate (which might hurt my professional reputation, not to mention pride) the better part of valor would dictate that I discontinue the feature. But I was not ready for that yet."

In a "last gasp" effort to instill new life in *The Spirit*, Eisner hired Wally Wood, an exceptionally talented artist who had worked for Bill Gaines at EC (Entertaining Comics) and who would eventually work for *Mad* magazine. Wood joined Eisner as a freelancer after a blowup with EC, but he wasn't interested in contributing only to the *Spirit*'s backgrounds, as Eisner hoped. Eisner worked out a system that found him discussing scripts with Feiffer, who would write dialogue for the installment. Eisner then did rough pencils and turned the art over to Wood. Given the talents of the three, this might have resulted in sensational work, but it didn't happen, mainly because these stories, which placed the Spirit in outer space, confounded readers and the comic's creators alike. Feiffer, no science fiction fan, hated the entire idea. Readers wondered what happened to the detective who walked the streets of the big city. The syndicate grumbled that the change was too radical, that the art was nothing at all like Eisner's. Eisner pleaded for patience, to no avail.

Outer Space Spirit, as the series eventually came to be known, while beautifully drawn and innovative for a time when the United States' exploration of space was still nearly a decade away, was an ignominious curtain call for Denny Colt and *The Spirit*. For all his considerable gifts, Wally Wood could be unreliable when he was drinking, which was often enough, and he struggled with *Spirit* deadlines, missing one entirely and forcing Eisner to throw together a weak installment that didn't fit into the series. Eisner pressed on, planning an unusual series called *Denny Colt: UFO Investigator*, but only one episode was ever published. As much as he would have liked to see *The Spirit* continue, Eisner realized it was impossible. Jules Feiffer was about to enter the service, Wally Wood was unpredictable, and Eisner had seen enough. The final *Spirit* entry appeared on October 5, 1952, ending a run that lasted 645 installments over a stretch of more than twelve years.

Eisner regretted his decision to let his groundbreaking series hang on for as long as it did: "Looking back I have to say that it's a blemish on my career that I allowed *The Spirit* to continue through this period," he confessed. "I compromised the character just because I was busy with other things. That's not to say that these were all bad stories but they don't have the consistent outlook they had when I was directly involved . . . I look at these stories and I want to cringe—again, not because they're bad, but because only the merest essence of the character is retained."

chapter eight

OUT OF THE MAINSTREAM

*I have to tell you how my father used to refer to my publishing business.
'What you have here," he would say, "is a wheelbarrow. Sure,
it's a machine, but if you don't push it, it won't go."*

When Will Eisner shelved *The Spirit* near the end of 1952, he vanished from public view. He would never again produce comics for newspapers, and two decades would pass before his familiar signature appeared in a comic book—and even then it would be in the form of *Spirit* reprints. For all his *Spirit* readers knew, he'd retired and moved to Florida. In reality, he was working as hard as ever, contributing art to *P★S* magazine and, through American Visuals, putting together a large variety of instructional and commercial comics for corporations and organizations. He was thirty-five years old, raising a family in upstate New York, traveling when his job required it, and conducting business as usual. The move to Florida would come later—much later.

His retirement of *The Spirit* came at an opportune moment, though he certainly hadn't timed it that way. Comic book opponents were again stepping up their efforts to legislate against the medium, though they were finding it difficult to make significant headway. There had been studies, conferences, radio roundtable discussions, newspaper and magazine articles, editorials, church meetings, and public forums, all scrutinizing the popularity of comic books and influences they might bear on young readers. The New York State Legislature twice attempted to pass restrictive measures against comic book content, only to see the submitted bills thwarted by Governor Thomas Dewey's veto. In 1950, the United States Senate Special Committee to Investigate Crime in Interstate Commerce, chaired by Estes Kefauver, a Tennessee Democrat with presidential aspirations, included comic books in its investigation, with public hearings examining a possible link between comic books and juvenile delinquency. Exhaustive testimony poured in from all sides of the debate, including public officials, comic book publishers, psychologists, prison officials, and even FBI director J. Edgar Hoover. There was general consensus that the more extreme crime and horror titles stepped outside the bounds of good taste and acceptable reading material for children, but no one could agree on whether policing these publications and their creators was the duty of legislators or the comics industry. Lawmakers strongly suggested that the comic book companies exert peer pressure to discourage other publishers from issuing objectionable material. Not only was there resistance to this idea, but the major offenders, emboldened by the failed efforts to block or censor comic book content, published even gorier and more violent material. Their rationale was purely business: they were giving the people what they wanted.

Fredric Wertham, staging a ceaseless drive against comic books, added more combustible fuel to his campaign with the publication of *Seduction of the Innocent*, a bestselling polemic that bypassed what Wertham considered to be ineffective leaders and took his case directly to the public. Wertham was neither subtle nor scientific in his approach. Instead, he served up general but incendiary claims, which he then attempted to back with sketchy anecdotal examples that hit readers with the impact of a fist to the throat. Danger lurked everywhere. Comic books seduced young readers with depictions of violent crime, sadism, perverse sexuality, bondage and sadomasochism, cruelty, homosexuality, disrespect for the country and law enforcement officers, torture, and racism. Wertham claimed that his interest was in crime comics only, though his broad definition included virtually every comic book on the market, including the superhero comics, westerns, and romance comics. He assailed Superman as a sadistic figure who taught children all the wrong lessons about justice. He went after Batman and Robin, who in his judgment might have been sending out subliminal messages about homosexuality. Wonder Woman was a double threat—a closet lesbian with a bondage fetish. All in all, not a single type of comic book, aside from the Disneyesque titles featuring talking animals, was spared Wertham's scrutiny and commentary.

Some of Wertham's criticism, such as his dismissal of comics as being poorly written and illustrated, leading to poor reading habits among youths, was old and tired, but that didn't prohibit him from repeating these assertions. He stopped short of stating that comic books were the *cause* of juvenile delinquency, or that every comic book reader would go on to engage in bad behavior, but he viewed them as influential to impressionable minds. He listed the areas in which comic books could have ill effects on their readers:

1. The comic-book format is an invitation to illiteracy.
2. Crime comic books create an atmosphere of cruelty and deceit.
3. They create a readiness for temptation.
4. They stimulate unwholesome fantasies.
5. They suggest criminal or sexually abnormal ideas.
6. They furnish the rationalization for them, which may be ethically even more harmful than the impulse.
7. They suggest the forms a delinquent impulse may take and supply details of technique.
8. They may tip the scales toward maladjustment of delinquency.

Wertham had been waiting years for this moment. He'd given lectures, participated in panel discussions, written for scholarly and general interest publications, appeared before committees. His body of work on the subject, incontestably the most voluminous in the world, had made him, at least in the public eye, *the* final word on the topic of comics and a protector of children's interests. A new electronic contraption called television, now finding its way into households across America, brought him even more of the national spotlight.

His timing couldn't have been better. By spring 1954, within days of the appearance of *Seduction of the Innocent*, another Senate subcommittee, this one focusing on juvenile delinquency and chaired by Robert C. Hendrickson, was ready to reexamine the comic book business. Hendrickson had begun his work months earlier, in November 1953, with lengthy hearings in Washington, D.C., Boston, Denver, and Philadelphia, covering such issues as gangs and gang violence, pornography, and drugs. The examination of comics was slated for New York, home of the huge majority of comic book publishers and, to cynical observers, the location where the most political hay might be made from the televised hearings. Estes Kefauver, still stinging from an unsuccessful bid for the 1952 presidential nomination yet hopeful for another shot in 1956, was a committee member, and history would eventually attach his name, more than Hendrickson's, to the proceedings.

The hearings opened on April 21, 1954, in the same Manhattan courthouse room that had housed the Kefauver committee four years earlier.

As in the previous hearings, the roster of invited witnesses was impressive—twenty-two spoke and answered questions over a three-day period, including the usual assortment of comic book publishers and distributors, comic strip artists, child psychologists, law enforcement officials, and authorities on juvenile delinquency. Fredric Wertham, absent from the 1950 organized crime hearings, was on hand this time around, taking full advantage of an opportunity to continue his crusade and, not coincidentally, the opportunity to stand before television cameras and promote *Seduction of the Innocent* by referring to it continually.

Wertham's testimony rehashed his old position, by now familiar to anyone with the slightest interest in the comic book controversy. As expected, he took aim at the horror and crime genre titles, holding forth at length on one example that he deemed to be particularly offensive, a seven-page story from *Shock SuperStories* entitled "The Whipping." Published by EC Comics, it addressed small-town racial prejudice, in which a group of hooded Klan-like vigilantes went after a Mexican man attracted to one of the members' daughters. To anyone paying attention, the story was a cautionary tale decrying bigotry, but all Wertham seemed to care about was the story's use of the slur "spick," uttered by one of the Klansmen. That the hateful term was used by a despicable character was beside the point.

"I think Hitler was a beginner compared to the comic book industry," Wertham told the committee. "They get the children much younger. They teach them race hatred at the age of four, before they can read." Wertham didn't bother to explain how a child might be influenced by offensive words published in a comic book he couldn't read.

The highly anticipated clash between Wertham's testimony and that of William Gaines, publisher of "The Whipping" and an aggressive opponent of what the EC publisher believed to be a witch hunt against comics, was memorable, but not because of the quality of the debate. Gaines had spent considerable time preparing a statement for the committee, but he grossly miscalculated the committee's disposition. EC was indeed publishing some of the goriest work around, but its horror line featured some of the highest-quality writing and art in the industry, which Gaines arrogantly believed would be enough to win the day. He fully expected to enter the courtroom, sit down, calmly but firmly present his case before the committee, and, by the hearing's end, squeeze Wertham and his case like a bothersome tick in the woods. After all, this was America, home of freedom and the First Amendment, and Wertham and his opinions were more of an annoyance than a real threat.

He withered under questioning, which he would later blame on the adverse combination of the lengthy testimony earlier in the day and the effects of the diet pills he was taking. "I felt that I was really going to fix those bastards," he told biographer Frank Jacobs, "but as time went on I could feel myself fading away."

The low point of his appearance arrived when Kefauver confronted Gaines with one of his own company's publications, featuring a cover depicting a murderer holding a woman's severed head in one hand and a bloody ax in the other. Only moments earlier, Gaines had stated that, in terms of what he would consider inappropriate, "my only limits are bounds of good taste, what I consider good taste."

"Do you think that is in good taste?" Kefauver asked Gaines, indicating the cover with the beheading.

"Yes, sir, I do, for the cover of a horror comic."

Gaines attempted to explain his position—how that particular cover might have crossed his bounds of good taste had it been presented in another way—but there was no saving the moment, either at that point or when Gaines addressed "The Whipping." The next day's papers, including the *New York Times*, excoriated Gaines's testimony, adding credibility to Fredric Wertham's attacks earlier that same day. In the weeks to come, newspapers rushed comic book features and editorials to their pages. Senator Hendrickson, in the interest of obtaining information, tacked on an additional day of testimony nearly two months later, but it was anticlimactic. The same public that bought into Senator Joseph McCarthy's Red-baiting was now turning against comics.

Rather than face the full wrath of the anti-comics crusaders, complete with new legislation, more comic book bonfires, and additional bad press and plummeting sales figures, comic book publishers acted as swiftly as possible. William Gaines, soon to announce that EC was suspending publication of all its horror and crime comics, called for a banding together of publishers. On August 17, 1954, thirty-eight publishers, printers, and distributors gathered at New York's Biltmore Hotel and, to Gaines's consternation, rather than developing strategies to fight the forces of censorship, founded the Comics Magazine Association of America, an organization designed to self-regulate comic book art and content. The CMAA drew up a new set of guidelines—a Comics Code—that capitulated in almost every respect to the criticism directed against comics by Fredric Wertham and the different comics hearings and conferences. The adopted standards addressed subject matter, dialogue, religion, costume, marriage and sex, and advertising matter, and those standards all but eviscerated the crime and horror books on the market. They put large dents in the romance and superhero titles as well. Comic book publishers, for instance, were no longer allowed to use the words *horror* or *terror* in their titles, and these words could be used only sparingly—"judiciously," as the Comics Code Authority called it—in the interior text. Criminals had to be punished for their deeds, with no exceptions. A stamp of approval would be placed on every comic book adhering to the new standards. Parents would know instantly if their children were looking at objectionable material.

Not every comic book publisher joined the CMAA or went along with its code. William Gaines and EC refused to have anything to do with them, for obvious reasons, and Dell, publisher of Disney and other innocuous comics, objected on principle. Gaines realized that he was all but finished as a comic book publisher, but he continued his new hit publication, a satirical magazine called *Mad*, which skirted the new code by coming out in an oversize format that distinguished it from comic books and exempted it from the code.

The Comics Code might have spared the industry from outright extinction, but it did irreparable damage to a business that had been expanding to reach an older, more mature readership. Will Eisner's dream of presenting stories for adult readers had backslid to such a point that had he written *The Spirit* as a newsstand comic book, he would have had to tone down the feature to meet the Comics Code Authority's standards. The violence would have been too intense, and his femmes fatales too sexually provocative, for the new guidelines.

Eisner kept up on all these developments, even though they didn't directly affect his current work. Watching Wertham promote his book on television convinced him that he had been right to discontinue *The Spirit*. He was tired of the fight, of arguing on behalf of comics' value as literature, of the constant reminders, now so prominent, that comic book artists were disdained by the public. He was disgusted by the efforts to connect comics with juvenile misbehavior. Aside from his general objections to censorship, Eisner was interested in how this criticism would apply to an industry that had evolved enormously in only a few decades. He'd watched with interest when Milton Caniff, his friend and early influence, eloquently addressed the Senate Special Committee to Investigate Crime in Interstate Commerce. He'd followed the Kefauver hearings and the development of the Comics Code, which he judged to be well-meaning but ultimately misguided. "We are constantly forming committees to protect people in somebody else's living room," he'd grouse, noting that this was an American tradition. "We try to protect people from ideas that we think are bad."

Comics would limp along for nearly two decades, staying within the framework of the code at the cost of insipid stories certain to offend—or challenge—no one. Many pre-code titles were discontinued, and companies went under. Artists and publishers disappeared from the business, took jobs in commercial art in advertising and mainstream magazines, or found other outlets for their talent, sometimes for the better. Harry Chesler and Victor Fox, whose shops were barely hanging on before the Comics Code went into effect, left the business, content to know that they had cast large shadows in the early days of comics. Charles Biro, whose writing for *Crime Does Not Pay* helped shape the explosion of true-crime comics in the late forties and whose crime fighter, Daredevil, became a tight combination of costumed hero and detective, had seen enough, as had Jack Cole, former Eisner employee, creator of Plastic Man, and contributor to EC's line of crime comics; Cole, noticed by Hugh Hefner, who was busy creating his own controversial magazine for adult males, would become one of *Playboy*'s most significant early contributors.

Ironically, things improved when the baby boomers, the ones the Comics Code was designed to protect, came of age and challenged the strict standards by producing comics that were bold and relevant, addressing the issues of the times. Underground comic books, preferring to go by the title "comix," the product of the sex, drugs, and rock 'n' roll counterculture of the sixties, would gleefully thumb their collective nose at the code.

When these times rolled around, Will Eisner would be ready.

Eisner might have welcomed the opportunity to exchange his ongoing problems with *P★S* magazine for a censorship tussle. The magazine had jumped off to a good start, at least in terms of the press runs and continuity, but after appearing six straight months between June and November 1951, production halted completely for the next seven months owing to problems with budgeting and infighting among the staff. Only nine issues would reach GIs over the next twenty-five months. By the summer of 1953, *P★S* was in such disarray that its future was in doubt. Seven years later, Eisner would sit down with Paul Fitzgerald, the magazine's managing editor, and characterize the period with disarming candor. "I have never known personal distress to equal the gloom, doom, despair, frustration, betrayal, and helplessness that enveloped me during that horrible summer of 1953," he told Fitzgerald.

His troubles had begun much earlier, with the breakdown of his working relationship with Norman Colton. Eisner, stubborn whenever his work was questioned or criticized, found himself locked in personal and professional battles with Colton that left him seething in frustration. Both Eisner and Colton wanted control of the magazine's direction, and neither was inclined to budge in a disagreement, especially after Eisner rebuffed Colton's demands for part ownership of the publication. Eisner was accustomed to working to order, to making changes in his work to accommodate the wishes of his customers, but on far too many occasions the dispute in the early years of P★S struck him as being petty or nit-picky. When he'd served in the army, he'd been a celebrity artist, highly regarded by his Pentagon superiors, who were more apt to defer to his knowledge and background than to set their jaws and demand changes. He'd endured some raw-nerve moments, but they were nothing in comparison with the battles he encountered as a civilian working for the military. Everybody in the army seemed to have something to say about the magazine.

As Eisner—and the army—eventually determined, Colton had issues that explained his behavior. One could have forgiven Colton his ambitions if he hadn't been so adept at working all sides against the middle for his own benefit. A master of office politics, Colton knew when to schmooze with the right people, how to drop the right piece of information guaranteed to create disputes that would place him in a favorable light, when to brownnose and when to plant his feet, and perhaps most important of all, how to plan for his own advancement. Eisner detested these calculating qualities, but he was living in suburban New York and P★S was coming out of the Aberdeen Proving Ground in Maryland. So as long as he could limit his personal contacts with Colton and the army, he couldn't have cared less about Colton's machinations.

Then Colton began making more frequent visits to New York, supposedly to consult with Eisner on the magazine's content. As it turned out, Colton had other things on his mind. Eisner resisted Colton's attempts to obtain part ownership in P★S, growing more uncomfortable with each of Colton's visits, until one day he answered his door and was greeted by two government agent types, dressed in black suits, demanding some of his time. Eisner insisted that he have an attorney present before he spoke to them, but that turned out to be unnecessary. The men were from the FBI, and they were investigating Colton on allegations that he might have fudged his travel expenses for the army. As if on cue, the phone rang. Eisner answered it and found himself talking to Colton, who wanted to meet him at Grand Central Terminal. The agents followed Eisner to the meeting and confronted Colton. His days at *P★S* were over.

The army wasn't happy with the way things were going at the magazine in any event, and shortly before the end of Norman Colton's tenure at *P★S*, in an effort to restore order to a situation that was spiraling out of control, officials brought in Jacob Hay, a columnist for the *Baltimore Sun*, to work as managing editor. After the departure of Colton, Hay was made acting editor, but he was so shocked by the disorganization at *P★S* that he quit his post after two months in September 1953, took a position at the *Greensboro Daily News*, and a short time later wrote a six-part exposé on just how bad things were at the magazine.

This dark period couldn't have arrived at a more inopportune time for Eisner. He and Ann were expecting their second child, he'd just purchased a new home, and while American Visuals had other clients bringing in income, *P★S* was supposed to be his meal ticket. Thirteen years earlier, when he'd gambled and left Eisner & Iger for *The Spirit*, his business and artistic instincts had been rewarded. Now, here he was, working for the government on an army publication being issued during a time of war, a venture that should have been solid enough, but his future looked shaky.

Fortunately for Eisner, the army made an excellent move with its selection of the magazine's third editor. James Kidd, a thirty-three-year-old veteran of World War II, teaching journalism at West Virginia University when he was offered the job at *P★S*, was as different from his predecessors as one could have imagined. Quiet, soft-spoken, straitlaced, and no-nonsense, Kidd brought stability and credibility to the chaos that had been *P★S* magazine. Twice decorated for valor during the war, Kidd was an officer and he knew the army, and with his recently earned Master of Arts degree to go with his Bachelor of Science Journalism degree, he knew reporting and editing. Not given to cursing, raising his voice, tossing things around the office, or showing much of any emotion, for that matter, Kidd took a laid-back approach to business that greatly contrasted with the kinetic energy that seemed to bounce off Eisner, yet there was never a question of his authority. Eisner took one look at Kidd and declared, "I don't think I want to play poker with that guy."

He would, however, work well with him for the next eighteen years.

The first issue of *P★S* magazine under Jim Kidd's guidance was published in January 1954, and from that date until Eisner left the magazine in 1971, 212 issues were published, with only two delays. Kidd and Eisner disagreed frequently, but Eisner never doubted Kidd's professionalism or intentions. For his part, Kidd acted as an effective buffer between Eisner and the army brass.

The magazine was a work in progress throughout the Korean War. The format remained the same: a five-by-seven digest-sized magazine, forty-eight pages, with a four-color wraparound cover done by Eisner in comic art, eight color pages of maintenance-focused stories by Eisner in the middle, and the rest devoted to articles, charts, and other graphic material related to preventive maintenance. Shortly after joining *P★S*, Kidd hired Paul Fitzgerald, a World War II vet and one of Kidd's former students at West Virginia University, to work as the magazine's managing editor. Fitzgerald assisted with the post-Colton office restructuring as well as some of the fine-tuning of the publication's content.

These were trying times for Eisner, who never adapted easily to change. ("If you moved his socks to another drawer, it was a crisis," his wife would joke.) He had to adjust to a new staff, hit his monthly deadlines, and deal with an army chain of command that bordered on the preposterous. Every month, Eisner would deliver a dummy of the magazine's layout, as well as rough pencils of the artwork, which Kidd would subsequently take to the Pentagon for review. From this point until the final proofs were delivered to the printer, there would be discussions over content and artwork, adjustments to editorial content, disputes over details, revisions, more discussion, and enough friction to make all parties involved wonder what the hell they were doing in this business in the first place. Eisner, the only artist in the bunch, fumed whenever others picked apart his work and insisted on changes.

"It would reach a point where Kidd or I would have to say to Will, 'You're right, and we know you're right, and you know that we know, but we can't do it that way,'" Paul Fitzgerald recalled. "Quite frequently, that would provoke him into coming up with a third alternative."

Dating back to his *Army Motors* days, Eisner could really find himself at loggerheads with others when they failed to understand or appreciate his original vision of approaching his readers on their level, in their language, in ways that would make the material easy to remember. The military, which devoted so much time and effort to shaping a GI's thought processes, wasn't interested in the informal or humorous. Joe Dope and his sidekick, Pvt. Fosgnoff, were perennial points of contention—and, in essence, prime examples of the never-to-be-resolved differences between Eisner and the army. Eisner believed—and correctly, if one could judge by the reader response to *P★S*—that these two misfits exemplified, through

The 'T-Slot" you carelessly clean
Will pit and soon form a space-seam
Ruptured cartrige at best
Will result, and the rest
Joe Dope best describes what we mean

Eisner's contributions to *P*S* magazine convinced him that comics could be used as an educational tool. (© Will Eisner Studios, Inc., courtesy of Denis Kitchen)

their failures, how something should *not* be done. Army officials felt otherwise. Joe Dope, they countered, invited ridicule of the training process and, by extension, the army itself. Soldiers might be amused by his foibles, but they were enjoying themselves at the expense of the officers who trained them. In addition, preventive maintenance was a difficult concept to address to begin with, since the military didn't want it even implied that its equipment was anything but top-notch.

"I was fighting something much more deadly than not being allowed to make fun of an officer," Eisner told Tom Heintjes in 1990. "I was fighting the huge internal bureaucracy of the military, which wanted to suppress information that would make them look bad. They would blame the soldiers for equipment failures, when in fact it was manufacturing flaws. That's one of the great villainies of the military, I've always thought."

To back his claim, Eisner mentioned a tank that was designed in such a manner that when a shell was fired, the gun's recoil would smash the breech into the gunner's chest, killing him instantly. "When I learned this, I told them the tank was poorly constructed, that it was costing lives because of some stupid engineer. They said, 'No, you've got to train the gunners to sit sideways in the tank,' even though the seat was designed to look forward! I was furious, but I was powerless."

The Joe Dope debate crested in 1955, when a memorandum of record laid down the law:

1. Effective immediately the separation from the service of Private Fosgnoff at the convenience of the government and in the best interests of the service;
2. A replacement having a good military bearing and appearance will be developed;
3. The use of, or reference to, the word "dope" as a last name for the character "Joe" will be discontinued and the heading of the continuity will be changed to read "Joe's Dope";
4. The appearance of Joe will be altered, including removal of his previously protruding teeth;
5. The appearance of incidental soldier-characters used for humorous and illustrative purposes will be prepared so that humor, where such is called for, will be connoted through the use of expression and attitude, rather than through grotesque distortion.

Eisner gritted his teeth and complied. Fosgnoff was immediately written out of the scripts, and a short time later, Joe Dope suffered serious facial injuries as the result of his ineptitude, and during cosmetic surgery, his buckteeth were straightened out. Eisner wasn't through with Joe Dope, though. Years later, after his term with *P★S* had ended, he tried to obtain legal rights to Joe Dope. Ironically, he had no claim to either the characters or the artwork, which the army destroyed almost immediately after it was used in *P★S*. In a legal action, Eisner tried to wrestle the rights to Joe Dope from the army, with no luck. He claimed to have no bitterness about it, but his words said otherwise.

"Some bureaucrat in the Department of Defense with too much time on his hands saw the notice and decided that they should own the character, not me," he said. "So I got into a legal battle with them, and the courts ultimately ruled that since I'd originally created Joe Dope during World War II, when I was in the full employ of the armed services, I didn't own the character. It was a work-for-hire type of thing, as it turned out."

Connie Rodd, a holdover from the *Army Motors* publication, was another point of contention, though for entirely different reasons. *P★S* might have been circulating among young men thousands of miles from home, caught in combat zones, and far removed from their wives and girlfriends, but the magazine's overseers, safe in warm, dry offices, constantly objected to material they judged to be too racy for soldiers. There was no question that Connie was intended to be a sexy, even provocative, character—a bit of eye candy even if she was a cartoon figure—but Eisner was continually skirting the border between what was good clean fun, delivered with a wink, and what the army considered to be inappropriate. The army nixed one cover for a Christmas issue that depicted Connie, discreetly covered with a man's shirt but wearing only underwear, changing into a Santa Claus outfit. Any cover depicting Connie in a bathing suit, single or two-piece, was also subject to discussion. Eisner had no alternative but to comply, though he ridiculed his bosses in private, not only for their Victorian attitudes, but also for their moral judgments, delivered from the comfort of the Pentagon.

Eisner experienced some of those conditions firsthand. As part of his job, to ensure that he understood the equipment he was illustrating, he was required to travel to military posts overseas—an interesting irony given the fact that he never left the States during his active duty in the service. Beginning with his first trip to Seoul, South Korea, in 1954, Eisner found his Korean experiences to be unusual—and educational. An armistice had been established between North Korea and the United Nations a year earlier, on July 27, 1953, but the truce was uneasy, especially around the demilitarized zone dividing North and South Korea, and troops were to be combat-ready at all times.

"When I went to Korea, I visited the repair shops, mostly," he recalled of the trips that usually lasted four to six weeks at a time. "I never saw direct combat; I wasn't there to study that. I would take notes, make sketches, take photos. I would talk to the guys. I was always accompanied by an editor who was more of a reporter than I was, and he would take notes as well. We would talk to the GIs and discover any 'field fixes' they had worked out for emergency purposes, because they can be quite important."

Eisner would joke that his ignorance of machinery acted as a positive influence on his drawings of machines, as well as his directions on how to maintain them; he was simply passing along what he himself was learning. What he *did* understand intuitively was human nature. He realized that in *P★S* he could go only so far in his depictions of army life, but what he saw and sketched on these trips benefited him greatly later in his career, when he was working on a series of graphic narratives published as

Last Day in Vietnam. "Hard Duty," one of the book's most moving stories, was the direct result of something Eisner had witnessed during a trip to Korea.

"I stayed with a particular unit," he explained, "and on Saturdays, these big, tough, rugged guys would take time to go up to a local orphanage, where the kids who were the result of American soldiers and Korean women were kept.

> The Koreans were particularly against mixed marriages; the taboo was very strong. And I met one young girl who kept hanging around the orphanage. I got to talking to her, and it turned out that she had a baby who was there, but she couldn't tell anyone at the orphanage or they wouldn't take care of her baby. She said she was hanging around, waiting for her husband to show up and gather the family together. She told me her husband lived in a place called Harlem, and that he was a sanitation engineer. Of course, I knew her husband was never going to show up to take her away from the orphanage, because a young black man bringing a Korean girl home to Harlem in 1952 wasn't likely to get very far. It was a sad moment.

Eisner's harshest critics would accuse him of selling out to commercial endeavors when he could have used his time and talent to produce the type of creative work that had defined his time with Eisner & Iger and the twelve-year run of *The Spirit*, when he was young and hungry and bursting with the types of ideas that made him a leader in the comics world. Eisner scoffed at such criticism. He openly admitted that he enjoyed the art of the deal, the bantering and negotiating that accompanied each new contract. He had a family to support. Besides, he'd point out, sometimes testily, the work he was doing in instructional comics was groundbreaking.

If nothing else, his résumé was impressive, covering an astonishing range of topics and clients. Besides the government contract for *P★S* magazine, American Visuals produced materials for such corporate clients as General Motors, the American Red Cross, Fram Oil Filters, the Baltimore Colts professional football team, the American Medical Association, and RCA Victor. His *Job Scene* booklets (produced for the Department of Labor and designed to offer career guidance to people unaware of career opportunities) and his educational supplements used in grammar schools supported Eisner's theory that comic art could be used in almost any kind of learning situation.

"I became far more interested in the use of comics as an instructional medium than I was as an entertainment medium," he told the *Comics Journal*. "I felt that was a new channel for the use of comics. All my life, professionally, I've been really obsessed with the idea of trying something new. I'm in love with innovation and experimentation. It's risky, but it's really very exhilarating."

Some of Eisner's projects bordered on the bizarre and were nothing but manifestations of Eisner the businessman. Mike Ploog, an artist and Marine Corps veteran with a style so uncannily close to Eisner's that it fooled even those close to the two, remembered the chaos he encountered when he joined American Visuals in 1970, late in the company's existence. Ploog had been hired to work on *P*S*, but as he quickly determined, there was a lot more going on in Eisner's Park Avenue offices than the army publication. "There were all kinds of goofy things going on," he said, referring to the piles of old *Spirit* plates stored at the facility, as well as Eisner's other business interests, including a program he called "World Explorer," which found him buying and selling trinkets from all over the world to school-age children subscribing to his newsletter and ordering these items from advertisements he placed in the newsletter.

"We used to get these strange boxes full of exotic bric-a-brac," Ploog said.

He used to bring in goofy things like pipes from Peru, and silk worms from Japan. They used to be stored in boxes all over the place, and they used to be shipped out in these educational supplements. I remember we had silk worms in the basement that the rats got. We ended up with boxes and boxes of empty silk worms, and beads from South America that somebody realized were highly poisonous. If somebody even so much as put one around their neck, it would kill them. Goofy things like that.

For all the business pouring in, money could still be tight. Overhead and payroll rose in proportion to the company's increasing number of artists, needed office equipment and supplies, telephone and postage costs, and insurance and other expenses, and Eisner often found himself scrambling to balance the books. Profit margins could be razor thin. Eisner never had trouble generating work; the issue, as it is with all small businesses, was to produce the work, bill the client, collect payment in a timely fashion, and move on to the next project before cash flow became problematic.

The challenge was apparent in the different permutations of American Visuals—and other Eisner companies—through the 1950s and 1960s. At one point, American Visuals filed for Chapter 11 bankruptcy protection and merged with the Koster-Dana Corporation. However, this turned out to be a big corporate headache for Eisner, who was unaccustomed to answering to stockholders. Koster-Dana was a media conglomerate with syndicated newspaper and radio companies to go along with its popular Good Reading Rack Service, which produced instructional pamphlets for schools and corporations; while he never admitted as much, it could be that as president of the company's communications divisions, Eisner had spread himself too thin. The company thrived under his leadership, doubling the value of its stock, but Eisner clashed with its board of directors as much as he'd clashed with the army over *P★S*. Ultimately, he broke with Koster-Dana and went back to running a small company.

The frenetic pace could be grueling. In addition to his obligatory travels for *P★S*, there was other work-related travel that kept him on the road more than Ann would have liked—on top of the long days he spent at his Manhattan office before commuting home to White Plains.

Eisner's career—or at least the public's awareness of it—received an unexpected boost with the 1965 publication of *The Great Comic Book Heroes*, a book-length essay that was part memoir, part comics history, and part appreciation, written by Eisner's onetime protégé Jules Feiffer. E. L. Doctorow, then working as an editor at Dial Press before embarking on his renowned career as a novelist, had contacted Feiffer about writing the book. Doctorow wanted a serious look at comics, something that went outside the usual comic-book-bashing screeds that popped up on publishers' lists from time to time. *Superman* and *Batman* were now on their second generation of readers, comics had withstood stiff challenges from their opponents, and it seemed like a good time to revisit the past.

Feiffer was a good candidate to write the book. He had been creating *Sick, Sick, Sick* (later entitled *Feiffer*), some of the edgiest, most intelligent cartooning in the business, for the *Village Voice* since 1956. Besides being a recognizable name helpful in the marketing of the book, and a talent giving him a voice of authority in analyzing comics, Feiffer had a history in the business dating back to the early years.

The Great Comic Book Heroes began with a brief description of Feiffer's own childhood love of comic strips, and from there he took a workman-like approach to dissecting comics history, detailing the development of early comic books and covering the births of Superman and Batman.

Never one to withhold an opinion, Feiffer offered caustic commentary about the superheroes' sidekicks, and he took a few potshots at Fredric Wertham and his theories about homosexuality and lesbianism in comics. His passage on the studios and sweatshops was as thorough as anything published to that point.

Will Eisner and *The Spirit* warranted a chapter, and Feiffer was generous in his appreciation of his former boss. He praised Eisner's use of German expressionist cinematic techniques in *The Spirit* and of his use of humor—a rarity in superhero comics at the time. Feiffer's wisecracking style, so prevalent when he worked with Eisner in the late forties and early fifties, seeped into his analysis and led to the airing of a long-standing point of contention regarding the Spirit's clothing. After describing the Spirit's suit, hat, and mask ("drawn as if it was a skin graft"), Feiffer joked about the Spirit's socks: "For some reason, he rarely wore socks—or if he did they were flesh-colored. I often wondered about that."

("It was kind of a massive ten-year oversight," Eisner said of the Spirit's socks. "I never paid any attention to it. Still to this day I don't know what color socks he should have. Jules picked it up because he was concerned, and it was always very funny with him, because he would say, 'Gee, look, he's got no socks on!' and we would laugh and think it was very funny.")

Feiffer's greatest enthusiasm was for Eisner' technique:

Eisner's line had weight. Clothing sat on his characters heavily; when they bent an arm, deep folds sprang into action everywhere. When one Eisner character slugged another, a real fist hit real flesh. Violence was no externalized plot exercise; it was the gut of his style. Massive and indigestible, it curdled, lava-like, from the page.

This was the stuff guaranteed to catch the attention of readers too young to remember *The Spirit* or to even know Eisner's name. The Spirit was a notable contrast to other figures—Superman, Batman, Wonder Woman, Sub-Mariner, Captain America—discussed in the essay, and when the book was excerpted in *Playboy*, a huge audience in the magazine's eighteen-to-thirty-year-old readership was introduced to a character that had slipped into the past. As for Eisner's importance and influence in comic book history, Feiffer pulled no punches in his assessment: "Alone among comic book men, Eisner was a cartoonist other cartoonists swiped from."

Despite his having no use for the work Eisner was doing for *P★S* magazine, or for his American Visuals productions, Feiffer felt that Eisner more than warranted inclusion in his book. "I knew Will had disappeared," he said four and a half decades later, "and I felt this was a crime. He deserved the critical attention he'd never had. I wouldn't have existed without him, without reading *The Spirit*, learning from *The Spirit*. He, along with Caniff, was an enormous presence in my life, long before I met him."

The book pleased Eisner to no end. Over the years he and Feiffer had remained in touch, although only occasionally, and reading his analysis brought back fond memories of good work that somehow was accomplished under backbreaking deadlines. An entire *Spirit* story had been included in the book, leading to inquiries about the possibilities of reprinting some of the old stories. Eisner, who figured he'd put *The Spirit* to rest for good more than a decade earlier, entertained the idea and, in a surprise to the feature's old fans, even produced a new story, a humorous swipe at New York City mayor John Lindsay for the January 9, 1966, *New York Herald Tribune*. Al Harvey of Harvey Publications saw the new *Spirit* and approached Eisner about issuing comic books with reprints and some new material. The first appeared in October 1966, with a new "origin story" for readers unfamiliar with the Spirit's background. A second book arrived five months later, in March 1967, with a new story and several reprinted episodes.

Reception of the comic books was disappointing, and no further issues were published. Eisner, despite enjoying a new dip into *Spirit* adventures, retired the title again.

The Vietnam War assured Eisner of steady, if somewhat controversial, work on *P★S*. By the mid-1960s, with an antiwar movement springing up on college campuses across the United States, anyone over thirty and working for the military was a target for protesters. Eisner didn't hear much directly from the antiwar factions, but as someone whose political views leaned left of center, he could understand how his work might be judged as contributing to the war effort. Nevertheless, he felt no internal conflicts over what he was doing.

> I wasn't training people to kill. I was training people to maintain and repair their equipment, and to save their lives. I had no way of preventing the war, or even getting involved in the morality of the war in Korea, or in Vietnam. While I was personally opposed to

Vietnam, I also felt I was doing something good for the guy who was drafted and was there whether he wanted to be or not. So at no time did I feel I violated my principles in producing a technical manual for GIs.

According to Eisner, he heard more negative commentary about his work on P★S in Europe than in the States, and on those occasions when he was questioned about his involvement with the army during the unpopular war in Vietnam, he offered up a favorite memory of an incident in Korea that occurred during one of his visits to the country, an anecdote that illustrated his point about saving lives rather than taking them.

"One guy, a big guy with a dead cigar in his mouth, came up to me, poked his finger in my chest and asked, 'Are you Will Eisner?' I said I was, and he said, 'You saved my ass.' His tank had broken down in a combat situation, and he used material from one of my stories for a field fix, and it worked and he was able to drive to safety."

The Vietnam War years presented challenges different from the ones Eisner had faced during the Korean conflict. The climate conditions, new equipment, draftee attitudes—all put a new spin on making preventive maintenance a voluntary part of a GI's daily routine. Eisner continued to walk the line between being informative and entertaining. He'd set some of his scenes in past wars, going as far back as Caesar and moving forward, including entries involving the Revolutionary War, Civil War, and the world wars—anything to get his point across. Chariots needed to be maintained as much as tanks; uniforms changed, but the chain of command remained essentially the same.

The operations on Eisner's end of the magazine had expanded enormously from the days when he was creating almost all the artwork himself, using a letterer as his only assistant. The many projects being undertaken by American Visuals called for expansion. Eisner hired his brother, Pete, to run the office, and over the years, a steady stream of talented artists contributed to P★S and other American Visuals projects. Ted Cabarga was hired as the magazine's art director. Artists Chuck Kramer and Dan Zolne were brought on board for their ability to do technical illustrations. Murphy Anderson and Mike Ploog became steady contributors. The staff expanded to fifteen, making the shop the largest Eisner had had since his Tudor City studio days.

"We had other people running a Photostat machine and making film negatives, making color separations, things like that," Eisner said.

One type of person we didn't have on staff was a writer—the writers were effectively the Army people who sent us manuscripts, usually from Fort Knox. Then I would translate their writing into the comics script that would be used.

We ended up using 3,000 square feet of space on Park Avenue South, so it really turned into quite a big operation. We were turning out about three magazines at any given time: one was just beginning, one was in production and one was being finished. You can't imagine how much work this type of operation is until you get into it.

The required travel for the magazine differed significantly from Eisner's previous experiences. He'd made his earlier trips without worries about any danger involved. He would be shuffled by helicopter from site to site, and he never saw a combat situation. The Korean conflict was all but over when he made his first visit to the country. When he journeyed to Vietnam for the first time in 1967, there was serious fighting—or the potential for it—almost everywhere. Americans had endorsed the war in Korea; when Eisner traveled to Vietnam, President Lyndon Johnson was under increasing pressure to stop the fighting and evacuate the country.

"The differences were like night and day," Eisner recalled. "In Korea, we were all John Waynes. In Vietnam, there was a feeling of shame; you could tell something wasn't right. You didn't see the flag that much. During that trip, I was traveling under the rank of brigadier general, so I got briefed. The stories we were told, about body counts and so on, just didn't jell. There was a sense of fear."

Knowing that his going to Vietnam would worry his wife, Eisner was less than forthcoming when he outlined his plans. He told Ann that he was going to Japan—which was true enough: he *was* going to Japan in the early part of his trip—but he said nothing about Vietnam. Ann boiled over when she heard from him after he reached the country.

"He lied to me about Vietnam," she recalled. "When he got there and told me he was in Vietnam, I was so mad. I said, 'Just wait until you get home . . .'"

Saigon, the destination for the first leg of Eisner's visit to Vietnam, while safe, had an almost surreal quality to it. These were the days before the Tet Offensive, when the American troop presence still secured much of South Vietnam and the fighting was far enough away from Saigon to give the people in the city a feeling of safety. Eisner had never witnessed any heavy fighting when he traveled to Korea, but there was never a question of combat preparedness or of GIs being aware that fighting could break out at a moment's notice. It was different in Vietnam.

"Saigon was like a stage set," Eisner said. "U.S. soldiers dwarfed the native Vietnamese. Correspondents drank at the sidewalk cafés. Hotels were encased in wire screens to protect them from the occasional bomb-throwing civilian. The remnant of a French law office held hundreds of files belonging to plantation owners who had fled the country a decade before. Because the city was under military control, it all seemed relatively benign."

All that changed when Eisner went out in the field, to the Mekong Delta, accompanied by a young officer at the tail end of his duty in-country. As Eisner would recall in the title story of *Last Day in Vietnam*, the major was edgy about being anywhere near a combat zone when he was about to be shipped home, and it only got worse when fighting broke out shortly after their helicopter landed. Eisner suddenly found himself in the middle of the war, with shells exploding all around him. He made a bee-line to a helicopter, jumped in, and was whisked away, safe but shaken. The experience fortified his belief that he was performing a service with his work with *P*S*, but it was unnerving for someone who had spent his own years in the service tucked away in an office in Washington, D.C.

Throughout his stay in Vietnam, Eisner took notes and photographs, made sketches, and filed away impressions that he couldn't use with *P*S*, but that three decades later would become part of *Last Day in Vietnam*. Before departing for Southeast Asia, Eisner had believed that the U.S. military would win the day in Vietnam. After seeing the war firsthand and witnessing the troops' morale, he feared that this was a war that could not be won.

By all appearances, Eisner's quiet suburban life away from work was designed by a man determined to avoid a repetition of his own childhood. White Plains, a short train ride from Manhattan, boasted tree-lined streets, one-family frame houses, good schools, and a feeling of order that was missing in the rushed foot traffic, honking cars, and twenty-four-hour neon lights of the city. Eisner loved both—the city and the suburb—but his wife was happy to escape the city of her youth and provide as idyllic a life as possible for their two children. Eisner reveled in New York's energy, but he too was determined to see that his kids would never experience a hint of the life he'd known while he was growing up in the tenements.

According to Ann Eisner, this focus on providing for his family was the precise reason he had abandoned his career as a comic book writer

Will, Ann, and John Eisner in an undated professional family photograph.
(Courtesy of Ann Eisner)

and artist and picked up a far less exciting but more stable life of working on *P★S* and creating instructional and industrial comics. "He had a wife and children he was supporting," she stated, stressing that he quit work on *The Spirit* at almost the same time their son, John, was born.

Will Eisner enjoyed fatherhood. His creativity spilled over into his domestic life, when he added artistic touches to his children's lives, such as the time he brought home a rowboat and converted it into a sandbox or when he painted scenes and cartoon figures on the walls of his children's bedrooms. John was bright, extroverted, and athletic, and he showed enough artistic promise that Eisner wondered if he might join him one day in the studio. Alice, the more introspective of the two, shared her father's keen powers of observation and his sensitivity toward the less fortunate. Ann remembered a time when Alice was watching a television program or commercial about impoverished children and demanded that they send a donation. Eisner was the soft touch, slow to scold his children and easily amused by them, and Ann often found herself in the role of disciplinarian in the raising of their children.

Ann remembered a time when Alice was about fourteen. She wanted a pair of expensive, fashionable boots that Ann deemed to be a little excessive. Alice waited until that Saturday, when her father was home for the weekend, and talked him into taking her to the mall for the boots. Ann hadn't discussed her prior refusal to get the boots with her husband, but she was fairly certain, in retrospect, that he knew the situation. "He did whatever the kids asked him to do," she remarked, adding with a laugh, "He was a patsy."

That incident, very insignificant in the grand scheme of a person's

Alice and John Eisner. (Courtesy of Ann Eisner)

lifetime, became a kind of photograph—one that Ann and Will Eisner preserved in their memories when life changed for all of them a year later, when Alice, now fifteen, began complaining of not feeling well. Ann took her to the family physician, and after the usual battery of tests, she and Will learned that Alice had leukemia and wasn't expected to live. Ann and Will decided not to tell their daughter how gravely ill she was, and for the next year, they struggled with her declining health in their own ways. Will buried himself in work, unable to confront the horrific reality that he was about to lose his daughter; Ann spent almost all of her time with Alice, in and out of the hospital. When Alice passed away at age sixteen, it was on her mother's birthday.

Eisner was overwhelmed, not as much by grief as by rage. Although he was not a religious man, he felt as if some kind of agreement had been broken, as if he had lived a decent, moral life only to be punished all the same—or, worse yet, that Alice had been punished.

"He said, 'She didn't get a chance to live! She didn't have a life! She was given nothing! Why?'" Ann recalled.

Eisner's anger peaked at Alice's funeral, when a rabbi spoke of her as if he had known her when in fact he barely knew her name. He raged at the cemetery when Alice was laid to rest on a hillside a short drive from the Eisner home.

"He didn't cry when Alice died," Ann recalled. "He was just very, very angry. He would not talk about it to anybody—*anybody*. There were times when somebody in the shop would say that Will was different. Of course he was different. You never recover from something like that."

Eisner internalized his daughter's death to such an extent that some friends and business associates didn't even know that he had a daughter who had passed away. Grief, he felt, was private—a family matter. His work was his therapy, and later, when the time was right, he would creatively combine his work and grief into a sequential art form that would help change the direction of comics.

chapter nine

BACK IN THE GAME

It's a little bit like being Rip Van Winkle. I go to a convention now
and I stand there and look around, like in San Diego, at thousands of
people milling about and hundreds and hundreds of comics and comic
book booths and I think to myself, "My God, in 1937, who would
have dreamed that this could really happen?"

Eisner loved to tell the story about a day in June 1971, when his secretary took a call from a man named Phil Seuling.

"I want to invite him to a comic convention," Seuling said when he
asked to speak to Eisner. He went on to explain that he was running a
convention that would take place on July 4 at the Commodore Hotel in
New York City. Eisner, he mentioned, would be a most welcome guest.

The confused secretary paused for a moment, put her hand over the
mouthpiece of the telephone, and called out to Eisner in his office:

"Mr. Eisner, were you once a cartoonist?"

That innocent question illustrates how far Eisner had withdrawn from
the comics scene. His secretary knew nothing about *The Spirit*. Eisner
had stored that past life in his home in White Plains, and he never spoke
of it at the office.

Eisner had to be talked into attending the convention. He couldn't
imagine what relevance he might have in such a setting. *The Great Comic
Book Heroes* had put his name back in the spotlight for a brief period, but
Eisner felt no compelling reason to bring back the Spirit for a series of
new adventures. Comic book heroes had been reinvented in the nearly
two decades that had passed since the Spirit made his last appearance on
a regular basis, and Eisner seriously doubted that young readers would be
interested in a detective who wore a fedora, gloves, suit, tie, and mask—a

hero without superpowers or, at the very least, a utility belt packed with cool gadgets.

Seuling, however, could be very persuasive. "Come on down," he insisted.

Eisner finally agreed.

Meanwhile, half a country away, a tall, angular, long-haired Wisconsin comic book artist and publisher named Denis Kitchen was about to embark on his first trip to that same New York convention. Although only twenty-four, Kitchen had put a lot of mileage on his artistic odometer, as a cartoonist and publisher, co-founder of a college humor magazine and, shortly thereafter, an alternative newspaper. He'd "met" Phil Seuling about six months earlier, when Kitchen and fellow Wisconsin cartoonist Jim Mitchell, broke and hungry, decided to sell some of their original art to pay bills and buy groceries. They placed an ad in the *Bugle-American*, the Milwaukee paper that Kitchen had co-founded. SAVE A STARVING ARTIST, read the ad's headline. The two received one response—from someone named Phil Seuling, who had somehow run across the ad even though he was out on the East Coast. In lieu of placing an order for artwork, Seuling sent Kitchen a Coney Island salami with an attached card that read, "Never let it be said that Phil Seuling let cartoonists starve." The two corresponded, and in the months following the Great Salami Episode, Kitchen had drawn some comic strip advertisements for Seuling, repaying Seuling's generosity and bartering some of his ads for original Al Capp artwork.

What Kitchen lacked in money he compensated for in ambition, chutzpah, hard work, talent, good timing, resourcefulness, and luck—the ideal recipe for a successful artist (or at least a constantly working one) in any field. Born August 27, 1946, Kitchen had been raised in the state known for its political extremes, for Fightin' Bob La Follette and Joe McCarthy, whose political ideologies were debated on the University of Wisconsin campus and in smoky corner taverns, where Friday night fish fries were treated like sacraments and the Milwaukee Braves and Green Bay Packers like seasonal deities. Like every kid growing up in the fifties, Kitchen loved comics, but unlike other kids at the time, he wanted to create them. Since art school wasn't an option, he'd taught himself to draw. He loved *Mad* magazine, particularly the work of Harvey Kurtzman, whom he tried to emulate when, as an undergrad, he started up *Snide*, the first (and only) humor magazine ever to come out of the University of Wisconsin–Milwaukee. According to Kitchen, the magazine failed after one of its editors, a New Yorker with some street smarts, took the magazine's profits and tried to invest them in pot, only to find himself arrested in Mexico.

Kitchen's gift for satire, along with his presence on a progressive college campus at the height of the Vietnam War, might have seemed like the perfect combination for his work as an underground comix* artist and publisher, but only a strange turn of events spared him from a much different fate. By his own description, he was as "straight as they come" when he enrolled as a freshman at the University of Wisconsin–Milwaukee. His father was a World War II veteran, and as a result of his upbringing, Denis felt a sense of patriotism not shared by some of his friends, who were appalled when he joined the Reserve Officers' Training Corps, donned a uniform, and marched around the campus twice a week. As Kitchen tells it, he might have enlisted in the service if not for one minor issue: he was allergic to wool, and his uniform pants itched like hell. He dropped ROTC and started hanging out at a coffeehouse called the Avant Garde, where UWM's hippies whiled away their hours and argued the finer points of the escalating war in Southeast Asia. Kitchen's friends praised him for finally coming to his senses about the war. He didn't have the nerve to tell them that his decision was based on itchy trousers. "Had the pants been made out of cotton, I might have been a lieutenant colonel today," he quipped decades later. "It astonishes me how we pick these paths."

Fate also played a role in Kitchen's choice of academic pursuits. Since UWM didn't offer art courses conducive to a comics career, Kitchen went into journalism, which, he reasoned, would prepare him for a career in cartooning. Thanks to the time he spent in his classes and at the coffeehouse, Kitchen's thinking changed radically. He joined the Socialist

---

* "Comix" was an informal term, adopted by publishers, artists, and fans to signify the difference between the usual mainstream comics of the day and the alternative publications springing up across the United States in the late sixties and early seventies. In *Comics in Wisconsin* comics creator and historian Paul Buhle wrote: "The *x* factor that changed comics to comix was first seen in San Francisco, in the poster shops where Day-Glo images and photos of very angry-looking Black Panthers pioneered a poster print business with advertising big enough to keep *Ramparts* magazine, then master of muckraking journalism, going for years. Young Robert Crumb was the foremost artist, by a long shot, but along with him came a dozen highly talented, definitely leftwing comics veterans, the oldest of them still not thirty, a pack of them (including Art Spiegelman) from New York. There were a handful of comix in traditional comic book form, but they had twenty-four to forty-eight pages, black-and-white insides, and a pricetag of fifty cents or a dollar."

Labor Party, and besides his work on the ill-fated *Snide*, he drew cartoons for the *Post*, UWM's student newspaper. More significant, he began assembling his own comic book, a work called *Mom's Homemade Comics*. The undergrounds were making a splash on the West Coast, where they fit nicely into the sex, drugs, and rock 'n' roll milieu of Haight-Ashbury and, by extension, appealed to hippies all across the nation who were listening to the Grateful Dead, Jefferson Airplane, Quicksilver Messenger Service, or Janis Joplin. Kitchen didn't aspire to reach a national audience with *Mom's*; he was happy loading his comic book with inside jokes and references to Wisconsin. When *Mom's #1* came out in 1969, Kitchen distributed it himself, hoofing it around Milwaukee's east side and setting up sales arrangements with drugstores, head shops, used-book stores, and anyone else willing to take a handful of the comics and sell them for a slice of the profits. Kitchen made a little money, but nowhere near enough to pay bills *and* self-publish a follow-up edition of *Mom's*.

At this point, his ambitions were sprinting far ahead of the returns he was earning for his efforts. In 1970, Kitchen partnered with four friends and co-founded the *Bugle-American*, an alternative weekly newspaper initially issued from Madison before settling a short time later in Milwaukee. As the paper's art director, Kitchen was responsible for many of the *Bugle*'s covers as well as a regular strip running in the comics section. The position put him in touch with all sorts of area cartoonists, and if he still wasn't earning any real money for all the work, at least he was becoming well connected. Kitchen was an easy name to remember, and his work, although not nearly as polished as it would become over the next year or two, caught the attention of artists throughout the region.

Two of these artists, Jay Lynch and Skip Williamson, hailed from Chicago and published *Bijou*, one of the earliest underground comix and by far the finest to come out of the Midwest. The two enjoyed *Mom's*, and they contacted Kitchen shortly after its publication. When Kitchen complained about how he was being worked to death yet starving at the same time, and about how he needed to find someone to publish and distribute his work if he ever hoped to birth another issue of *Mom's*, he learned that *Bijou* was being published by the Print Mint, a California outfit specializing in rock posters. Kitchen revised *Mom's #1* and submitted it, along with a follow-up issue, to Print Mint.

As a businessman, Kitchen was caught somewhere between the traditional and the hippie-dippy, which became very evident while he was dealing with Print Mint and its lax royalty reporting. The company was sporadic about reporting its sales, and defensive about it to boot, as

Kitchen discovered when he inquired about the sales figures for *Mom's #1*. He learned that Lynch and Williamson were similarly dissatisfied with the way *Bijou* was being handled. Kitchen vowed to dump Print Mint and publish the third issue of *Mom's* himself, only this time he was going to do it on a broader scale. The Print Mint versions of *Mom's* had been enthusiastically received on the West Cost, where the undergrounds were really thriving, and Kitchen had no reason to believe that his third issue wouldn't do as well, perhaps even better, without Print Mint.

Lynch listened to Kitchen's spiel, and when the Wisconsin artist was finished, Lynch made a proposal. The people at *Bijou*, like Kitchen, were looking to switch publishers. How would Kitchen feel about publishing future issues of *Bijou* under his proposed new publishing imprint? As Kitchen would remember, he responded with "what may have been the smartest or dumbest thing I ever said: 'Sure. Why not? Doing two is as easy as one.'" At that moment, he became "a publisher by default."

Phil Seuling conducted his conventions like a drill sergeant dragging buck privates through basic training—but without the charm. He would be remembered for his dictatorial manner of running his conventions, for his shouting and pointing and barking directions. He'd learned early on that comic book creators tended to be loners in need of someone to nudge them in the right direction—or *any* direction, for that matter. The fans were even worse. The circus needed a ringmaster, and Seuling was it. Friends would remember that once off the convention floor, Seuling was much more laid-back—engaging, funny, full of great stories.

Passionate about comics and the business of comics, Seuling, a high school English teacher from Brooklyn, had been devouring comics for as far back as he could remember, and he offered no apology for his affection for them as an adult. He knew his comics history—the titles, stories, artists, the evolution of the comics as a cultural phenomenon—and in very short order, he had graduated from fanboy to industry leader. He almost single-handedly ushered in the comic conventions that we know today, expanding them from small-time gatherings of geeks and dweebs to huge, high-profile, high-energy, moneymaking events attracting people from all over the world. There was still a higher percentage of dweebs and geeks attending these conventions than you'd find gathered in any one place on the street, but you'd also see a strong mixture of artists, serious collectors, publishers, and businesses attending the same conventions, all ready to talk shop, swap stories, mingle with the troops that kept their bank accounts solvent, or, in increasing numbers, plop down previously unheard-of sums of money for original artwork, bagfuls of the latest titles, or, God forbid, a pristine copy of *Action Comics #1* or *Detective Comics #27*.

Seuling's involvement with the comics conventions came gradually, dating back to July 1964, when he had his first experience in conventions. Besides teaching, Seuling ran a comics sales and memorabilia business on the side. Doug Berman, a fellow teacher, heard about a comics convention being held at a Manhattan union hall on Fourteenth Street and Broadway. Both sensed a business opportunity. Bernie Bubnis, the convention's organizer, offered Berman and Seuling a shot at selling refreshments. As Seuling remembered, the total concessions take at that first convention came down to a case of soda. Comics artist Tom Gill (*The Lone Ranger*), the convention's guest of honor, spoke to about a hundred attendees seated on folding chairs placed on the union hall's old wooden floor. It might not have seemed like much to people now accustomed to massive comics conventions thrown at Madison Square Garden, but at the time Seuling was impressed. "In 1964, I think the world was ripe for a comics convention," he declared years later.

The following year, the convention moved to the Broadway Central Hotel, and each ensuing year saw the convention growing in popularity. Bubnis dropped out of the business, and Seuling graduated from soda salesman to convention organizer. As Seuling saw it, the convention was too provincial for its potential: "In 1968, I said, 'Hell, why are we doing this on such a small scale? Let's get some people here from Oshkosh, Peoria, and Podunk.' We ran it at the Statler Hilton Hotel and called it the International Hotel."

Attendance rocketed, expanding exponentially, as Seuling knew it would. By 1971, the convention was pulling in sixty-five hundred attendees and still growing. Seuling was now earning enough money off his former hobby to seriously consider giving up teaching and pursuing a career in distributing comics and presenting conventions. His annual convention, held on the Fourth of July weekend, became a fixture in the industry.

After he started attending them in 1971, conventions energized Will Eisner through the rest of his career. He loved looking over the new books and chatting with their creators; he enjoyed the talk about the business of comics, from contracts to sales figures. He had a keen understanding of the evolution of comics, and he tried to anticipate the directions in which they were heading. To Eisner, conventions were sensory overload, and he would

Eisner's self-portrait appeared in the Kitchen Sink Press series of "Great Cartoon Artists"
buttons, issued in 1975. (Courtesy of Denis Kitchen)

walk away from them with a newfound enthusiasm for the future. Over
the years, he would repeatedly mention how, after attending a convention,
he couldn't wait to get back to work. It wasn't just a matter of a collision
between ambition and inspiration; Eisner hated the thought of being out-
done by the upstarts that he'd just met, regardless of how friendly and encouraging he could be toward them on the convention floor.

He hadn't seen any underground comix prior to attending the New
York Comic Art Convention in 1971, but he'd heard more than enough
about them to spark his curiosity. *Something* was happening, and it was
happening away from New York, Eisner's home base and the traditional
epicenter of comics operations. Marvel and DC were still at the top of the
charts in terms of sales and influence, but they were earning their keep
in the superhero game, even if such young writers and artists as Dennis
O'Neil and Neal Adams were pushing the boundaries of superhero entertainment by adding heavy doses of social consciousness to their work.
Eisner wanted no more to do with creating superheroes than he had while
he was working on *The Spirit*. From everything he'd heard, the undergrounds were entirely different, from the topics they addressed between
their colorful covers to the way they were being marketed and distributed. They had *shelf life*. They weren't being issued every month or so, only
to be pulled from the racks and replaced when a new issue came out.
They stuck around until they were sold, and in the cases of really successful ones, additional printings were issued. This was radically different
from anything Eisner had ever experienced.

He'd heard of Denis Kitchen and his continuously expanding operations, Krupp Comic Works and Kitchen Sink Enterprises, which in just a
few years' time had grown from publishing a handful of titles per year to
moving into merchandising and recording. Robert Crumb, the most recognizable name in comix, was publishing regularly with Kitchen; his
Home Grown Funnies had been Kitchen Sink's first bestseller. When Eisner
learned that Kitchen was attending the convention, he asked French comics

historian Maurice Horn to set up a meeting. Horn ran across Kitchen in the dealer's area of the convention floor, rifling through old comic books. "Will Eisner wants to meet you," he announced.

Kitchen wouldn't have been more surprised if he'd just heard that a head of state was requesting a private audience. Kitchen knew Eisner more by his reputation than by his work, but that was more than sufficient for him to know that he should be the one requesting a meeting, not the other way around.

Eisner and Kitchen met in a hotel room, where they could talk without interruption or having to shout over the din of the convention floor. Kitchen, in a ruffled shirt, purple tie-dyed pants, and tan corduroy jacket, and Eisner, in his gray three-piece suit, were the generation gap personified. It didn't take long, however, for both to realize that their interest in each other's work and experiences in comics transcended their age difference. Kitchen, quite naturally, wanted to know all about

Bridging the generation gap: Denis Kitchen created this sketch of his first meeting with Eisner in 1971. The two became close friends, working together from their initial meeting until Eisner's death in 2005. (Courtesy of Denis Kitchen)

Eisner's exploits in the Golden Age of comics and about his work on *The Spirit*. Eisner had other interests. Through Phil Seuling, he had been briefed about Kitchen's operations, of the way he distributed his comix on a no-return policy, how he paid royalties to his artists (as opposed to flat page rates), how he returned all the original art to the artists, and how the artists retained their copyrights. All this differed from the way the big companies conducted business, and Eisner, who was toying with the idea of starting his own magazine of *Spirit* reprints, wanted every bit of information Kitchen could supply. Eisner, Kitchen determined early in their conversation, had little interest in talking about his past. He would politely answer a question or two about the old days, then redirect the exchange back to the present and, ultimately, the future.

"I was impressed," Kitchen noted later. "This straight-looking fellow seemed to be a kindred spirit. I had been under the impression, like the rest of the industry, that Eisner had more or less retired from comics. In retrospect, we couldn't have been more wrong."

Eisner later admitted that he, too, had to dismiss his first impressions.

"To a buttoned-down type like me, this should have sent me running in the other direction," he said of his initial impressions of Kitchen. "However, it didn't take great genius to see that what was afoot was a reprise of the frontier days of 1938."

The more Eisner heard, the more he appreciated what the undergrounds had to offer. In the past, he'd always had to conform, one way or another, to firms purchasing his work, whether it was Fiction House buying work from Eisner & Iger or the Sunday newspapers picking up *The Spirit* supplements. The army had rigid restrictions for *P*S* magazine, and his bosses there wouldn't have considered returning his art. For all he knew, it was being destroyed as soon as the magazine appeared. Eisner and Kitchen talked and talked, and when Eisner eventually admitted that he had never actually seen one of these underground comix, Kitchen offered to take him back to the convention for a look. Kitchen was thrilled. When he'd left Wisconsin for the East Coast, he couldn't have predicted in his wildest fancies that he would be making friends with one of the most influential figures in comics history.

Unfortunately, the Eisner-Kitchen meeting ended abruptly, and on less than favorable terms, when Kitchen walked Eisner to the dealer area, to a grouping of several long tables stacked with nearly every underground book on the market. Kitchen intended to select a few titles that Eisner might appreciate, but before he could do so, Eisner reached down and grabbed a copy of *Zap*, which contained one of the most

over-the-top shock entries in early comix history, an S. Clay Wilson
number, *Captain Pissgums and His Pervert Pirates*, in which a pirate cuts off
the tip of another pirate's penis and proceeds to eat it.

"Will saw it and he just blanched," Kitchen remembered. "I mean, he
was virtually speechless. As I recall, he started to stutter. I said, 'This isn't
exactly typical.' He said, 'I had no idea they were this strong.' There were
fans standing nearby—fans who recognized Will—but there was also a
very young and virtually unknown Art Spiegelman, and as soon as he
saw Will start to harrumph about these undergrounds, he stepped in to
try to defend his buddies."

Eisner had no interest in engaging in a public debate with Spiegelman
or anyone else over the merits of the undergrounds. If this was the type of
material published by the underground publisher, he wanted no part of
it, regardless of how the business was run. Maybe the generation gap was
too much to overcome. Rather than continue the conversation, he politely excused himself and left the convention. To Kitchen's dismay, he
didn't return.

Given Eisner's age and background, it isn't difficult to understand why he
might have been offended by the Wilson comix feature. Nor is it difficult
to determine the appeal of comix to the underground artists and their
readers. In the rebellious decade between 1965 and 1975, when the undergrounds took root, thrived, and eventually lost some of their impetus,
the Comics Code of Authority stamp of approval stood nakedly in the
world of comics as the ultimate symbol of the Establishment. Following
the implementation of the code, comic books issued by the big publishing houses had been reduced to pabulum. With only an occasional exception, such as the Dennis O'Neil and Neal Adams *Green Lantern/Green
Arrow* contributions to DC, or a Steve Ditko or Jack Kirby story about
one of Marvel's conflicted superheroes, comics had no heart and soul.
They could be accomplished in their artwork, but their stories were va-
pid and their heroes predictable.

Stan Lee, though mainstream in his subject preferences and a good
company man while working for Marvel, was intrigued by the popularity of the undergrounds. There was obviously a market for this new
anti-Establishment material and money to be made. In 1974, he would
approach Denis Kitchen and enlist his services in the production of a new
Marvel title, *Comix Book*, but the title had no chance. The magazine-
sized hybrid, a kind of cross between the undergrounds and *Mad* magazine, lasted only three issues at Marvel. Lee admired some of the work of

a few comix artists, but, like Eisner at the convention, he had no tolerance for the excesses. "To be successful, they had to be outrageous and dirty," he said. "I didn't want to be dirty, so I abandoned it."

The excesses, of course, were precisely what attracted readers to the undergrounds. To teenagers and young adults schooled in the hurricane mixture of rock 'n' roll, radical politics, free and open drug use, and casual sex, the more excessive the comic book could be the better. There was no room for compromise in a country engaged in an extremely unpopular war, where political assassinations destroyed any faith they might have had in their futures, where a dissident voice might be silenced by law enforcement officials using petty drug busts and subsequent incarceration as a means of eliminating protesters. The undergrounds, sold in head shops next to black-light posters, rolling papers, and tie-dyed T-shirts, were further endorsements of their lifestyles. Freedom of speech, although wounded, wasn't dead.

Robert Crumb, who preferred to use only an initial for his first name when signing his work, was nothing less than a god in the underground canon. Crumb had loved comics as a kid, and along with his brother Charles, he had created comics as a teenager, including a series of adventures involving a cat named Fred, later renamed Fritz. Suave, fast-talking, and oversexed, Fritz the Cat was just about everything Crumb was not. Harvey Kurtzman, editing *Help!* magazine after his stint with *Mad*, saw the feature when Crumb moved briefly to New York, and he gave Crumb a job at the magazine, working as an assistant for future filmmaker Terry Gilliam. Crumb, however, was too peripatetic by nature to stay at any job for long, and his tenure at the magazine was brief.

Crumb had actually tried living in a more traditional American way, when he married and worked as a card designer for the American Greetings Corporation in Cleveland; but he wasn't happy. He abandoned that life without warning, leaving his wife and job behind and taking off for the West Coast, where he found a receptive culture in San Francisco's Haight-Ashbury district. Drugs—particularly LSD—gave him a new perspective on both his life and his art. "All the old meanings become absurd," he said later, long after his name had become synonymous with comix, "so it heightens your sense of the absurdity, or mine, anyway, of all the things you're taught or programmed to believe is important or significant about reality, so that it made it easier to poke fun at everything."

Crumb could have scoured the entire country and he wouldn't have found an environment more receptive to his art. The Bay Area, historically tolerant and freewheeling in its thinking, loved its eccentrics, misanthropes, antiheroes, outlaws, tricksters, pranksters, dissidents, and radicals. Peter Fonda's Captain America was a far better fit than the Jack Kirby/Joe Simon comic book hero by the same name, and Crumb's Mr. Natural, with his long hair, waist-length beard, and totally laid-back demeanor, was far more interesting than a tights-wearing, muscle-bound superhero defending truth, justice, and the American way. Crumb's characters had huge feet and big butts, legs like tree trunks, and overall physiques that seemed like polar opposites of the glamour cultivated by Hollywood a few hundred miles to the south. They were hairy as hell, smoked lots of pot, and jumped in the sack whenever the mood struck— which was often. Crumb urged his readers to "Keep on Truckin'" at a time when America was rocketing to the moon. His album jacket art for Big Brother and the Holding Company's *Cheap Thrills* attained iconic status before Janis Joplin's boozy blues voice had reached the ears of the young folks in the hinterlands.

Crumb inspired other comic artists and countless imitators, but lost in the hoopla was the fact that, whatever his image, he worked like a demon, more out of necessity than the Muse's constant calling. There still wasn't much money in comics—and especially not in the underground variety—and living on the West Coast wasn't cheap. Fortunately, there was a steady demand for Crumb's art, much of it in the Midwest, where publishers like Denis Kitchen, Jay Lynch, and others coveted Crumb's latest work. In San Francisco, Crumb produced his own titles and hauled them around the city in a baby buggy, selling them to people on the streets.

He wasn't alone by any means. Comix artists, some rebels without a cause and others more traditional practitioners unable to land work with the bigger publishers, either contributed to someone else's underground comic book or started their own. Circulation for these comix could be spotty and their lifetimes brief, but it was better to be a hometown hero than never to be seen at all. Gilbert Shelton's *Fabulous Furry Freak Brothers*, featuring the antics of three potheads named Fat Freddy, Freewheelin' Franklin, and Phineas, cracked up readers in their relentless pursuit of great dope. Shelton, an aspiring filmmaker, also created a stir with his *Wonder Wart-Hog* and *Smiling Sergeant Death and His Merciless Mayhem Patrol* titles, which skewered characters in the Marvel and DC stables.

Readers loved the undergrounds for their irreverence, wacky artwork, and taboo-shattering subject matter, but they also loved the energetic intelligence that rumbled beneath the surface of all the mayhem. The comix producers were offering the kind of lacerating social commentary you weren't finding in the more traditional media outlets. Like their cousins the alternative newspapers, comix could address off-limits topics and be as subversive as they wanted to be without fear of offending any corporate sponsors that supported them through advertising. Comix would eventually be threatened by legal action and the prospects of new obscenity laws, but in their heyday they celebrated a kind of freedom that would have made Fredric Wertham faint.

In future speeches and interviews, Will Eisner would remember his visit to the 1971 New York convention in a much more favorable light. He would joke about running into a group of hippie artists who smoked strange-smelling cigarettes and laughed at all the wrong times, and he would remember admiring their work for the way it addressed social issues and confronted the Establishment. "That's *exactly* what I felt comics should do as a literary form," he'd say.

That's probably how he wanted to recall it, given the way things turned out, but in reality, he might not have connected with Denis Kitchen again if Kitchen hadn't kept his business card and contacted him. Not long after the convention, Kitchen initiated a reconciliation by sending Eisner a letter and a sampling of comix. The carefully chosen selection, taken from Kitchen Sink Press catalog, included copies of *Bijou*, R. Crumb's *Home Grown Funnies*, and Kitchen's own *Mom's Homemade Comics*.

"Enclosed is a sampling of our line of underground comic books," Kitchen wrote in his July 14, 1971, cover letter. "I think you will find them generally more tasteful than the unfortunate titles you happened to pick up in the dealers' area of the Comic Art Convention." Those titles, Kitchen made a point of mentioning, had been the products of a competing publisher, not of Kitchen Sink Press.

Eisner responded favorably. "You are quite right!" he told Kitchen of the comix he'd sent him. "They are more tasteful and much more professional than most. I'm particularly impressed with your own work and I was glad to see that your books have something more to say than fornication! There's a lot of exciting promise here."

Eisner's enthusiastic response summed up in a very few words the basic difference, then and in the future, between Eisner and some of his contemporaries. Comic book artists, often afflicted with egos surpassing their talents or importance, could be quite dismissive and snarky in their comments about the works of others. Eisner possessed a substantial ego of his own, but with only an occasional, surprising lapse here and there, he tempered it into the kind of self-confidence that permitted him to be open-minded without the poison of negative competitiveness. He might not have cared for an artist's style or the theme or content of an artist's story, but he remained open to the possibilities of almost any form of expression.

Scott McCloud, graphic novelist and author of *Understanding Comics* and *Making Comics*, would recall a time, years after that New York convention, when he was sitting in on one of Eisner's classes at the School of Visual Arts in New York. He had approached Eisner before class with a book by Japanese manga artist Osamu Tezuka and wondered what Eisner thought of it. "He liked it instantly," McCloud said. "He really was quite fascinated by what he was seeing. He picked it up and held it aloft to his students and said, 'There, you see, this guy's not a slave to the close-up like you guys are.' I showed the very same book to another very accomplished artist. He picked it up, flipped through it for no more than fifteen seconds, put it down, and said, 'That's enough for me.' It really did point out the difference between the two men. Will was eternally curious. He could just turn on a dime when exposed to new ideas, even if he began with one idea in his head. He was always open, always ready to change, always ready to accept that there might be something else that didn't previously belong to his universe or perception."

Denis Kitchen reminded Eisner of his own youthful ambitions. Kitchen was as much an outsider as Eisner had been back in the 1930s, when he decided to enter a field with very little past and no predictable future. As a businessman, Kitchen showed the same type of gumption that Eisner himself had shown when he'd formed Eisner & Iger and, later, his own

Denis Kitchen and Will Eisner. (Courtesy of Denis Kitchen)

company, when he'd forged ahead with the belief that there had to be a market, perhaps a lucrative one, for quality comics aimed at all audiences, even adult ones.

"Maurice is at work putting together a dummy of 'The Spirit' magazine," Eisner wrote in conclusion to his initial response to Kitchen's proposal. "As soon as we have something in hand, we shall be talking to you on more specific matters."

"More specific matters" meant hammering out a basic publisher–artist agreement on the terms of royalties, payment schedules, copyright ownership, and other points of publishing and distribution common to any publishing business agreement. After talking to Kitchen about his business practices at the convention, Eisner felt confident that the agreement would be reached without some of the contentious back-and-forth that he had faced in the past. Kitchen had boasted of the way the undergrounds allowed artists to maintain ownership of their characters, and he had established a track record of reliably reporting sales figures and paying royalties to his artists. These hippies were loose and easy and anti-Establishment right down to the way they conducted their business. It was a fair, honest exchange between artist and publisher. Eisner didn't have to look far to see how artists had lost control of their creations— Jerry Siegel and Joe Shuster were still struggling for control of, or at least better compensation for, Superman; Bob Kane had been forced into a brilliant legal maneuver in order to see something for his creation, Batman; and the creators of Spider-Man, Captain America, and others were essentially out of luck at Marvel—and publishers had earned their oily reputations for being cheapskates, from the per-page rates they paid to the credits they gave their writers and artists. Maybe it was because he was an artist himself, maybe it was the pot that he was smoking, or maybe it was just a matter of his being a decent guy, but Denis Kitchen seemed to be different.

He was, as Eisner discovered shortly after they had reached a verbal agreement on the terms of their relationship. The deal was beneficial to both sides. Eisner was not only granting Kitchen Sink Press permission to reprint *Spirit* stories long out of print, he also agreed to produce new stories and artwork, including covers. For his part, Kitchen was offering a deal that included 10 percent royalty payments, total control of the material, and copyright ownership.

"Send me a draft of your proposed contract and we'll proceed," Eisner instructed Kitchen.

"Contract?" Kitchen responded. "I don't do contracts."

Kitchen went on to explain that contracts, as he viewed them, were "a product of an uptight, corrupt, and cynical capitalistic system that exploits creative people." Kitchen thought he was appealing to the artist in Eisner, to the man who had been abused by the system. Contracts, Kitchen insisted, had always been imposed on artists in the comics business.

"We're trying to do business in a more progressive manner," he said. "Besides, I don't want to give money to lawyers."

Eisner heard Kitchen out before delivering a lecture of his own. Contracts, he explained, shouldn't be looked on as impositions, not if both parties were in agreement; instead, they were protection for both parties, insurance that their agreement would be honored in the unlikely event something terrible happened to one of them.

"What happens," he asked, "if you are killed in a car accident tomorrow? Or vice versa, if something happens to me, how does my widow know what obligations I've burdened her with or what income she might expect from my literary dealings with you? Are there restrictions on her if she is presented with third party opportunities to license my work? Who controls the media or merchandise rights?"

Kitchen, who had only considered contracts in abstract, dogmatic terms, was knocked backward a couple steps. He had never considered the scenarios Eisner was presenting. There was clearly a difference in thinking between the twenty-four-year-old still feeling his way through the dark and the fifty-four-year-old with life lessons to support his arguments.

In recalling the conversation nearly four decades later, Kitchen could only laugh at the irony. "I had this notion that publishers force oppressive contracts on artists," he'd say, "and here was the artist forcing the contract on the publisher."

Eisner agreed with Kitchen on one point: He didn't like paying attorneys to review contracts, either. So he offered to draw up a contract using his own boilerplate language. If Kitchen agreed with the wording and terms, he could sign the contract and it would be a legally binding document.

Denny Colt, the detective who'd risen from the dead to become the Spirit, was about to be resurrected once again.

chapter ten

RESURRECTION

It's a literary dream to think that a character you created is going to live on. It's more than anybody in this field could ever ask for. So I'm very proud of it and very grateful for it.

Eisner caught the New York convention and met Denis Kitchen at the perfect moment. He liked people to believe that he was snug and happy with his life in educational comics and *P★S* magazine, that he was using these opportunities to further the growth of comics in other types of media. And although this was true enough, by 1971 he'd had enough of *P★S* and was ready to move on. In reality, some of his corporate experiences had been nightmares that he'd just as soon forget. He had applied his art to all sorts of endeavors and could feel accomplished at it, but he wasn't truly happy. For as creative as he could be in enterprises such as American Visuals, *P★S*, and A. C. Croft, a Connecticut-based firm that produced educational materials that Eisner purchased, he'd been removed from the comic book scene long enough that he missed the shop environment and the camaraderie among the artists, the energy of the comics industry, the joy of entertaining, and the challenge of finding new ways of writing comics for adults. The convention had brought all this home. He discussed this with Ann from time to time, until one day she encouraged him to divest himself of his business interests and do what made him happy.

Eisner had no interest in starting up new Spirit adventures; he was insistent about that from the onset of his relationship with Denis Kitchen. He would create new covers and add some interior artwork involving the Spirit character for the Kitchen Sink books, but he had no desire to reprise the old grind of coming up with complete, all-new stories on tight deadlines. He'd been on that treadmill nearly all of his adult life, at the cost of having to turn down other projects that demanded more time than his weekly or monthly commitments would permit. Reprints would have to suffice.

As it was, he had another *Spirit* reprint commitment, this one with Dave Gibson, a California comics publisher and packager who was issuing reprints as small comic books, packaged in polybags and aimed at collectors. Each bag would contain ten *Spirit* stories, published in black and white, with additional new commentary by Eisner.

Denis Kitchen, delighted to be publishing Will Eisner in any capacity, was fine with this arrangement. He was already publishing Robert Crumb and, through such publications as *Bijou* and *Bizarre Sex*, the work of Harvey Kurtzman, Art Spiegelman, Bill Griffith, and a host of other popular artists. Adding Will Eisner to the roster meant more diversity in content and style. No one in the business could boast of a cast of characters as diverse as Angelfood McSpade, Zippy the Pinhead, and the Spirit.

Eisner was having the time of his life. After more than twenty years of working in other sequential art adventures, producing to order for the army and corporate clients, he had returned to his first love, and he couldn't hide the pleasure he was getting from it. "This is fun—after all these years!" he wrote Kitchen.

Selecting *Spirit* installments for the Kitchen Sink books presented a problem. Eisner had piles of old *Spirit* comics, from original artwork to published Sunday supplements to photostats, but none it was cataloged. Worse yet, only a handful of pre–World War II *Spirit* original artwork was still in existence. Zinc had been a precious commodity during the war years, rationed out as parsimoniously as the paper upon which comics were printed, and Busy Arnold had protected his zinc plates by stacking them carefully with a sheet of original art sandwiched between each plate. When Eisner returned from Washington, D.C., after the war and tried to get his artwork returned, he learned that almost all his original art had been destroyed. He'd saved the Sunday supplements of his early work, but much of that wasn't in the best condition—certainly not good enough for Denis Kitchen to reproduce for the new magazine.

The approach to selecting *Spirit* reprints was scattershot, based entirely on originals most readily available and which of those Eisner preferred to publish. In addition, Kitchen Sink was in no position to reprint *The Spirit* in color—not that Eisner looked askance at this turn of events. If offered the choice, he would have preferred to see *The Spirit* published in black and white all along. He could never rely on printers to get his colors right, plus he felt that black and white added a cinematic film noir element to *The Spirit*.

"*The Spirit* seemed to look better to me in black and white than it did in color," he said, adding that even though fans and collectors preferred color, the black-and-white *Spirits* helped preserve the accent on story. "*The Spirit* was originally designed for color, but I found myself liking the work better in black and white. It seemed to have more of a mood and expression, everything I wanted to convey."

As soon as he'd signed on with Kitchen Sink, Eisner busied himself with major projects: designing a cover for the forthcoming Kitchen Sink comic book *Snarf #3*, choosing the entries for *Spirit #1* (informally marketed as the *Underground Spirit*), and coming up with the magazine's cover. The covers would place the Spirit in sexier, more violent settings, enough to prompt Kitchen to note on the covers that the contents of these comics were "adults only." The caveat, of course, all but guaranteed head shop browsing.

The *Snarf* cover, appearing in early 1973, combined the type of cover work seen on previous *Spirit* magazines with the more mature artwork common in the undergrounds. The Spirit is shown breaking through the door of a seedy, waterlogged basement comix studio, where long-haired artists are preparing an underground book. A thoroughly disgusted Commissioner Dolan follows the Spirit through the doorway, snarling, "I'm gonna arrest them, Spirit," to which the world-weary detective responds, "For what, Dolan?" The cover served as Eisner's commentary on his entrance into the undergrounds.

It also acted as a preemptive strike against the proponents of a new run on comic book censorship. The popularity of the undergrounds had stirred up talk of new regulations and obscenity busts. Eisner hated the thought of it, regardless of how put off he was by some of the more provocative comix he'd seen, and he wasn't shy about expressing his feelings. "I'm against any form of censorship other than the restrictions imposed by the creators' own tastes, or sense of responsibility to moral values," he said.

The first *Underground Spirit* presented four *Spirit* reprints (including stories featuring the popular P'Gell and Octopus villains), a full-color wraparound cover, several new one-page entries, and an introductory essay by Maurice Horn, all for a fifty-cent cover price. More than a quarter century separated the original appearance of the stories and the Kitchen Sink reprints, and the times and readers couldn't have been more

different. When the stories in the Kitchen Sink edition had first appeared
in the Sunday supplements, World War II had ended, America felt optimistic about the future, babies were booming, and Levittownesque sub-
divisions were sprouting up in suburbs across America. The country was
in a dramatically different mood now. The war in Vietnam was still
dragging on, and the sour winds of Watergate, following on the heels of
the sixties, found America mired in pessimism. Readers of the *Underground Spirit* books would be an entirely different breed from those who'd
picked up the old Sunday comic book newspaper inserts the first time
around.

Ebony, the Spirit's African-American sidekick, was the ultimate symbol of the changes Eisner had to address. When Ebony, with his minstrel
show character traits, backwoods English, and sense of servitude in his
relationship with the Spirit, made his first appearance in a *Spirit* story, the
Brown v. *Board of Education* Supreme Court decision was a decade away
and the civil rights movement two decades in the future. This characterization wasn't going to go unnoticed in the wake of the violence accompanying the civil rights movement, the Black Power manifestos, the fair
housing and busing confrontations, more than a decade of hotly con-
tested legislation, Cassius Clay changing his name to Muhammad Ali,
and a controversial new show called *All in the Family*, in which a couple
of white characters regularly sparred over racial bigotry. A character like
Ebony White was fodder for debate—and it wasn't always polite. Some
critics went so far as to hint that Eisner himself was racist. Eisner reacted
defensively or angrily, depending upon his mood. Knowing that a sizable
percentage of his current readership might take exception to his depiction
of Ebony, Eisner confronted the issue in the first *Underground Spirit* in a
one-page short, in which Ebony is interviewed by a young black reporter
who looks as if he just stepped off the set of *Shaft*. Although heavy-
handed, the dialogue cuts to the point in five panels:

Reporter: Ebony White, I'm here to interview you on behalf of Spirit
fans and collectors of your old adventures with the Spirit. Er, some of my
questions may be quite blunt . . .

Ebony: No sweat . . . ask anything!

Reporter: It is hard for many of us to understand why you have accepted the role of a sort of "Man Friday" . . . a form of Uncle Tomism
larded with a kind of humble servility the whites have always expected as
due them from blacks in those days!! What I mean is . . . how can you
have found pride in a secondary role . . . in an era of rising black identity
that was emerging during those years!?

The Spirit: (entering the room) Hey, Ebony Did you have any success tailing that pusher this morning? Dolan is howling for evidence!

Ebony: (pointing to trussed-up criminal on floor next to him) Well, Spirit . . . I took about 15 photos of this rat makin' a big buy . . . Then I took 9 shots of him selling the stuff in a schoolyard!! Then he spotted me! So I hadda ack fast . . . He chased me up an alley . . . I rolled a trash can at him . . . He tripped, knocked hisself out on a fire escape ladder, then I jes' dragged him in . . . You can book him with all the evidence!

The Spirit: Great!

Ebony: (turning back to the reporter) Sorry, now would you mind repeating that question?

The dialogue was as honest an appraisal of the character as Eisner could muster, a straight-on summation explaining his reasons for Ebony's continuing adventures with the Spirit. Whenever confronted with the Ebony issue in interviews—and there were many such occasions—Eisner would insist, first and foremost, that he felt no regrets for creating Ebony, that Ebony had been brought into *The Spirit* as a means of infusing humor into the stories. Ebony was a creation of his times, much the way Shylock—himself in a play its writer called a comedy—was the product of Shakespeare's times, Li'l Abner was a reflection of Al Capp's times, or Rochester was used as a foil in the classic Jack Benny comedy skits. No malice had been intended. Humor, Eisner insisted, often depended on the stereotypes and clichés of the day, and stereotypes, in and of themselves, were not necessarily harmful. To Eisner, it all boiled down to intent: if caricatures were drawn for evil purposes, such as Nazi propagandists' caricatures of the stereotypical hook-nosed, dark, curly-haired European Jews, there was no doubting the artist's intentions to injure. Ebony, Eisner submitted, was entirely different. He was the featured character in any number of *Spirit* stories; his actions were always positive, even heroic. In his early appearances in *The Spirit*, Ebony had been an older man, but Eisner fine-tuned the character over the years, first by making him younger in an effort to bolster the humor and then by giving him more to do.

"When the feature began in 1940, Ebony was perhaps more viable and valid than he is today," Eisner conceded to an interviewer, adding, "I would imagine that Shakespeare would have one hell of a time defending Shylock in *The Merchant of Venice* to today's socially conscious people. It doesn't make an author any less culpable for what he does, but it does indicate how difficult it is for an author to divorce himself from current norms, especially if he's being entertaining."

According to Eisner, his perceptions began to change during World

War II, when he witnessed troop segregation, and his views continued to change over the following two decades, when national consciousness turned to the civil rights movement. By then, the Spirit and Ebony had been retired and Eisner had moved on. The reprints kindled new disputes. Not only did Eisner have to address the criticism, he was also saddled with a position that younger readers, steeped in the conflicts of the 1960s, weren't inclined to accept. Nor did it matter that as *The Spirit* evolved, Eisner had introduced other African-American characters more in step with the times.

One of Eisner's most common defenses focused on two letters he had received at about the same time, one from an old DeWitt Clinton classmate who accused him of abandoning his youthful, liberal ideals, the other from an African-American newspaperman from Baltimore who praised him for his compassionate treatment of Ebony. Such was the nature of the conflict.

The debate would continue for decades, first with the Spirit and Ebony and later when Eisner published *Fagin the Jew*, his graphic novel addressing stereotypes and anti-Semitism in Charles Dickens's classic novel *Oliver Twist*. Eisner labored, sometimes awkwardly, to explain his position, but he was never able to fully resolve the issue.

The Eisner-Kitchen Spirit reprint deal was short-lived. The first *Underground Spirit* sold out, proving that there was still a market for the Spirit stories. Kitchen went back to press to produce another batch of the first *Underground Spirit* while Eisner prepared a second issue. Eisner was pleased with the results of the first issue, and he might have stayed with Kitchen indefinitely had he not received a phone call from a bigger publisher with a better offer.

It might have been expected. Eisner's reappearance in the comics world after such a long hiatus was big news.

At Marvel, Stan Lee, always on the lookout for emerging trends, heard about the sales figures for *Underground Spirit #1*. He loved the idea of having Will Eisner in the Marvel stable, but he wasn't interested in reprints. Marvel specialized in superheroes tormented by personality flaws or foibles, and the Spirit seemed like a good fit. Lee called Eisner and asked if might be open to creating new Spirit adventures or, at the very least, writing new story lines that could be developed by other Marvel artists.

He wasn't. Eisner thought the idea was wrongheaded for two basic reasons. First, he felt he had gone as far as he could with the Spirit during the character's newspaper lifetime, and he wasn't fond of the idea of up-

With Stan Lee. (Courtesy of Denis Kitchen)

dating the character or placing him in a more contemporary setting. Second, Marvel's comic book readership was younger than the *Spirit*'s newspaper readership, and Eisner wanted to create more adult work.

Marvel, Lee suggested, might have something along that line. Marvel had been developing a satire magazine aimed at college students and young adults, and Lee had writer/editor Roy Thomas meet with Eisner and sound him out about the idea.

"Stan wanted something in the *Mad* vein, only for a little older audience, because this was the time of *National Lampoon*," Thomas recalled. "He had me go out to lunch with Will, but not much came out of it."

What Lee really wanted was for Eisner to take over his duties at Marvel. Lee had been with the company since his teenage days, and he was anxious to move to the West Coast, to Hollywood, where in recent years a rebirth of the motion picture industry, led by a new wave of directors and such highly regarded films as *The Graduate*, *The Last Picture Show*, *Easy Rider*, and *The Godfather*, promised talented people the chance to earn big bucks and gain big exposure. Marvel, seeing the potential for huge earnings from movie adaptations from its comics and characters, was kicking around the idea of starting up a motion picture division within the company. Lee fancied himself to be a natural in this environment— which, as later years proved, turned out to be true enough—but he couldn't leave his job as editor and publisher at Marvel before hiring a replacement. The comic book industry was brimming with young talent, but none with Eisner's knowledge and background. Eisner seemed to know everyone in comics, which promised to be valuable in attracting new artists and writers to the company. Lee believed that Eisner was the ideal candidate to lead Marvel through the next decade or two of business. "I really wanted to make our company bigger than it was, and I thought he would be the greatest guy to get a handle on all these new things I wanted to do," Lee said.

Although flattered by Lee's proposal, Eisner wasn't interested in overseeing a huge list of characters he hadn't created. More important, he wanted no part of being another cog, albeit an important one, in the corporate world; he'd just escaped all that by signing on with Kitchen Sink Press. Marvel still did business the old-fashioned, work-for-hire way—the company paid by the page, maintained copyright ownership, and held on to the artists' work—and Eisner wouldn't work under those conditions. More than thirty years had passed since his initial dickering over copyright and character ownership with Busy Arnold and Henry Martin, and nothing had changed his opinion in the interim. To Eisner, it wasn't an issue of rights or of proverbial white hats and black hats. Publishers had rights, as did writers and artists. It was an issue of negotiation, of the artist having the chance to make a choice and living with his decision.

And so it went with Marvel. The salary would have been lucrative, but money wasn't the point. Eisner informed Lee that if he was put in charge at Marvel, he'd want to initiate changes that gave writers and artists ownership of their work. Lee was in no position to negotiate such changes.

"We had a long lunch," Eisner said of his meeting with Stan Lee, "and that was the end. I thanked him very much. And we were walking out to the elevator, and he said, 'Why aren't you interested?' I said, 'I think it's a suicide mission.' Really, it wasn't for me."

The two parted amicably, mutually respectful of each other, but Eisner would never work for Marvel. He would occasionally be offered one-shot opportunities to work on stories that featured the Spirit and Marvel superhero characters, but he found those offers easy to turn down. Denny Colt and Peter Parker were never going to meet.

Word of these inquiries bounced around the comics rumor mill, and Jim Warren, the colorful founder and publisher of Warren Publishing, eventually contacted Eisner and set up a meeting. Aggressive and competitive, Warren relished the thought of being able to stick it to Marvel and DC by signing Eisner to his company. Problem was, there was no way Warren could begin to offer Eisner the kind of money that Marvel or DC could wave at him. To have any chance of snagging Eisner, Warren had to appeal to the artist in him. He'd also have to hope that Eisner had forgiven him for hiring Mike Ploog away from *P★S* magazine a few years earlier.

Warren pitched his idea over lunch in a posh Manhattan restaurant. Eisner, no slouch as a salesman himself, listened closely to what Warren had to say. By the end of their lunch, he was convinced that Warren Publishing offered more than the other publishers he'd been dealing with, including Kitchen Sink. Warren's distribution network easily surpassed Kitchen Sink's, though it wasn't as extensive as DC's or Marvel's. Kitchen Sink, Marvel, and DC published standard-sized comic books; Warren offered to publish *The Spirit* in a larger, magazine-sized edition. Warren wanted to publish reprints, where Marvel insisted on new material.

One other important issue tipped the scale in Warren's favor. "I felt better dealing with a smaller publisher for very practical reasons," Eisner later explained. "To Jim Warren, I was one of maybe four properties he had. To Marvel, I was just one of 400 properties they had. I felt I would get better care and attention from Jim Warren than from Marvel."

Eisner and Warren discussed the terms of their agreement, and Eisner walked away with a sweetheart deal. Eisner would receive $1,000 per issue and royalties on sales, in return for onetime reprint rights. Eisner, of course, would own his properties.

One sticky problem remained: what to do about the small publisher Eisner was currently dealing with—the one already devoting great care and attention to his work. The second *Underground Spirit* had just hit the streets, which led to one final provision in Eisner's arrangement with Warren. Eisner hated the notion that Kitchen might lose money on the new *Spirit* issue if it failed to sell as well as anticipated, so before the deal became final, Jim Warren had to promise to buy out Kitchen Sink's inventory. Warren agreed without hesitation.

When breaking the news of his agreement with Warren, Eisner tried to appeal to Kitchen's own business instincts. The Kitchen Sink experiment had been valuable, Eisner said, but Warren Publishing offered an opportunity he couldn't ignore. The first *Underground Spirit* had sold in the twenty-thousand-copy range; Warren believed he could do much better. "He thinks he can sell a hundred thousand," Eisner told Kitchen. "I hope you understand. It's not personal, but I'm going to have to explore this other venue."

The buyout arrangement with Warren blunted the blow to some extent, but the sudden and unexpected change of plans left Kitchen angry, frustrated—and "heartbroken," as he later said.

He also knew better than to say or write anything that might jeopardize his chances of working with Eisner in the future, so as soon as he learned of Eisner's buyout arrangement with Jim Warren, he sent a letter to Eisner intended to keep all business doors open.

"It is apparent that Warren 'made an offer you couldn't refuse,'" he wrote, paraphrasing Vito Corleone's famous statement from Mario Puzo's bestselling novel and Francis Ford Coppola's movie, *The Godfather*, "and I am not at all resentful that you decided to go with him. THE SPIRIT certainly deserves a circulation and package which we could not deliver at this time. I am grateful that you gave us the opportunity to publish THE SPIRIT and I hope we will be able to take you up on your offer to produce some experimental, non-Spirit comix in the coming year."

"We'll do something again in the future," Eisner assured Kitchen.

At that time, neither could have estimated just how much they would be doing.

Jim Warren, like Jerry Iger, Busy Arnold, and other impresarios Eisner had dealt with throughout his career, was not a comics writer or artist. He operated by instinct and a strong understanding about his special niche in the comics market, and he could be very stubborn and assertive. He wasn't often called diplomatic, but even those who disliked him had to admit that, in surviving in an extremely competitive business, he must have known what he was doing. Warren Publishing's titles often sounded like knockoffs of what other publishers were producing, when in fact Warren was coming up with ideas that the bigger houses were imitating.

A comics aficionado since his youth, Warren started Warren Publishing in Philadelphia in 1957, fresh off the Senate hearings and the establishment of the Comics Code Authority. To circumvent the Comics Code Authority and its little corner cover stamp, Warren published in the standard 8½-by-11-inch magazine size, charged a magazine's cover price, and declared his audience to be older than the kids picking up *Superman* or *Batman*. His early magazines specialized in horror or science fiction, but by the mid-sixties, he was well established, with titles that included *Creepy*, *Eerie*, and (with the Vietnam War heating up) *Blazing Combat*. By the time he and Eisner connected, Warren had worked with such notable editors and artists as Archie Goodwin, Harvey Kurtzman, Richard Corben, Alex Toth, Wally Wood, and Al Williamson. Frank Frazetta, who gained international acclaim for his work on the *Tarzan* and *Conan* books, created sexy, over-the-top covers for the Warren horror magazine *Vampirella*. As he'd hoped, Warren saw many of his publications stocked on magazine racks next to general interest periodicals, rather than languishing on drugstore spin racks or buried among the ever-increasing number of new comic book titles.

Warren had crossed paths with Eisner a decade before their *Spirit* deal, when one of his early publications, *Help!*, a humor magazine edited by Harvey Kurtzman and featuring reprints by some of the Golden Age artists whom Eisner admired, reprinted a *Spirit* story in its February 1962 issue. But like so many of Eisner's reprints between 1953 and 1972, it was a one-shot deal. W. B. DuBay, one of Warren's top editors, had once interviewed for a layout artist job at *P★S*, but he had lost the job to Mike Ploog. Now, coincidentally, he became Eisner's editor at Warren.

Warren took an approach similar to that of Denis Kitchen in publishing *The Spirit*. Issued bimonthly beginning in April 1974, Warren's *Spirit* magazine reprinted eight Spirit stories per issues, all but one entry in black and white. Eisner would have preferred to see the stories reprinted in chronological order, but the disorganized state of his files, along with Warren's wishes, nixed the idea. Warren had projected lofty sales figures for the magazine, but since comics sales were volatile in the early seventies and he had no way of predicting how long interest in *The Spirit* might last, Warren hoped to present the very best of the character in each issue. To grab the attention of potential readers browsing through titles in the stores, Warren insisted on colorful, action-packed covers radically different from the inventive splash pages Eisner had used to introduce each newspaper supplement episode. The original splash pages were included with each story in the magazine, as they had to be, but the Warren covers, like the Kitchen Sink covers, gave the magazine a more standard comic book feel.

Eisner appreciated the care devoted to each issue of the magazine, although, true to his perfectionist nature, he was never totally satisfied with the final product. He tinkered with the stories before submitting them to Warren, redoing some of the panels that had been so hastily drawn and inked in the time-cramped, deadline-driven days of weekly publication, or fixing original art that needed touching up. Some of the stories were partially rewritten. Looking back over the old work, Eisner saw flaws and problems that he couldn't correct the first time around and, as he admitted, he would have revised even more if he'd had the time. "Just think of how lucky I am," he told an interviewer. "How many people had the chance to do it again?"

His biggest issues with Warren were over the covers, which he would design and pencil and others would color. Eisner wasn't fond of the arrangement, which he felt was a slight to his talents, but where Eisner viewed the covers from an artistic perspective, Warren approached them from a marketing angle.

"Jim had a different taste in cover art; he didn't feel that watercolors had enough power to sell," Eisner said. "He needed something that was brighter and more attractive. My paints are a little bit more subtle or pastel."

As part of his agreement with Warren, Eisner kept the right of final cover approval. As a practice, he refrained from touching up or changing any of the colorings, tempting as it might have been, but there were occasions when Eisner complained to Warren or DuBay about the way an artist colored his work. One particular cover infuriated him. The colorist lit Eisner's fuse by using what Eisner later called "circus colors," prompting a stormy meeting with Warren and DuBay in Jim Warren's office. "Over my dead body!" Eisner shouted.

"The cover was pretty awful," he would remember, "and I put a stop to it very quickly."

The first issue of Warren's *Spirit* magazine sold 175,000 copies, rewarding Warren's faith in the reprint's potential and Eisner's decision to leave Kitchen Sink Press for a bigger distributor. This was, however, the high-water mark for the magazine. The numbers fell off beginning with the second issue. Collectors gobbled it up, but the overall sales figures suggested that the Spirit, as a character, was more of a novelty than a serious contender for newsstand supremacy. Kids wanted their costumed superheroes; older readers were more attracted to the oddball material being published in *Mad*, the underground comix, and, on college campuses, the *National Lampoon*. All told, Warren published sixteen issues of *The Spirit Magazine*, plus one summer special, between April 1974 and October 1976.

The magazine might not have been an overwhelming financial success, but it served a higher purpose in Eisner's career. With Warren, Eisner was now back in the entertainment comics business, working steadily in a field he had abandoned long ago, learning more about the purchasing habits of comics fans, and preparing himself, even if he was unaware of it at the time, for his entry into the ultimate in comics for adults—the graphic novel.

chapter eleven

A CONTRACT WITH GOD

*I had trouble re-reading what I had written. Being honest is like being
pregnant—there's no such thing as being "a little bit" honest.
Once you start, there's no turning back.*

Eisner wasn't finished with *The Spirit*. The sagging sales figures for the
Warren reissues might have discouraged less determined artists, but
after seeing enthusiastic responses from those who did pick up *The Spirit
Magazine*, Eisner concluded that there still might be more life for *The
Spirit* in the reprint format. He called Denis Kitchen and asked the Wis-
consin publisher for his opinion.

"Are you kidding, Will?" Kitchen responded. "It may not be for newsstands, but I'm confident there is an interest in it in the collectors' market.
I'd be happy to continue it."

Eisner and Kitchen had remained close, despite the awkwardness
of Eisner's transfer of *The Spirit* from Kitchen's publishing house to Jim
Warren's, and the two had stayed in touch over the years. In 1974, a few
months after Warren began publishing *The Spirit Magazine*, Kitchen had
attended Phil Seuling's New York convention, staying as a houseguest
with the Eisners in White Plains. Eisner was brimming with ideas for
ways he and Kitchen could combine forces in the business world, including a proposed new company (which he called the Small Publishers Distribution Company) that would market their work and a syndicate that
would trade comics to college papers in exchange for ad space, which the
syndicate would then sell to advertisers. Kitchen was both intrigued by
the offers and impressed by Eisner's business acumen.

"There is no doubt that Eisner is a tough businessman," Kitchen wrote
in his journal, "and I feel terribly naïve in comparison, but still I feel an

innate trust. Eisner reinforces this feeling by his candidness and apparent affection for me. At one point he said, 'When I see you, I see myself forty years ago.' I think 30 is more accurate in terms of pure age, but the comment nevertheless staggers me."

Several things became evident to Kitchen while he and Eisner talked about having Kitchen Sink Press pick up *The Spirit*. First, Eisner clearly enjoyed the rejuvenation of *The Spirit*, even if he felt strongly that he had nothing new to add to the feature, that he'd exhausted the character's potential during the feature's newspaper run.

"If I devoted myself totally to new stories there would be almost no time left for other new projects," he told Denis Kitchen. "Besides, I could never fill a 64 page bimonthly without full-time working under a schedule I abandoned long ago. Then there is the consideration of the audience. Composed as it is of ½ collector fans, old timers and new readers I wonder what the reader reaction would be when they have the opportunity to compare the Will Eisner of 1940–1950 to today's Eisner."

Kitchen also realized that after spending two decades away from the comic book scene, Eisner was genuinely surprised by the potential he saw in the underground comix and the way the new artists wrote about compelling topics for older readers. Finally, he had new ideas that he wanted to pursue, and he needed an entrée—a publisher willing to let him explore these ideas on a regular basis. *The Spirit Magazine* could be a combination of reprints and new material.

Kitchen was all for it. Since the magazine had been numbered under Warren Publishing, he decided that for the sake of collectors, he would pick up where Warren left off, meaning that rather than start with #1, the first Kitchen Sink Press issue of the magazine would begin at #17. He would publish the magazine on a quarterly basis, and if Eisner had new material that he wanted to present, he'd take whatever he had to offer. The magazine's cover would be a team effort, with Eisner providing the pencil sketch and Kitchen Sink doing the rest.

"I would expect you to provide a tight pencil drawing of a wraparound cover design for each book we publish," Kitchen told Eisner. "I will absorb the cost of inking and coloring the covers. I have in mind Peter Poplaski . . . and have the utmost satisfaction that Pete can do a superb job. He has an uncanny ability to mimic styles. And if you had any reservations, I would submit inked stats for your approval."

If anything bothered Kitchen about the arrangement, it was the selection process for the *Spirit* reprints. The Warren magazine had published the very best of the *Spirit* stories, and Eisner feared that he had only "rather lightweight" stories to offer Kitchen, especially if Kitchen published the magazine on a bimonthly basis, which was his early projection. Kitchen had never seen Eisner's archives, and he had no idea what might be available for reprinting, so every shipment from Eisner became a new adventure—and not always for the better.

"It was a hodgepodge," Kitchen said of the selections sent to his Wisconsin-based offices from Eisner's office in New York. "He had his brother, Pete, working for him, and Pete would pick the stories. Sometimes he would break up stories that were two or three parts. It was frustrating. We started to get fan complaints, and Will confessed that he really didn't have that much memory of which stories belonged together and should have been reprinted together."

That was the downside. On the positive side, the publication's magazine-sized format, similar to the Warren format, meant larger panels that accentuated the exquisite artwork and made the lettering that much easier to read. The splash pages, always a high point in any given installment, were all the more impressive, especially on the creamy white paper that Kitchen used in his magazine—a stark contrast to the less expensive paper used by Warren. *The Spirit* had never looked so good.

As promised, Eisner delivered a variety of non-*Spirit* material to flesh out each issue. He submitted reprints of *Lady Luck*, the feature that had appeared in the *Spirit* Sunday comic book, as well as reprints of Jules Feiffer's *Clifford*, a clever, sardonic comic featuring precocious kids that pre-dated Charles Schulz's *Peanuts*. *Clifford*, like *Lady Luck* and Bob Powell's *Mr. Mystic*, had been part of the Sunday comic book. In future years, Eisner would broaden the magazine's scope by serializing his graphic novels, writing a series of instructional pieces on sequential art, and conducting workshop interviews with leading comic book artists under the heading "Shop Talk." If there were any doubts about Eisner's return to the comics arena, they were settled in the magazine, which found him moving forward while offering up hefty selections from his past.

One might imagine that for a financially secure man hitting sixty, Eisner might have considered his commitment to *The Spirit Magazine* more than enough work to keep him occupied. But he was only getting started. With obligations to American Visuals and *P*S* magazine no longer part of his daily routine, Eisner was free to pursue projects that he might otherwise have had to put aside. He liked the idea of publishing a book of prose, and with the Spirit back in circulation, he used the character's newfound popularity to knock off *The Spirit's Casebook of True Haunted Houses and Ghosts*, a book of paranormal tales narrated by the Spirit, lavishly illustrated, and published by Eisner's newly created company, Poorhouse Press.

The press was another of Eisner's innovations with business roots dating back to his days in the old comic book studios. He wasn't interested in publishing his non-comics work in the traditional way, which amounted to a loss of creative and financial control. Rather than going through the usual submission and production processes, Eisner could approach a publisher with a finished book, written and illustrated and laid out the way he wanted to see it in print, and upon accepting the project under consideration, the publisher would print and distribute the book, giving Eisner a better cut of the profits than the standard royalty rates. The publishing house imprint also enabled Eisner to market his books wherever he chose, he would no longer be tied down to a particular house.

According to Ann Eisner, the company's name was a humorous reference to the uncertainty and risks of the publishing business. "They had to make up a name for it," she said of the publishing imprint, "and Will said, 'Well, this is the best way I know of going to the poorhouse,' so he decided to call it Poorhouse Press."

Eisner, shown here in his Manhattan office, took great pride in his business acumen, often joking that he kept one foot at the drawing table and one foot under his desk. His skills in negotiating contracts kept him from experiencing the kind of money and ownership troubles that plagued most of the early comics artists. (Courtesy of Denis Kitchen)

All joking aside, Poorhouse Press was a safe enterprise. Between 1974 and 1985, Eisner cranked out every type of novelty book imaginable—more than twenty all told, most published by Poorhouse Press, with an occasional offering to another house, such as Baronet Press, Scholastic Books, or Bantam—bearing such titles as *Gleeful Guide to Living with Astrology*, *Gleeful Guide to Communicating with Plants to Help Them Grow*, *Gleeful Guide to Occult Cookery*, and *How to Avoid Death & Taxes, and Live Forever*. There were also two instructional books (*Comics and Sequential Art* and *Graphic Storytelling and Visual Narrative*), joke books, and even an illustrated bartender's guide and *Robert's Rules of Order*. The *Spirit Coloring Book* gave young artists the chance to provide the color to some of the comic's best-known splash pages. Eisner employed assistants and co-writers on many of the projects and treated the books, if not their subjects, seriously, requiring the same quality that he demanded in his other, more ambitious work. But he never regarded them as anything other than a means to make money.

Denis Kitchen recalled a time, not long after he'd begun reprinting *The Spirit* in magazine format, when he was chiding Eisner for his Poorhouse Press and Scholastic Books projects. "I said to him, 'Will, what are you doing that stuff for? Fans don't want to see this stuff.' He picked up one of those paperbacks that I thought was schlocky, and said, 'This sold forty thousand copies. This made my mother very happy.' Then he picked up *A Contract with God* and said, 'This made my father very happy.' He never let one prevail. Had he been strictly business, he never would have created the stuff he's justly famous for, but you could argue that had he just been focused on the art, he wouldn't have had the success, because it was the business side of him that negotiated the much better deals."

Eisner wasn't speaking literally when he held up his books and spoke of his parents' reactions to them. Neither, in fact, had lived to see him reach his peak in international acclaim. Fannie Eisner died in 1964 at age seventy-two, long before the birth of Poorhouse Press and her son's big push in commercial publishing, at a time when he was still working at *P*S* magazine and going through the ups and down of American Visuals. Sam Eisner, a dreamer until the end, passed away in 1968 at age eighty-two, a decade before the publication of *A Contract with God* and the ensuing praise of his son's graphic novels. Sam never abandoned his passion for art and was painting landscapes, some on a very large scale, as though he were trying to express the breadth of the dreams he'd never given up well into his old age.

★ ★ ★

A much bigger—and more time-consuming—occupation materialized from an unexpected source: the School of Visual Arts, a Manhattan-based facility specializing in training students in fine art, commercial art, photography, and filmmaking. The school had discontinued its courses in comics art until a couple of students requested that such courses be offered again. Will Eisner and Harvey Kurtzman were the first two artists recommended for teaching positions.

"I always read that if you wanted to be a cartoonist, go to the School of Visual Arts," recalled Batton Lash, a School of Visual Arts alumnus who went on to a successful career in comics. "Once I got there, I realized they had dropped their cartooning classes. I had met a lot of other like-minded students who went to the school for the same reason I did. We talked to Tom Gill, the artist for *The Lone Ranger*, who was head of the alumni department, and he went to the president of the school and proposed that they reinstate the cartooning classes. The school decided to start them again, and they asked Harvey Kurtzman and Will Eisner if they'd like to teach, and both of them said yes. It was a very exciting time."

Eisner loved the idea of teaching a class. He'd given many young artists their starts, of course, and he'd taught a brief course at Sheridan College in Ontario in 1974. He'd enjoyed the experience. He and the class had created a new *Spirit* adventure entitled "The Invader," and he'd found that he liked sharing tips, business advice, artistic shortcuts, and ideas with aspiring cartoonists. He didn't appreciate the fact that so many putative comics artists were interested only in learning how to draw superheroes in order to land jobs with DC or Marvel, but he could also remember a time, back in his youth, when he was creating similar characters to order for Busy Arnold and others.

He set up his class at the School of Visual Arts similar to the way he'd taught at Sheridan College. The room was arranged like one of his old shops, with rows of drawing desks facing his desk in the front. Huge windows looking out over Twenty-third Street gave the room lots of natural light. Eisner would lecture or, on occasion, bring in a guest speaker. He called his class "Sequential Art," but as he'd quip in interviews, no one seemed to know what that meant. He liked to differentiate between "comics," which had an entertainment connotation, and "sequential art," which included other types of art, such as the work he was doing for *P★S* and American Visuals. The officials at the school found it confusing. "In the catalogue they say, 'Mr. Eisner is teaching sequential art,' and then, in parentheses, 'See comics,'" Eisner quipped.

In preparing his syllabus, Eisner found himself in the unusual position of considering matters that for more than three decades had been coming to him instinctively.

"I had been dealing with a medium more demanding of diverse skills and intellect than I or my contemporaries fully appreciated," he wrote in *Comics and Sequential Art*, an instructional book based on his lectures, published by Poorhouse Press in 1985.

> Traditionally, most practitioners with whom I worked and talked produced their art viscerally. Few ever had the time or the inclination to diagnose the form itself. In the main they were content to concentrate on the development of their draftsmanship and their perception of the audience and the demands of the marketplace.

Trying to corral a lifetime's experiences into a class that met one day a week for three hours involved no small amount of planning, and the class was constantly evolving during Eisner's 1974–1993 involvement with the school, to such an extent that he wrote three textbooks—*Comics and Sequential Art* (1985), *Graphic Storytelling and Visual Narrative* (1996), and *Expressive Anatomy* (published posthumously in 2008)—as a result of the experience. It wasn't enough just to cover such topics as story breakdowns, panel construction, dialogue, narrative, and point of view in the class; one could understand all there was to know about the art of the comic book and never see his or her work published. Eisner believed that he had an obligation to share his knowledge about the *business* of comics and how it was as important for artists never to compromise the ownership of their work as it was to be notable.

His students would remember him as a supportive but no-nonsense teacher, a guy who wore a jacket and tie at a time when T-shirts, torn blue jeans, and punk hairstyles were in vogue among many of his students. Award-winning filmmaker John Dilworth, who attended the School of Visual Arts from 1982 to 1985, characterized the students as "paint-splattered torn jeans and sneakers, tee, oversize black portfolio, smokes, dirty fingers, swaggering pride, diamond ambition, and arrogant willfulness immune to objectivity and criticism." Eisner's teaching style, he said, was "one of amusement . . .

"He appeared to be amused by the students and the work they presented to him," Dilworth said. "He wouldn't approach the students. The students would present their studies to him for criticism. He was always chuckling. He rarely expressed dramatic comments. He was a gentleman.

The studies were 'corrected' with tissue paper. The results were immediate. As I reflect, Eisner may have contributed to my belief that comparisons make the best education. Eisner would simply redraw the assignment in front of you. What made the critique so effective was how fair he was in complimenting the good or promising qualities."

Eisner reminded Batton Lash of someone "sort of like a shop teacher. He had a good rapport with the class, but everyone in that class knew who was in charge. He wasn't going to put up with any nonsense, and I think that came from his years of running a shop."

Eisner's style, his former students all agreed, contrasted strongly with the teaching style of Harvey Kurtzman, whose class was as popular as Eisner's. Loose and easygoing, Kurtzman wanted his students to be his friends, to the point where he would invite some of them into his home. Students who had taken both artists' classes felt that Kurtzman let the more aggressive students walk all over him, whereas with Eisner there was no thought of disruption. On those occasions when someone did act out, Eisner didn't hesitate to throw the student out.

Eisner's own curiosity made him a different type of teacher. His class wasn't all shop talk and drawing, which pleased some of the students and irritated others.

"He was interested in everything, even though he was teaching a course about comics," Lash explained. "He always wanted to hear what was going on in the film department. If someone was taking a film class, he'd want to hear about it. He wanted to see a student's photography. He was always interested in what was going on."

The interest in film came naturally. Eisner had been influenced by movies as a young artist, and he was curious about what his students found interesting in the films they were seeing.

"One day, he said, 'Okay, put down your pens and pencils, we're going to screen this Chaplin movie,'" recalled David Mandel, a former student. "He screened the whole film, and afterwards he discussed it with the class. He related it to his own comic work."

The class objective, aside from the actual learning process, was to produce a comic book called *The Gallery*, to be published at the end of the semester. The project, Eisner believed, not only gave students a taste of the mechanizations of assembling a comic book, it also taught them important elements of business.

John Walker, a native New Yorker who attended the School of Visual Arts and wound up running a successful advertising agency in Connecticut, remembered the class as being much more than picking up a pencil or pen and creating art.

"He taught us a lot of fundamentals of business," Walker said. "He'd say to us, 'All right, how are we going to get this thing printed?' We'd say, 'Well, you know, the school must have some money.' He'd say, "No, if you guys want to showcase your artwork, get out there and see if the local pizzeria will take an ad.' I was taking a course in advertising, and he'd say, 'Johnny Walker, you're a salesman. Get out there and find a local bar that might take an ad in *The Gallery*. Sell space. That's how we're going to pay for printing.'"

A large portion of each meeting was devoted to looking at the students' work for the proposed comic book, and Eisner could be a tough task-master when a student disappointed him with inferior work—or, worse yet, a missed assignment.

"If you screwed up a deadline, he would chew you out," Walker recalled. "He'd say, 'You let yourself down and you let the class down. What do you have to say for yourself?' That kind of stuff. There were kids who didn't care, and they would know that this guy was going to be a drill sergeant and they would remove themselves from the class. He was a tough guy. He grew up in the Bronx and took no crap from anyone. He had that sort of steely gaze. It was his way of saying, 'You're letting me down, but you're letting yourself down, too.' It was a team effort, with give and take, and that's how he ran the class."

Teaching at the School of Visual Arts and seeing the creativity in student work inspired Eisner more than he could have predicted, stoking the fires of a decision that had been long in arriving. Eisner had never wavered in his belief in the potential of using comics to make a serious statement. Seeing the work published in the underground comix had strengthened this belief, but Eisner still lacked the motivation to pursue the ideas in his head until he saw some of the potential realized in his students' work.

"In the process of teaching, you get to test your own concepts," he explained in an interview with *Heavy Metal* magazine. "You look at the professional world with a different perspective. I began to discover that there were some things to do that hadn't yet been done in the world of comics."

Eisner had considered some of these other possibilities, but his obligations to other projects demanded that he relegate them to an ever-expanding file of future projects. He'd had a family to support and the youthful confidence to believe that there would always be time to accomplish whatever he wished. Now, with the endorsement of his wife, who encouraged him to pursue whatever he wanted to in comics, he concluded, "If I don't do it now, I ain't ever going to do it."

The "it," more specifically, was a lengthy, cohesive work exploring themes and topics that might appeal to older readers—perhaps readers in their thirties, forties, or maybe even older than that—readers who might have grown up reading *The Spirit*, readers no longer attracted to superhero adventures but still interested in comics.

Eisner was still haunted by his daughter's death, by the unspeakable sadness and anger he'd felt when he'd watched helplessly as Alice succumbed to leukemia. At the heart of his rage were questions and issues that he'd never thought of exploring in his work, all focusing on an individual's relationship to God. By his own admission, Eisner was not a religious man. He had been brought up to believe in a deity, but life had left him an agnostic grasping for faith. Alice's death had embittered him, but it had also deepened some of his reflections on the idea of a personal God. If such an all-powerful, all-knowing being existed, where was He when Alice became ill? Why had He let her suffer and die when she was so young? Religious leaders had preached that the virtuous were rewarded, that they had a *contract* with God that promised good things to those living an honorable life. Yes, human beings violated the contract from time to time—they were human, after all—but an omnipotent God had to be held to a higher standard. Alice's death had been a violation of a contract, a type of betrayal for which there could be no answer.

Eisner had pondered these issues since his daughter's death, and though years would pass before he was able to publicly admit that his long graphic story "A Contract with God" had emerged directly from those horrible times in his life, his tale about Frimme Hersh, a good man devastated by the loss of his adopted daughter, was as personal as anything he had published in four decades of comics writing.

"The creation of this story was an exercise in personal agony," he wrote in the preface to *The Contract with God Trilogy*, a grouping of three Eisner books set in a fictitious tenement building at 55 Dropsie Avenue in the Bronx and published in 2006, nearly four decades after Alice Eisner's death.

My grief was still raw. My heart still bled. In fact, I could not even then bring myself to discuss the loss. I made Frimme Hersh's daughter an "adopted child." But his anguish was mine. His argument with God was also mine. I exorcised my rage at a deity that I believed violated my faith and deprived my lovely 16-year-old child of her life at the very flowering of it.

Eisner set the tone for his story in its opening pages, picturing Hersh, a single, middle-aged man, stooped over in grief and walking through torrential rain. He is returning home from his daughter's funeral. Eisner had always used rain—Harvey Kurtzman dubbed it "Eisenshpritz"—to establish mood and a sense of reality to his art, from *The Spirit* to his work in *P*S* magazine; but the sheer weight of Nature's own grief, gathering in pools on the street, rushing down the stairs of the stoop leading to the tenement building, and forming watery footprints in the hallway inside, matches Hersh's sense of overwhelming loss. When Hersh pulls off his shoes and sits on a tiny stool near the window of his apartment, his head buried in his hands and a single candle burning on a table nearby, he almost disappears into himself. His despair is palpable. The story immediately flashes back to the days of Frimme Hersh's youth in Russia before Hersh's immigration to the United States, to accounts of his many acts of kindness that led others to believe that he was truly blessed, of his literally setting his contract with God in stone, and of his finding a baby girl abandoned on his doorstep—a girl he takes in and treats as his own. He believes, from his religious background and training, that he will be rewarded for living an exemplary life. And now this . . .

Emotionally hardened, Hersh abandons his faith and pursues monetary wealth. He begins his quest by purchasing a tenement building with money he's embezzled from his synagogue, and he eventually amasses a small fortune in real estate, making him a powerful and respected man. But he cannot escape the man he once was—a moral man capable of good deeds. He needs another chance, another contract, and to obtain it he makes amends, returning the stolen money and vowing to lead a good life. Hersh's story ends cynically when, after setting his life back in order and planning a future that might even include another daughter, he suffers a fatal heart attack.

Eisner wisely chose to set his story in Depression-era Bronx, giving it a feeling of life preserved in amber. The art is drastically different from Eisner's earlier comic book work, with open, borderless panels, strong lines that give an edgy feeling to the characters, and no washes to soften the backgrounds. The world of Dropsie Avenue is stark and relentless.

Page from the title story in *A Contract with God*.
(Courtesy of Will Eisner Studios, Inc.)

"In the telling of these stories, I tried to adhere to a rule of realism, which requires that caricature or exaggeration accept the limitations of actuality," he wrote in the preface to the original volume of *A Contract with God*.

To accomplish a sense of dimension, I set aside two basic working constrictions that so often inhibit the medium—space and format. Accordingly, each story was written without regard to space and each was allowed to develop in format from itself; that is, to evolve from the narration. The normal frames (or panels) associated with sequential (comic book) art are allowed to take on their integrity. For example, in many cases an entire page is set out as a panel. The text and the balloons are interlocked with the art. I see all these as threads of a simple fabric, and exploit them as a language. If I have been successful at this, there will be no interruption in the flow of narrative because the picture and the text are so totally dependent on each other as to be inseparable for even a moment.

Arriving at these decisions was largely a matter of trial and error, of writing and rewriting, drawing and redrawing. The entire process, from first draft to the finished book, took two years, and every step was a process of discovery. In his initial rough draft, he used his daughter's name rather than Rachele, as it appeared in the finished book, for the name of Hersh's daughter. He tried drawing the story in color, with overlays and washes, before deciding that sepia tones—the tones of dreams and memories—served his narrative better. Panels were enlarged and shrunk until he was satisfied with the way they looked on the page. He debated about how explicit he could be with some of the book's sex scenes, deciding, at least in the case of "The Street Singer," to combine a couple of scenes into one. Since he had no deadlines, he was free to experiment and piece together the stories to his liking.

Three stories followed "A Contract with God" in the book, all set in the same tenement building, all adhering to Eisner's theme of survival in the big city. "The Street Singer" is the account of a man who sings in alleyways and backyards for loose change, only to be seduced by an aging diva hoping to use him to reclaim some of her own lost youth. "The Super," a grim and ultimately violent tale of the apartment building's superintendent and the power struggles he faces every day, includes a shocking look at the way he mishandles a pubescent girl who offers him "favors" in exchange for money, only to blackmail him later. "Cookalein" (the title coming from the Yiddish for "cook alone") is a coming-of-age story about a teenage boy's initial brushes with sex and its powers at a summer retreat in the Catskills. In his past work, Eisner had hidden behind his characters, with any hints of autobiography so thoroughly buried in the story that a reader would never have noticed them. The four interlocking pieces that make up *A Contract with God* were so gritty and realistic that a reader couldn't help but wonder about their origins. In "Cookalein," the main character was even named "Willie," Eisner's boyhood nickname, and his parents and brother were named Sam, Fannie, and Petey, making "Cookalein" his most openly autobiographical work to date.

With the exception of "A Contract with God," which found Eisner silent for decades about the personal origins of the story, Eisner never attempted to conceal the autobiographical nature of these new graphic vignettes. These were fragments of his experiences of growing up in the tenements, where people settled for moments of contentment in a place where happiness was dreamt, not lived.

"Every one of the people in those stories is either me or someone I knew, or parts of them and me," he told Cat Yronwode in an interview for the *Comics Journal*. "How can you not be autobiographical if you're writing about something that you've seen?"

He was more specific in his preface to *The Contract with God Trilogy*.

"Cookalein," he wrote, was "a combination of invention and recall . . . an honest account of my coming of age." "The Super" was "a story built around the mysterious but threatening custodian of the Bronx apartment house where I lived as a young boy." "The Street Singer" existed vividly in Eisner's memory, as an out-of-work scrounge who survived by singing, "in a wine-soaked voice, popular songs or off-key operatic arias," with the hope that someone listening might toss down a penny, a nickel, or, if the singer was extremely lucky, a dime. Eisner remembered throwing down a few coins himself. "With this book about tenement life," he wrote, "I was able to immortalize his story."

Eisner wrote and illustrated the stories in *A Contract with God* with the understanding that when the time came, he was going to have great difficulty in finding a publisher for his book. Denis Kitchen was willing to publish it as part of the Kitchen Sink Press list, but Eisner turned down the offer. These were serious stories, and Eisner wanted them to be issued by what he called "a Park Avenue publisher."

"No offense, Denis, but I don't want this work to be from a publisher on 2 Swamp Road," he told Kitchen, referring to the Wisconsin address of Kitchen Sink Press.

Problem was, no one in New York was interested. This type of book was new, and publishers found it difficult to get excited about something they couldn't fit into a convenient slot. They certainly weren't at all enthusiastic about putting out another comic book, regardless of its merits, as Eisner discovered when he called Oscar Dystel, president of Bantam Books, and told him about his book. Eisner knew Dystel and knew that Dystel admired his work on *The Spirit*. Eisner also knew that he'd be rejected outright if he told him that he had a comic book for sale.

"I looked at it and realized that if I said, 'A comic book,' he would hang up," Eisner recalled. "He was a very busy guy, and this was a top-level publishing house."

"It's a graphic novel," he told Dystel.

"Oh, that's very interesting," Dystel replied. "Bring it up here."

Eisner ran it up to the Bantam offices, but Dystel took one look at the manuscript and shook his head.

"You know, this is still a comic," he declared, peering over the top of his glasses at Eisner. "We don't publish this kind of stuff. Go find a smaller publisher."

Eisner tried unsuccessfully to find a major publishing house for the book he was calling *The Tenement*. No one shared his enthusiasm for the potential of this new type of work. Eisner finally found a small New York press, Baronet Books, willing to put out the book, but even then the going was rough. Baronet was in dire financial straits, and Eisner wound up loaning the publisher money to stay afloat.

The book's title became a marketing decision. Believing that no one outside of New York City would know what a tenement was, Eisner's editor suggested that the book be given the title of its longest story—or, more fully, *A Contract with God and Other Tenement Stories*—and the book was marketed as "a graphic novel" even though it was a collection of stories and not a novel.

Eisner is often credited with inventing the term *graphic novel*, but in reality, he was neither the inventor of the term nor the first to publish one.

"I thought I had invented the term," Eisner admitted, "but I discovered later that some guy thought about it a few years before I used the term. He had never used it successfully and had never intended it the way I did, which was to develop what I believe was viable literature in this medium."

In years to come, when book-length works of sequential art expanded in scope to include biography, memoir, history, and other types of nonfiction, the term *graphic novel* would be dismissed by comics artists and writers, who complained that it limited the understanding of their work to a convenient label. Eisner himself, who experimented with the form over the next three decades, called it a "limited term," although his preferred "graphic literature" or "graphic story" came across sounding a little too academic for bookstore owners and readers alike, just as the term *sequential art* would rub some readers the wrong way. Eisner would never like it, but Oscar Dystel probably spoke for a majority of editors and readers when he told Eisner that the graphic novel, regardless of the new terminology, was ultimately a comic book.

Comics scholars, like their counterparts in prose fiction, will always haggle over the definitions, composition, inner workings, and merits of the works spilling off bookstore and library shelves. If nothing else, it gives them something to do—topics for lectures, panel discussions at conventions, books and magazine articles, and late night barroom debates. Literature has rigid schools of criticism that go in and out of vogue, as well as intellectuals and self-appointed arbiters of taste who are all too pleased to announce, with great fanfare, the writers and books one simply *has* to read. When *A Contract with God* came along, comics were too young for such a history, but they were working on it. The graphic novel gave critics, historians, and social observers a virgin field to explore, chart, and plow.

First came the issue of definition. The term *graphic novel* was unheard of when Eisner published *A Contract with God* in 1978, so defining it was open to debate. Was it held to a prose novel's standards? Was it, as Art Spiegelman once said, a big comic book that needed a bookmark? Storytelling and sequential art went back a long way, at least to the days of ancient Egypt, when stories were told in hieroglyphics. For all anyone knew, sequential art dated back to the cave drawings. No one argued that these early literary permutations should be considered novels, graphic or otherwise. Eisner had tossed out the term without giving it a lot of thought and attached it to a collection of longish stories as a means of announcing that this was serious work (as opposed to the superhero stuff on the comics market), but the immediate effect was confusion.

Robert C. Harvey, a comics scholar with a doctorate in English and a sideline career as a freelance cartoonist, joined a number of historians when he traced the modern graphic novel back to as early as 1827, when Swiss artist Rodolphe Töpffer combined words and pictures in his satirical tales. In his 1996 book, *The Art of the Comic Book: An Aesthetic History*, Harvey repeated one of Töpffer's statements about his work, which seemed to offer one definition of the graphic novel:

> The drawings without their text would have only a vague meaning; the text, without the drawings, would have no meaning at all. The combination of the two makes a kind of novel.

Harvey accepted this only to a point. Since Töpffer pre-dated the comic strip, he had nothing to which he could compare his work. Later comic strip artists such as C. W. Kahles (*Hairbreadth Harry*) and Alex Raymond (*Flash Gordon, Prince Valiant*) used a similar style of illustration with text running at the bottom of the panel, but to Harvey, these works weren't terribly dissimilar to illustrated children's stories, and they weren't necessarily comics, at least in the familiar sense. Comics, Harvey argued, gained their distinctive look and style by using dialogue balloons and in the way they broke down narrative into panels that gave the story action and pacing.

> Whatever the graphic novel is to be [or is], it seems to me that it must incorporate these two essential aspects of comics art if it is to be of the same species. The graphic novel may have other characteristics as well, but speech balloons and narrative breakdown seem to be vital ingredients: concurrence and action, and timing. Without these traits, the graphic novel will simply be something else—another kind of graphic story, surely, but not of the same order as the comics.

This explained some of the technical aspects of the art, but it still did not address the elements of story. What distinguished the graphic novel from a comic-book-length story? Or even a comic strip story that continued from day to day, week to week, until a story had been told?

Stephen Weiner, author of *Faster Than a Speeding Bullet: The Rise of the Graphic Novel* and coauthor of *The Will Eisner Companion*, conceded the difficulty of defining the graphic novel, especially as it evolved over the years, with the appearance of graphic memoirs, graphic nonfiction, graphic adaptations, graphic novellas, and graphic story collections. For the sake of simplicity, he defined the graphic novel in a way that covered all of these books under a single umbrella.

> Graphic novels, as I define them, are book-length comic books that are meant to be read as one story. This broad term includes collections of stories in genres such as mystery, superhero, or supernatural that are meant to be read apart from their corresponding ongoing comic book storyline.

Michael T. Gilbert, a comics writer and historian, took exception to the belief that Eisner was the creator of first graphic novel, a distinction he was willing to give Arnold Drake, coauthor of *It Rhymes with Lust*, which appeared in 1950. Gilbert agreed, however, that the issue was one of definition.

"Eisner is credited with the modern graphic novel," Gilbert said, "but it depends on how you define *modern*. It it postwar? Is it eighties? I could make the argument that any of the *Classics Illustrated* comics were graphic novels, by any reasonable definition. *A Contract with God* is all related short stories, with similar themes, but that doesn't make it a graphic novel, and it certainly doesn't make it the first graphic novel."

The essays, books, articles, arguments, and discussions at comics conventions invariably focused on the contents of the graphic novel when trying to define it, trace its history, and assign Eisner a place in contributing to its existence. N. C. Christopher Couch, a former editor in chief at Kitchen Sink Press, dealt with Eisner on a practical level, but his back round as a professor at the University of Massachusetts and his work as coauthor of *The Will Eisner Companion* placed him in the position of seeing both sides of Eisner, the artist and businessman, in relation to his work as a graphic novelist. Couch was not prone to quibbling over who came first—even though his editor at DC Comics insisted that the subtitle to his *Will Eisner Companion* include the phrase "Father of the Graphic Novel"—and he, as much as any of his colleagues, understood the difficulties of defining the form attributed to Eisner. In Couch's opinion, Eisner's familiarity with the mechanics of publishing, and his belief in the necessity of changing the physical look of his graphic novel, was a major contribution to the form.

Eisner was one of the few people in comics who had actually worked in trade publishing. At American Visuals, Eisner had produced hardcover books for the educational market on several topics, including one on space and rocketry. He had played a variety of roles, as coauthor, designer, art director, doing what is now called packaging. Eisner understood book marketing, binding, illustration, trim size and shelving by category. No one else in comics at that time had the same direct experience of the book market and editorial work that Eisner did. Someone else, editors and designers at the trade houses who licensed the publication from Marvel, packaged Stan Lee's books. Underground anthologies barely penetrated the bookstore market, finding shelf space in alternative book stores and comic shops. Eisner's knowledge formed part of the background for the creation of *A Contract with God*.

Using this knowledge of publishing, Eisner created a book that didn't look like a comic book. It was the size of a trade paperback, had lettering on its spine, boasted a cover design that didn't scream "children's book" to bookstore owners and librarians, and provided an interior that eschewed the panel-by-panel artistry typical of comic books. Eisner had always been a voracious reader, and besides his knowledge of what constituted serious literature, he knew what a book should *look* like. "When Eisner turned to creating a novel in comics," Couch concluded, "he had both a publishing professional's understanding and inveterate reader's physical, tactile grasp of what a novel should be."

Newspapers and general interest magazines didn't review comic books of any type—not in 1978—so Eisner had his hands full trying to reach potential readers. The book received extensive advertising in *The Spirit Magazine*, which was to be expected, and comics journals and fanzines noted its publication. (In a lengthy review in the *Comics Journal*, reprinted as an introduction to later printings of *A Contract with God*, comics writer and editor Dennis O'Neil, evoking the literature of Bernard Malamud, Philip Roth, and Isaac Bashevis Singer, called *A Contract with God* "a near masterpiece.") Beyond that, publicity for the book was all word of mouth.

Bookstores had no idea how to display or stock *A Contract with God*, as Eisner determined shortly after its publication, when he took a call from Norman Goldfine, Baronet's publisher, who informed him that the Fifth Avenue Brentano's in Manhattan was stocking his book. Eisner was elated. Having a store like Brentano's carry *A Contract with God* seemed to underscore his claim that adults would be receptive to serious graphic novels. To avoid looking like an overeager author checking in on his book, Eisner waited two weeks before venturing to the store. After looking for the book and not finding it anywhere, he approached the store manager, identified himself as the author of *A Contract with God*, and asked how it was selling. The manager replied that the book had been prominently displayed for a couple of weeks, had sold well, but had to be relocated when the new James Michener novel arrived in the store.

"What did you do with mine?" Eisner wanted to know.

"Well," the store manager said, "I brought it inside and I put it in with religious books since it's about God, and this little lady came up to me and said, 'What's that book doing there? That's a cartoon book. It shouldn't be in with religious books.' So I took it out and I put it into the humor section where they have people like Stan Lee and so forth. And someone came to me and said, 'Hey, this isn't a funny book; there's nothing funny in this book. Why do you have it here?' I took it out of there, and I didn't know where to put it."

Eisner had anticipated this sort of problem. Bookstores, like publishers, liked the convenience and comfort of labels. Genre fiction was ideal, with such categories as science fiction and fantasy, romance, westerns, humor, and horror making books easy to classify; everything else could be stocked under the category of general fiction. *A Contract with God* defied categorization. It wasn't a collection of comic strips, which usually found a place near the back of the store, but it wasn't prose fiction, either.

"Where do you have it now?" Eisner asked the store manager.

"In a cardboard box in the cellar," the manager responded. "I don't know where to put the damn thing."

One of Will Eisner's favorite pieces of his own work was a single-panel drawing, a self-portrait with no caption or dialogue balloon. Eisner portrays himself, leaning casually against a crude, makeshift newsstand stocked with copies of his graphic novels. The stand is set up in the middle of nowhere. The land around him is hilly but barren. Three birds fly in a cloudless sky.

Eisner looks off into the distance.

On the horizon, far away, a cloud of dust is being raised by a throng of people heading in his direction.

Eisner could wait.

chapter twelve

OUTER SPACE, THE CITY— NO LIMITS

Think of me as a one-man band, walking down the street with a sign saying "Sequential Art," every once in a while looking around and there's somebody following me, but the line isn't too big at the moment.

Pleased with the results of *A Contract with God*, Eisner started another graphic novel, this one to be written and published in a radically different way. Beginning with the third Kitchen Sink issue of *The Spirit Magazine* in 1978, Eisner serialized *Life on Another Planet* (later published in book form as *Signal from Space*), which presented more drama and less humor than had been the trademark of *The Spirit*, with a larger cast of characters plopped down in a world that allowed Eisner the opportunity to comment on the human condition more than ever before. A year prior to the publication of the first installment of Eisner's story, *Star Wars*, George Lucas's space opera, had shattered box office records and jacked interest in science fiction and fantasy to a new level. But *Signal from Space* was light-years from *Star Wars*, more James Bond than Luke Skywalker, complete with a cold war, international espionage, murder and mayhem, exotic settings, crooked politicians and corporate officials, a Nixon-like ex-president named Dexter Milgate, an Idi Amin–like African dictator named Sidi Ami, treacherous female villains, and conflicted heroes. The feature, running in sixteen-page installments, appeared in eight consecutive issues of *The Spirit Magazine*, beginning in October 1978 and concluding in December 1980.

In this case, creating the story and art was the equivalent of working without a safety net. Eisner had begun the project with the idea of building a story about the repercussions roiling around the discovery of another form of life on a planet a mere ten years' travel distance from Earth. But whereas with *A Contract with God* he'd carefully plotted out the stories before penciling them, here Eisner was virtually improvising, with no real idea where he was taking this graphic novel. The first installment/ chapter opened with two scientists receiving a transmission from somewhere out in space, and from that point on Eisner just let his imagination take him wherever it chose.

"I'm gonna let it happen, just do it and let it happen," he told the *Comics Journal* shortly after the first installment's appearance in *The Spirit Magazine #19*. The uncertainty, Einser said, added to the excitement of creating a new story. "I don't know what the second chapter is going to be yet," he admitted, "but I'll do that very shortly."

Eisner's plans for presenting the continuing installments differed greatly from anything he'd done before. Rather than publish in the traditional comic book way, he and Denis Kitchen decided to experiment with a pull-out section that readers could remove from the magazine and cut and fold, creating a booklet in the process. The idea sounded good in theory, but Kitchen received complaints from distraught collectors who didn't want to tear apart their magazines.

"There has been a universal 'nay' vote from readers in response to the format of 'Life on Another Planet,'" Kitchen wrote Eisner. "Fans seem to like the story but resent having to clip their copy or reading in a helter-skelter manner."

Eisner was disappointed by the news, but he agreed to drop the insert idea. "In view of information relating to the consistently 'NAY' vote on the format for LIFE ON ANOTHER PLANET, I have to accept the reality that the insert idea just won't work," he wrote in response to Kitchen's letter. "Too bad . . . I guess I misjudged the attractiveness and practicality of this 'gimmick.'"

Kitchen later admitted to having reservations about the feasibility of the project. "I knew instinctively that my generation had this 'collector's gene,'" he said. "They didn't want to cut things up. They didn't want to turn the magazine sideways. But we had to test it to prove it. If it worked and we got a lot of people writing and saying, 'Hey, I really dig this,' we'd do more, and if they complained, we'd rethink it. We couldn't afford a real market survey."

Signal from Space posed problems that Eisner hadn't encountered with *A Contract with God.* He had mastered the short form of comics writing dating back to his earliest years in the business, and the longer pieces in *A Contract with God*, although more challenging, had involved his fleshing out the elliptical elements of comics writing. Pacing and exposition weren't major considerations. *Signal from Space* was not only significantly longer and more complex than anything he had ever attempted; since it was being published in installments, Eisner had to find subtle ways to keep readers connected to his graphic novel's characters and subplots from issue to issue of the magazine. Prose writers faced similar challenges when writing by installment, but they weren't trying to align image and text the way comics writers were, and the difference between a phrase (or even a paragraph) of prose and a comics panel was monumental. For the sake of clarity and pacing, Eisner generally preferred to limit a scene to a single page, but that didn't give him much wriggle room in each installment's sixteen pages, especially when one of them was a splash page. *Signal from Space* was full of the usual Eisner trademarks: innovative camera angles, lighting, and movement, with more dialogue than usual.

Fortunately for Eisner, he had ample input from a publisher and, for the first time in his career, an editor. The former, Denis Kitchen, was vastly experienced in comics; the latter, Dave Schreiner, was more heavily involved with the written word.

As a publisher, Kitchen was aware of the market, and he knew, as a fan and collector, what appealed to him personally. Kitchen Sink Press was a small operation, with a small staff and very limited funding, and as pleased as he was to be publishing Will Eisner, Kitchen was by no means in the position to absorb many losses. The graphic novel was unexplored territory, and Eisner and Kitchen were mapping out its terrain as they went along. Schreiner, a Wisconsin freelance editor and old friend of Kitchen's, possessed extensive knowledge in contemporary literature and was brought on board to act as a buffer between publisher and artist.

Kitchen and Schreiner went back a long way, to their days at the University of Wisconsin–Milwaukee, when both were contributing to the student newspaper, Kitchen as a cartoonist, Schreiner as the paper's sports editor. The two became close friends and, eventually, co-founders of the *Bugle-American* alternative newspaper. "You get to know a person pretty well when you work with him all night, week after week, pasting bits of paper on layout sheets," Schreiner wrote of Kitchen in *Kitchen Sink Press: The First 25 Years*, his history of Kitchen's publishing enterprise.

The demise of the *Bugle-American* hit Schreiner hard. He had been the driving force behind the paper, and he took the loss personally. For a longer time than he'd ever care to admit, he drifted aimlessly, working a string of menial jobs and drinking so heavily that he almost lost his life. The rehabilitation was slow and difficult, but once he was sober and

Artist and editor: Dave Schreiner worked with Eisner as an editor and advisor on all but his first and last books. Eisner looked for an editor who could be brutally honest with him, and Schreiner fit the bill. (Photo by Doreen Riley, courtesy of Lesleigh Luttrell)

rebuilding his life, he reconnected with Kitchen and began working at Kitchen Sink Press as an editor.

Taking the job with Kitchen Sink, he wrote in his history of the company, was "equal parts rewarding, frustrating, exciting, and boring." His editing of Eisner and others, he continued, was the source of his greatest satisfaction.

It gave me the opportunity to do some real editing; that is, trying to facilitate their work. Acting as a sounding board, working out problems, debating story points—that was all stimulating. Comics still offers that type of atmosphere to editors. In the book publishing world, it's all marketing; in comics, editors can still actually work with creators. And, if these editors aren't too stupid or egotistical, they can perhaps make that work better.

Kitchen and Schreiner treated Eisner's work very cautiously in the beginning. Eisner's credentials had been established before either of them was born. They felt fortunate just to be working with him, and they were reluctant to be too forceful in stating their opinions about his new work. Eisner, however, felt differently. He wanted direction, not patronizing from fanboys or sycophants.

"When I was reprinting *The Spirit*, I remained very respectful," Kitchen noted of his early working relationship with Eisner. "There was nothing to say about the stuff from that long ago, other than 'Wow! This is really great!' But right after *A Contract with God*, when I started publishing his graphic novels, he requested feedback. Will had a conversation with me on the phone one day. He said, 'I expect honest editorial feedback. You're not a good publisher if you aren't completely honest with me. Look at the work objectively. Tell me if you think I'm wrong. I demand objective feedback.' I remember turning to Dave after that conversation and saying, 'Will doesn't want us to pull our punches,' and Dave said, 'Good.' It went better than ever at that point, because it was like the gloves were off. Dave was very good at what he did, and Will recognized that early on. Dave was an editor's editor. It wasn't about his own ego; it was about making the work better."

"He often referred to the publishing operation as being no more than a conduit between the creator and the reader, and the work published during his tenure reflects that," said graphic novelist Jim Vance (*Kings in Disguise*), who succeeded Schreiner as editor in chief at Kitchen Sink Press after the company moved to Massachusetts and Schreiner decided to stay in Wisconsin. "Dave was soft-spoken and had a wit so dry you could cut yourself on it. He was utterly blunt when it came to discussing your work. If he thought you were painting yourself into a corner, he'd let you know in no uncertain terms, but there was never the sense that you were being bullied or insulted. On the job, he was a no-nonsense guy who had to deal with his share of flakes and prima donnas, and he was apparently unflappable no matter what was presented to him."

Not that Eisner went along with all—or even a majority—of Schreiner's or Kitchen's suggestions. According to Kitchen, Eisner would listen to his (or more often Schreiner's) suggestions, consider them, and make a decision. Much of this work was done through the mail, with Schreiner handling the bulk of the correspondence from the Kitchen Sink end. The exchanges were almost always cordial, but they could get a little chippy if Eisner felt that Kitchen or Schreiner didn't understand his position. Kitchen recalled one particular series of exchanges that occurred when he and Schreiner were pushing Eisner to expand an autobiographical vignette that eventually became *The Dreamer*, Eisner's third graphic novel. Eisner was satisfied with it at story length, similar to the pieces he'd published in *The Spirit Magazine* and, later, *Will Eisner's*

Quarterly, but Kitchen and Schreiner, captivated by Eisner's anecdotes from his earliest experiences in comics and believing that readers would respond in a similar way, asked for more. Eisner wasn't eager to comply. "He did it with great resistance," Kitchen allowed. "We got that one expanded from about sixteen pages to about fifty. We would have wanted it to be one hundred–plus pages, but he just wouldn't do it."

Eisner wanted his work to be judged as literature, and Schreiner held him to literary standards. Schreiner read Eisner's work as he would a novel, and he expected Eisner to honor the rules of the novel, from characterization to plotting, from point of view to pacing. The key to dealing with Eisner was to be straightforward but diplomatic. Eisner had a favorite expression—"Don't tell me how to do it, just tell me what's wrong"—and Schreiner would work off that.

Denis Kitchen would often overhear the telephone conversations between Schreiner and Eisner, and he was impressed with Schreiner's methods of critiquing Eisner's work. "Dave would say, 'I don't think this transition works,' or, 'This character isn't plausible,'" Kitchen explained. "He'd then say, 'You can take this in several directions, but here's what's wrong with it.' And Will would say, 'Oh, I got it. Okay. Here's what I'm going to do. What do you think?' And Dave would say, 'Well, you could take him in that direction, or you might throw the reader a curve and do this.' They would have these conversations, and Dave would follow them up with letters."

Over time, the two developed a very strong, trusting writer–editor relationship. Schreiner worked closely with Eisner on all of his longer graphic works, editing every one with the exception of *A Contract with God* and *The Plot*, Eisner's final book.

When Denis Kitchen initially set up arrangements to publish *The Spirit Magazine*, it was with the hope that Eisner would be contributing new material to complement the reprinted *Spirit* stories. He had more than six hundred *Spirit* episodes to choose from—enough to sustain the magazine for years to come—but he was convinced that, for as much as collectors might want to see old episodes of the old comic, they would also clamor for something other than reprints. Since new Spirit adventures were out of the question, Kitchen depended on Eisner to come up with other supplemental material for the magazine.

Eisner more than held up his end of the bargain. The twenty-five Kitchen Sink *Spirit Magazine* issues, presented quarterly over the six-year

stretch from 1977 to 1983, caught Eisner in one of his most creatively fer-
tile periods. His new material, besides each issue's wraparound cover and
the *Signal from Space* graphic novel entries, was astonishing in its range and
quality—enough to eventually make up his book *New York: The Big City*
and form the foundation for the instructional book *Comics and Sequential
Art*. Eisner's "Shop Talk," featuring his interviews with such comics leg-
ends as Gil Kane, Milton Caniff, Joe Simon, Jack Kirby, and Joe Kubert,
would also be gathered into a book. The centerpiece of *Spirit Magazine
#30* was a "jam," in which fifty comics artists contributed to a single new
Spirit story. It was reaching the point where the Spirit was fighting for
space in his own magazine.

The *Big City* project, years in the making, was particularly close to
Eisner's heart. Eisner had used New York City—renamed "Central City,"
to satisfy editors in newspapers across the country—as the setting for *The
Spirit*, and in interviews he spoke candidly about his passion for the city.
He could live in a suburban setting, as he did now, or he could move away
completely, as he would do in years to come when he and Ann moved to
Florida, but New York would always be home. Writers, he'd say, were
encouraged to write about what they knew best, and New York was
where he grew up, where he learned the rules of the neighborhood, where
he sold newspapers and opened his first studio. He'd seen countless dramas played out; he'd seen joy and despair. "I know it and understand it,"
he said. "The city is my area, and I want to talk about it."

"Just call me a Jewish Frank McCourt," he said on another occasion.
"I'm a city boy. I love New York. That's what I know and that's what I
write."

The project began in 1980, when Hollybrock Graphics published
a limited-edition, six-plate portfolio called *City: A Narrative Portfolio*.
Each plate focused on some element, good or bad, of city living and
was accompanied by a brief Eisner poem. The portfolio had been very
well received, including overseas in Europe. Eisner then began a book-
length follow-up combining black-and-white work with color chapter
lead-ins—a celebration of the city that had been his home for almost all
of his life.

In the early stages of its development, Eisner entitled his New York
book *The Big City Project*, and, as would be the case throughout his life,
he spoke very little about his work in progress, even to Denis Kitchen.
The book, he'd say, would be different from the usual perception of New
York City. Rather than present the city on a grand scale, as it was usually

depicted in the movies, Eisner preferred to portray New York through a "worm's-eye view" perspective—which, he explained, is how the city is seen by its inhabitants.

"We're used to seeing it from the skyscrapers, and generally with a symphony in blue playing in the background as the camera pans in across the city and you see the tops. But no one ever sees the city the way I see it—the way all of us who live in it [see it]—with the sewers, the fire hydrants, the stoops, the grills, the grates, the fire escapes. *That's* what the city people who live in the city see all day. That's the city."

Eisner, however, was not interested in producing realistic, picture-perfect renderings. He didn't use photographs, and any research he conducted for the project was accomplished during his walks through the city, when, for the sake of accuracy, he would make notes on such details as how many steps there were to the average apartment building's stoop. It was important, he told Dave Schreiner, that he rely on his memory rather than extensive research when sketching New York.

"Once you get too accurate in your art," he stated, "something gets lost. Artists in Europe tend to do accurate renderings of city scenes. It's brilliant and beautiful, but somehow or other, the art gets so strong and powerful that the mood is lost. To me, the important thing is mood. Ultra realistic art tends to draw attention to itself. That's exactly the point I want to avoid."

The vignettes in *New York: The Big City*, many only a single page in length, presented under such chapter headings as "Subways," "Windows," Stoops," and "Walls," offered the humor, irony, heartbreak, frustration, hope, and small victories often seen but overlooked in day-to-day city life, the images of people and events that rush by city dwellers too preoccupied in their own daily routines to realize that this is the fabric of urban life. Eisner thought of himself as a social reporter, and these vignettes, when originally published alongside Spirit stories in *The Spirit Magazine*, proved that for four decades Eisner could use environment as a critical element in his storytelling. The city, and the demands it placed on its inhabitants, changed and shaped fortunes in subtle yet all-important ways.

The different aspects of *New York: The Big City* never quite coalesced the way Eisner intended. After its serialization in *The Spirit Magazine*, the book was published by Kitchen Sink Press, in black and white only, without the originally planned color paintings; Kitchen Sink simply couldn't afford the additional expenses. Nevertheless, Eisner was pleased with the results. New York, as he'd always known, was a great environment to use in graphic works, and *The Big City*, as it turned out, was only the beginning of his explorations of it.

As 1982 drew to a close, Eisner and Denis Kitchen both realized that *The Spirit Magazine* had run its course, at least in its current format. Eisner was set to begin yet another major project, an ambitious graphic novel set in Depression-era New York, and this, along with his "Shop Talk" interviews, the occasional instructional pieces, and other work, amounted to more non-*Spirit* material than the magazine could possibly manage. As it was, *Spirit* fans were complaining that the new material was inappropriate for the magazine. After discussing their options, Eisner and Kitchen decided to suspend publication of *The Spirit Magazine* and create two separate publications, one a monthly comic book devoted exclusively to *Spirit* reprints and another a magazine entitled *Will Eisner's Quarterly*, dedicated to the publication of Eisner's new work. The comic book would present every post–World War II *Spirit* episode in chronological order.

The comic book was made possible largely through the efforts of Cat Yronwode (pronounced Ironwood), a fan and scholar who knew more about *The Spirit* than anyone other than Eisner himself. Eisner had hired Yronwode to sort through and catalog his work, and her "Spirit Checklist," a detailed, comprehensive list of every *Spirit* appearance, in newspaper and reprint, ran in three consecutive issues of *The Spirit Magazine* and became the final word on the feature's history. Yronwode spent weeks at the Eisners' home, poring over an extensive archives that, although carefully preserved, had no sense of organization. "Will Eisner never threw anything away," she recalled. "He lost a lot of things, and I went up there and I found things that he didn't know he had."

Strong-willed and intelligent, Yronwode was in parts an academician and a barefoot hippie, a solid writer and editor with an interest in esoterica, an obsessive comics historian, and an archivist with an instinctive feel for the importance of the tiniest scrap of prose or art. Born Catherine Manfredi, Yronwode was the daughter of a special collections librarian at UCLA, and she appears to have inherited his meticulous eye for detail and organization. At the time of her initial meeting with Will Eisner, she was living in a cabin in the Ozarks and freelance writing for a meager living. She'd hoped Eisner might have back issues of *The Spirit* newspaper sections to fill the holes in a friend's collection, and she reasoned that the best way to approach him would be through an interview, where she could ask him face-to-face about the issues. Armed with an interview assignment for the *Comics Journal*, she set out for New York. Eisner not only gave her the interview, which ran in two parts in consecutive issues of the magazine, he saw how broke she was and also gave her the job of arranging and cataloging his archives as a means of helping her earn some money. Thus began an association that lasted nearly twenty years and found Yronwode working extensively with Eisner, assisting with the writing and editing of some of his books and comics, appearing with him at comics conventions, compiling the checklist of Eisner's work from high school through *The Spirit*, and representing his art as an agent until their friendship evaporated after a bitter falling-out around the time of Eisner's eightieth birthday.

Yronwode's work on Eisner's archives yielded an immediate harvest of publishable material: *Color Treasury* and *Spirit Color Album*, published in 1981, and *The Art of Will Eisner* and *Spirit Color Album Volume Two*, published a year later, all by Kitchen Sink Press, all in simultaneous hardcover and paperback editions. *The Art of Will Eisner*, edited and with written text by Yronwode, was a lavishly illustrated biography, with work dating back to Eisner's DeWitt Clinton days and running through his early graphic novels. Some of Eisner's earliest published work, including posters and comic strips, had been buried in his archives and never seen by the public, and the book gave Eisner fans the chance to see his development as an artist, as well as glimpses of such rarities as "Muss 'Em Up Donovan" and selections from *P★S* magazine. The *Color Treasury* published full-color reproductions of two of Eisner's portfolios—*The Spirit Portfolio* and *The City Portfolio*—both previously issued in limited editions and never reprinted elsewhere.

The Spirit comic book premiered in November 1983 and ran through December 1992, eighty-seven issues in all. Every month, Eisner designed a new cover related to one of the four stories in the issue, and as was his practice with *The Spirit Magazine*, he tinkered with the original artwork, revising and improving what had once been written under intense deadlines.

"Stage Settings," one of the comic book's regular monthly features, gave readers a close-up view of Eisner's creative mind. Written by Dave Schreiner in an interview/article format, "Stage Settings" generally occupied two or three pages of the comic book, with Eisner commenting on the stories in that month's issue, in effect creating a logbook detailing what inspired the stories, how they were drawn, who worked on such

NEW YORK, FRIDAY, DECEMBER 8, 1933

AT THE "FORGOTTEN" GHETTO

Bronx's "Forgotten" Ghetto Revealed;
"Is School For Crime," Doctor States

Eisner's first published art, an
illustration for a DeWitt Clinton
High School newspaper article
on tenement life in the Bronx,
appeared on December 8, 1933.
(*Will Eisner Collection, the Ohio
State University Billy Ireland
Cartoon Library & Museum*)

Two high school works: the cover for the
Clinton "Class Nite" minstrel show (1935)
and the cover for *Magpie*, his school's
literary magazine (1935). (*Will Eisner
Collection, the Ohio State University Billy
Ireland Cartoon Library & Museum*)

(© Will Eisner Studios, Inc., courtesy of Denis Kitchen)

While in the army, Eisner designed training and maintenance materials for the military, leading to the introduction of Joe Dope, the most inept GI in history, seen here in a poster for *Army Motors*. *(© Will Eisner Studios, Inc., courtesy of Denis Kitchen)*

Eisner's use of the elements for establishing mood is brought into sharp focus in this November 30, 1947 *Spirit* splash page. (© *Will Eisner Studios, Inc., courtesy of Denis Kitchen*)

The notorious—and immensely popular—P'Gell in an Eisner poster of the *Spirit* femme fatale. (© *Will Eisner Studios, Inc., courtesy of Denis Kitchen*)

*P*S* magazine gave Eisner his first test of using comics as a learning tool. In times of war, the preventive maintenance tips saved lives. (© *Will Eisner Studios, Inc., courtesy of Denis Kitchen*)

The army was less than pleased with Eisner's use of humor in some of his *P*S* illustrations, but marketing tests showed them to be very effective. (© *Will Eisner Studios, Inc., courtesy of Denis Kitchen*)

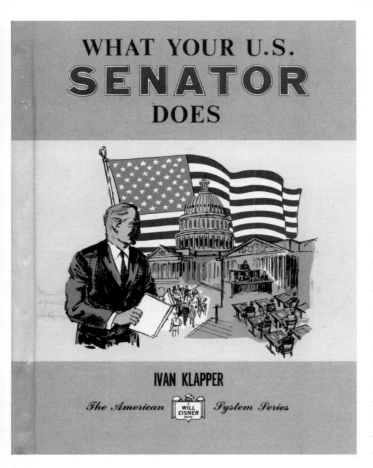

Eisner's company, American Visuals, produced a wide variety of books and pamphlets, training manuals, and educational tools, all using comic art as illustrations. (*Will Eisner Collection, the Ohio State University Billy Ireland Cartoon Library & Museum*)

(© *Will Eisner Studios, Inc., courtesy of Denis Kitchen*)

(© *Will Eisner Studios, Inc., courtesy of Denis Kitchen*)

The *Underground Spirit*: Eisner's cover art for *Snarf* #3, inspired by Eisner's introduction to underground comix, signaled a bolder, more adult direction for both character and artist. (© *Will Eisner Studios, Inc., courtesy of Denis Kitchen*)

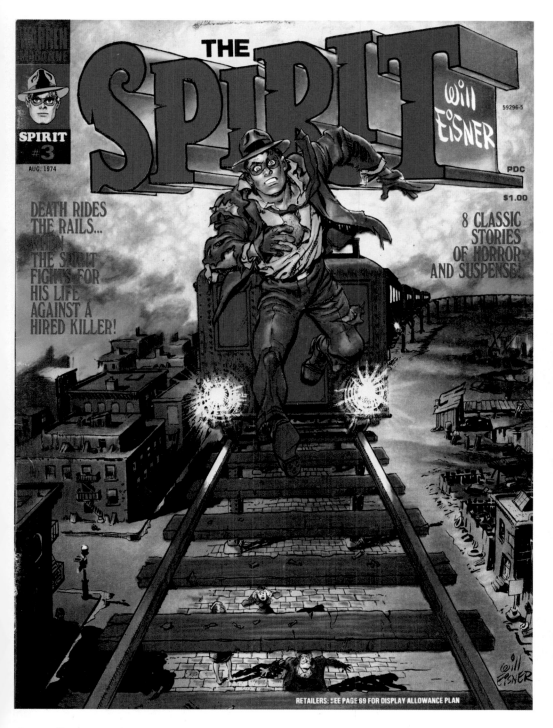

Cover illustration for the Warren version of *The Spirit Magazine*. Eisner created cover art for each of Warren's reprints of the best of his old *Spirit* newspaper adventures. (© *Will Eisner Studios, Inc., courtesy of Denis Kitchen*)

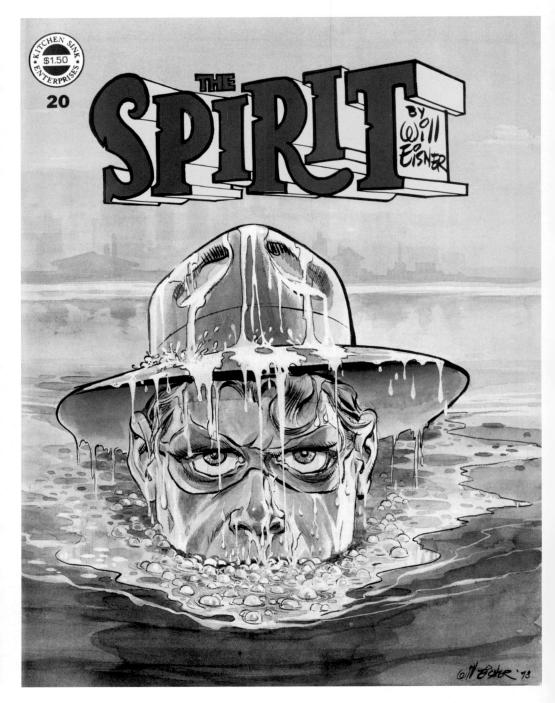

Kitchen Sink Press continued *The Spirit* reprints, along with new material, after Warren quit publishing *The Spirit Magazine*. (© *Will Eisner Studios, Inc., courtesy of Denis Kitchen*)

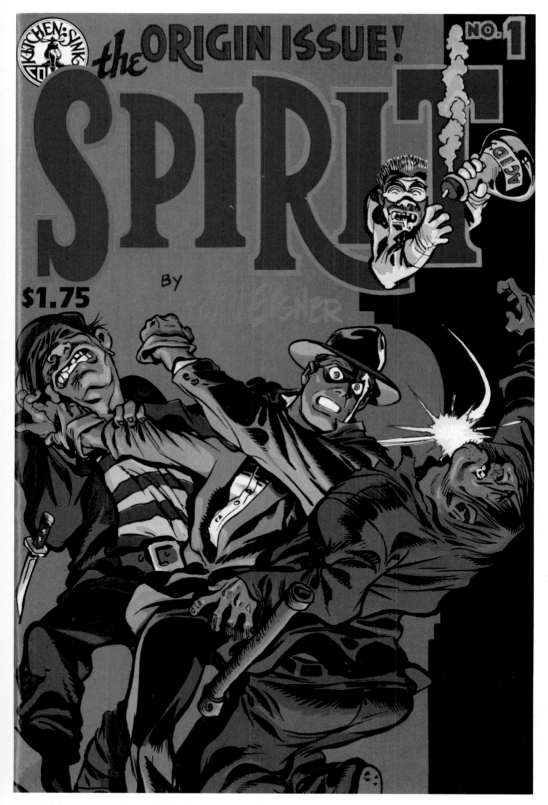

The Spirit comic book, published monthly and reprinting every post-War Spirit story in sequence, featured some of Eisner's most accomplished work, including his collaborations with Jules Feiffer. (© *Will Eisner Studios, Inc., courtesy of Denis Kitchen*)

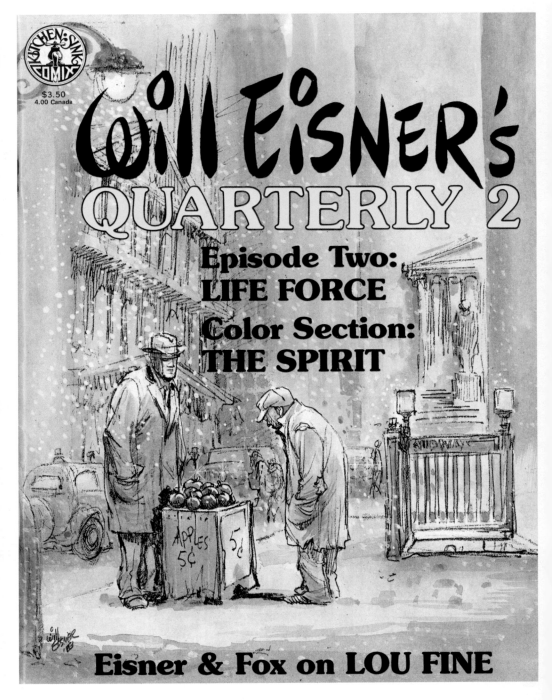

Will Eisner's Quarterly published Eisner's non-Spirit work, including the serialization of graphic novels, his "Shop Talk" interviews with time-honored comics artists, instructional pieces on comic art, and graphic short stories. (© *Will Eisner Studios, Inc., courtesy of Denis Kitchen*)

The U. S. and Hebrew editions of *A Contract with God*, Eisner's breakthrough work of connected stories about life in the Bronx tenements. (© *Will Eisner Studios, Inc., courtesy of Deni Kitchen*)

"Life," an entry from *Eisner's City: A Narrative Portfolio* (1980). (© *Will Eisner Studios, Inc., courtesy of Denis Kitchen*)

"The Last of Yesterday," an Eisner watercolor (1988), portrays the artist's love of (and disappointment in) his city. (© *Will Eisner Studios, Inc., courtesy of Denis Kitchen*)

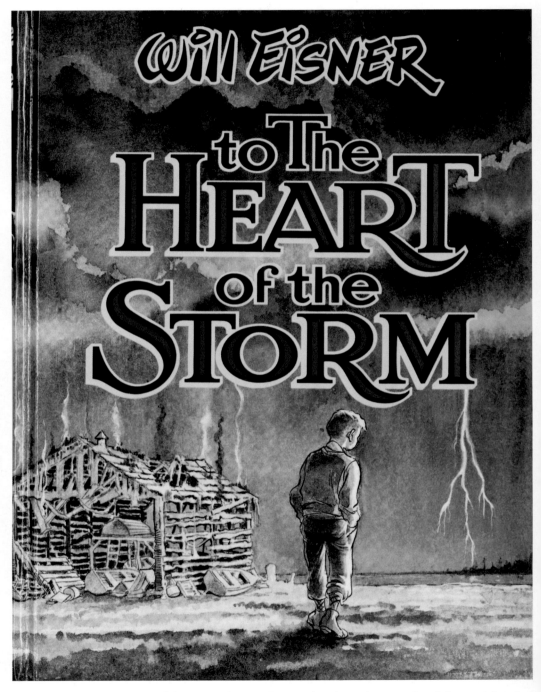

The cover of *To the Heart of the Storm*, the autobiographical graphic novel widely considered to be Eisner's most fully realized work. (© *Will Eisner Studios, Inc., courtesy of Denis Kitchen*)

elements as the lettering and inking, and anything else that Eisner wished to address. Eisner clearly enjoyed talking shop.

"He was an amazing combination of artistic dreamer and hard-nosed pragmatist," said Tom Heintjes, who took over "Stage Settings" for Dave Schreiner in 1989 and wrote the feature until the comic book ceased publication. Heintjes had worked for Fantagraphics, one of the leading publishers of graphic novels and comics studies, where he became acquainted with Denis Kitchen, and he inherited "Stage Settings" after Kitchen relocated his Kitchen Sink to Northampton, Massachusetts, and Schreiner, back in Wisconsin, became too busy with other work to continue it. Heintjes, a comics historian who created his own magazine called *Hogan's Alley*, was impressed by how quickly Eisner thought on his feet.

"What was interesting to me," he pointed out, "is how much of what we take now as standard comics storytelling devices was, to him, problem solving on the fly, because he was having to produce so furiously. I guess I went in with this impression that he sat at his drawing board, scratched his chin, and developed these genius ideas. I found out that it wasn't like that at all. He was having to crank this stuff out and solve problems, because the form was so new in those years that there was no well to go to, really. He was digging the well."

Eisner had plenty of help on the comic book and other projects. Some of his assistants, like Robert Pizzo, were former students hired to help around the studio. Pizzo had studied at the School of Visual Arts from 1978 to 1980, and the circumstances behind his hiring had to have seemed like a case of déjà vu to Eisner, a parallel to his initial meeting with Jerry Iger.

"I saw him on the train one day and found out that he lived near my neighborhood," Pizzo remembered. "On the last day of school, I asked him, 'Would you mind if I took a ride out to the studio one day?' And he said, 'By all means, come up.' I went up the next week, and when I got there, it was really like one of those movie moments. The place was crowded and busy, with people running all around. One panel of an illustration was bad, and Will was complaining about how they had to fix it and couldn't get a hold of the guy to do it. I literally heard myself saying, 'I could do that.' He put me down at a drawing board and said, 'All right, this is what I need. Take a shot at it.' I did it, and he said, 'That's perfect.' Then, as I was leaving, he followed me outside and said, 'Listen, do you want to come up here and work a little bit?'"

Pizzo reported to the studio several days a week and was put to work on a variety of projects. He added stars to some of the panels in *Signal from Space*. He worked on some of the background revisions and color overlays for *The Spirit* comic book. Eisner, acting every bit the role of the studio head, would assign the activities and supervise his assistants' work.

"We were surprised to find that he had another whole studio in his house," Pizzo said. "He had a room set up with a drawing board and everything, and we found out that this was where he got the main work done. In the studio, he sat at his desk with his phones. He wasn't at a drawing board that often, though there was one that was kind of reserved for him."

The studio was a special place for Eisner. A few years earlier, in 1975, he and Ann had decided to downsize their living quarters. With Alice gone and John no longer living with them, they were alone in a fairly large house. A real estate agent had shown them several places in White Plains, but none had captured their fancy. Then one day the agent called Ann and asked if she could talk her husband into coming back early from his New York office. "I have a house I really want you and Will to see," he said.

The house, at 51 Winslow Road in White Plains, not far from where the Eisners were currently living, was a modern wood-and-glass structure designed by an architect for his own residence and office. It sat on three quarters of an acre of land, much of it wooded, in semiseclusion near the end of a dead-end road. The architect had built a beautiful detached studio in back of the house.

"It's absolutely beautiful," Ann declared after taking a tour of the house and grounds, "but it's too big for us."

Eisner couldn't argue that point. With five bedrooms on the second floor, the place was more house than the one they were thinking of leaving. Still, the detached studio, the woods . . .

"That house just spoke to me," he said to his wife. "It said, 'Buy me.' "

"He just fell in love with it," Ann recalled. "It was just about perfect."

John Walker was another School of Visual Arts student who wound up working for Eisner after taking his class. For Walker, the job was an extension of the classroom, a place for further learning, especially about the business aspects of comics art. Eisner, it seemed, was always passing on his knowledge to anyone willing to listen. Walker drew illustrations for one of Eisner's Poorhouse Press joke books, which turned into an exercise of practical business.

"He'd say, 'You are going to illustrate and I'm going to pay you to do that. What are you going to charge me for the rights to use your illustration?' I'd say, 'I'll be happy with whatever you pay me.' 'Don't be a schmuck,' he'd say. 'Let's sit down and look at this contract. I'll pay you x amount to do the drawings, but you have to come up with a number for me to own the rights to these illustrations forever. Do you want a thousand dollars? Fifteen hundred?' I'd say, 'I don't know what I want,' and he'd say, 'Well, let's do some research on it.' He'd send you to the library and you'd research business law and contracts. He really opened my eyes that way, on my value as an artist. He would say, 'Your art has value. Your art will have value decades from now, even after you're dead. You don't know, a Walker cartoon might be famous.' "

Walker, like other Eisner students, was constantly amazed by how Eisner could turn almost anything into a learning exercise. One Friday, Walker recalled, Eisner approached him and asked him what he was doing that upcoming weekend. When Walker replied that he had nothing special planned, Eisner pulled out an envelope with two tickets to the ballet. "I'm not using these," he said. "You're gonna go."

"The ballet?" Walker responded, hoping not to disparage his boss's generosity. "I'm not into the ballet, Will. But thanks."

Eisner wasn't taking no for an answer. "Go to this and bring a sketchbook. I want you to draw while you're at the ballet. Just do it for me, please."

What Walker didn't realize was that Eisner had done his own sketching at the ballet, back when he was in the Art Students League and would head to the ballet on Fifty-ninth Street in Manhattan—a point that Eisner drove home when Walker, after attending the ballet and sketching some figures, showed him his work. Rather than spending a half hour or so in a life drawing class at the School of Visual Arts, sketching a model standing stock-still, Walker had drawn the human body in motion and enjoyed the ballet at the same time. "It's amazing how quickly you can capture the human form and an appreciation for it by watching ballet," Eisner observed.

Walker stayed in touch with Eisner after his apprenticeship, leading to an informal collaboration on a famous television commercial that Eisner never spoke about in interviews. Walker, working for an advertising agency, needed to come up with a symbol to represent a fabric softener, something soft and fuzzy, representative of the product's name: Snuggle. Walker designed a number of candidates—puppies, kittens, rabbits, a teddy bear—but he never came up with anything that jumped off the page and said, "This is it!" Finally, he called Eisner, told him what he was up to, and asked if he could show him some of the illustrations. Eisner looked over

Walker's samples and reached a quick decision. "It's the bear," he announced. "Tell them you like the bear."

The two worked on Walker's drawing, Eisner adding touches that made the bear more endearing, more squeezable. The drawings were turned over to Kermit Love, the master puppeteer and major influence to Jim Henson, and Love brought the bear to life. Snuggle the Bear became the fabric company's longest-running symbol.

As soon as he saw his first Snuggle commercial, Eisner called Walker.

"They chose the goddamn bear," he declared, clearly pleased with his role in seeing the idea through fruition. "I told you I was right, Johnny."

He paused for a moment, then asked: "Do we get royalties on this?"

According to Ann Eisner, her husband showed very little interest in balancing his personal checkbook—she managed the household's finances—but as a professional, from his earliest days with Eisner & Iger through his final day on earth, Eisner kept a close watch on where the money was coming from and how it was being spent. In the years following the Depression, when he was running his comics studios, he earned a reputation for pinching pennies—using scraps of discarded paper as notepaper or even using pencil extenders to prolong the lives of the nubs that passed as pencils. Employees such as Bob Powell, Lou Fine, and Jules Feiffer battled him over their salaries, and Feiffer referred to him as a "stingy boss." Eisner never disputed his reputation. When reminded of the Feiffer quote, he laughed and admitted, "Oh, that's true. Jules and I used to argue over nickels all the time."

Because of his publisher-artist relationship with Eisner, Denis Kitchen had occasion to see Eisner in action, professionally and privately. Pete Eisner, Kitchen said, would calculate the royalty payment to the exact decimal point, rather than rounding off the numbers, which resulted in at least one almost surreal experience.

"His brother must have calculated it to twelve decimal points," Kitchen remembered, "and when we sent a check and a statement, Pete compared it to the contract and said, 'You're thirty-seven cents short.' I said, 'You gotta be kidding me.' I mean, I sent him a check for three thousand dollars, and he says it's thirty-seven cents short. I said, 'What do you want me to do?' He said, 'Send a check.' He was punctilious when it came to that sort of thing. I learned to live with it.

"After I first met Will," Kitchen continued, "I went to White Plains and was their houseguest for a weekend. They took me out to dinner to this very fancy, expensive place, and Ann was exceptionally generous. We got the menu and Ann said, 'Do you like lobster?' I said, 'Well, I very, very rarely have it, Ann. It's just too expensive. Where I live, it's kind of a specialty.' She said, 'Order the lobster.' I could see Will kind of raise his eyebrow. And then—and I'll never forget this—she said, 'You're a growing boy. I bet you could eat two lobsters.' I said, 'Well, I probably could.' She said, 'Well, order two.' This time I saw Will's brow furrow, and there were serious wrinkles in the brow. It was subtle. He just thought it was excessive, and he was picking up the tab. I was paying him a lot of money then, and certainly a lobster, two lobsters, was a tiny fraction of what I'd been paying him. But nonetheless, it was the principle for him."

Kitchen reasoned that much of Eisner's frugality was the result of his Depression-era upbringing and the struggles his family had faced when Sam Eisner couldn't find work. Kitchen noted, as did others, that Eisner could be as generous as he was frugal. He had supported his family, put his sister through college, and, through his shops, provided the livelihoods for numerous families.

Eliot Gordon, who married Eisner's sister, Rhoda, recalled how a newly wed Eisner had continued in his generosity toward his family. "Despite being newly wed to Ann, Will insisted on continuing to pay Rhoda's tuition. He had paid the first three years, while he was a bachelor, but after he was married, it could have been, 'Do I really have to continue? I'm a married man now. Maybe enough is enough.' It was a sign of character that he was able to assert himself and persuade Ann to understand."

Money had been tight in those early days. In later years, after he was well established and earning a good annual income, he was able to loosen up.

W. W. Norton editor Robert Weil, who later bundled Eisner's graphic novels into attractive hardcover volumes, reissued his entire catalog of graphic novels and instructional books, and worked closely with Eisner on his final book, bristled when he heard stories accusing Eisner of being a tightwad.

"I'm still offended by this talk about how he was cheap, how he was penurious, how he saved things. Will was unfailingly generous, if not overgenerous, in my working relationship with him. I remember the first meal I ever had with him. He treated us to a meal at the Princeton Club."

John Walker also disputed the idea that Eisner was overly tightfisted with his money.

"I wouldn't say he was cheap," Walker said. "One time, I needed a compressor and he lent me the money. He gave me an advance on my salary to get it. He was kind that way. I think people said he was cheap because he lived simply. He drove this beat-up old Dodge Dart. His house was a nice suburban home, but it wasn't some McMansion kind of thing. But I wouldn't say he was cheap. He paid us well when we worked for him. It wasn't a sweatshop or anything."

chapter thirteen

A LIFE FORCE

I want my reader to feel that he is watching something real. I start
everything I do with the words "believe me." "Believe me," I say,
"let me tell you this story."

Eisner's sixty-fifth birthday found him in a reflective mood. Although
he was in the autumn of his life and had no way of predicting how
many more years lay ahead, he felt hopeful and ambitious: he had
much left to do. His health was still very good. He played tennis almost
every day, usually in the early afternoon, after his morning work session
and lunch, and he still had great stamina. He and Ann enjoyed active
social lives. This was encouraging, yet he couldn't help but seriously
ponder what he had accomplished and what he might do in the future.
He worried that he wouldn't accomplish everything that he hoped to
do, that the "sands of the hourglass"—a phrase that he bandied about
often with friends and business acquaintances—would run out when he
was in the midst of his next great new idea.

What rose out of these ruminations was *A Life Force*, perhaps the most
ambitious graphic novel he would ever create, which addressed issues
that had gnawed at the edges of his imagination for the better part of half
a century. In the preface to *The Contract with God Trilogy*, he explained:

The debate over Darwinism and Creationism continues over the
decades, but the Meaning of life remains scientifically unanswer-
able. It is one thing to deal with How we got here. It is another to
deal with Why. I undertook this book after my 65th birthday, a hall-
mark that seemed to arrive too soon. For someone who has always

felt caught in a mortal struggle with time and who has an enormous number of yet undone projects ahead, this was a sobering event. Suddenly, enduring memories that were accumulations of the detritus of living seemed more ephemeral.

In *A Life Force*, Eisner created two characters to address his past and present selves, the aging process, and how simple lessons in life help form a much greater perspective: Jacob Shtarkah, an aging carpenter who suddenly finds himself unemployed and questioning the purpose of his life; and Willie, a politically active young artist who finds his youthful ideology challenged by the realities of the day. Both reside at 55 Dropsie Avenue, the Bronx tenement building that Eisner used as a setting in *A Contract with God*.

At the opening of the story, Jacob Shtarkah learns that the job he's had for five years, building a library at his synagogue, has come to an end. This is Depression-era New York, and finding any kind of new employment is going to be difficult. Worse yet, in Shtarkah's mind, is the knowledge that the library is going to be named after the men who funded its construction rather than the man who actually built it. A library bearing his name was Shtarkah's one chance at immortality, a reward for a life that otherwise had very few rewards, and now it has been denied him.

On his way home from the synagogue, Shtarkah suffers a mild heart attack and collapses in the alleyway next to his tenement building. As he sits on the ground, waiting either to die or regain his strength, a cockroach, shaken out of a rug two floors above, plops down on the ground near him, prompting a one-sided conversation that encapsulates the essence of the book.

"You, being only a cockroach, just want to live!" Jacob declares. "For you it's enough! But me . . . I have to ask, why!?"

The answer, Jacob believes, lies in whether man created God or vice versa. "If man created God, then the reason for life is only in the mind of man," Jacob says. "If, on the other hand, God created man, then the reason for living is still only a guess! After all is said and done, who really knows the will of God? So, in either case, both man and cockroach are in serious trouble, because staying alive seems to be the only thing on which everybody agrees."

"When Jacob talked to the cockroach in the alley, he is speaking my thoughts," Eisner stated in an interview published shortly after the completion of *A Life Force*. "I wanted to draw some parallels between man's

Page from *A Life Force*. (Courtesy of Will Eisner Studios, Inc.)

and the roach's survival. My objective was to present this debate Jacob
has with himself to the reader. All of the things expressed in this novel
are for readers to decide. It's in the nature of an intellectual exercise."

Willie, like Eisner in his own youth, is politically left of center, a union
sympathizer, and a true believer in society's potential for social justice.
The Communist Party, a mainstay in the intellectual circles of New
York's Greenwich Village during the Depression, has caught the attention
of the union organizers, and a rally, guaranteed to attract the news media,
is planned. Willie, an aspiring artist, along with one of his friends, volun-
teers to make signs for it.

While Willie busies himself designing ways to save the workers of the
world through social and economic revolution, his father, owner of a
tiny fur factory (similar to the one once owned by Sam Eisner), is visited
by a couple of union strong-arms trying to muscle their way into the
shop. Willie's father and the plant foreman attempt to explain that theirs
is a small shop employing only three workers, and that those workers are
currently earning union wages, but the thugs won't listen to reason.
During an ensuing scuffle, the shop foreman is beaten on the head and
sustains wounds that will leave permanent brain damage. When Willie's

father returns home to find his son working on pro-union, pro-Communist signs, he flies into a rage and throws Willie's friend out of the house, forcing Willie to make an immediate decision: the cause or his family. Willie chooses family, ending his brief life as a revolutionary.

Eisner worked other autobiographical details into *A Life Force*. Elton Shaftsbury, a young stock market player ruined in the crash and pondering suicide, shared some of the characteristics of Ann Eisner's father. A rabbi offering cut-rate bar mitzvah lessons in the tenement gave Eisner opportunity for subtle commentary on the relationship between God and money—a lesson he and his father were taught on the steps of the synagogue many years earlier during the High Holy Days, when Sam Eisner couldn't afford the standard donation necessary for entry. A brilliant but mentally disturbed young man named Aaron, isolated from the world and tormented by his own raging thoughts, bore a resemblance to Eisner's son, John, who began to display signs of psychological trauma following his sister's death and would struggle with mental illness from that point on.

With the exception of the novel's villains, who are largely caricatures motivated by greed or a lust for power, Eisner's characters in *A Life Force* are complex individuals trapped in a harsh world of daily survival, forced to make decisions that under other circumstances they might never have faced. They are the victims of *life*—not the one they were raised to believe was possible, but the one they are forced to live. The Depression and the European immigration to New York City brought on by Hitler's persecution of the Jews brings into fine focus the way otherwise decent human beings discover sometimes shady ways of surviving. People find ways to rationalize their behavior and overlook the behavior of others, all for the sake of survival. They are no different from the cockroaches scurrying around the dark corners of the city, struggling to stay alive.

Lengthy installments of *A Life Force* appeared in the first five issues of *Will Eisner's Quarterly*, but unlike *Signal from Space*, which Eisner essentially wrote on the fly to accommodate each individual installment's deadline, this new graphic novel was carefully plotted in its entirety before the first installment's publication. At 139 pages, the story was easily the longest Eisner had yet created; and with a demanding historical setting that covered the Depression and the origins of World War II, Eisner had to make use of every storytelling device in his arsenal—including newspaper clippings, handwritten letters, weather reports, and lengthy passages of prose—to construct his narrative. Images weren't enough. He had employed some of these devices in *Signal from Space* with mixed results. Comic book readers, he was learning, weren't interested in reading long passages of prose. The images were the main attraction. "We have two mediums which are not necessarily meant to replace each other," he concluded. "Visuals can't entirely replace words; they can replace descriptions and actions, often in exciting ways."

After reading *A Life Force*, Robert Crumb contacted Denis Kitchen, first by telephone and then by mail, to tell Kitchen the profound effect the book had on him. Kitchen made a habit of sending Crumb regular samplings of new Kitchen Sink publications, though he never bothered with Spirit magazines or comic books, since Crumb had no interest in superheroes or adventure stories. He did send Crumb Eisner's graphic novels, however, but Crumb had never commented on them. *A Life Force* was the exception.

"Robert told me on the phone that, at that point in his life, he was very depressed and contemplating suicide," Kitchen recalled. "He said, 'I got the package and it really motivated me to continue in the business.' Then he followed up with a postcard."

The postcard, reprinted in its entirety in *Kitchen Sink Press: The First 25 Years* and excerpted in Kitchen Sink ads, didn't repeat Crumb's feelings of depression. Crumb did admit that he hadn't expected much when he started *A Life Force*. "It's really an uplifting book!!" he wrote, calling it the best work recently produced by an artist of Eisner's generation. "You can tell 'im I said so!! Sort of a masterpiece!!"

Certain that Eisner would appreciate Crumb's compliments, Kitchen photocopied the postcard and forwarded it to him. Eisner and Crumb had met on one previous occasion, at a restaurant in New York, but they found then that they didn't have much to talk about. According to Kitchen, Crumb spoke directly to Eisner only once, after the two had been together for some time in silence, when a beautiful young woman passed their outdoor table. "Look at those gams," Crumb remarked, pointing at the young woman. Eisner didn't know what to make of him.

Crumb's postcard was different.

"He knew that Crumb didn't hold him in particular regard," Kitchen recalled, "so for Crumb, the leading guy in his generation, to go out of his way to compliment him was very meaningful to him."

Three years would pass between the appearance of the last installment of *A Life Force* in *Will Eisner's Quarterly* and its publication in book form—an unfortunate time lapse. The book fit better as a follow-up to *A Contract with God* than in the order in which it was presented, but the timing was a necessity given the large volume of his work being published by Kitchen Sink Press. Besides *Will Eisner's Quarterly* and *The Spirit* comic book, which demanded a chunk of his time and assured him of regular appearances in the Kitchen Sink catalog, Eisner was busy preparing *Life on Another Planet*, which he was now calling *Signal from Space*, for publication in book form.

Signal from Space was more than just a recycling job. Two of the book's eight installments in *The Spirit Magazine* had been published in a sideways, pull-out format, with smaller panels and less background than the other six installments, which were presented in the standard *Spirit Magazine* size and format. So before it could be bound together, Eisner had to overhaul one fourth of the book. As long as this was the case, Eisner decided to revise the rest of his story by reworking parts that, in retrospect, he deemed weak. On top of that, *Life on Another Planet* had been black and white, but the book was to be in color. Eisner was far too preoccupied with other projects to color it himself, so he brought in his old colleague André LeBlanc for the job. *Life on Another Planet* became the only Eisner graphic novel ever published in color.

Although she had been born and raised in New York, Ann Eisner did not share her husband's enthusiasm for the city. She enjoyed much of what the city had to offer, particularly the arts scene, but she preferred the tranquillity of White Plains to the energy of Manhattan. She hated the New York winters, and now that she was ready to retire from her job at a hospital, she yearned to move somewhere warm, as far away from the snow and blustery winds as possible. Will's brother, Pete, and his wife, Lila, had relocated to Florida when Pete had taken a job with Dannon yogurt—a job that Will had lined up for Pete when he could no longer afford to keep him as an employee—and Ann reasoned that Will might be happy living in Florida and reuniting with his Pete and his family.

Eisner, as Ann expected, initially opposed the idea. He felt Florida was a place where people retired and vegetated, where people went to finish out their lives. He was still very active, producing more art than ever, teaching at the School of Visual Arts, and keeping a busy social calendar. New York City was his home, not some godforsaken town in Florida, where he'd be as far removed from his business as he could imagine. His relationship with Pete, while loving, was complex, built largely on a lifetime of looking out for his younger brother. Pete had worked for him for a long time, and he'd been a loyal, outstanding employee. Still, having a brother as an employee had built-in complications that others didn't have to face, and Eisner was happy for Pete's success outside of his sphere of influence.

Ann was insistent, Will relented, and in the summer of 1983, they began the process of finding a place in Florida and packing up their belongings. They moved on July 1, but it wasn't easy. Eisner was a pack rat who kept every scrap of paper he'd ever drawn on, every letter he'd ever written or received, every book he'd ever read. His personal archives included original art, tear sheets, published books, magazines and comics in which his work (or interviews) had appeared, newspaper clippings, awards, memorabilia, and business correspondence. The long-distance move simply would not permit the transfer of all this from one place to another.

Fortunately, largely through the efforts of Cat Yronwode, there was now an order to Eisner's archives. A lifetime's work had been organized and cataloged. Some of the memorabilia could be sold off to collectors. The rest of the archives would be divided between Eisner's new home and a university library. Yronwide contacted Ohio State University, which housed the Milton Caniff collection, and the university's Library for Communication and Graphic Arts agreed to add the Eisner papers to a collection that already included extensive holdings of editorial cartoonists, the Association of American Editorial Cartoonists, and art by magazine illustrators.

For the library, obtaining the Eisner collection was a major event, adding to its reputation of being one of the finest cartoon archives in the academic community. "Eisner's work has been of major importance in the development of both comic book art and narrative," Lucy Caswell, the library's curator, declared when the university formally announced its procurement of the Eisner collection. "His creative use of layout and design in the 1940s influenced a generation of cartoonists."

One unexpected offshoot of the Eisners' move to Florida was a new, twenty-eight-page graphic story, "A Sunset in Sunshine City," published in *Will Eisner's Quarterly* #6 and reprinted later in the miscellany *Will Eisner Reader*. It is the story of Henry Klop, widower, father of two daughters, and owner of a well-respected small business, who has bought a retirement condominium in Florida. It's a bittersweet move. As he wanders down the snowy streets of New York, Henry is haunted by the memories of his youth, marriage, children, and business—all preserved, it seems, by the mundane objects of the city itself. "After all, what else is there to bear witness to the past?" he wonders, repeating an Eisner theme explored in *New York: The Big City*. "Only lampposts, fire hydrants . . . a street, a sewer, a building . . . They are monuments to my memories."

"That was his getting used to things," Ann Eisner said of "A Sunset in Sunshine City." Like Henry Klop, Eisner couldn't imagine himself as a retiree so far removed from the memories of his youth—a point that Ann Eisner readily acknowledged. "It's mostly retirees in south Florida where we moved," she said, "and it took some getting used to."

Ironically, Ann made a significant contribution to the story when she suggested the montage of Henry Klop's New York memories presented early in the story. Ann's involvement with her husband's work had developed slowly over the years: from the earliest days of their relationship, when she had no use for comics and didn't even visit his office until after they were married, to her much greater interest and more active involvement in his art after he began his graphic novels.

Denis Kitchen watched this evolution from the perspective of a publisher. On one occasion, shortly after he and Eisner began working together on *The Spirit Magazine*, he visited the Eisner home in White Plains. During a lull in their dinner conversation, he asked Ann, innocently enough, to name her favorite *Spirit* story.

"There was a silence," Kitchen remembered, "and she kind of glanced at Will, and then looked at me and said, 'Well, honestly, I've never read any of them.' My jaw dropped. As a fanboy and a guy making a living publishing this stuff, that was incomprehensible to me. I think she saw my response and felt slightly embarrassed. She said, 'I married the man, not the cartoonist'—which I thought was a great comeback. I didn't bring it up again."

Eisner valued his wife's feedback. Although they had very different tastes in entertainment—he favored public television, she network programming, for instance—she was well-read and had strong instincts on what might work or be appropriate in a story, and she wasn't shy about stating her opinions. She strongly objected to one scene in *Signal from Space*, which depicted one of the characters urinating in a rainstorm. ("Will, that's not you," she scolded. "You shouldn't do that.") On another occasion, she protested her husband's intention of putting together a never-to-be-released Poorhouse Press book entitled *30 Days to a New Beautiful You* (or, in its original working title, *30 Days to a Brick Shithouse Figure*).

"He wanted her opinion," Denis Kitchen said. "I can remember one time when Will had a character having an affair in the story, and Ann proofread it and said, 'This isn't plausible. The wife would know he was having an affair.' Will said, 'How?' and Ann said, 'The woman would just know.' Will respected Ann's opinion enough that he rewrote the scene."

The Eisners impressed their friends as an ideal couple. Even after thirty-plus years of marriage, they were playful, openly affectionate, clearly still very much in love. Every year on their anniversary, Will would tease Ann about signing on for "one more year," and on those occasions when Will would bring home flowers, Ann would tease him about what he must have done wrong to warrant the purchase of such an unexpected gift. As extensive as his business travels had been, Will still missed Ann when he was away, and after she retired and they moved to Florida, Ann would accompany him on almost all of his journeys. Ann enjoyed watching her husband bask in his popularity at comics conventions and lectures, yet she had a way of seeing that none of it went to his head.

"To me, they were the role model of a married couple," noted Denis Kitchen. "I saw them in their natural environment, where you can only fake things so long. I would especially notice it in the morning, at breakfast, or at dinner. Will was obviously the famous one, but at home he was just Will. He'd leave his ego at the door, and Ann would reprimand him if he would even say anything that seemed a little pompous. It was a complete give-and-take."

Jackie Estrada, a longtime volunteer and administrator of the San Diego Comic-Con, the largest annual comic book convention in the world, had many occasions to see the Eisners together. She and her husband, cartoonist and former Eisner student Batton Lash, traditionally had breakfast with the Eisners on the Friday morning of the convention, when the four of them could relax before going off to face the bedlam on the convention floor.

"It was so funny when Will and Ann were together," Estrada said. "Will would start to tell a story, and Ann would go, 'That's not the way it went at all. That's not what happened.' And Will would go, 'I'm giving her one more year.' They were a great match."

Ann Eisner's biggest concern about their move to Florida was the effect it would have on her husband when he could no longer teach. But those worries were put to rest when Eisner told the School of Visual Arts that he was moving and submitted his resignation. The school officials, shocked to be losing one of their high-profile teachers, countered with an offer to fly Eisner to New York every other week for classes. Eisner accepted. Those forays to the city, along with a couple of other longer visits, gave Will the "carbon monoxide fix" he needed to keep his yearnings for the big city at bay.

Eisner found an office near their home and set up shop. It had two rooms—an outer office and a studio in which to work—and was located in

a small professional building in a strip mall. Eisner found himself surrounded by doctors, dentists, lawyers, and accountants—hardly the environment he'd enjoyed in New York City or in his studio in White Plains,
but it was functional.

He already had a couple of projects in mind that he wanted to develop:
an autobiographical work and a textbook on sequential art. Neither approached *A Life Force* in ambition, but both reflected his nostalgia for his
lost youth and the city he'd left behind.

The Dreamer, a roman à clef of his early days in comics, started out at
approximately the same length as "A Sunset in Sunrise City," but Denis
Kitchen and Dave Schreiner were so taken by it that they pressed him
into extending it to include more detail and anecdotes.

"Dave Schreiner and I both were badgering him, urging him to put
more flesh on the bone," Kitchen recalled. "We were fascinated with
early comic book history, and we had been asking him to do kind of a
memoir in comics form. When he did that, I said to him, 'Will, this is
a great outline, but we want the whole story.' And he very reluctantly
said, 'All right, all right, I'll add eight pages.' He would, and we'd say,
'More.' We pushed him and pushed him until it got to around fifty
pages, and then he said, 'That's it. That's it.' We could tell it was an em-
phatic one, so we said, 'All right, all right, fine.'

The idea for *The Dreamer* originated at the School of Visual Arts. His
young student artists were all dreamers hoping to use their talents in one
way or another to earn a living, but soon enough, they learned that there
was quite a gulf between dreams and reality.

"At the end of the semester, students were always wringing their
hands over having to get out into the field," Eisner stated. "What would
happen to them? Where were they going to go? And I thought, Gee, let
me tell you my story. It's to say to the kids who are growing up and going
out into the field, 'Look, it's always been this way and if you stay with it,
and remain the dreamer that you really are, you'll prevail.'"

The Dreamer started out as a fictional tale, with Billy Eyron, the main
character, stepping into a cafeteria and meeting a fortune-teller who offers to tell his fortune for a dime. It's New York City, 1937, and like the
young, post-Depression Will Eisner, Billy is lugging around a portfolio,
hoping to find work. Billy laughs off the fortune-teller's predictions of
success, but he later stops at a fortune-telling machine on the street. Its
message, too, is that he will be a success in his chosen career.

Eisner shifted at this point to his actual experiences in comics, using the
real people and events. He reasoned that nonfiction was better than any-

At the drawing board, 1985. (Courtesy of Denis Kitchen)

thing he could have invented; plus, in relating his experiences, he was giving the history of comics—or at least his part of it. Readers were introduced
to such players of the Golden Age as Jerry Iger, Major Malcolm Wheeler-
Nicholson, Harry Donenfeld, M. C. Gaines, Victor Fox, and Busy Arnold,
as well as to such up-and-coming artists as Bob Kane, Lou Fine, Bob
Powell, Jack Kirby, George Tuska, and others in the Eisner & Iger shop.
Eisner discreetly changed their names, but to anyone familiar with comics,
the name changes were more the source of a humorous "name the character" game than a way of disguising identities. Jack Kirby became "Jack
King" in homage to Kirby's "King of Comics' nickname; Lou Fine became "Lou Sharp." Even the comics and their characters were given fictitious names: *Superman* translated to *Bighero: Man of Iron*, while *Batman*
became *Rodent Man*. For Eisner, it was a playful exercise and a way to avoid
potential litigation, but for aficionados like Dave Schreiner and Denis
Kitchen, who were eager to see history played out in graphic form, it was
a source of consternation.

"We were so frustrated that he didn't just call people who they were,"
Kitchen complained. "I remember saying to him, 'Why must you dis-
guise those people?' He said, 'Well, some of them are still alive, and I
don't want to embarrass them or their families.' It was the gentleman in
Will. And part of it was there was a clear implication that Donenfeld and
Liebowitz, the guys who ran the early DC Comics, were crooks. I said,
'Will, everybody knows those guys were crooks. What's the problem?' He

said, 'I don't know firsthand that they were crooks.' I said, 'Well, is there anyone still around who even knows *second*hand?' He laughed but said, 'No, I'm not going there. This is the way I want to do it.' I wanted to have some annotations early on, but he said, 'No, no. Let people figure it out. That's part of the fun.'"

Eisner crafted his book in tight, compact episodes. He included the major moments of his development as a comics artist, including his early work with *Wow, What a Magazine!*, the formation of the Eisner & Iger studio, the *Wonder Man* fiasco with Victor Fox, and his initial meeting with Busy Arnold and Henry Martin. Colorful episodes such as Jack Kirby's confrontation with the Mafia thug, George Tuska punching Bob Powell, and even Eisner's brief fling with Toni Blum spiced the narrative. Through it all, Eisner never lost sight of his "dreamer" motif. The comic book world was a place where dreamers came face-to-face with ne'er-do-wells, crooks, grifters, and hungry businessmen, all looking to make a name and a buck, regardless of the compromises they had to make. At the end of the forty-six-page story, with World War II looming in the not-so-distant future, Billy again drops a coin in a fortune-telling machine. The message is the same: He will be a success in his chosen profession.

Ultimately, *The Dreamer* is a fascinating failure, a book that should have been two or three times as long. It could have told a more detailed story about the early history of comics, which would have highlighted Eisner's important contributions, and it could have addressed the larger issue of anti-Semitism that had forced so many talented artists into the business. The book includes an abundance of interesting stories, but the reader walks away dissatisfied, like someone expecting a feast, only to be served delicious but insubstantial appetizers.

Though he'd been working in comics for nearly fifty years, Eisner found his instructional text *Comics and Sequential Art* a difficult book to organize and write. At the School of Visual Arts, he lectured off the top of his head, using minimal notes. Student questions and interests guided him when he needed to add emphasis to a topic or when he wasn't being clear enough for his art students to understand. When he set out to write the book, which began as a series of essays in *The Spirit Magazine*, Eisner was on his own.

"I couldn't find any textbook on the medium that dealt with comics as a discipline, as a true discipline," he told interviewer Jon B. Cooke. "Most of the comic books at that time—books on comics, rather—dealt with how to draw feet, and how to draw noses, and [took] a very simplistic approach to the drawing aspect of it. Very few of them had attempted to develop a theoretical discussion on the discipline of the medium."

The lack of available texts, Eisner felt, could be traced to the continuous perception of comics as a type of pop art unworthy of serious scholarly study. "While each of the major integral elements, such as design, drawing, caricature and writing, have separately found academic consideration, this unique combination took a long time to find a place in the literary, art and comparative literature curriculums," he wrote. "I believe that the reason for slow critical acceptance sat as much on the shoulders of the practitioner as the critic."

Comics and Sequential Art was not an instructional book on how to draw feet, noses, or any other part of the human body. In one chapter entitled "Expressive Anatomy" (which he would expand into a book-length study of the same name twenty years later), Eisner wrote and gave examples of how an artist could use the body and gestures as means of expressing emotion; but this was not a book that intended to teach someone how to draw. Instead, Eisner directed *Comics and Sequential Art* at the artist who already knew how to draw and ink but needed guidance on how to apply those skills to creating comics. Chapters included "Imagery," "Timing," and "The Frame," and in writing the book, Eisner was revealing as much about his thoughts and methods as he'd ever allowed outside the classroom. Heavily illustrated with examples from his graphic novels and his work on *The Spirit*, the book showed how to write scripts, do breakdowns and rough pencils, create catchy splash pages, and move on to the finished work. Later editions included a chapter on how to create comics with computers.

One of the more arresting examples offered in the book was a complete ten-page modern adaptation of the "To Be or Not to Be" soliloquy from *Hamlet*. Eisner and writer/editor Dennis O'Neil had been at a party, engaged in a spirited discussion about the limitations to comics, and Eisner's piece seemed to rise out of their disagreement.

"I said there were intrinsic limits to what comic books could do," O'Neil recalled, "and I cited Hamlet's soliloquy as an example. Six months later, *Will Eisner's Quarterly* came out with Hamlet's soliloquy, done by a teenager on a tenement roof."

Eisner included "Hamlet on a Rooftop" in *Comics and Sequential Art* as an example of how body language and facial expressions could be used to accentuate the written text. Eisner would always insist that *The Spirit* had been influenced by the movies, while his graphic novels were informed by plays he'd seen.

Eisner applied his love of plays to his later graphic work, particularly in his graphic novels. "Hamlet on a Rooftop" became an exercise in applying body language as a means of enhancing text. (Courtesy of Will Eisner Studios, Inc.)

"*The Spirit* was originally done with a cinematic approach because I felt that the language at the time was being impacted by cinema and cinematic ideas," he told *Time* magazine's Andrew D. Arnold in 2003. "[But] I was never really satisfied with it. It was interesting and fun to experiment with, but for me live theatre is a reality."

"Hamlet on a Rooftop" provided concrete evidence of how to bring the theatrical elements of a story to the printed page. The creation of each panel was fully explained with an annotation affording readers a rare glimpse into Eisner's creative process. More significant, the piece illustrated Eisner's lifelong insistence on the importance of writing in comics.

"This represents an example of a classic situation—that of author vs. artist," he wrote. "The artist must decide at the onset what his 'input' shall be; to slavishly make visual that which is in the author's mind or to embark on the raft of the author's words onto a visual sea of his own charting."

In analyzing "Hamlet on a Rooftop," Dennis O'Neil, lauded for his work on the *Batman* and *Green Lantern/Green Arrow* books, saw the piece as representative of the marriage of story and art that made Eisner so effective.

"That was his art—catching the precise moment when the body is most expressive of what's going on in the mind, and then sort of freezing that and exaggerating a little bit," O'Neil said. "The art skill is subordinate to the narrative. It's not showing off and saying, 'Look what pretty pictures I can draw.' That's a happy skill to have, but it's not comics. With comics, everything should be subordinate to the narrative. He was doing it with Shakespeare, and he was doing it with the stuff he wrote, too."

The Dreamer, published by Kitchen Sink Press in 1986, told a story that was half a century old. As Eisner already knew, there were plenty of contemporary dreamers hard at work on graphic novels, and 1986 turned out to be a breakthrough year in the form. In that one year alone, Art Spiegelman, one of the best-known names in the underground comix scene and widely regarded as one of the comics industry's leading literary practitioners, published *Maus: A Survivor's Tale*; Frank Miller, who had already garnered critical acclaim for his reworking of *Daredevil*, released his four-part novel, *Batman: The Dark Knight Returns*, a recasting of the character's legend accredited with saving the character from extinction; and Alan Moore and Dave Gibbons, a British writer/artist team, were publishing the initial installments of their influential twelve-part *Watch-men* series. In *Faster Than a Speeding Bullet: The Rise of the Graphic Novel*, comics scholar Stephen Weiner labeled 1986 "a turning point" in the comics industry: "From then on," he wrote, "cartoonists aimed higher and hoped more than ever that their books would break—or at least peek—out beyond the traditional comic book readership, and focused more on stories holding appeal to readers who didn't care for traditional comic books."

Although all four were young enough to have been Eisner's children, and had learned aspects of their craft by looking at his oeuvre, they were all fiercely individualistic and dedicated to their own work, with colorful histories in comics prior to the publication of these seminal graphic novels.

Spiegelman, a product of the undergrounds, shared Eisner's passion for the literary possibilities of comics as well as his distaste for superheroics. The son of Polish Jewish concentration camp survivors, Spiegelman grew up in New York, where he attended Manhattan's High School of Art and Design. He connected with the publishers of underground comix in the late sixties, and his work appeared in a variety of publications, including *Bijou Funnies*, *Bizarre Sex*, *Comix Book*, and *Snarf*. His more commercial work included a twenty-year stint with Topps, the chewing gum company best known for its sports cards. Spiegelman, who cited *Mad* magazine's Harvey Kurtzman as one of his major influences, created the Garbage Pail Kids and Wacky Packages for the company. In 1980, he and his wife, Françoise Mouly, founded *Raw*, an influential annual book-length anthology of innovative sequential art, which included early installments of *Maus*.

Maus was the most complex work of sequential art ever created. It is the story of one family's survival of the Holocaust, but it is also a memoir of how a young artist came to terms with his complicated, prickly relationship with his father and of the relationship between an artist and his art. Spiegelman was unsparing in his portrayal of the book's characters, including himself, leaving to readers the tasks of sorting through the details and answering the book's crucial questions about what is right and good in the face of annihilation and, perhaps more complicated, what is right and good once that threat is gone.

By the time *Maus: A Survivor's Tale* was published by Pantheon Books, Spiegelman had been living with the project for what seemed like a lifetime, literally and figuratively.

When I began to work on *Maus*, there wasn't such a thing as a graphic novel, but there also wasn't a body of literature about the Holocaust that would take several lifetimes to read. So it was really just a matter of time to figure out "What happened to my parents, and how did I get born?" When I started the book, my father was very much alive, and by the time I was halfway through with it, he was dead.

The Holocaust, of course, was a monumentally tragic story, and any telling of it could not be diminished by the wrong kind of writing or art. On a personal level, Spiegelman had tremendous loss as deep background to his writing: his older brother and only sibling, Richieu, had been a victim of the Holocaust, poisoned by his caretaker-aunt rather than be deported from the Zawiercie ghetto and sent to almost certain death at the camps; and his mother, Anja, had committed suicide in 1968. Spiegelman's decision to use anthropomorphic animals to tell his story—the Jews were mice; Germans, cats; Polish, pigs; and Americans, dogs—was bold and risky and almost certainly would have backfired in a writer/artist of lesser talent. Even so, it took a while for this creative process to ferment. The first volume of *Maus*, eventually subtitled *My Father Bleeds History*, concentrates mainly on Spiegelman's relationship with his father and his process of self-discovery and is populated almost exclusively by Jews as mice; a second volume, *Maus II: And Here My Troubles Began*, published five years later in 1991, flashed back to the horrors of the concentration camps and required the delicate working in of the other zoomorphic ethnic groups and nationalities.

Frank Miller, who would eventually become involved in the movie business, including as director of a film adaptation based on Eisner's *Spirit*, was heavily influenced by film and by the violent urban setting he saw after moving from Vermont to New York. Although, like Eisner, he was more interested in telling adult stories than in depicting superheroes in tights, he was also astute enough to recognize that the superhero presented him with his entrée into the comics world. When he had the opportunity to work on *Daredevil*, a slowly sinking Marvel title about a blind crime fighter, he added hard-edged elements of film noir that would later become his trademark in his *Sin City* graphic novels. His work was daring, uncompromising, flashy, brutally authentic, moody, and violent—and readers responded enthusiastically, boosting the title's circulation to the point where Marvel started publishing it on a monthly rather than bimonthly basis. The success of his *Daredevil* series led to other assignments, most notably a short run on the *Wolverine* spin-off of Marvel's immensely popular *X-Men* series, and the *Ronin* miniseries, which he created. His involvement with *Batman* began with a one-shot appearance as the illustrator in a 1980 Dennis O'Neil–written Christmas story.

Batman had gone through a number of permutations since Bob Kane created him, including a television run as a parody, and Miller saw potential for further development of the character, not as the heroic "Caped Crusader slavishly devoted to the law," but as the "Dark Knight," a wealthy vigilante working almost as far outside the law as the criminals he was facing. Miller's Batman was in his late fifties, retired from crime fighting, haunted by his past, and angered enough by the present violent society to leave retirement. There were no *POW*s and *BAM*s in Miller's version; Batman was as apt to throw a bad guy off a building as offer him a chance to surrender. In *The Dark Knight Returns*, Miller ushered in a Batman for adults, a female Robin, a seriously unfunny Joker, a Gotham City that was darker than ever, and action that moved at a breakneck pace from frame to frame.

Will Eisner lauded *The Dark Knight* series as a significant breakthrough in superhero comics—a move toward satisfying readers who had grown up reading *Batman* and were still fond of the character but now insisted on more realistic, mature stories. "The superhero largely survived because big publishers had the courage to have other people do adaptations of the superheroes," he stated. "They had the courage to let Frank Miller take Batman and carry him on into another dimension, so to speak."

Watchmen took superheroes another step forward. Like Frank Miller, Alan Moore was fascinated by the vigilante reputation of the superhero, and he too was intrigued by the possibilities of exploring the world as it would be without these costumed characters. Born in 1953, Moore had witnessed the clash between culture and counterculture, the evolving of the Beat Generation into the hippie movement, the mushrooming of radical politics, the growth of the music industry, the acceptance of science fiction and fantasy as serious literature, the use of psychedelic drugs as a means of expanding the mind, and the development and expansion of performance art. In short, he was far from the mainstream in his interests and work, and perhaps more than any comics writer, he was able to integrate a vast range of popular culture into his work. After gaining a lofty reputation in England, he began working on American comic books, bringing his esoteric ideas to DC Comics' *Swamp Thing*.

Four years older than Moore, Dave Gibbons took a more traditional route to his success in comics. The prolific artist contributed to the popular *Harlem Heroes*, *Dan Dare*, *Judge Dredd*, and *Doctor Who* series in the United Kingdom in the late 1970s, and for American comics, he illustrated *Green Lantern* and *Superman* stories for DC. He and Alan Moore teamed up on several issues of *Tharg's Future Shocks* before jointly tackling Superman in "For the Man Who Has Everything" in the 1985 *Superman Annual*, and they discovered that they worked well together.

Watchmen was a culmination of their experiences and a compelling combination of diverse styles and influences. Comic books had certainly never seen anything like the nonlinear, episodic storytelling that Moore brought to the series, a sort of *Naked Lunch* world populated by ex-superheroes, in which superheroes have been banned (or employed by the government), cynical politics dominate, and the world, as always, seems to be on the verge of extinction. Gibbons's exquisitely detailed artwork, set on a traditional nine-panel page, came across as order amid anarchy, while Moore's new mythology, propped up by literary and cultural references, fragments from popular songs, and even long prose passages presented as memoir, gave *Watchmen* a complexity never before attempted in comics.

The arrival of these and other graphic novels didn't usher in immediate acceptance in the larger cultural landscape, as a young British journalist and comics writer named Neil Gaiman discovered when he approached newspaper editors with a proposal to write an article on the phenomenon.

"I wanted to write about comics and graphic novels," he recalled, "and I went to an editor of a major English newspaper and said, 'Alan Moore is doing *Watchmen*, Art Spiegelman is doing *Maus*, Frank Miller is doing *The Dark Knight*. All of them will talk to me. I want to do an article on this thing that is happening right now.' I was told, 'Neil, it was English comics character Desperate Dan's fiftieth anniversary six months ago. We wrote about it. Why would you write about this now?' I went to the Sunday *Times* magazine in England, and I sold an editor on letting me do it. I talked to Alan and Art and Frank, and to the Hernandezes and Dave Sim, and wrote an article about this crazy thing that was happening right now. I handed it in and, not hearing anything back, I called the guy and said, 'What did you think?' He said, 'Well, we have a problem with it. It's not balanced.' I said, 'What do you mean it's not balanced?' He said, 'You seem to think they're a *good* thing'—meaning that in order to get proper balance, I needed to have somebody saying that comics led to juvenile delinquency or whatever.'"

Gaiman was learning a lesson that Eisner had learned during the early days of comic books: Acceptance was going to be a long, tough process. Graphic novels would go through the same process of naysaying and skepticism, critical examination, opposition, and ridicule before the public eventually came around. But it was going to take some time.

Eisner adapted well to his new home in Florida, settling into a routine busy enough to rival any work period of his career. He complained to friends that he had too many ideas and not enough time to pursue them. Rather than tie up a year or a year and a half to create a lengthy graphic novel of the scope of *A Life Force*, he decided to develop smaller projects addressing some of his philosophical musings—books that would take much less time—and he would stay on this path for the better part of the next decade. His next book, *The Building*, was one such project.

While living in the orbit of New York, Eisner had taken the changes in the urban landscape for granted. Stores and restaurants came and went, businesses failed and new ones started up. After moving to Florida, Eisner saw New York as a kind of expatriate, revisiting the scenes of an earlier life; and in revisiting those scenes, he couldn't avoid noticing that the structures of the city, like living organisms, had a kind of life expectancy.

"I became obsessed by the fact that the buildings in New York City that I grew up with were being torn down," he said. "Every time I came back to the city, another building was missing, and a new glass building was there instead. At first I was outraged and said that this was terrible, but then I asked myself: why? What happened? Can it be that when a building is torn down that nothing is left?"

Like *A Contract with God*, *The Building* was a grouping of four stories connected by location, in this case a Manhattan building modeled after the Flatiron Building on Twenty-third Street. And like *New York: The Big City*, the new book continued Eisner's obsession with how human drama is played out in plain view, unnoticed by the public. Once again, the four stories' main characters were dreamers whose lives are altered—and ultimately destroyed—by their pursuit of those dreams. Monroe Mensh is a man who keeps to himself and minds his own business until one day, when an innocent child is caught in the crossfire of a shooting in front of the building. Haunted by the fact that he might have saved the child if he'd pushed the boy to the sidewalk or even shielded him with his own body, Mensh devotes the rest of his life to making amends, working for a number of children's organizations, never satisfied that he is making a difference. Gilda Greene, a beautiful woman, falls for an as-

piring poet but marries a dentist for the security he will provide, however unsatisfying. Every Wednesday she meets the poet in front of the
building, and they have a lifelong affair; but ultimately it is no more satisfying than her marriage. Antonio Tonatti is a talented violinist who's
not quite good enough to earn a living in music and eventually winds up
in front of the building, busking for passersby. P. J. Hammond, the son of
a real estate tycoon, obsessively schemes to purchase the building; eventually he succeeds, but at the cost of his business and ultimately his life.

Their stories are played out through extensive flashbacks. They now
exist as spirits who gather in front of the building, invisible to those on
the sidewalks, forgotten, anchored to their pasts. The building is replaced by a steel-and-glass high-rise, leaving the spirits in a kind of limbo
until an accident—a window washer's safety belt breaks and he falls
onto a sign overhanging the building's entrance, where he dangles precariously while a horrified crowd watches below—gives them a purpose, perhaps even an opportunity for redemption. The book's happy
ending negates what might otherwise have been an overwhelmingly
cynical set of stories.

When he first saw the rough pencils for the book—which Eisner was
then calling *City Ghosts*—Dave Schreiner projected a lot of work ahead.
He liked the premise, which he called "thought provoking," but Eisner's
execution of it was sloppy and not credible. "You've stressed to me before
that you want a strong editor, or at least strong opinions," Schreiner reminded Eisner in a letter expressing his first reaction to the rough pencils
of the book. "With that in mind, I have to say there are some things I feel
are not right with 'City Ghosts' in its present configuration."

This was not what Eisner wanted to hear. He had hoped for a quick
turnaround on the book, and in a phone call responding to Schreiner's
letter, he told Denis Kitchen that he would consider Schreiner's suggestions but added that he had already lettered half the book—a sure indication that he would listen to positive criticism but probably wouldn't be
making a lot of changes.

In an effort to keep his message—that the building, like all buildings
in the city, "somehow absorb[s] the radiation from human interaction"—
front and center, Eisner intentionally kept his allegorical stories simply
told and illustrated, which only highlighted the book's inadequacy in
character and plot; prose writers would have struggled to get any of these
stories published. The theme of the book was sound, but the stories
seemed to be filled with stock characters behaving in predictable ways.
The element of surprise, a staple in Eisner's best work, was absent, as was

the sense of play that made *The Spirit* stories so entertaining. Eisner could only hope that his readers would be emotionally attached enough to his stories to accept these shortcomings.

Gary Groth, editor of the *Comics Journal*, was not one of those readers. Groth, who was born in 1954, had not grown up reading *The Spirit*, and when he was finally introduced to Eisner's work, he was not inclined to lump Eisner in with Carl Barks, Harvey Kurtzman, or Jack Kirby, his favorites of the classic comic book artists. Although he had no personal issues with Eisner, Groth wasn't terribly fond of his book-length work, which struck Groth as "frivolous and tepid compared to the underground comics I was also devouring at the time." Nor was he pleased by what seemed like the free pass Eisner was given by the critics and comic book historians. When Eisner's books were reviewed—usually by fanzines, since newspapers still weren't reviewing graphic novels on a regular basis—they were treated as if they were stone tablets issued from on high, and Eisner was treated as if he were the man destined to deliver comic-dom to the Promised Land. He even seemed immune to the criticism, now becoming very public, of editors and publishers who treated their artists like slaves, holding on to their works' copyrights and keeping their artwork long after it had been published. As Groth saw it, despite Eisner's benevolent reputation, he was really no different from the others. He'd run a comic book sweatshop, held on to copyrights and artwork, and de-nied artists their artistic identities when they were working for him at Eisner & Iger.

These thoughts were brought into fine focus when Groth read *The Dreamer* and *The Building*, both of which he judged to be subpar efforts but which were nevertheless getting strong notices in the comics fanzines. Groth reasoned that it was time *somebody* took Eisner to task, and his re-view of *The Dreamer* and *The Building* did just that.

"The review was harsh," Groth admitted in a reflective overview of Eisner's career published in the *Comics Journal* after Eisner's death, "but it was honest, accurate, and, of course, utterly politically suicidal."

Eisner was hurt and angry when he saw Groth's review, which he felt was unfair and unnecessarily mean-spirited. Groth had the reputation of being esoteric in his tastes and of mincing no words when stating his opinions or his likes and dislikes, but in Eisner's view, the review was nasty even by Groth's standards. Worse yet, on a personal level, Eisner felt as if a professional friendship had been betrayed. He'd given the magazine numerous interviews over the years, supplied it with art, and, in his mind, done his part to see that the publication maintained high visibility on the market. In his heart, if he stepped back from the work and looked at it objectively, applying the same standards he used in judging the work of others, Eisner might have admitted that *The Dreamer* and *The Building* were substantially inferior to *A Contract with God* or *A Life Force* and that the two books might never have seen the light of day if not for his relationship with Dave Schreiner and Denis Kitchen and their efforts on his behalf.

Still, the review was too much. Eisner stewed over it for months and decided that he was finished with the magazine. In the years ahead, the *Comics Journal* tried to line up interviews with Eisner, but he rejected all requests. Eisner and Groth would eventually exchange pleasantries at the 2000 Comic Book Legal Defense Fund cruise, but as far as Eisner was concerned, his professional relationship with that magazine had ended.

chapter fourteen

WINNERS AND LOSERS

The big joke in my shop was that I always had one foot under the front office desk and one foot under the drawing board.

At the end of 1986, Eisner became involved, in a very limited way, with the creation of the Comic Book Legal Defense Fund, an organization founded by Denis Kitchen and dedicated to assisting artists and writers in a variety of legal issues, from copyright matters to freedom of speech court cases. As a rule, Eisner preferred to keep his life away from comics, including his political views, as private as possible. If asked in interviews, he would provide frank answers to questions regarding his opinions about censorship and the long abused rights of comics creators, but he was guarded about allowing his name to be attached to organizations that might eventually cause him grief at the marketplace.

Kitchen called to request a sheet of art to be included in a portfolio he was assembling to raise funds for Michael Correa, a Champaign, Illinois, comic book store employee who found himself in a storm of trouble when six police officers walked into the establishment, confiscated seven titles, and arrested him for having obscene books on display. One of the seized books had been *"Omaha" the Cat Dancer*, a Kitchen Sink title written by Kate Worley and illustrated by Reed Waller. Kitchen readily admitted that *Omaha* was sexually explicit, but he also pointed out that it was critically acclaimed internationally and that "it was also one of the very few comics in 1986 that could boast a high female readership."

Kitchen might never have heard of the arrest had it not been for a call from Frank Mangiaracina, a comic book distributor who also owned a small chain of Illinois and Indiana comic book stores called Friendly Frank's, which employed Correa. A short time after hearing from Mangiaracina, Kitchen attended a comics convention in Minneapolis, where he ran into comics artists Sergio Aragonés (*Mad*), Hilary Barta (*Plastic Man*), and Reed Waller. Kitchen told them about the bust, which was unsettling enough on principle alone—no minors had been sold any of the comics, and Kitchen was especially outraged when one of the officers suggested that these comics had a strong element of Satanism in them—but it also posed serious problems to Correa, who faced a prison term and/or a steep fine if convicted. The four came up with the portfolio idea, and Kitchen began contacting artists he felt might be sympathetic to the cause.

Fourteen artists, including Eisner, donated plates for the portfolio, which was issued in a signed, numbered edition of 250 and in an unsigned edition of 1,250. The effort wound up raising more than $20,000, which turned out to be urgently needed when Correa was convicted in a lower court and funds were needed to hire a First Amendment attorney for the appeal. Correa was eventually exonerated, and with the money left over from the fund-raising, Kitchen founded the Comic Book Legal Defense Fund, for which he would serve as president from 1986 to 2004.

Comic book creators' legal rights had improved since the beginning of Eisner's career, although at a painfully slow pace—and only then as the result of the efforts of a very few. Artists had fought for ownership of the characters they created, for copyright of the stories they wrote, for the return of their artwork after its publication, and for protection against censors who would impose their will on the creative process.

Neal Adams, one of the most highly regarded artists in comics, knew of these struggles. He'd leveraged his standing in the industry to advocate

Eisner enjoyed appearing at comics conventions and sitting on panel discussions, where he was able to promote his lifelong agenda of seeing comics realized as entertainment for adults. (Courtesy of Denis Kitchen)

for the rights of others with less influence. He could recall a time when, as a young graduate from the School of Industrial Arts, he'd wanted to go into comics but had been advised that comic books were on the way out, that he should find another way to apply his considerable skills in the job market. He wasn't one to surrender easily. He created shorts for *Archie Comics*, contributed to other titles, kicked around in advertising, earned his chops on the *Ben Casey* newspaper comic strip, and finally settled in at DC, where he became the company's star artist by virtue of his cover art and, later, his groundbreaking team-up with writer Dennis O'Neil. He'd reluctantly gone along with some of the industry's long-standing business practices until one day, while working for DC, he saw one of the company's employees cutting up original art.

"I got up hypnotically and walked toward him," Adams remembered. "He was slicing original art into three pieces. I stopped him. I said, 'What are you doing?' He said, 'I'm cutting up the art and throwing it away.' I said, 'Hold on a second. Please stop. I really don't know exactly how to say this, but you really shouldn't be cutting up that artwork.' He said, 'Yeah, yeah. I'm the low man on the totem pole. I get the crap jobs. Every three months, we pull the art out of the cabinets and chop it up and throw it away.' Once I got a hold of my soul, which had shriveled to the size of a peanut, I said, 'Look, I don't want you to cut up any of these pages anymore. I'm not kidding. I have to go talk to some people, but while I'm talking to them, I don't want any of these pages cut up.'"

Adams's journey was only beginning. After leaving the befuddled employee wondering why discarded art mattered to anyone, Adams visited his friend and DC art director, Carmine Infantino. Adams hoped that Infantino, an outstanding artist himself, would be sympathetic to his appeal. Infantino agreed in principle that the art shouldn't be destroyed and that it belonged to the artists and not the company, but he also noted that this had been DC's practice for as long as he'd been with the company.

"Okay, let me put it one more way," an increasingly frustrated Adams told Infantino. "If another piece of artwork gets cut up, I'm going to be leaving here. I'm not going to work for DC."

This caught Infantino's attention. Adams was a huge presence at DC. Comic book readers bought certain titles just because Adams was illustrating them. Losing him would be disastrous.

Infantino, still sympathetic to Adams's cause, told Adams to hang on until he'd talked to DC's powers-that-be. He conferred with the company officials and, a half hour later, returned with the verdict. The company would store the art and quit destroying it.

This, however, only solved part of the problem.

"What about the idea of returning it to the artists?" Adams wondered.

"They'll get back to us on that," Infantino replied.

Seven years passed with no further movement Adams would inquire about it on occasion, with nothing to show for his efforts. DC higher-ups, not entirely convinced that Adams was correct when he argued that the artwork had monetary value, decided to test the theory by auctioning one of Adams's covers at a Detroit convention. The artwork, they determined, was worth money—a lot of money—which only created a new set of problems. They obviously couldn't toss out valuable work, but could they return it to the artists, knowing that they, and not the company, would be benefiting from sale of the art?

This provided Adams with his game-winning strategy. The company had paid for a *service*, for the right to reproduce the art, not for the artwork itself. If DC had purchased the artwork, the company would have been required to pay a sales tax, and given the company's decades-old policy of operating the way it had, there was no telling how much it would owe in back taxes if, say, a disgruntled employee contacted the tax people in Albany and briefed them on the situation. A few weeks after hearing Adams's argument, DC decided to return the artwork to the artists. Not coincidentally, Marvel began doing the same, probably more out of fear of losing their artists to DC than out of the sudden realization that it was the upstanding thing to do.

"It was a little bit of a game," Adams said of his back-and-forth with DC. "I tried to keep it light as much as possible. I wasn't aggravating, and I wasn't angry or yelling at them. I tried to be sensible and logical and practical. I said, 'Look, if the artwork is returned to the artist and he discovers, God forbid, that it's worth something if he could sell it, isn't he going to put more effort into making a piece of artwork? Isn't it in his behalf to do that for you? Doesn't it then fall to you to profit by this sincere effort to do a better piece of artwork?' Sometimes it's very hard to convince people that things are in their best interests, which is shocking to me, but in the end, we did it."

His work as an advocate was even tougher when he tried to help get Jerry Siegel and Joe Shuster their due for the creation of *Superman*. The two former kids from Cleveland had grown older, much older, and had been on the outs with DC, National Periodical, and most recently Warner Communications for longer than either cared to remember. Much of their misfortune had been their own doing. They'd voluntarily signed away ownership rights to *Superman* shortly after they'd created the character, and later, they'd really buried themselves when they sued for money they felt they had coming to them for having created arguably the biggest character in comics history. Their advancing years weren't being kind. Shuster was nearly blind and living with his brother in a small New York apartment, while Siegel, living with his wife in Southern California, was in declining health. Neither had any money to speak of.

Adams and Jerry Robinson, a Golden Age artist responsible for the creation of the Robin and Joker characters in *Batman*, mobilized the comic book community, distributed petitions, gave television and radio interviews, and in general tried to shame corporate minds into offering Siegel and Shuster at least a minimal annual stipend, along with health insurance benefits, in return for all the money Superman had earned for the company over the years. A film adaptation of *Superman*, starring Marlon Brando and Christopher Reeve, was in the works, and the huge sums of money being sunk into that project were widely publicized. By this point, the creators of *Superman* had all but given up on the idea of remuneration for their character, though both, particularly Siegel, wanted their names attached to the movie, Superman merchandising, and other Superman-related books, magazines, and products. This, they felt, was only fair, and the movie adaptation gave them another shot. "The first *Superman* movie was the big leverage we had," recalled Robinson, a past president of the National Cartoonists Society. "They didn't want any bad press at that time."

While Adams worked on the comic book organizations, Robinson contacted board members and artists in the National Cartoonists Society as well as members of the Association of American Editorial Cartoonists, Writers Guild of America, the Screen Cartoonists Guild, and the Overseas Press Club. He even managed to secure the involvement of Kurt Vonnegut and Norman Mailer, two of his Cape Cod summer home neighbors. Warner Communications felt the pressure but also believed that the company faced a problematic legal bind: If it agreed to the terms of the Siegel and Shuster case, it might be up against other legal turmoil.

As Robinson remembered, the battle took its toll on the two artists.

"It was terrible, the state they were in," he said. "They had no self-confidence. Their identity was lost. Imagine creating one of the biggest properties of the twentieth century and not having your name on it. My argument was you didn't take the author's name off Sherlock Holmes because Arthur Conan Doyle died. Or Shakespeare. It was a tenuous negotiation. The big sticking point was getting their name restored to the property as creators. That was the last thing we had to settle.

"The night before we settled, I got a phone call from Jerry [Siegel]. He was in bad health at the time. He had already had a heart attack. He called and said we had to settle the next day because he was worried he wouldn't survive the negotiations, and if he didn't, he wouldn't have anything to leave to his wife. So I knew we had to settle the next day."

The two sides did reach an agreement the next day, on December 19, 1975. Siegel and Shuster would receive $20,000 annually, with cost-of-living allowances added. Their heirs would also receive benefits. Their names would be attached to all Superman products—comic books and books, television programs, and motion pictures—but not toys.

Robinson lauded it as a landmark decision. "It established the protocol of restoring the creators' names," he said.

All this had happened in the 1970s, before neoconservatism, when unions were still strong, strikes and work stoppages could bring a company to its knees, and the residual effects of the 1960s kept people suspicious of "the Man," of big corporations that would screw the daylights out of the little guy if there was a dollar to be earned or quietly stolen. Evening network news programs still wielded tremendous clout, and a news item such as the television and newspaper reports on the Siegel/Shuster battles over Superman could trigger a wave of activity. But now, in the 1980s, a scene like the one in the Illinois comic book store, while perhaps not encouraged by the public in the same way comic book burning had been several decades earlier, was tolerated or overlooked.

Eisner supported efforts to help comic book creators with their rights, but as a businessman he also felt a conflict. After all, he'd run a comic book studio not all that different from the others of the time. Granted, he'd created almost all the characters originating from the Eisner & Iger shop, but it was his name, or a generic nom de plume, that was affixed to the comics, and his shop maintained ownership and the copyrights on the art. He'd negotiated what he thought was a fair deal with Busy Arnold for ownership of the Spirit and other characters that he'd created for Quality Comics. At the same time, he resented losing ownership of the characters and art he'd produced while he was with P★S magazine, and he made certain that would never happen again. As he saw it, comics were business, and there would inevitably be a give-and-take between the artist and the company buying his or her work. The individual was ultimately responsible for negotiating his or her rights.

Still, it rankled him when he heard about other comics artists—especially the pioneers who had paved the way for the big companies—having to struggle to gain credit for their creations or fight to have their artwork returned. When Jack Kirby became involved in a protracted battle with Marvel to get his original art returned, Eisner was compelled to act on his old friend's behalf. In an "Open Letter to Marvel Comics," published in the *Comics Journal*'s August 1986 issue, Eisner chastised the company for keeping what he considered to be Kirby's property.

"This matter has gone beyond whatever legal merits there may or may not be to your position," Eisner wrote. "By your public intransigence you are doing severe damage to an American cultural community that is now emerging from the dark years of trash and into an era of literary responsibility."

Eisner's tone was firm and direct, as close to open anger as he would permit himself in print. The Kirby story had been perplexing and very public. Kirby had produced thousands of pages of art for Marvel during the 1960s, but when he asked for its return, Marvel offered him a mere eighty-eight pages—and only under the condition that he sign a document in which he all but disclaimed any connection to the characters he had produced for the company. Copyright and ownership weren't negotiable. Kirby refused to sign the document, but he also balked at the suggestion that he sue the company. Like Siegel and Shuster, he was getting old and was in poor health, and he wasn't certain he'd live to see litiga-

Eisner enjoyed great international appeal, and it was never more evident than when someone painted *The Spirit* on the Berlin Wall. (Courtesy of Denis Kitchen)

tion worked out in court. The *Comics Journal* took up his cause, closely following and reporting the case, which was gaining momentum by the time Eisner wrote his letter in 1987. Marvel was under no legal obligation to return the art, and like DC before them, they feared that capitulating to Kirby's request might set a precedent the company didn't want to deal with in the future.

But this was precisely Eisner's point.

"A whole new generation of creative people [is] watching your conduct," Eisner warned Marvel at the closing of his letter. "Don't fail them!"

Marvel eventually returned more than two thousand pages of Kirby's art, though the company retained the copyrights on the work and ownership of the characters Kirby had created or co-created for the company. For Kirby, it was a bittersweet victory, but about the best he could have expected.

Over the course of his career, Will Eisner received numerous inquiries from Hollywood producers about the possibilities of optioning the rights to *The Spirit* for a motion picture or television adaptation, but he could never work out an arrangement that accommodated the demands of the entertainment industry while maintaining the integrity of the character. Those making the inquiries were always looking to update the character in a modern urban setting, convert him into an action hero, dress him in

Signing his art in São Paulo, Brazil, in 1987. (Courtesy of Denis Kitchen)

tights or a cape—anything but that hopelessly dated fedora and suit—or give him superpowers. Eisner rejected such offers without hesitation. *If* a theatrical motion picture or made-for-television movie were to be made out of *The Spirit*, it would have to remain faithful to his vision. What gave the Spirit his appeal was the fact that he was good-looking and strong, yet vulnerable, capable of getting into life-threatening binds or even being outwitted by a beautiful woman; he had to use his wits, rather than gadgets, to save the day. Eisner favored James Garner, who played this type of character in the 1960s television western *Maverick*, but they never hooked up while Garner was young enough to play the Spirit.

Some of those interested in *The Spirit* were worthy of consideration.

In the early sixties, Anthony Perkins, still flush from his breakthrough role in Alfred Hitchcock's *Psycho*, contacted Eisner with the hope of optioning *The Spirit* for the movies. There was a fair amount of money involved, but after talking to Perkins, Eisner had to decline.

"I asked him what his idea was for a movie," Eisner recalled, "and he said, 'Well, I see the Spirit as a sort of a mystic, as a magician of some kind.' That's clearly not what I had in mind. The deal never went anywhere, of course, because I wasn't interested in a Spirit movie where he was a supernatural figure, even if it would be a successful movie. It's not that I dislike making money, but I am very loyal to the ideas I hold about my characters."

William Friedkin, director of *The French Connection* and *The Exorcist*, succeeded in optioning the motion picture rights to *The Spirit*, but bringing the character to the big screen proved to be elusive. Harlan Ellison, the award-winning writer and screenwriter whose work touched upon every type of fiction imaginable, worked on a screenplay, as did Jules Feiffer, who had successfully adapted *Popeye* for Robert Altman's film. Even Eisner gave it a shot. None of the scripts met Friedkin's approval, and the project died in development.

There had also been an attempt to launch an animated version of *The Spirit* in the early 1980s, and when Eisner agreed to option the film rights to the character, he was confident that he had a good team working on the feature. Gary Kurtz, producer of *American Graffiti*, *Star Wars*, and *The Dark Crystal*, was on board in a similar capacity, while relative newcomers Jerry Rees and Brad Bird were hired to write the screenplay. Bird, who would eventually make his name as director of such films as *The Iron Giant*, *The Incredibles*, and *Ratatouille*, had created a rough pencil trailer of a possible *Spirit* project with Rees and several Cal Arts students, and Eisner was impressed when he was shown the work.

"I will be interested to see it," Eisner told an assembly of reporters covering the Tenth Annual International Salon of Comic Books in Angoulême, France, where he was the 1984 convention's guest of honor. Although he'd tried to distance himself from comparisons of comics and the movies after he began producing graphic novels, Eisner still saw a connection between the two media. "In the beginning were the comics, then the movies," he stated. "Cinema came from comics; I regard film as an extension of comics."

Unfortunately for Eisner and the others, the timing for finding backing for such a project was bad, and Eisner's original hopes of aiming the *Spirit* newspaper feature at adults worked against him in the movie project. These were times before animated films were geared for adults, and Walt Disney Studios, the standard-bearer for movies marketed to children, was financially troubled and in a state of flux. Development on the movie was shelved, and the option eventually expired.

When a made-for-television movie was finally produced in 1986 and broadcast a year later, it was an unqualified disaster, not for a lack of effort on the part of those making the film, but for reasons no one could have predicted when the project was in the planning stages. The deal with ABC and Warner Brothers Television called for a ninety-minute movie, which would be used as a pilot for a television series—which, in theory, sounded like a good idea. After the Spirit and his origins were introduced to television viewers in the pilot, the ensuing programs could follow Eisner's old episodic structure. Rather than try to set the movie in the past, which the budget wouldn't permit, or update the character to the present day, which Eisner wouldn't allow, the director and screenwriter placed the Spirit in a stylized limbo, a place that was neither past nor present, with buildings and cars that could have existed at any time. Ebony, for obvious reasons, was out, replaced by a new sidekick named Eubie. The script was written by Steven E. de Souza, whose 1982 film, *48 Hrs.*, had been a major screen success.

Unfortunately, for reasons beyond the understanding of de Souza and others working on the film, ABC insisted that the role of the Spirit be given to Sam J. Jones, a handsome young actor who looked like Denny Colt but couldn't act the part. Will Eisner's character was a man of action, which Jones could play convincingly, but he was also highly nuanced—thoughtful, funny, vulnerable, not unlike George Lucas and Steven Spielberg's Indiana Jones—and for all his efforts, Jones couldn't master these qualities. Instead, he came across as an action hero indistinguishable from those viewers had seen before.

Even so, *The Spirit* might have caught on as a television series, and Jones might have had the chance to grow into his part, if big business hadn't entered into the picture. While *The Spirit* was in the midst of production, ABC changed hands, and the new powers-that-be didn't share the previous management's enthusiasm for the project. Rather than air the movie in an opportune, prime-time slot during the regular programming season, ABC broadcast it in the middle of the summer, on July 31, 1987, in the heart of the rerun season, when viewers traditionally stayed away from their television sets. The ratings were awful, and the movie was never rebroadcast. *The Spirit* television series never materialized.

After seeing the movie, Eisner, reminded of why he had resisted offers for a *Spirit* movie adaptation for all those years, was relieved by the cancellation. "It made my toes curl," he said.

Not that he was surprised by the project's failure. In a letter to Denis Kitchen written a year prior to the movie's airing, Eisner lamented the state of the project. He'd screened a tape of the film and wasn't fond of what he saw.

"They have about 2 million dollars invested in this 'dud,'" he told Kitchen, "but I can't weep for them because they never consulted me—or let me near the project. I'm only sad that the hopes we had of widening our audience has gone up in smoke."

By now, Eisner was accustomed to receiving his share of industry accolades and to seeing his name included on the short list of the influential founding fathers of the comic book, but he was unprepared for the call he received from Dave Olbrich, an administrator of the annual Kirby Awards handed out for excellence in the comics industry. The awards, Olbrich informed Eisner, were being discontinued. Would Eisner consent to having his name attached to similar awards?

Eisner had reason to pause before answering. The Kirby Awards, named after comics great Jack Kirby, his friend and former protégé, were being discontinued because of a dispute between Olbrich and Gary Groth, Olbrich's former boss at the *Comics Journal*. Olbrich's split with Groth had been nasty. There had been a power struggle over the Kirby Awards, to such an extent that Kirby himself had asked that his name be removed from the awards. Fantagraphics was starting up a new set of awards named after Harvey Kurtzman. Aside from his own falling-out with Groth, Eisner had other issues to consider. Kurtzman was still one of his close friends, so other awards might be seen not only as competing, but even as an affront to another great artist.

At the 1989 San Diego Comic-Con with comics giants Burne Hogarth, Jerry Robinson, and Jack Kirby. (Courtesy of Denis Kitchen)

According to Ann Eisner, her husband gave a lot of thought to the awards before accepting the offer. "At first he was very wary," she remembered. "He was always very suspicious of awards. He put down some very, very firm conditions—that they be objective, that he have nothing to do with selections, that it be done by a group, that it not be a favoritism or popularity thing. You could like or dislike the cartoon or the person, but that had nothing to do with it. It had to be based on merit."

Even with these stipulations, Ann had strong reservations about her husband's winning such an award, which was entirely likely.

"I felt that if the award was named after Will, he should not be able to participate. I said, 'You ought to disqualify yourself,' but he said, 'I can't very well . . .' Burne Hogarth, who for some reason didn't like Will, was interviewed, and he said, 'What do you think about a man who has an award named after himself so he can win it?' That's the kind of stuff that people say, even though you know it isn't true and it's done completely out of your control. People are always going to say that you had an *in* on that award. I said, 'Will, it's just not you. You shouldn't have people think that about you.' But he did not listen to me."

Dave Olbrich bowed out of his administrative post shortly after the awards were introduced, and Jackie Estrada, a volunteer organizer with San Diego Comic-Con, took over. "Dave and Will and Denis Kitchen came to Comic-Con and said, 'Since you're nonprofit, would you be willing to take over these awards and have them under your umbrella?'" she recalled. "They suggested that I be the one to administer them."

Estrada was well qualified for the job. She had attended the very first San Diego Comic-Con back in 1970 and became involved in it as a volunteer four years later. What started out as a part-time seasonal job blossomed into a year-round adventure. She eventually wound up inviting guests and working on the souvenir book, which put her in touch with a large number of artists, including Eisner, who contributed art to the annual souvenir book.

By this point, conventions bore almost no resemblance to Phil Seuling's old Fourth of July gatherings in New York, and none was bigger than the annual gala event in San Diego, which featured enormous crowds arriving from all over the world, many decked out in the costumes of their favorite characters; panel discussions with some of the biggest names in the industry; and displays and booths selling, advertising, or showing off anything related to comics, from memorabilia to the latest offerings. The convention, with its high energy and noise, was not for the faint of heart. People were packed in so tight that just walking from display to display required resolution and patience. Art and commerce collided, with predictable results.

Having been around since the early days of the conventions, Eisner had watched them grow and evolve from the modest to the overblown, and he observed their effect on the industry. "It is to me a most important development in the history of the comic book marketplace," he said of the comics convention. "I believe it will be seen by historians as an underlying force that changed the direction of comic book content."

The Eisner Award ceremonies became one of the cornerstones of the convention in San Diego. In her early days with the awards, Jackie Estrada was given a crash course in the logistics of organizing and administering the industry's version of the Oscars. Planning began months prior to the awards ceremony, and the schedule was tight.

"We mail out a call for stories," she said, explaining the process that has evolved over the years, "and tons of books come pouring in. I have five judges, selected to get the full spectrum of background. I have a retailer, somebody from book distribution, someone who actually creates comics, a journalist of some kind, and a reviewer. I bring these five people

to San Diego, to a hotel for a three-day weekend, and they have a meeting room where all the submitted material is laid out. They have to narrow everything down to the most worthy items in each category, then
make sure they've read all those items in every category, and then vote
on them to determine what goes on the ballot. The ballot goes out to
creators, publishers, and retailers in the comic book industry. There's an
online ballot today. To be nominated is to draw attention to the best
material being done in comics, so we try to publicize that as much as
possible. Then we start to prepare for the big ceremony in San Diego. All
of the nominated items have to be scanned to Photoshop and set up for
PowerPoint. Then I work with an MC for the awards. We line up celebrity presenters. We have to set up the whole event itself, with VIP seating
and dealing with hotels, food, and publicity."

Will Eisner himself presented the awards to each of the winners, and
for many of them, the handshake from the comics legend was as big an
honor as winning the award itself. Eisner enjoyed the attention, but even
for someone half his age, standing onstage in one place for a couple of
hours could be physically difficult. Eisner soldiered through the ceremonies, refusing to be seated, until one year he faced a situation that was in
parts a tribute, a practical joke, and a means of getting him off his feet.
The idea originated with comics artists Jeff Smith and Kurt Busiek, who
were concerned about having Eisner stand throughout the ceremony.
They contacted Jackie Estrada and outlined their plan.

With DC editor Julius Schwartz and *Batman* creator and high school friend Bob Kane.
(Courtesy of Denis Kitcher)

"We've got to get some kind of throne," they said.

One of the convention workers had connections with the San Diego Opera, and it was through the opera company that Estrada was able to borrow a throne upholstered in red velvet. The prop, everyone involved agreed, was perfect. Smith and Busiek hid the throne behind a curtain until after Eisner had been introduced and was onstage, and then they brought it out, to the laughter and applause of the awards ceremony attendees. Eisner, though slightly embarrassed, played along, taking a seat and posing for pictures until the hoopla had died down. Then he stood up—and stayed that way for the remainder of the ceremony.

J. Michael Straczynski, winner of an Eisner Award for Best Serialized Story for his work on *Amazing Spider-Man* in 2002, probably offered the best summation of the experience of receiving the award from Eisner when, after taking it and shaking Eisner's hand, he held the award up in the air and said, "You know, you get the Emmy, you don't get it from Emmy. You win the Oscar, you don't get it from Oscar. How freakin' cool is this?"

While organizing his office and files after his move to Florida, Eisner came across a small book's worth of artwork originally intended for *New York: The Big City*. The pieces, like those in *The Big City*, were short takes—graphic essays, he called them—that hadn't fit into the other book's thematic structure, but the art was too good to be discarded. In looking over the work, Eisner decided to gather the pieces into three basic themes—Time, Space, and Smell—and release them as a small book.

Eisner never intended *City People Notebook* to measure up as a literary work against his ambitious graphic novels or even to *New York: The Big City*. It was more of a confection, a grouping of thirty-two pieces, some only a page or two in length, all dealing, like the vignettes in *The Big City*, with what Eisner called "the most influential and pervasive environmental phenomena" found in the daily life of New York City. The pieces, Eisner said, were very personal—the kinds of sketches he might have slipped into other graphic novels—and he included self-portraits in some of the art, depicting the artist as an observer.

Eisner's decision to release the sketchy, disparate pieces was based largely on a writer's ultimate nightmare: he was suffering through a prolonged period of writer's block and couldn't come up with a topic for a full-length graphic novel. Work on *The Dreamer* and *The Building* had drained him, and as he complained in a letter to Dave Schreiner, he was struggling to find the enthusiasm that fueled each new project.

"While it is true that I go through periods of 'blockage'—generally after the completion of a work—it usually lasts only until I get 'revved' up for a new project," he wrote. "What I did reveal to Denis was my feeling of dissatisfaction with the lack of real challenge among the stored up notes for new projects that fill my desk-top file next to the drawing board. I told him I was always in search of new departure and finding them these days was hard work. At any rate finding them these days was not as easy as heretofore. And adding to the agony was the fact that working behind or with a writer (as Denis suggested) does not solve my frustration a bit. It is very exhilarating being a pioneer but it loses some of its euphoria when the time comes to move on and find another mountain to conquer."

The mountain he was talking about was just up ahead. Conquering it would involve one of the biggest struggles of his career.

chapter fifteen

THE HEART OF THE MATTER

*I think many of us in this business are Don Quixotes. Anybody
in the business of innovation is in pursuit of something that
nobody else believes exists.*

In the spring of 1989, Eisner began work on his lengthiest graphic novel
since *A Life Force*. This new book, eventually published as *To the Heart
of the Storm*, was designed to focus on the insidious forces of anti-
Semitism in the Depression-era New York of Eisner's youth. It was to be
a work of fiction, but after numerous reworkings, it would become the
most autobiographical work Eisner would ever create.

Earlier books had addressed compelling personal issues in his life,
but aside from *The Dreamer* and "Cookalein," his autobiographical
coming-of-age short story in *A Contract with God*, Eisner consciously
avoided depicting actual events from his private life in his work. Whether
this choice was a matter of dignity or courage is a subject for debate.
According to Eisner, he had changed the names in *The Dreamer* to avoid
embarrassing living people depicted in the book, but as he would admit
in interviews after the publication of *To the Heart of the Storm*, he found
"standing naked in the drill field," his description of the self-reflection
required for the process of autobiographical writing, exceedingly difficult.

"When I was younger, I couldn't bring myself to do it," he confessed.
"I didn't dare bare those details of my life. I think autobiographies are
done mostly by older people because they have reached the point where
they don't have much to lose."

In writing about the Depression and the uneasy period leading up to
World War II, Eisner almost inevitably included incidents from his own

life. After all, he had lived through the period, and he adhered to the old axiom that a writer should write about what he or she knows. As a young boy, he'd coped with anti-Semitism in his own neighborhood, and his brother, Julian, had permanently lost a precious part of his identity because of a flashpoint moment on the street and the resulting name change. Sam Eisner's story, from his days in Vienna to his eventual move to the Bronx, exemplified the European Jewish immigrant experience and the hardships of adjusting to life in America. And to illustrate the way Jews were socially shunned, Eisner needed only to deliver a heartbreaking story from his own youth, when a girl whom he fancied, not knowing that he was Jewish, invited him to a party, only to learn the truth from one of Eisner's rivals and panic about how her parents would react to her bringing a Jewish boy into their home. The book, Eisner decided, would achieve its greatest impact as a straight-on memoir rather than a fictionalized account.

Still, for a man accustomed to controlling the flow of public information about his private life, Eisner found writing about his family especially problematic. Even though both of his parents had died years earlier, Eisner agonized over how to portray them in his book. He didn't trust the accuracy of his memory, and he knew that if he was as truthful as his memory permitted, his parents—or at the very least his mother—would not be seen as sympathetic characters.

"To write about your parents and their lives is very painful," he said, likening the process to the catharsis of psychotherapy. "You have to fight the feeling of betrayal if you want to tell something honestly, like the relationship between my mother and father. This was something that I always held very private. I wouldn't tell that to anybody before, and now I'm about to tell it to the world. I ask myself, if my mother and father were alive, would they not feel betrayed by that; am I telling the truth?"

And what, he wondered, *was* the truth? As he pointed out in an interview with journalist Shawna Ervin-Gore, his relationship with his mother and father had changed significantly over the years. He'd gone through periods when he was very angry with them and saw them in a negative light, only to soften in later years when his own experiences added texture and color to what had at one time seemed very black and white. Furthermore, Sam and Fannie were remembered in different ways by each of their children, as Eisner discovered after the publication of *To the Heart of the Storm*. "When I showed the finished book to my brother," Eisner recalled, "he said to me, 'I don't remember Mom and Dad like that.' And when I showed it to my sister, who is thirteen years younger than I am, she said she remembered them the way I did."

To get around some of these concerns, Eisner decided to narrate the story of his youth through a series of extended flashbacks. He opened *To the Heart of the Storm* with Willie, his protagonist, sitting on a train in his army uniform, talking with two other draftees on their way to basic training. One of his two fellow inductees is the Catholic editor of a Turkish-American newspaper in Brooklyn, the other a redneck southerner whose coarse opinions immediately send Willie into meditations about his childhood and the bigotry he'd seen. As a literary device, the flashbacks work effectively: Willie's memories are selective, reliable but not necessarily complete. These impressions, the diamond-hard truths of what remained with him over the years, are what matter most.

To the Heart of the Storm was a masterwork, comparable to, or even surpassing, the excellence of *A Contract with God* or *A Life Force*. But as Eisner's correspondence with Dave Schreiner indicates, the writing did not come easily. Schreiner, by now totally frank with Eisner about his work, was immediately impressed with the rough dummy of the book, but he had serious issues with it as well.

"I think it's your most powerful work to date," he wrote to Eisner in July 1989, "and if it were published as is, it would probably be all right. I see no need for you to feel apprehensive about it. It *is* intense, and rightfully so. It is your perspective on your early life, and in a novel, you get to call 'em as you see 'em."

Schreiner went on to offer detailed criticism of what he perceived to be the technical and editorial flaws of the book. He had serious reservations with the balance of the book's characters, who, he felt, "on the whole . . . [were] either Jewish or anti-Semitic." It would work better, he suggested, if the characters were further fleshed out. "It would perhaps be a bit more authentic if you could humanize these characters a little more. Add a little grey, perhaps, to the black and white. In a good novel, the reader is given a hopefully complete picture of a human being, good and bad, and draws an overall judgment of that character from the picture drawn in the book."

One of Schreiner's strongest objections was to Eisner's working title: *A Journey to a Far-Off Thunder*. The title, he told Eisner, fit the book, but it wasn't the best from a marketing standpoint. "Would you consider thinking of a *short* and *punchy* main title, and using the *Journey* line as a subtitle?"

Eisner considered Schreiner's suggestions, made some revisions, especially on the characters, and submitted a new draft to Schreiner. While conceding that the characters in the new version were more nuanced than in the previous version, Schreiner still wasn't satisfied. "Ambiguity and ambivalence—this is what can make good books," he wrote, exhorting Eisner to take it even further. In addition, he gently prodded Eisner toward using his mother's real name rather than "Birdie," as he was calling Fannie in the draft. He appreciated the power Eisner's autobiographical segments about his parents already had, but he believed they could be revised to be even more effective. The biggest technical problem, in Schreiner's view, involved the flashbacks: as written, they could be confusing, especially because there were sometimes flashbacks within the flashbacks; he encouraged Eisner to clean them up. He still didn't like the title, although (perhaps because he knew he could push Eisner only so far) he mentioned it only in passing.

And so it went, for more than a year. Eisner revised, and Schreiner pushed for more. Finally, Eisner was reaching the end of his patience. On September 4, 1990, he sent what he considered to be the final draft, with a terse note: "Enclosed: it's *The Book* !!! Note I've settled on a shorter title 'To the Far Off Thunder'—based on your advice. Hope you can work on this before your wedding—I really cannot expect you to take this book on your honeymoon."

Pending nuptials didn't prohibit Schreiner from reading and responding. After the difficulties he and Denis Kitchen had experienced with Eisner over the lengthening of *The Dreamer*, Schreiner recognized, in the stubborn tone of Eisner's letters and telephone calls, that Eisner felt he had reached his limit. Schreiner was very fond of the book, but he still felt compelled to toss out a few final suggestions that he hoped would strengthen it. Most were of the technical variety: the newspaper headlines that Eisner used were often incorrect. In one panel, for instance, Eisner had a headline with the Nazis invading Belgium in 1942. "In 1942," Schreiner informed Eisner, "that battle was over for two years. I suggest . . . NAZIS ADVANCE IN NORTH AFRICA."

This was small but important stuff, as were the misspellings and typos. But Schreiner still had big problems with Eisner's title, and he now made one last ditch effort to convince him to change it.

"My major misgiving is the title," he stated. "I still don't like it. It just doesn't reach out and grab me. Are you open to suggestions for change, if we can find a suitable one? Please say you are: by far and away, the weakest part of this book is its title . . . It would be a dirty shame if people were not drawn to this book because of its weak title.

"This is your strongest work to date, Will," he continued. "I know you seem to care more for the writing than the art, and ordinarily I do, too. I don't even feel competent usually to comment on art. But I know good art when I see it, and I can't let this opportunity pass without saying that I see it here . . . I think you've done a particularly masterful job this time."

To Schreiner and Denis Kitchen's great relief, Eisner relented and retitled the book *To the Heart of the Storm*, putting an end to one of the longest-running disagreements he'd ever had with his editor and publisher. The work on this book signaled Schreiner's finest hour as Eisner's editor, and Eisner seemed to recognize it. "My gratitude to Dave Schreiner, who edited this book and persevered with me through the painful revisions," he wrote in the book's acknowledgments. "His judgment is unfailingly dependable."

The reviews ran the spectrum from lukewarm to breathless. In one that probably made Eisner wince, *Publishers Weekly* praised Eisner's story but objected to what the reviewer dismissed as "schmaltzy" and "melodramatic" graphics, calling the book "a vivid but flawed work from an acknowledged master of the comics medium."

Don Thompson was much more generous in his review in *Comics Buyer's Guide*, one of the industry's most influential publications. "This is an outstanding work even by Will Eisner's standards," Thompson wrote. "Don't miss this. Keep a copy handy for any *truly* intelligent friend who asks you why you are still reading comic books at your age. If this doesn't answer him/her, maybe he/she is less intelligent than you thought."

Eisner was often asked where he came up with the ideas for his graphic novels and how he chose his projects. He'd reply that some were from scenes he had witnessed; some came from thinly disguised but deeply personal autobiographical material he'd carried around in his head for decades, waiting for the proper moment and inspiration to motivate him to work it into a story. He'd overhear bits of conversation, see a compelling news item on television, or maybe find something worthwhile in the newspaper. He kept an idea file of notes, clippings, and rough pencil drawings, every scrap representing a seed for a story. His emotions played a heavy role in his decisions about what projects to pursue.

Such was the case in early 1991, when he read a newspaper account about a woman named Carolyn Lamboly, a disabled, destitute woman who, in the throes of loneliness and depression, had hanged herself with a light cord a few days before Christmas 1990. Her body lay for two months in a funeral home, and when no one stepped forward to claim her, she was buried in an unmarked grave in Dade County's Memorial Park. As sad as the story was, it got worse. The woman had spent a year trying to get help from government and community services, but she had become lost in the system, just another name on an endless list of faceless, "invisible" people you see every day but never notice. On January 3, 1991, just days after her suicide, she was formally approved for housing and medical coverage.

Angered by the story, Eisner set out to work on three comic book–length stories about people who, like Carolyn Lamboly, went about their lives unnoticed. Published by Kitchen Sink Press as three individual comic books, the stories, entitled "Sanctum," "The Power," and "Mortal Combat," were eventually bundled into a single book and published as *Invisible People*.

"Sanctum," the story most closely modeled after Lamboly, is a tale about Pincus Pleatnik, a bland, middle-aged bachelor who works as a clothes presser, keeps to himself, and tries to blend into the scenery, believing that anonymity "is a major skill in the art of urban survival." His life takes an irreversible turn one day when he opens the newspaper and sees his name listed on the obituaries page. He suddenly has to prove—to his boss, his landlord, the newspaperwoman reporting his death, and the police—that he's alive. It doesn't go well. After a series of misadventures bordering on the absurd, he winds up homeless and jobless and ultimately loses his life as a result of his quest to prove that he's not dead. In a bitter postscript to the story, the person who wrote his obituary, now retiring and being honored at a party thrown by her employer, receives an award and a $5,000 savings bond for the accuracy of her reporting.

Pincus Pleatnik, Eisner explained in an introductory note to the story, was a composite of the people he'd seen on the street during his youth. Like most other New Yorkers, he passed by without paying them a shred of attention.

"I grew up accepting this as a normal phenomenon of metropolitan life," he wrote. "Only years later did I realize how pervasive was this brutal reality and how people often accept, even welcome, invisibility as a way to deal with urban danger."

If "Sanctum" dealt with the worst possible results of *predictable* invisibility, "The Power" showed how even great promise might slip into such a state. There's no question that Morris, the main character in this story, is special. He discovers early in his life that he has the power to heal humans and animals, and rather than manipulate that power for fame and wealth, he decides to use it for the greater good. He wanders aimlessly from job to job, hoping to make a difference, only to slip into obscurity. When a scam artist from a circus finds him, she announces that he is the father of her young boy, who is hobbled by a birth defect and needs someone to heal him so he can walk. Morris hopes to be a good father, while the boy and woman are interested in him only for his powers. But Morris is unable to heal the child, and the woman and child abandon him in his final obliteration.

The third story, "Mortal Combat," is an account of a spinster librarian named Hilda, who has no life other than as caretaker to her aging, demanding mother. When she meets and falls in love with Herman, a colleague at the library, her mother, who doesn't want to share her daughter with anyone, threatens her relationship. Their love is all that gives Hilda's and Herman's lives any definition, and their life together is brought to a horrible conclusion when Hilda's mother, now bedridden, accidentally sets the apartment on fire, killing the two women and leaving Herman permanently disabled.

"In relating the story of Herman, who became the unwilling prize in a clash of wills, I hoped to evoke the helplessness of a person caught in an intersection of the traffic of life," Eisner wrote of the story. "Herman's dilemma is one of the dangers of group living."

Coming on the heels of such a lengthy, ambitious work as *To the Heart of the Storm*, *Invisible People* seemed like a minor work retracing steps already taken elsewhere. Eisner worried about this in a letter to Dave Schreiner. "I expect I'll be criticized by the younger critics for repeating myself," he predicted. "But I've wanted to deliver myself of these themes for some time—maybe on the next book I'll try some new arena." Schreiner, aware of the inspiration for the stories, was sympathetic. "You have to let these things out or they keep on bothering you," he advised. "You are an artist and writer and, while you can't do these things in a vacuum, I think it would be very dangerous to let a critic guide you. You wouldn't be true to yourself then."

Eisner labored over the three stories, from the naming of his characters to the titles of the stories themselves. He knew what he wanted to accomplish, but he seemed lost as to how to get there. "Sanctum" went through numerous drafts as Eisner struggled to fit the message of the Carolyn Lamboly story within the framework of his tale about Pincus Pleatnik. He drew several different rough pencil covers for the proposed single-story Pincus book, using such titles as "The Hider," "Safety," "Sinkhole in the City," "Sinkhole," and "Invisible," before eventually settling on "Sanctum." But he grew so frustrated that he wrote Schreiner and begged for help. "Still flailing at the title," he told his editor, undoubtedly remembering his issues with Schreiner over the title for *To the Heart of the Storm*. "For heaven's sake pick one and help me go on with this monster in peace!!!"

The *Invisible People* trilogy was marketed with a unified cover design and logo, with Eisner's name prominently displayed on each of the three covers, each book distinguished by its different art and title. However, readers weren't as compelled to buy all three books as they might have been if it had been a continuing story, and sales lagged behind expectations. The sales figures were similarly disappointing when the stories were gathered into a single volume. It could be that Eisner had gone to the proverbial well one time too often, that readers weren't drawn to the book as intensely as to some of his earlier efforts, as Eisner had originally feared, or it could have been that a downturn in the market affected sales. Whatever the reason, *Invisible People*, for all Eisner's passion and the work that went into it, was now officially a minor work in the Eisner line.

When Eisner celebrated his eightieth birthday on March 6, 1997, Ann marked the occasion by throwing a surprise party at the International Museum of Comic Art, a huge affair attended by friends, family, and

To those who knew them, Will and Ann Eisner were a model couple, as happy together late in life as they were when they initially met. (Courtesy of Denis Kitchen)

business acquaintances. Eisner was in remarkably good physical condition for someone his age—or even two decades younger—and he was producing more than ever. Nearly twenty years had passed since the publication of *A Contract with God*. In the years since the book's publication, he had produced more graphic novels than anyone in the business. He had reached the age where he was the subject of career retrospectives, he'd received more awards than he could keep track of—including the Milton Caniff Lifetime Achievement Award in 1995—and the University of Massachusetts had hosted an important conference on the graphic novel.

His international fame only added to his sense of accomplishment. His books had been translated into more than a dozen languages and had appeared in Europe, South America, and Asia, published by prestigious houses willing to give him the kind of exposure and circulation that American comics artists would have envied in their own country. He was invited to global comics conventions, where he was greeted as an icon. In 1996, he designed a special mural from his "Gerhard Shnobble" story for the side of a building in Copenhagen, and *The Spirit* had even appeared on the Berlin Wall before it was brought down.

Still, the acclaim wasn't enough. He was approaching his career goals, but he still felt confined in a comics ghetto. His awards were industry awards; his books were still limited to the comics section of bookstores, next to the superhero books and away from general interest or literary fiction shelves. Art Spiegelman had won a Pulitzer Prize for *Maus*, and newspapers were now devoting at least token space to reviewing higher-profile graphic novels, and while these were important steps forward, Eisner was growing impatient.

The key, he felt, was survival—waiting for the world to finally put the final pieces in place and his living long enough to see it happen.

New, unexpected projects popped up out of nowhere. One, originating from a Florida public television channel in the mid-1990s, combined Eisner's love of adapting classic literature to sequential art with his continuing interest in using comics as a teaching tool. The Florida television station had come up with the idea of producing a series of what could best be described as electronic comic books, in which there would be very little animation other than dialogue balloons that would be read by young viewers. Eisner's job was to supply the artwork, which was similar to storyboards used in movies.

"I developed what I called a reading experience on television," he explained. "I took the classics and reduced them to a little half-hour show in which there was no animation in the art, but the balloons were animated, so the language would pop in as the characters spoke it, and that would force the reader to read it. Well, it never went anywhere. They couldn't get enough funding to pursue it, and I was left with a bunch of stories."

The stories, in the form of pencil dummies, were filed away but not forgotten. Eisner, who never threw away a scrap that might eventually be recycled or worked into something, talked about the ill-fated television project with his agents and publishers overseas, and to his surprise, he learned that libraries were interested in stocking these comics as children's books. By then, Eisner had moved on to other graphic novel projects, but he found a way to satisfy the demand for these children's books without compromising his work on adult material. He worked on the adaptations after he'd completed one of his graphic novels, using them as sort of a cool-down exercise. "After I finish a heavy book," he explained, "I find that doing something very light is a great antidote."

Self-portrait from the unpublished *Count of Monte Cristo*. Eisner hoped to use comics to adapt the classics for young educational television viewers, but a lack of funding killed the project. (© Will Eisner Studios, Inc., courtesy of Denis Kitchen)

Unpublished panel from *The Count of Monte Cristo*.
(© Will Eisner Studios, Inc., courtesy of Denis Kitchen)

Eisner enjoyed the break. Aside from adapting some of the stories he'd enjoyed as a boy, he was able to put his own spin on some of the classics, such as in *The Last Knight*, his adaptation of *Don Quixote*, where he included a scene in which Don Quixote meets Miguel de Cervantes, his creator. Publication of the books was spaced over a period of years, in Europe and Brazil and, eventually, the United States. Four titles—*Moby Dick* (1998), *The Princess and the Frog* (1999), *The Last Knight* (2000), and *Sundiata: A Legend of Africa* (2003)—were issued by Nantier, Beall, Minoustchine Publishing in hardcover and paperback editions, including limited, signed, and numbered editions.

Another project, requiring far less attention, involved Eisner's return to his most famous character in a series of new Spirit adventures. Denis Kitchen had always favored such a project, but Eisner, fearing that it would turn *The Spirit* into a "mausoleum" piece, resisted creating, or allowing others to create, new stories. Kitchen persisted, arguing that *Spirit* fans would want to know what had happened to the Spirit after all these years, and when they finally came to an agreement, Eisner did the worst possible thing: he turned in an insipid story entitled "The Spirit: The Last Hero," a piece guaranteed to disappoint the character's most loyal readers. Kitchen had no choice but to reject it.

Kitchen wasn't finished, though. The comic book industry was staggering through an economic downturn in the mid-1990s, and Kitchen Sink Press, never a corporate giant like DC or Marvel, was in trouble. Kitchen and his staff tried to keep the company afloat through innovative merchandising and reprints of classic comics, but with the exception of their tie-in with the immensely popular film *The Crow*, sales figures lagged far behind

expectations. New *Spirit* stories, Kitchen reasoned, could only help prop
up his business. If Eisner, now totally focused on his graphic novels, wasn't
up to producing new stories, maybe others could. It would be a way of
showcasing the talents of the top comic creators of the day while simulta-
neously paying tribute to the artist who had influenced them.

When Eisner finally relented, it was under two conditions: He would
not be responsible for creating or editing the new material; and he had to
approve all material that others produced, "to be sure that they would
not warp or defame, or otherwise alter the basic concept of The Spirit's
character." He wasn't about to allow other artists, regardless of their talent, to kill or marry off the Spirit, turn him into a tormented street character hooked on drugs or alcohol, or otherwise tarnish the standard set
half a century earlier.

"It was a little like putting your child up for adoption," Eisner said of
his allowing others to create stories for his character. He was relieved
when the new stories in *The Spirit: The New Adventures* were assigned to
some of the best writers and artists in the comics business, including Alan
Moore, Neil Gaiman, Frank Miller, and Dave Sim. "I was astounded at
what some of them were doing with him," he admitted. "Clearly, I would
never have done stories the way these guys did. Guys like Alan Moore and
Neil Gaiman are very much in touch with today's reader, and they were
talking to them in that vein. I had no sense of violation or concern; they
just saw The Spirit from their perspectives."

He was especially pleased by the focus on story. Moore (*Watchmen*),
Gaiman (*The Sandman*), and Sim (*Cerebus*) were master craftsmen known
for elevating the level of storytelling in their work, and they clearly had
an understanding of Eisner's character before they began their work on
The New Adventures. This was evident in the series' first issue, when Moore
wrote and Dave Gibbons illustrated three Spirit origin stories, including
a retelling of Eisner's own account of how *The Spirit* came to be: there
was a familiarity to the work, but it was obviously not Eisner's. The same
was true of Neil Gaiman's entry, illustrated by Eddie Campbell, an account of a frustrated screenwriter who suddenly finds himself caught up
in a Spirit story.

"I did not try writing a Spirit story," Gaiman explained. "I tried writing a story about the Spirit, which is rather different. What I felt was fun
was just sort of going, 'Okay, what would happen in somebody's life if he
keeps bumping into a Spirit story?'"

Gaiman had to be talked into writing the story. When Denis Kitchen
called and asked him to contribute to *The New Adventures*, Gaiman

turned him down, despite the fact that he'd been hooked on the Spirit since he'd picked up the second Harvey reprint issue at age fourteen. What Gaiman hadn't counted on was Eisner's powers of persuasion.

"He was determined that he would have me in his book, and I was just as determined that I wasn't," Gaiman recalled, "because my attitude is that you can't do a Spirit story as good as the classic Spirit stories that burned my brain.

"I remember the moment he closed me, and it was like being closed by a really good salesman. You had no plans to buy that car, and you walk out of there with the keys in your pocket. We were in Gijón in northern Spain at a week-long convention. All of the events took place at night, so you didn't do very much in the afternoon. And one of those afternoons, Will told me we were going for a walk. Will and Ann and I walked for several miles on the beach and stopped at a little café. Will and I had this very, very long conversation, in which we both wound up realizing that what I wanted to do with *The Sandman* was what he'd done with *The Spirit*, which is create a character who is a machine for telling stories."

The two talked on and on about comics—about their history, the direction they were taking, and *The Spirit*. Eisner kept trying to convince Gaiman that he was a good candidate for writing a new Spirit story and Gaiman kept resisting until Eisner finally closed the sale by promising Gaiman the original cover art to the published issue of *New Adventures* containing Gaiman's contribution. Eisner was doing the pencils for the covers and letting others ink and color, which led to an awkward scene when the issue with Gaiman's story appeared.

"I had this really weird and embarrassing conversation with [inker and colorist] Mark Schultz," Gaiman remembered. "I said, 'Can you send me the cover?' And Mark said, 'Will promised me the cover.' I mentioned it to Denis, and shortly thereafter he sent me the pencil sketch for the cover— Will's sketch, which I honestly preferred to the finished thing, because it's Will's pencils. The way Will sent it to me was absolutely fascinating. He just rolled it up and taped it. There wasn't even a cardboard tube. I thought that was wonderful, how little Will valued that part of the thing."

Eisner bristled whenever he heard criticism that his books were too sentimental. He admitted that his own philosophy of inherent human goodness had been influenced by his boyhood reading of Horatio Alger, but he did not find anything objectionable about depicting triumph over adversity, or survival in urban grit. He saw nothing wrong with giving his books happy or wistful endings. He could have chosen another route, one reflecting the hardships of his life, and while some of those difficulties had been addressed in *A Contract with God*, *A Life Force*, and, most recently, *To the Heart of the Storm*, bitterness was something that he felt was best left to others. He could point to any number of his *Spirit* or other graphic stories that had ended unhappily, but his harshest critics didn't seem to notice. *Family Matter**, the darkest original story he would ever produce, and the last graphic novel he would submit to Kitchen Sink Press, seemed to be a direct response to those critics. Readers would have to look hard to find anything uplifting about it.

The story, about a family's gathering for its patriarch's ninetieth birthday, contained disturbing elements of greed, lust, euthanasia, incest, alcoholism, and violence—all told over a brief period of time, through flashbacks and some of the most pointed dialogue Eisner would ever write. Placing this dialogue in the familiar comics balloons, Eisner realized, was problematic in a novel so serious. He knew that to much of the public, dialogue balloons not only gave comics their distinctive look, but had the unintended effect of making otherwise adult subject matter appear to be something less than good, valid work.

"I'm coming to the reluctant conclusion that there is a stout wall of prejudice out there among adult readers against anything with dialogue that's encapsulated within a speech balloon," he told interviewer R. C. Harvey. "It makes the book suspect and translates it into a totally different category. If there's a balloon, it's comics; and if it's comics, it's for kids or idiots."

Eisner was inspired to write the book as the result of his conversations with Ann, who told him of the travails of some of her acquaintances in the Florida retirement community. One old woman's story especially infuriated him. Her husband had died, leaving her money, and her two grown children were constantly looking for ways to rob her of it. Eisner ruminated about their character, motivation, and actions and decided to take a reporter's approach in telling his story: he would tell the story without serving up any kind of judgment or otherwise interfering with it. If it was successful, readers would react with the same kind of anger that he felt when he heard Ann's accounts.

Family Matter tells the story of five siblings—two brothers and three sisters—as they gather for a birthday party for their wheelchair-bound father. None have any use for the old man, but all have secrets and ambitions that tie them to their father and reasons to demand a say in his

---

* Later editions of the book carried the title, *A Family Matter*.

future. The old man, unable to speak or walk, sits in a wheelchair in a room and listens in as his children argue over his fate in an adjacent room. As a story, *Family Matter* doesn't approach the ambition and detail of *The Name of the Game*, the family saga that Eisner published three years later, and with only a couple of exceptions, the characters behave too predictably to be as memorable as some of Eisner's characters in previous books and stories. Still, for its raw emotion, the book ranks high among Eisner's graphic novels.

"It was pure, unadulterated anger," observed Frank Miller, one of the novel's admirers. "That was a side of Will that I just wanted to see more of, because I always felt that he stopped himself at the edge of something. He was a deeply angry man, like any man who'd lived through what he did would be.

"He and I actually argued over one letter in the title of *Family Matter*. I thought that it would have been a wonderful double entendre if it had been called *Family Matters*, and I felt that by making it *Family Matter*, he shortchanged what was really one of his most bitter and brilliant books."

After nearly three decades of operating on a tight budget in an ever changing market, employing what, by industry standards, amounted to a skeleton crew working overtime to push out product, and reprinting the seminal work of such comics pioneers as Milton Caniff, Harvey Kurtzman, R. Crumb, Al Capp, and Will Eisner, Kitchen Sink Press finally went under in early 1999. It had been a slow, painful, ugly death.

Kitchen, quite naturally, was crushed.

"I didn't know what to do," he recalled of the period immediately following the demise of Kitchen Sink Press. "I was in a very deep funk—and possibly clinically depressed. I spent a lot of time just walking in the woods, sorting through stuff, not knowing what to do next.

"Will called me and said, 'What are you going to do?' I said, "I don't know. I'm thinking.' He said, 'How would you like to be my agent?' It had never crossed my mind. It is not something I would have suggested to him. He could have handled his own books, but he wanted to help me—he was being a friend—and he didn't want to be distracted from the actual creation of books, he saw time slipping away and he wanted to take advantage of what was left."

Actually, the agency proposal wasn't entirely new. In 1997, two years before the demise of Kitchen Sink Press, Kitchen and Judith Hansen, a former deputy editor at KSP, had discussed the idea of forming an agency together, and had run the idea past Eisner. Hansen, an attorney with extensive background in both mainstream trade book publishing and comics publishing, including stints at Random House and Simon and Schuster, had known Eisner since 1994, and had started her own literary agency in Sydney, Australia. When Kitchen Sink finally sank in 1999, Kitchen and Hansen moved forward, with Eisner and former Kitchen Sink author Mark Schultz as founding clients.

Eisner, who had begun work on the book that would become *Name of the Game*, only to suddenly find himself without a publisher or anyone to market his work, was delighted to have Kitchen and Hansen representing him. "As you know, we have a long 25 year relationship which I don't want to abandon," he wrote Dave Schreiner, referring to his business and personal relationship with Kitchen.

Eisner was equally concerned about retaining Dave Schreiner as an independent editor. "I see no reason why we cannot continue our editorial relationship on future works when & where appropriate," he wrote Schreiner, who had remained in Wisconsin following the Massachusetts relocation of Kitchen Sink Press and taken a job with a publisher in Madison. Schreiner was happy to continue the relationship.

Not surprisingly, it didn't take long for the new agents to find a new home for Eisner's work. Paul Levitz at DC Comics, an admirer of Eisner's work from the moment he'd seen his first *Spirit* comic, was immediately interested in adding Eisner to the DC roster. Hansen, however, was looking for more than a one-shot deal: She wanted DC to reprint his entire backlist of graphic novel titles. DC was open to this, and a deal was struck.

One of DC's book publishing division's highlights was its "Archives" series, featuring reprints of *Superman*, *Batman*, and other popular long-running features, all published in handsome hardcover volumes and featuring beautifully restored color artwork. *The Spirit*, Levitz figured, would be an ideal addition to the series. DC would start at the beginning, with the *Spirit*'s very first 1940 appearance in the Sunday comic book supplement, and present the full run of Eisner *Spirits*, running in chronological order, marking the first time the feature had been available in its entirety, in full color, in bound books. Each book would feature an introduction written specifically for that volume by a comics authority. To be complete, the company would have to publish more than two dozen volumes, at a hefty price tag of $49.95 each, but Levitz reasoned that there

Spirit bookplate, distributed in Europe, but unpublished in the United States.
(© Will Eisner Studios, Inc., courtesy of Denis Kitchen)

were enough libraries looking for bound copies of the legendary comics
feature, as well as fans with discretionary cash, to make the series profitable. Eisner, quite naturally, was very pleased with the arrangement, especially when he learned that the first volume was outselling similar volumes
featuring Superman and Batman.

Minor Miracles, Eisner's first new book with DC, veered sharply away
from *A Family Matter*, as if Eisner needed to cleanse his mind after the
psychological brutality of his last graphic novel for Kitchen Sink. In *Minor
Miracles*, Eisner returned to Dropsie Avenue, where anything was possible
in the drudgery of everyday life. A wealthy merchant just might pass by
a down-and-out cousin digging through the trash and offer to stake him
the money needed to start a business and turn his life around. A quick-
thinking kid might come up with an ingenious plan to avoid a beating
at the hands of neighborhood bullies. A new kid of mysterious origins
might appear out of nowhere and touch off a series of good fortune to every-

one in the neighborhood. A crippled young man might meet and marry a young woman who, as the result of childhood trauma, is unable to hear or speak, and, with any luck, live happily ever after with her. The four stories in *Minor Miracles* sprang from these possibilities, and under Eisner's writing and drawing, they became shards of magic glistening in the otherwise drab city streets. Ordinary occurrences had extraordinary consequences, becoming little miracles that no one seemed to notice.

"The stories in this work resemble the stories my parents referred to as 'meinsas,'" Eisner wrote.

> And while they are apocryphal, they were nevertheless distilled from my remembrance of those that were the common property of our family. For example, my mother would point to an old man feeding pigeons in the park and tell me, 'That is an uncle on your father's side . . . let me tell you about him . . . it's a miracle.'"

DC Comics soon learned what Denis Kitchen had known at Kitchen Sink Press: Will Eisner was so prolific that it was impossible to publish his books as quickly as he was writing them. He had a backlog of material that he wanted to publish, including a new collection of graphic stories based on what he observed during his travels for *P*S* magazine. He'd worked on the book during the last days of Kitchen Sink Press, even though he didn't have a market for it, but when he insisted that this new book be published in time for the upcoming San Diego Comic-Con, DC, unenthusiastic about the book to begin with, declined, stating they couldn't meet Eisner's publishing timetable.

The book, *Last Day in Vietnam*, landed with Dark Horse Comics, an Oregon-based company founded in 1986 and specializing in graphic novels and comic books for mature readers as well as in serious studies of their creators and comics history.

Diana Schutz, an editor at Dark Horse, was assigned the task of preparing *Last Day in Vietnam* under the tightest production schedule imaginable. The book landed on her desk in April, and with the San Diego convention looming only three months in the future, she had to accomplish the copyediting, design, story sequence, and photo work in one-third the production time to which she was accustomed. She'd never worked with Eisner before, and had no idea what to expect. On the business end, she had to solicit advance orders in a time-crunch that, by comics standards, was preposterous.

"Those orders guide your print numbers," she explained. "It was

April, and we were already soliciting for July. To solicit without any part of a book to send is crazy, impossible. But those were my marching orders.

"Will had already worked with Dave Schreiner on the various stories in the book. All the stories were done and the pages were drawn. The book was finished. That's why Will wanted it out for San Diego. In his mind, all we really needed to do was publish the damn thing, and, in a sense, that was true. Will was perfectly amenable all the way through, never once was there any kind of tussling or arguing."

Eisner believed that *Last Day in Vietnam*, with only limited use of dialogue balloons, marked a new approach that comics could take in the future. In these stories, the character is speaking directly to the reader, making the reader a participant in the story.

"It's an innovation which I thought has been coming for some time," Eisner explained in an interview that appeared when *Last Day in Vietnam* was published in 2000. "Anybody who has followed my work will probably know that I make a very major effort to make contact with the reader—almost directly. That's one of the reasons I use rain and weather and so forth in many of my stories—it seems like it involves the reader more heavily, brings them more into the story being told."

Eisner had attempted this type of narrative on one previous occasion, in a *Spirit* story in which a character, a sea captain, spoke directly to the reader. Eisner liked the approach, but he never followed up on it, partially because his frenetic work schedule prohibited his experimenting further and partially because this type of storytelling could be used only in very specific kinds of stories. "It only works on material where all the dialogue comes from one person," he pointed out. "I don't know how you could eliminate the use of balloons in other situations."

The artwork for the stories was similarly inventive. During his visits to Korea and Vietnam, Eisner had drawn numerous sketches of what he saw. With this new book, he wanted his readers to feel as if they were looking through his sketchbook, seeing what he saw, reacting to events the way he had reacted to them decades earlier.

"I wanted to keep it as close to a kind of diary as I could," he said of the approach. "As a matter of fact, originally I thought it might work to emulate a loose leaf binding on the inside, with lined paper, but I decided it was just too much, it was too gross. But the reason for this pencil technique was to create a very rugged, rough sketchbook look, almost."

The art has a grainy, gritty look, as if the pictures had been hastily penciled into a notebook by someone in the field. To further achieve the

Eisner carried a sketchbook whenever he traveled, creating studies of people, buildings, and places. These previously unpublished sketches are from a notebook Eisner kept while visiting China. (© Will Eisner Studios, Inc., courtesy of Denis Kitchen)

effect of authenticity, Eisner included archival photographs from Vietnam between stories.

The six stories in the volume were nonfiction "memories," as Eisner labeled them on the book's cover, based on events that Eisner witnessed in person. Only one—the title story—takes place amid actual fighting, but even so, they are heartbreaking, frightening, uplifting, ironic, and violent, with the kind of tension, drama, and boredom that GIs felt when they were safe on a base or on leave, knowing that combat was up ahead. One story, presented with no dialogue or narrative, offered one of the most violent scenes in the book, when a young soldier is seriously injured by a prostitute. Fear rumbles just beneath the GIs' tough talk, and Eisner makes it very clear that the most dangerous soldiers are the ones itching for battle—the ones who will kill or be killed, contributing to statistics. Senseless death is at the core of the two stories eliciting the greatest emotional response from Eisner—and, presumably, the reader. In "A Dull Day in Korea," the only story set outside Vietnam, a loudmouth GI, bragging about his hunting abilities back home in West Virginia, decides to display his marksmanship by shooting an innocent woman out gathering wood, only to be stopped by his commanding officer before he can kill her. "A Purple Heart for George" tells the story of a gay GI named George, who gets drunk every weekend and writes a note requesting dangerous combat duty; the weekly notes are intercepted and destroyed by friends working in the base commander's office, until finally—and tragically—George gets his wish when no one is in the office to tear up his note.

"'A Purple Heart for George,'" Eisner wrote in the book's introduction, "left a residue of guilt in many of us. I don't know about the primary actors in that event, which I witnessed, but for me it has never left my mind. I simply cannot forget it."

Dark Horse published four other Eisner titles—Shop Talk, Eisner/Miller, a reprinting of Hawks of the Sea, and a coffee table book called Will Eisner Sketchbook—during Eisner's brief but productive association with the company. Shop Talk, a gathering of the interviews that Eisner published in The Spirit Magazine and Will Eisner's Quarterly, featured in-depth conversations with such comics icons as Milton Caniff, C. C. Beck, Jack Kirby, Harvey Kurtzman, Gil Kane, Joe Simon, and Joe Kubert, speaking in an informal setting and talking about their work habits and contributions to comics. All had known Eisner for a long time prior to the conversations and felt comfortable about providing the kind of anecdotal detail that made the interviews a delight to read.

Eisner/Miller offered a different kind of interview. As originally planned, the book was to be the first of a series of book-length interviews with a younger generation of comic book and graphic novel creators, with such giants in the field as Neil Gaiman, Alan Moore, and maybe, with luck, the usually reclusive R. Crumb. But Eisner lived to see only one to fruition. *Eisner/Miller*, as published, was an informative, occasionally contentious discussion between two of the industry's heavyweights, but getting to that point was more work than anyone had anticipated in 2000, when the book was planned. Miller was busy on a *Dark Knight* project and unavailable, and Eisner was impatient, unhappy about the delays. When the two finally got together in Florida in May 2002, the early going was awkward and, at times, nasty. Eisner hadn't bothered to read Miller's latest *Sin City* book, yet he didn't shy away from critiquing it. Miller, unhappy with Eisner's condescending posture, grew justifiably defensive. Interviewer Charles Brownstein became a referee trying to keep the conversation on track. During one of the breaks in the conversation, when Eisner had gone into his house, Ann Eisner approached Brownstein and asked what exactly he wanted from her husband. As Brownstein remembered, she then went into the house and talked to her husband. When he returned, Eisner was much more relaxed.

"It didn't go as smoothly as we would have expected," Dark Horse founder and publisher Mike Richardson said of the interview sessions. "I think that both went in respecting each other, but when you have two people with egos and differing opinions about what they do, there might be a little bit of friction during the course of something like that."

When retracing the weekend's conversations, Miller shrugged off the tension as nothing outside of the ordinary whenever he and Eisner got together.

"It was mild compared to what we'd do privately," he said. "There are probably people who thought we didn't like each other, when in fact we loved each other. When I was working on the movie of *The Spirit*, I designed Commissioner Dolan after Will, and his conversations with the Spirit after the conversations that Will and I had. Very frequently, a conversation between Will and me would end with him saying, 'I don't know why I even talk to you anymore.' I used that line pretty much every time Dolan and the Spirit talked."

Both men enjoyed a good verbal tussle over comics and where they were headed, and while they did loosen up considerably during their discussions for *Eisner/Miller*, they still sparred as often as they agreed, making for an eye-opening, entertaining exchange. The finished book, lavishly illustrated with art from both and presented in a straight Q&A format, was published in 2005, just months after Eisner had passed away. It would stand as his ultimate "Shop Talk."

Eisner wasn't yet ready to abandon his obsession with family. He knew that in Ann's family, he had enough material for a graphic novel that would be a kind of combination of the family saga presented in *To the Heart of the Storm* and the close-up family drama depicted in *Family Matter*. Ann's family had a long, colorful history, bathed in the wealth acquired from banking and Wall Street, and Eisner was intrigued by the possibilities of exploring the dynamics of a family so unlike his own. He'd grown up in a world of tenements and survival; Ann's relatives and immediate family were more concerned with social position.

Eisner had begun the new book, tentatively entitled *A Good Marriage* but quickly changed to *The Name of the Game*, in 1998, when Kitchen Sink Press was in its death throes; but without a publisher, he'd set it down until after he'd secured a contract with DC and had marketed *Minor Miracles* and *Last Day in Vietnam*. It was a good move. He'd worked on the book in fits and starts, wrestling with how much he should say about Ann's family and how much he should fictionalize. The first draft was a mess, and he wasn't sure if he should even continue. As always, he sent a rough pencil dummy to Dave Schreiner, with a cautionary note expressing some of his misgivings about the project. "I've been concerned about its 'validity' and whether it has enough value for me to undertake its finish," he admitted.

Schreiner responded with a positive, detailed report proposing changes to characters and the plot. He liked the book, he told Eisner, but he agreed that there was a lot of work ahead. "I know this will lead to many revisions for you, if you go ahead with them," he said.

That had been July 1998. More than two years and numerous drafts later, Eisner was still at it, adjusting the plot to satisfy Schreiner and Denis Kitchen, double-checking the book's timeline, adding depth to characters—trying to make it work. Eisner had to think back to *A Life Force* sixteen years earlier to find a book that had challenged him artistically to this extent. *The Name of the Game* was a multigenerational epic covering more than a century's time, and Eisner not only had to present a multitude of characters in proper period costumes, he'd also decided to include more prose, aside from the usual dialogue balloons, than he'd ever attempted in a book, and he had to strike a balance between what to show and what to tell. Schreiner, convinced that Eisner had a "strong book" on his hands, cajoled and prodded, drawing up lengthy lists of suggestions, all with the hope that Eisner wouldn't grow frustrated and give up. The narrative and pacing of this book were better than in Eisner's other ambitious, multigenerational book, *Dropsie Avenue: The Neighborhood*, largely because of Eisner's willingness to adopt Schreiner's suggestions for expanding, cutting, or rewriting scenes. By fall 2000, *The Name of the Game* was nearing completion.

Since this is a story about how people marry (and stay married) for power and social position, Eisner opens the novel with lengthy accounts of how the Arnheim and Ober families acquired their wealth, the Arnheims through a successful corset company, the Obers through a dry goods business and, eventually, banking. Both families descended from

Pencil sketch for the cover of *A Good Marriage*, the working title of an early version of the graphic novel that would become *The Name of the Game*.
(© Will Eisner Studios, Inc., courtesy of Denis Kitchen)

German Jewish backgrounds, although, as Eisner carefully points out, the Arnheims were Ashkenazim, part of a wave of "crude and noisy" but "intelligent, resourceful and innovative" immigrants settling in East Coast seaport cities, and the Obers were part of a group of Jewish immigrants who headed west shortly after their arrival in America. As Eisner mentions in the book's foreword, supposedly written by Abraham Kayn, whose son married into the Arnheim family, marriage was a game played out for social and financial security.

> There were bad marriages and there were good marriages. Marrying beneath oneself was bad. Marrying outside of your religion or race was worse. However, marrying a rich girl (if you were a boy) or marrying a successful man (if you were a girl) was good. After all, the family into which one married was most important.

The Arnheim and Ober families become connected when Conrad Arnheim marries Lilli Ober in a marriage arranged by their successful fathers. Conrad, loosely modeled after Ann Eisner's father, is the ultimate product of privilege: spoiled as a child, uninterested in the family business if it means work, self-centered and unfaithful to his wife, and occasionally violent; over the course of the story, he rapes one of his two wives, beats both, kidnaps a daughter from her grandparents, neglects the business to its demise before starting up a stockbrokerage firm. In general, he is one of the least sympathetic characters Eisner ever created. Lilli stays with him because she enjoys the life of wealth and privilege, as does Conrad's second wife, Eva, who finds him repulsive but refuses to grant him a divorce because she will not give up the life to which she's become accustomed.

Ann Eisner was the model for Conrad's daughter, Rosie, and like Ann Eisner, Rosie is openly rebellious, uninterested in the family money, and even less interested in the kind of person her parents would like her to marry. She is more taken by Aron, a poet and the novel's Eisner character. Their courtship and wedding strongly resemble Ann and Will's own—including a touching scene depicting how out of place Sam and Fannie Eisner were in the Weingarten circle—and Conrad even pulls Aron aside and offers him a job, as Ann's father did with Will.

At this point, Eisner breaks away from autobiography. Rather than refuse his father-in-law's offer, as Eisner did in real life, Aron takes him up on it. He discovers that he is very good at the job, and by the end of the novel, he has taken on many of Conrad's characteristics. He's ruthless in business, cheats on his wife, and has settled into a loveless marriage of convenience. "We'll pretend to be a happily married couple . . . just the way most of the others do in our set," Rosie taunts when she confronts her husband at the end of the novel, after reminding him that it will be her family's money that sustains them. "You can have the kind of life you wanted . . . with the *better* people . . . but on *my* terms."

Visually, *The Name of the Game* might be the most theatrical of Eisner's graphic novels. The characters' gestures are exaggerated, as if the actors and actresses are playing to the cheap seats; there is nothing subtle about their movements. Some of the characters, such as Conrad's drunken yet sensitive brother, Alex, seem gratuitous, but the major players are well-rounded and fully developed, owing mainly to the constant prodding of Dave Schreiner, who had little patience with the predictability of the characters as originally designed. Eisner always pushed for credibility, and Schreiner held him to it. When discussing Eva, Schreiner chided Eisner for creating what he felt was a stock character.

"You show that Conrad and Eva haven't had sex before their marriage," he wrote after seeing what Eisner hoped would be the final rough pencil draft. "I find this hard to believe after seeing Conrad trying to have sex with anything in a dress and being very aggressive about it . . . I think something is badly needed here. I don't suggest that you delve into her childhood of abuse or something like that—avoid the pop psychology, please. But you have to show something about Eva that shows why sex is not an option with her. Good luck on this one, but I think you need to do it in order to convince the reader that this is a strong enough woman to keep Conrad at bay."

Schreiner was even tougher on Eisner with Rosie. As written, she was rebellious but ultimately far too passive for Schreiner, who pushed Eisner to make her tougher. "If Aron cheats on her and beats her, the Rosie you have presented would walk. Or kill him," he suggested. "I think you have to do something here."

Eisner took these recommendations to heart and changed the characters, especially the women—an irony, given Eisner's propensity for creating such intelligent, independent, and motivated female characters during his *Spirit* years. Perhaps Eisner held back in earlier drafts because he was modeling these characters after real people in his life. Perhaps he was in a rush to complete the book. Or perhaps he simply needed an editor's input on how to strengthen his characters. Whatever his reasons, the strong women in *The Name of the Game* gave credibility to the upper hand they held with men of such wealth and position.

With the publication of *The Name of the Game* in 2001, Eisner finished his cycle of books about family on a high note. This was his strongest work since his 1991 autobiographical book, *To the Heart of the Storm*, but by the time it hit bookstores, Eisner was moving on.

chapter sixteen

POLEMICS

Up until now, my books were essentially entertainment—or, perhaps,
art, if you will. Now, I'm entering a whole new area, where I'm taking
a stand on serious matters of injustice. I want to stimulate change—
change the way people think. I'm standing on a soapbox.

When Michael Chabon's *The Amazing Adventures of Kavalier & Clay*
won the Pulitzer Prize for Fiction in 2001, Eisner was as pleased as if
he had won the award himself. Chabon had assigned some of Eisner's
characteristics to his Joe Kavalier character, and this novel about the early
days of comics represented, in Eisner's mind, yet another step forward in
the quest for acceptance of comics as literature, not to mention one of the
finest written accounts of the powerful connection between the Jewish
immigrant experience and the establishment of the comic book.

When he'd first heard from Chabon in a 1995 letter, Eisner figured he
had another fanboy on his hands—someone wanting to meet him, shake
his hand, or, if he was as cheeky as some of the people he met, request a
personalized drawing. He knew nothing about the highly acclaimed author of *The Mysteries of Pittsburgh* and *Wonder Boys*, other than the fact
that he was another writer. Nor was he aware of Chabon's deep love for
comics. Chabon's grandfather had been a typographer for a company that
printed comic books, and he'd brought them home by the bagful for his
son, Michael's father, to enjoy. Chabon had inherited his father's interest
in superhero comics. He had read Jules Feiffer's *The Great Comic Book*
Heroes when he was an eleven-year-old kid, and he'd managed to get his
hands on an original April 17, 1949, *Spirit* insert from the *Pittsburgh Post-*
Gazette, which, he told Eisner in his letter requesting an interview, was
one of his "proudest possessions."

Chabon the novelist was interested in authenticity. As he noted in his letter, he could have written almost anything about the early days of comics and passed it off to the casual reader, but it would have seemed false to anyone who, like Eisner, had been around during the Golden Age. He had all kinds of information about New York City during that period, but nothing about the artists themselves. "I want to understand the marketing and production side of the business in those days," he told Eisner. "I want to know where you all lived, what you ate, if you took the subway, what music you listened to, etc. Sure, I could make all that up, but I think my book, for all its eventual flights of fancy, will be great only insofar as it is rooted in the way things really were."

Eisner consented to giving Chabon an hour of his time when he and Ann were attending the 1995 WonderCon in Oakland. In a relatively brief period of time, Chabon questioned Eisner about all aspects of comics, including the way they were when comic books were still in their infancy. As Chabon recalled:

> I interviewed Will Eisner when I'd written very little of the book. About 60 pages or so was written. I went up to WonderCon and interviewed him. He gave me an hour of his time, in the middle of a very busy day full of things he had scheduled for him. And actually, his wife sat down with us, too. I just got them trying to reminisce about their life in the late '30s, early 1940s. And it was great talking to him because he was not only an artist and writer of the period, but he was a businessman, too . . . I think that's one of the unique things about Eisner [as a comics creator], is that he actually ran businesses, and yet at the same time he was also an artist and a writer.

Chabon's Josef Kavalier and Sammy Klayman were a combination of the author's imagination and a composite of the characteristics of the artists he interviewed—comics creators such as Eisner, Stan Lee, and Gil Kane. Reviewers and comic book fans detected Joe Kavalier to be particularly similar to Eisner, but Chabon denied modeling his characters after any one artist. He did admit that Kavalier's faith in the potential for comics came directly from his conversation with Eisner.

"I gave him Eisner's rather surprising and unshakable faith in the medium of comic books," Chabon said. "That was rare at the time. In fact, I think Eisner was unique in feeling from the start that comic books were not necessarily this despised, bastard, crappy, low-brow kind of art form, and that there was a potential for real art. And he saw that from the very

After winning the Pulitzer Prize for *The Amazing Adventures of Kavalier & Clay*, his novel set in the early days of comics, Michael Chabon began *The Escapist*, a comic book based on his fictional characters' creations. Eisner's contribution to it was his last work. (© Will Eisner Studios, Inc., courtesy of Denis Kitchen)

beginning, which was very unusual, and I took that quality and gave it to Joe Kavalier. I think that was the only direct borrowing I really did."

Eisner's happiness for Chabon when he won the Pulitzer Prize contrasted strongly with his feelings of nine years earlier, when Art Spiegelman won a special Pulitzer Prize for *Maus*. Eisner deeply and openly admired Spiegelman's accomplishment, but he also harbored a resentment that after all his years of contributing to comics, he had never received such recognition. After hearing of Spiegelman's Pulitzer, Eisner called Denis Kitchen and inquired about the award, and he was surprised to learn that these awards didn't just materialize out of nowhere, out of a literary community's purist affection for great literature; one had to submit the work for the formal nomination process. This bothered Eisner more than he let on in his gracious public statements praising Spiegelman and his accomplishments in comics. For all his outward modesty, Eisner possessed a competitive streak that demanded the kind of attention his peers received.

Chabon, a prose writer, posed no threat. Spiegelman was another matter. Eisner could honestly state that he felt the Pulitzer for *Maus* was good for comics in general, but he could never overcome his ambivalent feelings about the fact that it was Spiegelman who won it and not him.

According to those who knew him, Spiegelman had a similar ambivalence about Eisner. He could appear with Eisner at comics functions, sing Eisner's praises, and talk about his contributions to the medium, but out of the public view there was always an uneasiness between them, a feeling that neither could—or perhaps even cared to—overcome.

Jules Feiffer, another Pulitzer Prize–winning friend of Eisner's, could understand how Eisner felt. "Everybody needs validation," he pointed out. "Will was the transition between the comic books and their truly lowbrow approach to everything, and the comics he was doing, which were becoming an art form. By his own will he had turned comics into something else. When others ran off with the prizes and attention, Will was confused, befuddled, and irritated: 'Wait a minute! I began this.'"

Florida had never taken the city out of Will Eisner. The September 11, 2001, destruction by terrorists of the World Trade Center had given him pause to consider, first, the boundless possibilities for inhumanity in a human world and, second, the temporary nature of cities themselves. So much of his identity was still connected to New York City, but the city, like his own life, was no longer youthful. Eisner had set graphic novels in the Bronx, in the tenement buildings on fictitious Dropsie Avenue, and by the end of 2002, he had decided to compose a graphic novel dedicated to the history of the neighborhood.

Dropsie Avenue: The Neighborhood stretches out over a century, starting with a rural stretch of land that over the decades grew into the South Bronx. By Eisner's own admission, a project of this nature posed daunting challenges.

"Writing with images so inherent to this form means dealing with reality within the limitations of the graphic narrative," he stated in his introduction to the book. "On the other hand, portraying internal emotions and real human experiences is abetted by the impressionism of cartoon art. The demands of the task were enough to make the undertaking worthwhile."

The book was ultimately visually stunning but dizzying from a narrative standpoint, as Eisner pulled his readers through tales of nepotism and corruption, greed, racism, and anti-Semitism, wealth and poverty, joy and despair, framed by four wars, the Depression, immigration, crime and violence, and a constantly changing society. Eisner had observed much of it when he was growing up in the Bronx: intense research provided the rest. The neighborhood provided a huge roster of characters, but precisely because of their number, only a few were fully developed. The rest pass through in a matter of a page or two, adding texture to an overarching story told through brief vignettes.

Eisner was in over his head, and—if one can judge by his remarks in the book's introduction and interviews he gave after its publication—he knew it. Three decades earlier, in *The Spirit*, he'd struggled to tell a fully realized story within the limitations of seven or eight pages; now he was attempting to depict, in 170 pages, the rise and fall of a neighborhood. He had no choice but to compress time and narrative.

Ultimately, Eisner's biggest accomplishment in *Dropsie Avenue: The Neighborhood* was his ability to present Dropsie Avenue as both a setting and a character. The neighborhood acted as a stage for all of Eisner's dramas, yet in the greater scheme, it symbolized human life itself, from sturdy developing youth to deteriorating old age. "Neighborhoods have life spans," Eisner explained. "They begin, evolve, mature and die. But while the evolution is displayed by the decline of its buildings, it seems to me that the lives of the inhabitants are the internal force which generates the decay. People, not buildings, are the heart of the matter."

Seven decades of working in comics hadn't dulled Eisner's enthusiasm for learning about whatever was new in sequential art. He was buoyed by the fact that libraries across the country were routinely stocking graphic novels and that universities were now offering courses in comics history and art. Manga, a form of comic art from Japan, heavily influenced by cinema and appealing to young readers raised on the electronics revolution, was flying off the shelves of comic book and general bookstores, offering further evidence that young readers even those addicted to video games and not inclined to read, were still letting their eyes travel from panel to panel of highly stylized art. Movies based on graphic novels drew long lines at the box office. At one time, comic books had been described as little movies on paper; motion picture producers and directors finally seemed to have taken notice.

"We're in a visual era," Eisner offered.

We have to communicate today with imagery because there's need for speed of communication. Comics—the comic medium, the idea of sequentially arranged images with some text to convey an idea and tell a story—have found the place between text and film. We deliver information at a very rapid rate of speed. Very often, our information is not as deep as a body of text, but a lot of people haven't got time to read a large body of text any longer. So I would say the growth of our society, the conduct of our civilization, is on our side.

To create something new for this quick-paced society and readership, Eisner turned to straightforward social commentary—an area offering great potential but rarely explored in comics. Newspapers had a tradition of pushing the limits in one-panel editorial cartoons or in daily cartoon strips. Garry Trudeau had successfully skewered social and political issues in his Pulitzer Prize–winning *Doonesbury*, and before Trudeau, Walt Kelly (*Pogo*) and Al Capp (*Li'l Abner*) had issued stinging commentary in their newspaper strips. These had been satires, however, maintaining the comic in comics.

Eisner wanted to present commentary as serious as he had in his other graphic works, but in a bold, new way. In the past, he had been reluctant to assert his political beliefs on his work, other than his obvious stance against anti-Semitism or occasional references to social issues, both sub-text to his stories. He was now prepared for a full-scale assault, to use his art as pamphleteers used prose in their polemics.

In the 1990s, while reading European fairy tales and classic literature for possible adaptations in his children's book projects, he'd noticed that many modern stereotypes could trace their roots to these tales. Eisner had no quarrel with stereotypes per se: comic book writers and artists, like co-medians, used stereotypes for the sake of brevity, as a type of shorthand not needed in prose but almost required in comics, where time and space were limited. What mattered, in Eisner's view, were the *ways* in which stereotypes were used—the intentions of the writers and artists. The more Eisner pondered the use of stereotypes over the years, especially in books regarded as classics, the more concerned he became about racism, sexism, anti-Semitism, xenophobia, and other poisonous ideas that could be planted in literature with damaging effects. When introduced to children, stereotypes wormed their way into a lifetime of thought and action.

One classic that caught Eisner's attention was Charles Dickens's *Oliver Twist*, a tale that had originally been serialized in a magazine for adults, then issued as a book by an adult trade publisher, but which over the years had become a children's story. On a number of occasions in the novel, Dickens had identified Fagin, one of the book's central characters,

simply as "the Jew," which Eisner found repulsive and damaging, especially since Fagin was the ultimate lowlife, a criminal who preyed on
children to earn his income. The illustrations in the early editions of the
book, focusing on the stereotypical look of European Jews, took it one
step further.

> Upon examining the illustrations of the original editions of *Oliver
> Twist*, I found an unquestionable example of visual defamation in
> classic literature. The memory of their awful use by the Nazis in
> World War II, one hundred years later, added evidence to the per-
> sistence of evil stereotyping. Combating it became an obsessive
> pursuit, and I realized that I had no choice but to undertake a truer
> portrait of Fagin by telling his life story in the only way I could.

Eisner's graphic novel, *Fagin the Jew*, was a biography of Dickens's fictional character. In interviews following the publication of the book,
Eisner strongly defended his appropriation of another man's character,
stating that he had made no changes in his depiction of Fagin's background that conflicted with *Oliver Twist*. In Eisner's book, Fagin was still
a criminal; he was still hanged at the end of the story. Fagin was useful as
a tool for constructing a new type of graphic novel.

"Actually I am not intending this as an adaptation but rather a polemic," he wrote Dave Schreiner in a cover letter accompanying an early
pencil dummy of *Fagin*. "I hope I can attract sympathetic readers."

What Eisner intended to do was present Fagin's background in such a
way that readers would see the reasons for Fagin's criminal behavior and
that those reasons had nothing to do with the fact that he was Jewish. By
referring to Fagin's Jewish background, Dickens had unwittingly rein-
forced a stereotype, similar to the way Shakespeare had in his portrayal of
the moneylender Shylock in *The Merchant of Venice*. The illustrations in
Dickens's book did further damage.

Eisner conceded that his own cartooning history left him open to
further criticism for his own stereotypical treatment—including the
illustrations—of Ebony White in *The Spirit*. He'd taken a beating from
critics and readers when the first *Spirit* reprints were issued, and he'd addressed the criticism at that time; he anticipated more of the same if he
criticized Dickens for his portrayal of Fagin in *Oliver Twist*. Eisner learned
during his research that Dickens was no more anti-Semitic than he, Will
Eisner, was a racist, and that Dickens, troubled by his depiction of Fagin,
had removed most of the references to his character's Jewish background

in later editions of *Oliver Twist*. Eisner addressed this in *Fagin the Jew* by working in a clever literary device: at the opening of his story, Eisner showed Fagin in prison, awaiting his execution, being visited by Charles Dickens himself. "Tarry a bit, Mister Dickens," Fagin says, "while ol' Fagin here tells you, sir, what I really was and how it all came to be!!"

What follows is Moses Fagin's narration, the story of his life, as offered to the writer who created him. Eisner's Fagin is the product of bohemian parents who, after fleeing a pogrom, wind up in London, only to find life slightly more tolerable than in their own country. Fagin's father puts him to work on the street, selling buttons and needles to supplement the family income. But it's a meager, steal-or-starve existence, and Fagin's father learns how to swindle and steal in order to survive—a skill that he passes on to his son.

An orphan in his teens, Fagin grows up quickly, working as a servant to Eleazor Solomon, a wealthy and influential Jewish merchant who hopes to use his power to build a school for Jewish children. Fagin's life might have gone well had he not become romantically involved with the daughter of the man building the school. Fagin is tossed out, forced to survive by using his wits as a common thief and swindler. He is eventually caught and sentenced to ten years of hard labor, but after a series of misadventures, he catches the second big break of his life when he saves the life of another businessman named Jack Dawson, who subsequently hides him from the authorities, employs him, and offers to stake him enough money to start his own business. Fagin might have become respectable again, but these plans, too, fall through when Dawson dies suddenly and unexpectedly. Once again, Fagin is out on the streets, this time permanently. He meets Bill Sikes, and the two team up to run a thievery ring, carried out by a group of street urchins who, like Fagin himself, have little choice than to steal to stay alive. One of them is an orphan named Oliver Twist.

From this point on, Eisner's story is largely an adaptation of Dickens's *Oliver Twist*. When Fagin is implicated in a murder and sentenced to hang, he is visited by Oliver Twist and Charles Dickens, Oliver because he needs Fagin's help in tracing his lineage and claiming a large sum of money left to him after his father's death, Dickens because Fagin requested his visit. Upon completing his story, Fagin and Dickens have an exchange about Dickens having attached the word *Jew* to Fagin in his book. "A Jew is not Fagin any more than a Gentile is Sikes!" Fagin shouts at Dickens. Writers, he accuses Dickens, are guilty of perpetuating the hurtful stereotypes. Dickens responds by promising to amend this problem in future editions of *Oliver Twist*.

The meeting between a fictitious character and his creator was an interesting device, requiring a suspension of belief on the part of the reader. Not only was such a meeting literally impossible, it was also impossible within the framework of Eisner's story, since Dickens couldn't have written his book while Fagin was alive. The contradiction, Eisner felt, was necessary.

"This book was intended as a polemic," he insisted. "The confrontation between Dickens and Fagin is a way of adding realism to an otherwise fictitious character. I also felt it was necessary and fair to show Dickens as he really was, not anti-Semitic."

To ensure that readers would not miss his points, Eisner bookended *Fagin the Jew* with two essays addressing the topic of stereotypes. In the foreword, as if to launch a preemptive strike against the criticism he was certain to receive when the book was published, he wrote of his feelings about Ebony and his use of stereotype in creating the character. In the afterword, he supplied a brief history of *Oliver Twist*, the illustrations for the book, and how the stereotyping, while not intended to be anti-Semitic, played into the hands of those who wanted Jews to be perceived a certain way.

Ironically, Eisner caught some flak from the Jewish press as a result of the title of his book. To these critics, including the word *Jew* in the title was an invitation to trouble.

"One man, a leading editor in Jewish publishing circles, wanted to know why I had to use the word 'Jew' in the Fagin title," Eisner said. "I could only point out that was the precise point I wanted to address."

In looking for a publisher for the book, Eisner sought a large house as opposed to a small press or publisher specializing in comics. Judith Hansen was able to place *Fagin the Jew* with Doubleday, meaning the book would receive first-rate publicity, marketing, and distribution, not to mention serious review consideration from the nation's biggest newspapers. As expected, Eisner was questioned about how he, as creator of a character like Ebony White, could justify criticizing Dickens for his treatment of Fagin, and just as predictably, Eisner wearily repeated his old arguments, now three decades old, about his reasons for creating Ebony. What Eisner could not—or refused to—understand was that in arguing what he felt were the pros and cons of stereotyping, he was fighting a battle he could not possibly win: *stereotype*, as a word, always carried a negative connotation and was indefensible under any circumstances. Eisner was no more convincing this time around than he had been when the *Spirit* reprints were being issued by Warren and Kitchen Sink. People either bought his explanation or they didn't. Eisner could only hope that time would be as kind to him as it had been to Dickens.

Eisner probably knew that his reputation would carry the day. He had spent a lifetime carefully cultivating an image that, with only a rare exception, was accepted industrywide—the image of an extremely talented artist who managed to stay congenial, generous, and highly professional despite the demands placed on him by a very competitive business—and he was as skillful as anyone in dealing with the press and seeing that the focus of the interviews remained on his artistic, rather than private, life. Not that he had much to hide, in any event: his life was devoted to and defined by his work, and away from the office he lived a quiet existence. He liked to travel, especially when he and Ann could attend conventions overseas, and he enjoyed the stream of visitors, including other comics artists, that he and Ann received in Florida. But in the end, he was still a child of the Depression, committed to working as if his livelihood might someday be yanked away from him.

All this was brought into sharp focus when he heard from two young men with a compelling new project.

Andrew Cooke was a documentary filmmaker with television credits under his belt. His brother, Jon, edited and designed *Comic Book Artist*, one of the leading magazines covering all aspects of the comic book industry. Neither had much money to finance the project, but both wanted to team up and make a full-length documentary on the life and work of Will Eisner.

By the end of his life, Eisner had become an iconic figure in comics, instantly recognizable at conventions, popular as a speaker, and still in demand as an artist.
(Courtesy of Denis Kitchen)

The project started modestly in 2002 and snowballed—or snowballed as much as their limited budget would allow. Jon had been watching *American Masters*, the PBS documentary television series, and he wondered why there hadn't been a segment devoted to a comic book artist or, more specifically, to Will Eisner. The next morning, he called his brother and suggested that they work on such a documentary. Andy, a comic book aficionado in his youth, liked the idea. Jon knew Eisner from past dealings with the magazine, and when he approached Eisner with his proposed project, Eisner responded enthusiastically.

"He was immediately very agreeable to it," Jon remembered, "but he did have some caveats. We had to contact Tom Powers, who had started a documentary that had been put on hold. Will wanted everything aboveboard, and he wanted everything on paper. It was the first time that I worked in a business deal with Will, and it was a wonderful introduction to working with him in a business concern. Comic book people are notoriously bad businessmen, but he was quite the exception. He had some very practical ideas, and he was looking out for us, as well as for himself."

Even though he had abandoned his plans to make a documentary, Powers turned out to be an important contributor to the Cooke brothers' project. Powers had shot a lot of interview footage—including footage of Eisner in his studio—that wound up in the Cookes' documentary.

"He was incredibly gracious," Andy Cooke noted. "He had interviewed Kurt Vonnegut and Gil Kane; he'd shot an interview with Ann, and a couple of interviews with Will. There was some really great stuff."

Eisner, of course, had been dealing with the media for decades. He knew of the high mortality rate of proposed movies and documentaries, of the great ideas that never saw the light of day through lack of time, money, or lost interest. A Brazilian documentary, *Will Eisner: Profession: Cartoonist*, produced and directed by Marisa Furtado de Oliveira and Paulo Serran, had been issued in 1999. He supported the Cooke brothers' documentary, but he knew it could be years in the making, especially if the filmmakers had difficulty raising funds.

The Cookes shot and edited the film over a five-year period, conducting interviews at conventions, where they were guaranteed to find a number of comic book artists gathered in one place at one time. Like others before them, they found Eisner to be a gracious but elusive subject, willing to talk about his work but reluctant to discuss his private life. Early in the project, they decided that the theme of their documentary would be how Eisner had spent his life trying to legitimize comics and how he'd done so by telling personal stories. Eisner, they discovered early in their research, was fully aware of his historical standing in comics, but he somehow managed to keep his modesty and perspective.

"This is an industry of both monstrous low self-esteem and incredible egomania," Jon Cooke remarked, "but he had his feet planted on the ground. You might not get that from a number of veterans. I was surprised by the amount of professional jealousy that took place. There was enormous jealousy for his success."

The finished product, *Will Eisner: Portrait of a Sequential Artist* was a tightly edited, quickly paced examination of Eisner's life, covering all the essentials of more than eighty years, complete with footage of Depression-era New York, rare photos of Eisner and his family, clips from Eisner's own home movies, sound bites from Eisner's *Shop Talk* tapes, interviews with the Eisners and numerous industry notables, and lots of art, including paintings from Eisner's youth.

The film debuted, to enthusiastic response, at the 2007 Tribeca Film Festival in New York. Sadly, Eisner, who had passed away two years earlier, wasn't around to see it.

One day, while researching a potential new project on the Internet, Eisner came across an English translation of *The Protocols of the Elders of Zion*, a work of anti-Semitic propaganda long discredited and proven to be a fraud of hatred and literary thievery. Originally published in Russia as a means of implicating Jews as agitators in times of political turmoil and denying Jews their basic human, social, and political rights, *The Protocols* was a cooked-up account of a Jewish plot to take over and dominate the world. Eisner had heard of the book but had never read it, and he was under the impression that it had no current global influence. He read the translation, and aside from being angered by what he read, he was shocked to learn that *The Protocols* was still very much in print all around the world and that it was being used as propaganda in Middle Eastern countries to incite hatred and violence toward the Israelis.

"I was amazed that there were people who still believed *The Protocols* were real," he said, "and I was disturbed to learn later that this site was just one of many that promoted these lies in the Muslim world. I decided something had to be done."

Anger had moved Eisner to action in the past, but after reading *The Protocols*, he became obsessed with learning everything possible about the book's origins, its publishing history, the efforts to use it as a tool to promote anti-Semitism, its exposure as a fraud, and where and why it was

Page from *The Plot*, a nonfiction graphic work especially close to Eisner's heart.
(Courtesy of Will Eisner Studios, Inc.)

still in print. Hitler had cited *The Protocols* in *Mein Kampf,* making it one of his rallying points against the European Jews, and it had been effective enough to set into motion the fear and hatred that made the Holocaust possible. Three decades before that, in Russia, the document had been influential in launching the pogroms. It was the inaction and misguided beliefs of the masses that made possible such horrific actions against the Jews. Eisner had even seen signs of it at home when he was a boy, dealing with anti-Semitism in the streets and resignation to it at home. "I remember being angry at the shtetl attitude of my parents, who advised that we should be 'quiet and not offend the goyim,'" he recalled. "To them the Holocaust was another, only much bigger, pogrom."

The Protocols, Eisner learned, had a long, winding, secretive history dating back to nineteenth-century France, where a satirist and political gadfly named Maurice Joly wrote a book entitled *The Dialogue in Hell Between Machiavelli and Montesquieu.* Published in 1864, the book attempted to present a similarity between the political philosophy of Machiavelli and Napoleon III's dictatorial reign. Not much came of the book, and Joly died, a suicide, in 1878.

The book resurfaced three decades later, although not by its original title and authorship. In the pre-revolution turmoil under Czar Nicholas II, Russian traditionalists feared that the czar was leaning toward adopting modern, much more liberal government policies in the near future. Something had to be done to convince the czar that this would be harmful to the country. The traditionalist leadership proposed that a document be produced—a document that would serve two functions. First, it would show how modernization would be harmful; and second, it would distract the czar by producing a new enemy of the state. That enemy would be the Jews.

The document, a book called *The Protocols of the Elders of Zion,* outlined a plot by influential Jewish leaders, supposedly hatched at an international meeting, in which the Jews planned a way of achieving world domination. The major points of the plan—and the heart of *The Protocols*—written by Mathieu Golovinski, a Russian agent, propagandist, and forger living in Paris—were lifted, almost verbatim at times, from Joly's now forgotten work. The Jews, the book insinuated, were behind the liberal reforms being proposed for Russia. *The Protocols* worked as intended: Czar Nicholas II dismissed his most trusted adviser, liberal factions fell out of favor, and ultimately, pogroms eliminated much of the Jewish population.

Years later, in 1921, Philip Graves, a correspondent for the *Times* of London, researched *The Protocols* and, by comparing *The Protocols* with

The Dialogue in Hell, exposed the book as a fraud. This should have been the end of the book's credibility, but as Eisner learned, it was a powerful propaganda tool, easily sold to the masses looking for a group to blame for its troubles. In 1920, automaker Henry Ford had published a series of articles in his newspaper, the *Dearborn Independent*, which used *The Protocols* as a source; he recanted six years later, well after the *Times* of London exposé. A suit in Switzerland, filed to prohibit the Nazis from distributing *The Protocols*, once again exposed the fraudulent nature of the book—to no avail. The book would not go away. The Ku Klux Klan had used the book in its campaign against the Jews, and it was used similarly in countries around the world.

While conducting his research, Eisner discovered that there was no shortage of books or newspaper and magazine pieces on *The Protocols*, but this was scholarly material aimed at the academic community—at people already interested in it and aware of the book's history. To Eisner, these were worthy endeavors, but they were really a matter of preaching to the choir. Sequential art would reach a lot more readers. For Eisner, it had been an effective educational tool in the past, whether used to show a soldier how to maintain his equipment or to inform an inner-city kid about job possibilities, and it could work now to dispel the myths and misconceptions about a propagandistic book.

"Am I trespassing onto academic territory?" he wondered aloud in an interview with journalist and author David Hajdu. "I didn't see the signs saying 'No comics allowed.' I refuse to acknowledge limitations in the art form. I say, 'Don't bother me with the formal details—we've got to climb a hill.' At this point in my life, I feel, 'What the hell.' If I'm wrong, I won't be around to find out about it anyway."

Eisner divided his book project into three parts. The opening portion of the book would address the history of *The Protocols* and how the book came to be written. The second part would focus on the successful efforts to expose the book as a propagandistic sham. Finally, the book would examine the current state of *The Protocols*, how it was still in print and still being used as a weapon against the Jews despite all that was known and published about it. Eisner wrote a script, broke it down to the page, and penciled a rough draft of what he proposed to do. He showed it to Dave Schreiner, who deemed it a project worth pursuing.

Eisner enlisted the help of others with his research. Benjamin Herzberg, who acted as an adviser on *Fagin the Jew*, acted in a similar capacity on the new project, to the point of helping Eisner restructure the book when it seemed to be losing its compass. N. C. Christopher Couch, a former senior editor at Kitchen Sink Press, a professor at the University of Massachusetts, and coauthor (with Stephen Weiner) of *The Will Eisner Companion*, a book examining all of Eisner's work from *The Spirit* through his graphic novels, translated the Joly book into English and charted a page-by-page comparison of *The Dialogue in Hell* and *The Protocols*. Upon receiving the comparison, Eisner took on the laborious task of committing the comparison to the printed page, devoting side-by-side illustrations of the text. For Eisner, it was utterly important that readers of his book see the extent of the plagiarism.

The more he worked on the book, the more he believed that this was one of the most important projects he had ever taken on. It was the ultimate marriage of subject matter and sequential art, a work that could influence the way people felt about a compelling topic. Finding the right publisher became critical, even more so than it had been with *Fagin the Jew*. Once again, he wanted to avoid publishing with a company specializing in comics. He wanted as large an audience as possible, but perhaps more important, it was crucial that the publishing house be highly respected, one certain to entice international sales, especially in the Middle East.

After reading the manuscript, Judith Hansen agreed that this was an important book and needed the right publishing house to market it properly.

"I submitted his book's proposal to selected houses, held an auction, and two houses, Metropolitan Books and W. W. Norton wound up with matching bids," Hansen recalled. "I was looking for a publishing house that would be interested in later picking up Eisner's graphic novel backlist if the rights could be reverted from DC, and I advised Eisner to speak to the editors from both houses. After talking with them, Eisner settled on Norton, one of the most prestigious houses in the United States."

Robert Weil, Eisner's editor at Norton, said: "He told me that he was looking for someone who had a history background because he felt very passionate about the subject and knew his graphics, but he needed someone who knew history, and he was comfortable with my knowledge of history. He knew that I knew a lot about European history.

"We worked very, very closely on that, and I made him redo it many, many times. Part of my job was to vet it for him. I sent it to two experts, one on the West Coast and one on the East Coast, because I didn't trust my judgment. We went over the language in those [dialogue] bubbles many, many times. There was this section where he compares the 1864 work by the French author to the false version, laid out page by page. I told him he had to cut it down. He said, 'I have to show this. No one will believe it.' And I said, 'No one's going to read it. I won't read it, Will.' "

This section became a bone of contention between Eisner and those reading the different drafts of the book. In his past projects, Eisner preferred to maintain secrecy about what he was working on, showing drafts to Denis Kitchen and Dave Schreiner but no one else. This book was different. Eisner sent drafts to people whose opinions he trusted, hoping for feedback that would improve the book. No one seemed to agree, especially on the prickly issue of the comparisons.

"I need your opinion," Eisner wrote Schreiner on August 21, 2003. "Denis K. feels that the 100 pages of comparison between Dialogues and Protocols is deadly dull and should not be where it is in the center of the book. He would see it as a 'footnote' in the end. Chris Couch does not agree. While I intend to leave the final decision to the publisher—I need your opinion."

It was an opinion he would never receive. On August 27, six days after Eisner sent the letter off to his longtime editor, Dave Schreiner lost a lengthy battle with cancer, less than three months shy of his fifty-seventh birthday. His health had been in decline for several years, but Eisner had hoped that he would somehow beat this latest setback. He wept when he heard the news.

While Eisner worked on *The Plot*, Judith Hansen worked on brokering a deal that would place Eisner's other graphic novels with the company. This, too, was extremely important to Eisner: He'd had no qualms about the way DC had re-issued his books, but DC was a comics publisher and Eisner was almost desperate to be published by a respected generalist house. After a meeting at DC in Paul Levitz's office with Levitz, Eisner, Hansen, Denis Kitchen, and DC attorney, Jay Kogan, Hansen and Kogan had extensive negotiations over the reversion of copyrights to all of Eisner's graphic novels except *Last Day in Vietnam* and *Fagin the Jew*. Part of the negotiations involved Hansen's proposal of combining the various individual works into hardcover editions and publishing the individual titles in trade paperback format. Hansen had read a French edition of Eisner's work that combined several of his graphic novels into one large volume, and she reasoned that this would be an interesting approach in the United States—presenting anthologies of the graphic novels with related stories or themes collected into attractive hardcover volumes.

Hansen discussed this with Eisner and suggested that hardcover anthologies of the graphic novels, followed by trade paperback publication of the individual works, would be a way to keep the works in print, present them in a fresh way, and still allow for publication of each individual title.* Eisner was thrilled. With any luck, his books might finally escape the comics ghetto and find their way to the shelves of serious literature.

"Will's quest in all of this," said Paul Levitz, "was for the respectability of the medium, not just for himself, but with himself as sort of a Moses: 'Can I please at least get into the Promised Land?' This was one of the debates that I had with Will that led to his doing the books [with Norton]. We were half-equipped, and the Nortons of the world were half-equipped: we knew how to physically make a book and reach the core audience; Norton knew how to reach the libraries and how to publicize it in a different environment. I was highly confident that we would reach that point in the next couple of years, but I remember Will sitting there and saying, 'I'm not sure I've got a couple of years.' That was the irresistible argument for his taking that body of work and going to Norton, and our freeing the backlist for him. We try not to give stuff up, but Will had a unique role in the history of all of it, and he was a total gentleman to do business with, and as long as we were getting something that we could look ourselves in the mirror and say, 'All right, we got a fair value in the deal,' we had to let him go."

Norton agreed to reissue Eisner's graphic novels in volumes designed to look more like traditional trade paperbacks as opposed to the old comic book look. With any luck, Eisner thought, his books might finally escape the comics ghetto and find their way to the shelves of serious literature.

He worked on *The Plot* throughout 2004, assembling the book like a scholarly work of history. He annotated the book, wrote a lengthy introduction giving the history of his involvement in its creation, enlisted Chris Couch's help on a bibliography, and even put together an index. Meanwhile, Robert Weil contacted Umberto Eco, an internationally acclaimed novelist and comic book fan, to write a preface for *The Plot*.

---

* There were three published anthologies of graphic novels, including *The Contract with God Trilogy: Life on Dropsie Avenue*, which included *A Contract with God*, *A Life Force*, and *Dropsie Avenue*; *Will Eisner's New York: Life in the Big City*, which gathered *New York*, *The Building*, *City People Notebook*, and *Invisible People*; and *Life, in Pictures: Autobiographical Stories*, with three graphic novels and two stories ("A Sunset in Sunshine City," *The Dreamer*, *To the Heart of the Storm*, *The Name of the Game*, "The Day I Became a Professional").

Eisner was delighted when the preface arrived in December. Aside from a few last minute adjustments, the book was ready for publication.

Eisner had been blessed with good health throughout life. At eighty-seven, he still had strength and stamina. He had decent eyesight and a steady hand—both essential to his art. He'd seen talented younger men have to abandon their work because of shaky hands, and it was sad to watch a creative mind hampered by an uncooperative body. He had the usual aches and pains associated with advancing age, but he still took his morning swim and moved about well. If he had a complaint, it was about a damaged right rotator cuff that forced him to give up his tennis game, which had been one of his passions throughout his adult life. His physician had told him that surgery would be necessary to repair the rotator cuff and allow Eisner to continue playing tennis, but Eisner declined, fearing that he wouldn't be able to work during the lengthy recovery period. He had passed his eightieth birthday at that point.

He was feeling poorly, however, as 2004 drew to a close. He was tired and had shortness of breath, but he pushed himself to complete work on *The Plot*, create a new *Spirit* story for Michael Chabon's *Escapist* comic book, make notes for and assemble a new instructional book, and conduct his usual day-to-day business. He insisted on finishing the *Plot* and *Escapist* projects before visiting his doctor. He pushed himself until, finally, he had to go to the emergency room After an angiogram, he was informed that he had serious arterial blockage and needed quadruple bypass surgery.

The surgery, performed in mid-December, initially appeared to have gone without a hitch, but the recovery was slow. Eisner still struggled with his breathing, and after he collapsed while getting out of bed one day, his surgeon decided that another operation was necessary, this time to eliminate fluid that had built up around his heart. As before, the surgery was declared a success, and Eisner hoped to be released from the hospital sometime in early January.

What he and the hospital's medical personnel didn't realize was that he was bleeding internally as a result of the surgery, not from a bleeding ulcer, as a gastrointestinal doctor diagnosed. An endoscopy was scheduled for January 4.

January 3 was an eventful day. Eisner had written a highly personal introduction to *The Contract with God Trilogy*, a hardcover gathering of *A Contract with God*, *A Life Force*, and *Dropsie Avenue: The Neighborhood*, in which he wrote about how the death of his daughter had influenced his most famous graphic novel. Robert Weil, his editor at W. W. Norton, had worked on the introduction, and he called Eisner to discuss some of the edits. Weil tried to keep the conversation light, but at one point they discussed Eisner's decision to talk about Alice in the piece.

"We discussed the autobiographical material about his daughter," Weil remembered, "and I said I never knew the relevance of *A Contract with God*. He felt it would be appropriate. We spoke about the revelations about Alice, but we didn't speak at length about the origins. I had some questions about the introduction, but he said, 'You deal with Denis on that. Denis is great.'"

Weil was impressed by Eisner's determination to get a clean bill of health and go back to work. "He was tired of the hospital and he was eager to get out," Weil said. "His voice was clear and very strong. He sounded like Will."

Later in the day, in the late afternoon, Weil called with news on another front: He'd just heard from Norton's rights director in Spain, who told him that Grupo Editorial Norma had agreed to publish *The Plot*. Eisner was glad to hear this, first because he liked the Spanish publisher's editor and enjoyed working with him, and second because Spain was one of those countries with an available edition of *The Protocols*. Eisner hoped that his book would refute any credence *The Protocols* might have in the country. As Weil remembered, it was a good conversation, cut short only when a nurse came in the room and intervened.

Weil was so excited about the prospects of seeing Eisner back at work that he immediately e-mailed Denis Kitchen with a brief account of their earlier conversations.

Will be sending you by overnight tomorrow my edited copy of Will's gorgeous Contract. When I spoke to Will on the phone at the hospital today, he said he would be delighted that I send you my editorial parts now. From his strong baritone voice and demeanor today, it sounds as if he's eager to plunge back to his work.

Ann hung around the hospital, as she had on every previous day of her husband's stay, until both she and her husband needed to get some rest.

"It was about ten o'clock that night," Ann recalled. "I said, 'Good night, honey. I'll be back at eight.' And two hours later, I got a call. He was dead."

Eisner had passed away in his sleep.

★   ★   ★

Obituaries and tributes poured in. The *New York Times*, in a half-page notice that included the high points in his career, noted the value of Eisner's
innovative writing, from his work on *The Spirit* through *P★S* magazine
and his graphic novels. "His seriousness," the *Times* writer stated, specifically citing *A Contract with God*, "helped bring mainstream attention to
works like Art Spiegelman's 'Maus' and Marjane Satrapi's 'Persepolis.'"

Following private family funeral services, Will Eisner was buried near
his daughter, Alice, in the family plot in the Mount Pleasant Cemetery
near White Plains, New York. A plain headstone lists his first name as
"Will," marking the resting place of a man who, in death, would be as
unassuming as he was in life. A short time after the private services, a
public memorial service was held in Manhattan, where, in a dignified yet
casual setting, fanboys mingled with some of the comic book community's
most influential contributors, all celebrating a life that somehow seemed
too brief, despite Eisner's almost eighty-eight years on earth. Such comics
magazines as *Comic Book Artist*, *Comics Journal*, and *Alter Ego* published issues devoted to remembrances of Eisner's life, all agreeing that Eisner's
considerable influence would continue to be felt for many years to come.
The 2005 San Diego Comic-Con held panel discussions about the man
and his work.

In the years immediately following his death, Eisner was never far removed from the public light. The annual awards bearing his name continued to be given to significant contributors to the comics medium. Bob
Andelman's biography, *Will Eisner: A Spirited Life*, with an introduction
by Michael Chabon and an appreciation by Neal Adams, was published
within months of Eisner's death, the first of what promised to be a line of
biographies and studies of the artist's life. Andrew D. Cooke and Jon
B. Cooke's highly anticipated documentary, *Will Eisner: Portrait of a Sequential Artist*, was released in 2007. *The Spirit*, a theatrical motion picture
directed by Frank Miller, hit theaters at Christmastime in 2008.

More significant, Eisner's own work continued to be published. In an
irony that Eisner would have appreciated, his final *Spirit* adventure, the
last work he'd delivered before entering the hospital, was published in
Michael Chabon's comic book series, *The Escapist*. Eisner had been feeling poorly while working on the story, but he was determined to drop it
in the mail before visiting a doctor.

The Plot, which might have signaled a new direction for Eisner, had
he'd lived to do more work, was published to generally favorable reviews. "His final book combines literary biography and criticism into
an activist work striking a blow against anti-Semitism," wrote *Time*'s

Andrew D. Arnold. "Though not without flaws, *The Plot* carries through Eisner's ambitious legacy to the end."

Jonathan Dorfman, in a review for the *Boston Globe*, praised *The Plot*'s economy in words and pictures. "It is a testament to Eisner, and his skill in the genre, that he packs so much historical narrative into so few pages. 'The Plot' tells the story of 'The Protocols of the Elders of Zion' with a wallop, and makes you writhe in disbelief at how this rubbish has served as a justification for so much political and human wreckage."

R. C. Harvey, a reviewer who knew Eisner and had interviewed him when he was just beginning his work on the book, called *The Plot* "an unprecedented, pioneering undertaking . . . an impressive manifestation of this kind of bold venturing . . . quintessential Eisner.

> [I]t is not entirely successful like much of Eisner's latterday literary endeavor. But, again like most of his work, it dares to go where few, if any, have gone before, and it is therefore typical of the artist's life-long crusade for the literary status of his chosen medium.

Eisner would have appreciated the care put into publishing the book: a hardcover, dust-jacketed volume, with the introduction by Umberto Eco, afterword by *Protocols* scholar and Rutgers professor Stephen Eric Bronner, and full notes, index, and bibliography. Eisner had spent seven decades charting unexplored territory in the sequential art, and the last book he would complete continued the tradition.

Then, in 2008, W. W. Norton published *Expressive Anatomy for Comics and Narrative*, the instructional book Eisner had been working on at the time of his death. As its title indicated, the book went beyond the kind of anatomical study usually associated with art school. A painter needed to understand skeletal and muscular structure, as well as posture and gesture, for his or her work, but the narrative of sequential art placed additional demands upon the artist. There was movement and changes in facial expression, exaggeration of body language typical of actors onstage. "In this whole process of creating a visual story," Eisner wrote in the introduction to the book, "the artist functions like a theater director choreographing the action.

> The expression of human emotion is displayed by behavior articulated by meaningful postures. Often, to achieve a particular expression the gestures may require distortion or exaggeration. To create an idea of individual personality and physical differences, the knowl-

edge of the anatomical structure and the weight of the human body are most important. If he is going to communicate his ideas effectively, an artist must have a complete understanding of the body grammar of the human figure and how to use it.

At the time of his death, Eisner had written the book's text, roughed out its layout and design, and chosen a large number of illustrations to use as examples for each of his topics; but there was still much work to do. The book lay fallow for a while during the period of grief following Eisner's death, while his affairs were put in order. Finally, after some discussion between Ann Eisner, Carl Gropper (Eisner's nephew, who was now in charge of the Will Eisner Studio), Robert Weil (Eisner's editor at W. W. Norton), and Denis Kitchen and Judy Hansen (who acted as agents for Eisner's art), a decision was reached to continue the project. Peter Poplaski was hired to finish the book.

Poplaski was highly qualified for the job. A former Wisconsinite who had known Denis Kitchen for nearly thirty-five years, Poplaski was a gallery painter, cartoonist, writer, archivist, and art historian who, as art director at Kitchen Sink Press, had worked extensively with Eisner, particularly on *The Spirit Magazine* and comic book. He had a large collection of anatomy books to consult, and as both a fine artist and a cartoonist, he understood the distinctions Eisner wanted to make between gallery and cartoon art.

"I wish I had been with him on it from the ground up, because it would have been fun to go over it with him and argue different things. I have an interest in silent movies, so I have an interest in how pantomime and gestures work in communicating a story idea. The biggest omission in the book is he doesn't really compare feminine gestures with masculine gestures, and because he had these students who wanted to work for Marvel Comics, he starts out with some muscle anatomy to show how to draw superheroes. He doesn't really get very deep into analyzing the aging process and the whole structure of how anatomy works in that regard. This is where you say, 'I wish we could have dealt with this.' It would have been great.

"He did a rough dummy that ran about 112 pages. He had a lot of false starts. It was my job to sift through all this stuff and kind of structure it. I started the book based on Will's notes and what I thought it should be. I made a list of what I thought should be changed, because he already used material in previous books when he was discussing this basic idea. He was repeating stuff from the other two sequential art volumes, and you don't want to repeat yourself. I had to go through everything he ever did and find more appropriate examples."

Expressive Anatomy, although not as strong as *Comics and Sequential Art*, was a worthy addition to the Eisner instructional canon, expanding upon what he had written in the earlier book and underscoring his value as a teacher. In the classroom and his two previously published instructional books, he'd taken a practical approach to sharing a wealth of experience with a strongly diverse group of students and readers. In *Expressive Anatomy*, he was teaching from beyond the grave.

Neil Gaiman once asked Will Eisner why he continued to work well into an age when so many of his contemporaries had retired. Eisner considered the question and responded by mentioning a movie he'd once seen about a jazz musician who kept playing because he was in search of "The Note"— the elusive symbol of perfection, the indication that he had achieved all he could ever hope to achieve. This search was what kept Eisner in the game.

"I never felt, in talking to Will, that there was a list of things that he had to do before he died," Gaiman said in 2009, "that he had this book and that book, and that book and that book, all lined up in his head like planes coming in, all in a holding pattern, and they had to be landed before the night comes. What I felt was he was pursuing The Note, and it's as if there was somebody just beyond the horizon, just out of sight, playing something on a flute, and Will wanted to try to reach that person before the night came. But in order to reach that person, he was going to have to keep walking down that street, and he was going to have to head into the forest or wherever you went next."

"The wonder of Eisner is he never stopped questioning," Frank Miller observed, agreeing with Gaiman's assessment of Eisner's life and art as a continual quest. "Had he lived another thirty years, we still would have been asking that question: Where else was he going to go?"

NOTES

NOTE: In its long history, *The Spirit* was printed and reprinted in newspapers, magazines, and books. The feature had its own magazine with two different publishers and its own standard-sized comic book. In these chapter notes, when I quote directly from one of the specific *Spirit* entries I cite the specific date on which the episode appeared in the Sunday newspaper supplement. When citing interviews and columns appearing in the magazine or comic book, I draw a distinction by citing *The Spirit Magazine* when I'm citing an entry in the Warren or Kitchen Sink magazines or *The Spirit*, followed by the number of the comic book and the parenthetical CB, indicating that it is from the Kitchen Sink Press reissue.

CHAPTER ONE: THE DEPRESSION'S LESSONS

1   Epigraph: Will Eisner, preface to *The Contract with God Trilogy* (New York: W. W. Norton, 2006), p. xiii.

1   Eisner family background and Will Eisner's childhood: Will Eisner, "Art and Commerce: An Oral Reminiscence by Will Eisner, interview conducted and edited by John Benson, *Panels #1* (summer 1979). Jon B. Cooke, "Will Eisner: The Creative Life of a Master," *Comic Book Artist* 2, no. 6 (November 2005). Interviews with Ann Eisner, Carl Gropper, Allan Gropper, and Eliot Gordon. See also Will Eisner, *To the Heart of the Storm* (Princeton, WI: Kitchen Sink Press, 1991).

1   "The city, to me": Cooke, "Will Eisner: The Creative Life of a Master."

2   "a kerosene miner": Eisner, "Art and Commerce."

4   "Julian": Eisner, *Heart of the Storm*, p. 9. The other citations in this passage are from this source.

9   "From those pulps": Cooke, "Will Eisner: The Creative Life of a Master."

9   "I grew up": John Benson, "Will Eisner: Having Something to Say," *Comics Journal #267*.

11 "As always": Eisner, "Art and Commerce."

11 "Seeing people": Ibid.

11 "He had been a dress-cutter": Interview with Stan Lee.

12 "Your father isn't": Bob Andelman, *Will Eisner: A Spirited Life* (Milwaukie, OR: M Press, 2005), p. 114.

12 "I got there": Dave Schreiner, "Stage Settings: Drawing from Experience," *The Spirit #24* (CB).

14 "We couldn't afford": Interview with Nick Cardy.

15 Eisner at DeWitt Clinton High School: Eisner's earliest published work, including cartoon strips, single-panel illustrations, paintings, and sketches, many published in the *Clintonian*, Eisner's high school paper, were reprinted in Will Eisner's *The Art of Will Eisner*, edited by Cat Yronwode (Princeton, WI: Kitchen Sink Press, 1982), and Will Eisner, *Edge of Genius* (New York: Pure Imagination Pubishing, 2007).

15 "Garry is so proud": Interview with Stan Lee.

17 "[it] represented": Eisner, *Art of Will Eisner*, p. 7.

17 "She had an aunt": Eisner, *Edge of Genius*.

17 "My mother stepped in": Cooke, "Will Eisner: The Creative Life of a Master."

18 "She was extremely shocked": Ibid.

18 Ham Fisher meeting: Tom Heintjes, "Stage Settings: Harried holidays," *The Spirit #64* (CB); R. C. Harvey, "Untitled Homage to Will Eisner," *Comic Book Artist* 2, no. 6 (November 2005).

19 "I almost fainted": Heintjes, "Stage Settings: Harried holidays."

19 "What kind of pen": Harvey, "Untitled Homage."

20 "One of the difficulties": Danny Fingeroth, "The Will Eisner Interview," *Write Now! #5*.

21 "They buy from everybody": Andelman, *Will Eisner: A Spirited Life*, p. 36.

CHAPTER TWO: A BUSINESS FOR THIRTY BUCKS

22 Epigraph: Maggie Thompson, "Will Eisner," *Golden Age of Comics #2*.

22 Eisner/Iger meeting: Will Eisner, *The Dreamer* (Princeton, WI: Kitchen Sink Press, 1986), pp. 9–10.

23 "I went up": Interview with Nick Cardy.

23 "I don't have time": R. C. Harvey, "The Shop System: Interview with Will Eisner," *Comics Journal #249*.

23 "Excuse me": Ibid.

24 Early comics history: Ron Goulart, *Ron Goulart's Great History of Comic Books* (Chicago: Contemporary Books, 1986); Davd Hajdu, *The Ten-Cent Plague: The Great Comic-Book Scare and How It Changed America* (New York: Farrar, Straus, & Giroux, 2008); Gerald Jones, *Men of Tomorrow: Geeks, Gangsters, and the Birth of*

the Comic Book (New York: Basic Books, 2004); Coulton Waugh, *The Comics* (New York: Macmillan, 1947), Will Eisner, "Getting the Last Laugh," *New York Times Book Review,* January 14, 1990.

24   "counter-cultural, lowbrow": Jones, *Men of Tomorrow,* p. 62.

26   Major Malcolm Wheeler-Nicholson: *Alter Ego* 3, no. 88 (August 2009) devoted most of its issue to Wheeler-Nicholson, with interviews with Christina Blakeney (his granddaughter), Douglas Wheeler-Nicholson (his son), Nicky Wheeler-Nicholson Brown (his granddaughter), and Antoinette Wheeler-Nicholson (his daughter). Not only did the interviews supply readers with information about this unusual character in comics' history, they also dealt with some of the myths and misconceptions, repeated in books and interviews (including Eisner's *The Dreamer*) for more than a half century. Dennis O'Neil, a writer and editor at DC, admitted that his thinking about Wheeler-Nicholson had been shaped by the standard, long accepted characterization of the major, but that thinking changed after he saw the Wheeler-Nicholson issue of *Alter Ego.* "All these years, Wheeler-Nicholson was kind of a clown in my mind," O'Neil said in an interview for this book. "Well, that's because that was the way he was portrayed by the guys who cheated him out of his company."

29   Formation of Eisner & Iger: Eisner, *The Dreamer,* pp. 11–12; Harvey, "The Shop System"; Jon B. Cooke, "Will Eisner: The Creative Life of a Master," *Comic Book Artist* 2, no. 6 (November 2005); Jean Depelley, "Will Eisner Speaks!," *Jack Kirby Collector #16;* Will Eisner, 'Art and Commerce: An Oral Reminiscence by Will Eisner," interview conducted and edited by John Benson, *Panels #1* (summer 1979). Not surprisingly, Jerry Iger had his own account of his business relationship with Eisner. In a 1985 interview with *Cubic Zirconia Reader,* Iger claimed: "I had gone into a brief partnership with Will Eisner in mid-1938, only to buy him out in 1940 when Will was drafted [*sic*] into the Army to do military posters. Will had become so accomplished— and so expensive!—as a freelance artist that the only way I could afford his services was to make him a partner." As we'll see, Iger's account of the creation of *Sheena* was equally creative.

29   "my name was first": Harvey, "The Shop System."

29   "Y'know, Billy": Eisner, *The Dreamer,* p. 12.

30   Chesler and the shop systems: Interviews with Joe Kurbert, Irwin Hasen, and Carmine Infantino. Ron Goulart, "Golden Age Sweatshops," *Comics Journal #249;* Harvey, "The Shop System." Hajdu, *The Ten-Cent Plague,* pp. 32–33.

31   "Chesler never did manage": Goulart, "Golden Age Sweatshops."

31   "Harry was extremely kind": Interview with Joe Kubert.

31   "I loved Harry": Interview with Carmine Infantino.

32   "Just don't work": Interview with Irwin Hasen.

32   "You needed a guy": Ibid.

32   "pretty much the way": Goulart, "Golden Age Sweatshops."

33   "ten-year-old cretins": David Hajdu, "Good Will," *Comic Book Artist* 2, no. 6 (November 2005).

33   "It was the bottom": Interview with Bob Fujitani.

33   "Comic book writing": Interview with Stan Lee.

33   "He said": Interview with Nick Cardy.

33   "It doesn't seem possible": Waugh, *The Comics*, pp. 333–334.

34   "comic book ghetto": Arie Kaplan, "Looking Back," *Comics Journal #267*.

34   "We were living": Will Eisner, "Keynote Address from 2002 'Will Eisner Symposium.'"

34   "There were a lot": Ibid. All other quotations in this passage are from this source.

34   "One was Willis R. Rensie": Mike Barson, Ted White, and Mitch Berger, ". . . and I Threw In a Hat . . . ," *Heavy Metal*, November 1983.

35   "The trouble with you": Harvey, "The Shop System."

36   "There was a great deal": Dave Schreiner, "Afterword" to Will Eisner, *Hawks of the Seas* (Princeton, WI: Kitchen Sink Press, 1986), p. 125.

CHAPTER THREE: SUPERMEN
IN A WORLD OF MORTALS

38   Epigraph: John Benson, "Will Eisner: Having Something to Say," *Comics Journal #267*.

39   *Sheena*: See "Sheena: Queen of the Iger Comics Kingdom" issue of *Alter Ego* 21 (February 2005) for extensive coverage of the Eisner & Iger shop and the creation of *Sheena*, including the reprinting of the Jerry Iger biography, *The Iger Comics Kingdom*, written by Jay Edward Disbrow and published in 1985 by Blackhorne Publications. Based largely on Disbrow's interviews with Iger, the biography is marred by historical inaccuracies, the result of Iger's revisionist history and insistence on taking credit for just about everything that happened in early comics history. Roy Thomas, *Alter Ego*'s editor and a comic book artist and historian, interjects with sidebars and commentary whenever necessary, and his "A Footnote on the Eisner and Iger Shops," listing all the shops' personnel, along with their dates of employment, is an indispensable resource.

40   Artists at Eisner & Iger shop: It's noteworthy that, with the exception of Baily, the artists at the Eisner & Iger shop were very young and, at best, minimally experienced in comics when they hooked up with Eisner & Iger. Most would do their breakthrough work after the breakup of Eisner & Iger, when Eisner was running a studio on his own and supplying a steady stream of material to Quality Comics. Powell (*Mr. Mystic*), Nordling (*Lady Luck*), and Mazoujian (*Lady Luck*) worked on various projects before becoming major contributors to *The Spirit* newspaper supplement, and Cardy, who in time would be known for his artistry with female characters, eventually

took over *Lady Luck* after Mazoujian left the studio. Fine (*Black Condor, The Ray*), Meskin (*Sheena*), Crandall (*Doll Man, Blackhawk*), and Tuska (*Uncle Sam*) were invaluable contributors to other comics produced for Busy Arnold and Quality Comics. Kane produced short features for Eisner before deciding that the money was better elsewhere and making his name as the creator of *Batman.* Several (Tuska, Henkel, Crandall, Fox) wound up creating crime comics for such publications as *Police Comics* and *Crime Does Not Pay.* Kirby, who worked at Eisner's shop long enough to warm a seat, turned out to be one of the greatest comics artists ever, from his collaborations with Joe Simon (*Captain America*) to his work with Stan Lee and Marvel (*Fantastic Four, Thor*). A few, most notably Fine and Fox, moved away from comics and into advertising, while Kirby and Cardy (*Teen Titans, Aquanan*) had lifelong careers in comics and did their most lasting work long after leaving Eisner.

41   "When his work came out": Interview with Joe Kubert.

41   "Lou had never": Mike Barson, Ted White, and Mitch Berger, ". . . and I Threw In a Hat . . . ," *Heavy Metal*, November 1983.

42   "When Eisner would leave": Interview with Bob Fujitani.

42   "He was a hell of a nice guy": Interview with Nick Cardy.

42   Tuska/Powell dustup: Nick Cardy disputed this account, first in an interview with comics historian Michael T. Gilbert and later in my interview with him. According to Cardy, he approached Tuska at a convention and asked him about the fight, and Tuska told him he'd punched Rafael Astarita while he was working for Harry Chesler, not Bob Powell while he was working for Eisner & Iger. "The story I heard from George is that he was working at Chesler, and this other guy was picking on a young kid. George said, 'Why don't you lay off. Pick on somebody your own size.' When the guy up and said something nasty, George cleaned his brush, rinsed it out and put it on his taboret, got up, and smacked the guy. The guy went through several tables. And that was the end of the story." When reminded that Will Eisner had witnessed the altercation and immortalized it in his novella *The Dreamer,* Cardy admitted that something like that could have happened before he was employed at Eisner & Iger or when he was absent. "Maybe Tuska hit Powell, too, I don't know. He could have, because Powell was the type who would get into trouble."

43   Kirby confrontation: Ronin Ro, *Tales to Astonish: Jack Kirby, Stan Lee, and the American Comic Book Revolution* (New York: Bloomsbury, 2004), pp. 4–5; Will Eisner, *The Dreamer,* p. 26; Jean Depelley, "Will Eisner Speaks!," *Jack Kirby Collector #16.*

43   "Look, we don't want": Ro, *Tales to Astonish,* p. 6. All other direct quotations in this passage are from this source.

44   "Jack was a little fellow": Depelley, "Will Eisner Speaks!"

44   "I was kind of": Interview with Stan Lee.

45   "I was upset": Interview with Nick Cardy.

45   "We had a whole bunch": Mark Evanier, "POV," *POV Online*, posted September 1, 2000.

45   "I wrote them": Joe Siegel, "An Interview with Will Eisner," *Spirit Magazine #2*.

46   "We were all concerned": Ibid.

46   "The creation of": Danny Fingeroth, *Disguised as Clark Kent: Jews, Comics, and the Creation of the Superhero* (New York: Continuum, 2007), p. 17.

47   *Superman*: Gerard Jones's award-winning book, *Men of Tomorrow*, offers the best available history of *Superman* and its creators, the disputes over ownership, and early comics history in general. His account of the acceptance of *Superman* can be found on pp. 121–125.

47   Wheeler-Nicholson's loss of his company: Harry Donenfeld's hostile takeover of National Comics has been recorded, disputed, and debated to the point where all the specifics may never be known. While admitting that the Major had poor business sense, Wheeler-Nicholson's descendants, quite understandably, hotly disputed the belief that the Major was solely responsible for his loss of the company. In an interview with Jim Amash, published in *Alter Ego* 3, no. 88 (August 2009), Douglas Wheeler-Nicholson, one of the Major's sons, maintained that Donenfeld and Jack Liebowitz had duped his father into believing that his company was failing by overprinting his publications and returning bundles of supposedly unsold comics, using these comics as proof that Wheeler-Nicholson's comics just weren't performing on the market. According to Douglas Wheeler-Nicholson, the Major took an early and active interest in *Superman* and intended to use it as the centerpiece of his proposed *Action #1* comic book. "It was a major source of discussion in the house," Douglas told Amash. "He thought it was extremely timely, and he was very specific about a Nietzschean kind of hero at this time of the Depression, and that this would be a perfect thing to put forth to the public at this time. He talked about it extensively." This memory doesn't match other accounts, including Eisner's, of the feature's making the rounds in early 1938, though his account of his father's losing his business, while differing somewhat with other accounts, does lend credence to the popular belief that Donenfeld and Liebowitz probably bilked Wheeler-Nicholson out of his company.

48   "pure luck" and "a fluke": Jones, *Men of Tomorrow*, p. 157.

49   "I've got dreams": Eisner, *The Dreamer*, p. 31.

50   Victor Fox: See Jones, *Men of Tomorrow*, pp. 148–149; Joe Simon (with Jim Simon), *The Comic Book Makers* (Lebanon, NJ: Vanguard Productions, rev. ed., 2003), pp. 29–33; Eisner, *The Dreamer*, pp. 34–35, 38–41; Will Eisner, "Art and Commerce: An Oral Reminiscence by Will Eisner," interview conducted and edited by John Benson, *Panels #1* (summer 1979).

50   "Fox was like": Evanier, "POV."

50 "a Wall Street hustler" who "didn't have": Simon, *Comic Book Makers*, p. 29.

50 "Kooba Cola": Ibid, p. 33.

51 "a thief": Eisner, "Art and Commerce."

52 "It's his magazine": Ibid. All other direct quotations in this passage are from this source.

53 "Don't pay any attention": Jim Amash, "I was Doomed to Be an Artist," *Alter Ego* 3, no. 48 (May 2005).

CHAPTER FOUR: A SPIRIT FOR ALL AGES

55 Epigraph: Will Eisner and Frank Miller, with an interview conducted by Charles Brownstein, *Eisner/Miller* (Milwaukie, OR: Dark Horse Books, 2005), p. 45.

55 Busy Arnold: Jim Amash's interview with Dick Arnold, "Men of Quality" (*Alter Ego* 3, no. 34 [March 2004]), provides a detailed look at Busy Arnold and Quality Comics. Amash's interview with Eisner, "I Always Felt Storytelling Was as Important as the Artwork, published in *Alter Ego* 3, no. 58 (May 2005), gives Eisner's perspective. See also Robert C. Harvey, *The Art of the Comic Book* (Jackson, MS: University Press of Mississippi, 1996), pp. 68–69.

56 "Busy Arnold was": Amash, "I Always Felt."

58 "That kind of rubbed me": Interview with Al Jaffee.

59 "To the syndicate": Tom Heintjes, "Stage Settings: Rolling toward five decades," *The Spirit #49* (CB).

59 "We agreed": Tom Heintjes, "Stage Settings: The accidental tourist," *The Spirit #71* (CB).

60 "Your dream": Eisner, *The Dreamer*, p. 44.

61 "There were a few": Will Eisner, "Art and Commerce: An Oral Reminiscence by Will Eisner," interview conducted and edited by John Benson, *Panels #1*.

62 "When I decided": Norman Abbott, "'The Spirit' of '41," *Philadelphia Record*, October 13, 1941.

63 "You read Sherlock Holmes": Tom Hentjes, "Interview with Will Eisner," *Hogan's Alley* (online), n.d.

63 "I didn't want": Dave Schreiner, "Stage Settings: A commonality of experience," *The Spirit #40* (CB).

63 "I like using": Tom Heintjes, "Stage Settings: The Spirit at work and play," *The Spirit #61* (CB).

63 "patterned after": Jim Amash, "I Was Doomed to Be an Artist," *Alter Ego* 3, no. 48 (May 2005).

64 "He suggested": Cat Yronwode, "Will Eisner Interview (Part 1)," *Comics Journal #46*.

64 "He's got a mask": Christopher Irving, "A Whole Lotta Spirit," *Richmond Comix* (online), n.d. All other direct quotations in this passage are from this source.

64 "When you draw": Ibid.

65 "It's an interesting point": Tom Heintjes, "Stage Settings: The healing Spirit," *The Spirit #51* (CB).

66 "It was just an attempt": Amash, "I Always Felt."

67 "I was just starting": Interview with Joe Kubert.

68 "I had to create": Interview with Al Jaffee.

68 "I hired guys": Amash, "I Always Felt."

68 "Everything had his name": Interview with David Hajdu.

70 "Since the comments": Will Eisner, "Ask Will Eisner," *Spirit Magazine #35.*

70 "open to criticism": Ibid.

71 "He offered Bob Powell": Mark Evanier, "POV," *POV Online,* posted September 1, 2000.

71 "I didn't like": Jim Amash, "I Created Blackhawk!," *Alter Ego* 3, no. 34 (March 2004).

71 "I wanted to knock": Ibid.

72 "It always struck me": Interview with Mark Evanier.

72 "He's the guy": Evanier, "POV."

72 "After the panel": Interview with Mark Evanier.

73 "I created *Blackhawk*": Amash, "I Created Blackhawk!" It should be noted that Cuidera's memory proved to be faulty at the time this interview was conducted, as well as during his appearance at the panel discussion, with Amash having to insert several clarifications in the published version of his conversation with Cuidera. The difficulties in tracing ownership and creation of characters originating in the early days of comics is illustrated in a 1976 exchange of letters between Will Eisner and Denis Kitchen. Kitchen hoped to create an updated version of *Sheena, Queen of the Jungle* as part of his Kitchen Sink Press line, but he ran into all kinds of problems when trying to trace ownership of the character. Jerry Iger claimed to own the rights, but Kitchen heard from others that this wasn't the case. Kitchen contacted Eisner, who in an August 10, 1976, letter said, "The last conversation I had on Sheena was with T. T. Scott, owner of Fiction House (now defunct) who asked me if I was interested in picking it up. I said I would be. He told me he was working on the complex matter of clearing it . . . for the property was part of the family estate . . . I had the distinct impression that the ownership of Sheena is still in the hands of the Scott family." After some literary detective work, Kitchen determined, through two 1938 letters, that Eisner & Iger had, in fact, retained the rights to the character and that Iger had retained the rights as part of the breakup agreement of the Eisner & Iger partnership. After examining photocopies of the documents, Eisner conceded that the documents were

authentic, but he was still unclear about the ownership, which is why he advised Kitchen to take a cautious approach to his proposed project. "As a friend I wanted to help you stay out of the courts," Eisner wrote Kitchen. Unable to gain final proof of ownership, Kitchen took the logical approach and abandoned the project.

74   " I wasn't ready": Will Eisner, *Will Eisner's Shop Talk* (Milwaukie, OR: Dark Horse Comics, 2001), p. 160.

74   "I discovered that": Danny Fingeroth, "The Will Eisner Interview," *Write Now! #5*.

74   "It gave him": Tom Heintjes, "Stage Settings: Earning stripes," *The Spirit* #77 (CB).

74   "The editor opened": Ibid.

75   "The comic strip": Abbott, " 'The Spirit' of '41."

75   "There was no precedent": Interview with David Hajdu.

76   "We're vaudevillians": Sarah Boxer, "Meeting of Comic Minds but No Bam! Splat! Zap!," *New York Times*, January 2, 1999.

76   "I got back": Will Eisner, "Keynote Address from the 2002 'Will Eisner Symposium.' "

76   "Here is a terrible": Letter from Everett "Busy" Arnold to Will Eisner, July 11, 1941.

76   "There are at least": Letter from Everett "Busy" Arnold to Will Eisner, July 7, 1941.

76   "Whenever anyone complained": Cat Yronwode, "When Partners Collide," *Will Eisner's Quarterly 4* (January 1985).

77   "I can get": Letter from Everett "Busy" Arnold to Will Eisner, August 20, 1941.

77   "Nick has too many": Letter from Everett "Busy" Arnold to Will Eisner, June 25, 1941.

77   "the last eight": Ibid.

78   "I knew if I didn't": "A.V. Club: Will Eisner," *The Onion*, September 27, 2000.

78   "My audience was transitory": Jon B. Cooke, "Will Eisner: The Creative Life of a Master," *Comic Book Artist* 2, no. 6 (November 2005).

80   "I was ambivalent": Brian Jacks, "Veterans Day Exclusive: 'The Spirit' Creator Will Eisner's Wartime Memories," published online on November 11, 2008.

CHAPTER FIVE: A PRIVATE NAMED JOE DOPE

82   Epigraph: Maggie Thompson, "Will Eisner," *Golden Age of Comics #2*.

82   "[I] talked to him": Eisner, *Will Eisner's Shop Talk*, p. 159.

83   Eisner in the army: Archivist/author Cat Yronwode compiled comprehensive

Spirit and Will Eisner checklists, with dates and extensive commentary on Eisner's work. These checklists appeared as a regular feature in *The Spirit Magazine* beginning with #22 and running through #32. In addition, she edited and wrote the text for *The Art of Will Eisner*, which reprints a strong sampling of Eisner's work while he was in the army.

83   "The Spirit was": Brian Jacks, "Veterans Day Exclusive: 'The Spirit' Creator Will Eisner's Wartime Memories," published online on November 11, 2008.

86   "I feel": Jim Amash, "I Always Felt Storytelling Was as Important as the Art-work," *Alter Ego* 3, no. 58 (May 2005).

86   "I don't know": Ibid.

86   "Except for the ownership": Mike Barson, Ted White, and Mitch Berger, ". . . and I Threw In a Hat . . . ," *Heavy Metal*, November 1983.

87   "What arguments": Cat Yronwode, "Eisner's P★S Years," *The Spirit Magazine #33* (February 1982).

90   "Captain America was created": Goulart, *Great History of Comic Books*, p. 154.

90   "Here was the arch villain": Simon, *Comic Book Makers*, p. 42.

91   "Only when": Gerard Jones, *Men of Tomorrow*, p. 210.

93   "During the war": Tom Heintjes, "Stage Settings: A new Spirit world," *The Spirit #73* (CB).

93   "I had to assure": Ibid.

94   "blonde, slim": Andelman, *Will Eisner: A Spirited Life*, p. 89.

CHAPTER SIX: FLIGHT

95   Epigraph: Eisner and Miller, *Eisner/Miller*, p. 271.

95   "When I came out": "Catch the Spirit," *Four-Color Magazine*, January 1987.

96   "Those who are": Shawna Ervin-Gore, "Will Eisner," *Darkhorse News* (un-dated press release).

97   "For some reason": Tom Heintjes, "Stage Settings: The Spirit that almost wasn't," *The Spirit #52* (CB).

97   "As far as": Ibid.

98   "I said": Will Eisner, "Art and Commerce: An Oral Reminiscence by Will Eisner," interview conducted and edited by John Benson, *Panels #1* (summer 1979).

98   "quite casually and disarmingly": Jon B. Cooke, "Jules Feiffer: His Early Years with Will Eisner," *Comic Book Artist* 2, no. 6 (November 2005).

98   "He had no choice": Ibid.

99   "Every time": Ibid.

99   "intensity": Eisner, "Art and Commerce."

99   "If you think": Cooke, "Jules Feiffer."

100 "He had a real ear": Tom Heintjes, "Stage Settings: The guarding of the change," *The Spirit #69* (CB).

100   Eisner/Feiffer working relationship: In *Panels #1*, Jules Feiffer talked exten-
      sively about the way he and Eisner worked together, and in a lengthy sidebar,
      he detailed his contributions to each individual *Spirit* entry, beginning on
      February 23, 1947, and running through September 28, 1952. Some of Feiffer's
      memories are vivid, others cloudy, reflecting the unique nature of his col-
      laboration with Eisner. In many of his interviews over the years, Eisner could
      be very generous in his recollections of Feiffer's contributions to *The Spirit*; in
      some cases, however, he could be possessive, even testy, about his creation.
      One gets the impression, when talking to those who knew the two artists at
      the time, that they felt both affection for and envy toward each other, Feiffer
      for Eisner's superior talents as an artist, Eisner for Feiffer's superior talents as a
      writer. Feiffer conceded that he was nowhere near as talented artistically as
      Eisner, yet he'd won a Pulitzer Prize, not Eisner, and this was a form of ac-
      ceptance that Eisner craved but would never receive. "Will felt a little irri-
      tated by me," Feiffer said in an interview for this book. "I achieved what he
      hadn't. I could see how he'd feel that way."

100   "I can't keep": Maggie Thompson, "Will Eisner," *Golden Age of Comics #2*
      (1982).

100   "It made for": Tom Heintjes, "Stage Settings: A doubly heralded new year,"
      The Spirit #65 (CB).

100   "Maybe I had": "A Listing of Jules Feiffer Scripts," *Panels #1* (summer 1974).

100   "Our fights were always": Interview with Jules Feiffer.

101   "the left intellectual": Jules Feiffer, *Backing into Forward* (New York: Double-
      day, 2010), p. 53.

102   "Kanegson was brilliant": Dave Schreiner, "Stage Settings: Looking in mem-
      ory's closet," *The Spirit #33* (CB).

102   "To me, lettering": Tom Heintjes, "Stage Settings: The Spirit at work and
      play," *The Spirit #61* (CB).

102   "There's always been": Dave Schreiner, "Stage Settings: Summer in the stu-
      dio," *The Spirit #34* (CB).

102   "the first visible hippie": Maggie Thompson and Cat Yronwode, "Will Eis-
      ner, Part II," *Golden Age of Comics #2*.

102   "I said": Ibid.

103   "I was always faced": Dave Schreiner, "Stage Settings: Summer in the stu-
      dio."

103   "I don't think": Interview with Jerry Grandenetti.

104   "It will take you": Will Eisner, "Ten Minutes," *The Spirit*, September 11,
      1949.

104   "That was mine": "Jules Feiffer Talks About The Spirit," *Panels #1* (summer
      1979).

105   "The philosophy": Maggie Thompson, "Will Eisner," *Golden Age of Comics #2*.

105   "really a Spirit story": Feiffer, *Backing into Forward*, p. 68.

106   "It goes like this": Tom Heintjes, "Stage Settings: Toys, time, love and death," *The Spirit #48* (CB).

106   "baptism of reality": Dave Schreiner, "Stage Settings: The beginnings of a roll," *The Spirit #20* (CB).

106   "We'll have a little": Ibid.

106   "I *caught* your *stuff*": Ibid.

107   "I always harbored": Ibid.

107   Fredric Wertham and comics censorship: Bart Beaty, *Fredric Wertham and the Critique of Mass Culture* (Jackson, MS: University Press of Mississippi, 2005), pp. 155–164; Goulart, *Great History of Comic Books*, pp. 268–274; Hajdu, *The Ten-Cent Plague*, pp. 250–295; Jones, *Men of Tomorrow*, pp. 270–277; Amy Kiste Nyberg, *Seal of Approval: The History of the Comics Code* (Jackson, MS: University Press of Mississippi, 1998), pp. 53–128.

108   "We found": Judith Crist, "Horror in the Nursery," *Collier's*, March 29, 1948.

109   "Wertham was a nest": Hajdu, *The Ten-Cent Plague*, p. 99.

110   "the greatest intellectual": Marya Mannes, "Junior as a Craving," *New Republic*, February 17, 1947.

110   "the marijuana of the nursery": John Mason Brown, "The Case Against Comics," *Saturday Review of Literature*, March 20, 1948.

111   "This is a public service": Will Eisner, "The Spirit's Favorite Fairy Tales for Juvenile Delinquents: Hänzel und Gretel," *The Spirit*, July 13, 1947.

111   "This was before": Schreiner, "Stage Settings: The beginnings of a roll."

114   "I walked a tightrope": Tom Heintjes, "Stage Settings: The Spirit that almost wasn't," *The Spirit #52* (CB).

116   "The stories with her": Tom Heintjes, "Stage Settings: The guarding of the change," *The Spirit #69* (CB).

116   "The thing about women": Will Eisner, "Thorne Strand and . . . The Spirit," *The Spirit*, January 23, 1949.

116   "When I did": Tom Heintjes, "Stage Settings: Back in the U.S.A.," *The Spirit #58* (CB).

117   "It was the first time": Dave Schreiner, "Stage Settings: Some of the great ones," *The Spirit #35* (CB).

117   "Do not weep": Will Eisner, "The Story of Gerhard Shnobble," *The Spirit*, September 5, 1948.

119   "I had been wanting": Dave Schreiner, "Stage Settings: Looking in memory's closet," *The Spirit #33* (CB).

119   "You didn't need": Will Eisner, "Reminiscences and Hortations," transcribed by Steve Freitag, edited by Gary Groth, *Comics Journal #89*.

119   "I guess I could be": Tom Heintjes, "Stage Settings: On the road again . . ." *The Spirit #54* (CB).

120   "*Baseball Comics* was": Dave Schreiner, "Rube Rooky triumphant," *Baseball Comics #1* (Princeton, WI: Kitchen Sink Press, 1991).

CHAPTER SEVEN: ANN

122   Epigraph: Will Eisner, in the documentary *Will Eisner: Profession: Cartoonist*, produced and directed by Marisa Furtado de Oliveira and Paulo Serran, Scriptorium, 1999.

123   Will Eisner and Ann Weingarten: Interviews with Ann Eisner, Carl Gropper, and Allan Gropper; Blake Bell, *I Have to Live with This Guy* (Raleigh, NC: (TwoMorrows Books, 2002); Jon B. Cooke, "Just My Will," *Comic Book Artist* 2, no. 6 (November 2005).

123   "Did you promise": Interview with Ann Eisner.

123   "Susan and I": Ibid. All other direct quotations in this passage are from this interview.

125   "I saw a different": Ibid.

126   "Sammy and Delilah": Interview with Ann Eisner; Tom Heintjes, "Stage Settings: On the road again," *The Spirit #54* (CB).

126   "I was sitting": Interview with Ann Eisner.

126   "They claimed": Tom Heintjes, "Stage Settings: On the road again."

129   "I felt there was": Mike Barson, Ted White, and Mitch Berger, ". . . And I Threw in a Hat . . . ," *Heavy Metal*, November 1983.

129   *P★S* magazine: Paul E. Fitzgerald's self-published book, *Will Eisner and PS Magazine* (Fincastle, WV: Fitzworld.US, 2009), is the most complete, comprehensive look at Eisner's work on the magazine available, with copious illustrations, interviews with *P★S* staff editors and artists, extensive commentary from Eisner, and more. See also Cat Yronwode, "Eisner's *P★S* Years," *The Spirit Magazine #33* (February 1982).

129   "It was a very": Tom Heintjes, "Stage Settings: Sam Spade and the Nature Boy," *The Spirit #82* (CB).

130   "Army personnel": Fitzgerald, *Will Eisner and PS Magazine*, pp. 15–16.

131   "he felt as if": Ibid, p. 21.

133   "it was a dilemma": Tom Heintjes, "Stage Settings: Stabilizing the Spirit," *The Spirit #74* (CB).

133   "The obvious was": Will Eisner, "An Introduction to the Wally Wood Spirits," *The Spirit Magazine #20*.

133   "last gasp": Will Eisner, "Reminiscences and Hortations," transcribed by Steve Freitag, edited by Gary Groth, *Comics Journal #89*.

134   "Looking back": Tom Heintjes, "Stage Settings: Stabilizing the Spirit."

CHAPTER EIGHT: OUT OF THE MAINSTREAM

135 Epigraph: Eisner, *Will Eisner's Shop Talk*, p. 23.

135 Comic book hearings and Comics Code: Beaty, *Fredric Wertham and the Critique of Mass Culture*, pp. 155–164; Goulart, *Great History of Comic Books*, pp. 268–274; Hajdu, *The Ten-Cent Plague*, pp. 250–295; Jones, *Men of Tomorrow*, pp. 270–277; Nyberg, *Seal of Approval*, pp. 53–128; Simon, *The Comic Book Makers*, pp. 118–130.

137 "The comic-book format": Fredric Wertham, *Seduction of the Innocent* (New York: Rinehart, 1954), p. 118.

138 "I think Hitler": Senate hearings, as quoted in Hajdu, *The Ten-Cent Plague*, p. 264.

139 "I felt that": Frank Jacobs, *The Mad World of William M. Gaines* (Secaucus, NJ: Lyle Stuart, 1972), p. 107.

139 "my only limits": Senate hearings, as quoted in Nyberg, *Seal of Approval*, p. 63.

139 "Do you think": Senate hearings, as quoted in Nyberg, *Seal of Approval*, p. 63.

140 "We are constantly": David Gallagher, "The Portrait of a Sequential Artist: Will Eisner," *Comics Bulletin* (online), n.d.

141 Shake-up at *P★S* magazine: Paul E. Fitzgerald, *Will Eisner and PS Magazine* (Fincastle, VA: Fitzworld.US, 2009); interview with Paul Fitzgerald.

141 "I have never known": Fitzgerald, *Will Eisner and PS Magazine*, p. 19.

143 "I don't think": Ibid., p. 30.

144 "If you moved": Interview with Ann Eisner.

144 "It would reach": Interview with Paul Fitzgerald.

145 "I was fighting": Tom Heintjes, "Stage Settings: A new Spirit world," *The Spirit #73* (CB).

145 "When I learned": Ibid.

146 "1. Effective immediately": "Memorandum of Record, June 28, 1955," as reprinted in Fitzgerald, *Will Eisner and PS Magazine*, pp. 82–83.

146 "Some bureaucrat": Heintjes, "Stage Settings: A new Spirit world."

147 "When I went": Tom Heintjes, "Stage Settings: Stabilizing the Spirit," *The Spirit #74* (CB).

148 "I stayed with": Tom Heintjes, "Stage Settings: Refried fiends," *The Spirit #81* (CB).

149 "I became far more interested": Will Eisner, "Reminiscences and Hortations," transcribed by Steve Freitag, edited by Gary Groth, *Comics Journal #89*.

149 "There were all kinds": Dirk Deppey, "Mike Ploog on Will Eisner," *Comics Journal #267*.

149 "We used to get": Ibid.

151 "Drawn as if": Jules Feiffer, *The Great Comic Book Heroes* (New York: Dial Press, 1965; updated 1977), p. 35.

151 "For some reason": Ibid.

151 "It was kind": Maggie Thompson, "Blue Suit, Blue Mask, Blue Gloves—and No Socks," *Golden Age of Comics #2*.

151 "Eisner's line had": Feiffer, *The Great Comic Book Heroes*, pp. 34–35.

151 "Alone among comic book men": Ibid., p. 37.

152 "I knew Will": Interview with Jules Feiffer.

152 "I wasn't training": Heintjes, "Stage Settings: A new Spirit world."

153 "One guy": Ibid.

153 "We had other": Tom Heintjes, "Stage Settings: Few regrets," *The Spirit #76* (CB).

154 "The differences": Heintjes, "Stage Settings: Refried fiends."

154 "He lied to me": Interview with Ann Eisner.

155 "Saigon was like": Will Eisner, introduction to *Last Day in Vietnam* (Milwaukie, OR: Dark Horse Comics, 2000), p. 5.

156 "He had a wife": Interview with Ann Eisner.

156 Eisner as father: Interviews with Ann Eisner and Denis Kitchen.

156 "He did whatever": Interview with Ann Eisner.

157 "He said": Jon B. Cooke, "Just My Will: An Interview with Ann Eisner," *Comic Book Artist 2*, no. 6 (November 2005).

157 "He didn't cry": Interview with Ann Eisner.

CHAPTER NINE: BACK IN THE GAME

159 Epigraph: Mike Jozic, "Will Eisner: The Godfather of Comics," *Meanwhile* (online), interview conducted March 7, 2000.

159 "I want to invite": Interview with Denis Kitchen.

159 "Mr. Eisner": Ibid.

160 "Come on down": Jon B. Cooke, "Will Eisner: The Creative Life of a Master," *Comic Book Artist 2*, no. 6 (November 2005).

160 "Never let it be said": Interview with Denis Kitchen.

161 "straight as they come": Ibid.

161 "Had the pants": Ibid.

163 "what may have been" and "publisher by default": Ibid.

164 "In 1964": Eisner, *Will Eisner's Shop Talk*, p. 286.

164 "In 1968": Ibid.

166 "Will Eisner wants to meet you": Interview with Denis Kitchen.

167 "I was impressed": Denis Kitchen, "How I Met Will Eisner, Businessman," *Comic Buyer's Guide*, November 29, 1996; reprinted under the title "A Kindred Spirit" in *Comic Book Artist 2*, no. 6 (November 2005).

167 "To a buttoned-down type": Will Eisner, as published in Dave Schreiner, *Kitchen Sink Press: The First 25 Years* (Northampton, MA: Kitchen Sink Press, 1994), p. 32.

168 "Will saw it": Interview with Denis Kitchen.

169 "To be successful": Interview with Stan Lee.

169 Comix history: Interviews with Denis Kitchen, Paul Buhle, and Jay Lynch. Robert C. Harvey, *The Art of the Comic Book*; Matthew J. Pustz, *Comic Book Culture: Fanboys and True Believers* (Jackson, MS: University Press of Mississippi, 1999).

169 "All the old meanings": Gary Groth, "The Straight Dope from R. Crumb," *Comics Journal #121*.

171 "That's *exactly*": Cooke, "Will Eisner: The Creative Life of a Master," *Comic Book Artist* 2, no. 6 (November 2005).

171 "Enclosed is a sampling": Letter from Denis Kitchen to Will Eisner, July 14, 1971.

171 "You are quite right": Letter from Will Eisner to Denis Kitchen, July 27, 1971.

172 "He liked it": Interview with Scott McCloud.

173 "Maurice is at work": Letter from Will Eisner to Denis Kitchen, July 27, 1971.

173 "Send me a draft": Denis Kitchen, "How I Met Will Eisner and Signed My First Contract," *Comic Book Artist* 2, no. 6 (November 2005). The rest of the dialogue from this exchange is from this source.

174 "I had this notion": Interview with Denis Kitchen.

CHAPTER TEN: RESURRECTION

175 Epigraph: R. C. Harvey, "An Affectionate Appreciation," *Comics Journal #267*.

176 "This is fun": Letter from Will Eisner to Denis Kitchen, November 2, 1972.

177 "*The Spirit* seemed": Cat Yronwode, "Will Eisner Interview (Part One)," *Comics Journal #46*.

177 "I'm gonna arrest": and "For what": Will Eisner, from the cover art in *Snarf #3*, Kitchen Sink Enterprises, 1973.

178 "Ebony White": Will Eisner, "The Spirit," *The Spirit #1* (*Underground Spirit*), Kitchen Sink Enterprises, 1972.

179 "When the feature began": Dave Schreiner, "Stage Settings: Killer ships, dogs, birds, and rays": *The Spirit #22* (CB).

181 "Stan wanted something": Interview with Roy Thomas.

182 "I really wanted": Interview with Stan Lee.

182 We had a long": Harvey, "An Affectionate Appreciation."

183 "I felt better": "Catch the Spirit," *Four Color*, January 1987.

183 "He thinks": Interview with Denis Kitchen.

183 "heartbroken": Ibid.

184 "It is apparent": Letter from Denis Kitchen to Will Eisner, October 16, 1973.

184   "We'll do something": Interview with Denis Kitchen.

185   "Just think": Yronwode, "Will Eisner Interview (Part Two)," *Comics Journal* #47.

186   "Jim had a different": Jon B. Cooke, "A Spirited Relationship," *Comic Book Artist* 2, no. 4 (1999).

186   "circus colors": Andelman, *Will Eisner: A Spirited Life*, p. 199.

186   "Over my dead body" and "The cover": Cooke, "A Spirited Relationship."

CHAPTER ELEVEN: *A CONTRACT WITH GOD*

187   Epigraph: Mike Barson, Ted White, and Mitch Berger. ". . . And I Threw In a Hat . . . ," *Heavy Metal*, November 1983.

187   "Are you kidding": Interview with Denis Kitchen.

187   "There is no doubt": Denis Kitchen, journal entry, July 5, 1974.

188   "If I devoted": Letter from Will Eisner to Denis Kitchen, December 9, 1976.

188   "I would expect": Letter from Denis Kitchen to Will Eisner, April 8, 1977.

189   "rather lightweight": Letter from Will Eisner to Denis Kitchen, March 16, 1977.

189   "It was a hodgepodge": Interview with Denis Kitchen.

190   "They had to": Interview with Ann Eisner.

191   "I said to him": Interview with Denis Kitchen.

192   "I always read": Interview with Batton Lash.

192   "In the catalogue": Maggie Thompson, "Will Eisner," *Golden Age of Comics #2.*

193   "I had been dealing": Will Eisner, *Comics and Sequential Art* (New York: Poorhouse Press, 1985), p. xii.

193   "paint-splattered" and "one of amusement": Interview with John Dilworth.

193   "He appeared to be": Ibid.

194   "sort of like": Interview with Batton Lash.

194   "He was interested": Ibid.

194   "One day, he said": Interview with David Mandel.

195   "He taught us": Interview with John Walker.

195   "If you screwed up": Ibid.

195   "In the process": Barson et al., ". . . And I Threw In a Hat . . ."

196   "If I don't": Ibid.

196   "The creation of this story": Eisner, *The Contract with God Trilogy*, p. xvi.

196   "My grief": Ibid.

198   "In the telling": Will Eisner, *A Contract with God* (New York: Baronet Press, 1978), unpaginated.

199   "Every one of the": Cat Yronwode, "Will Eisner Interview (Part Two)," *Comics Journal #47.*

200   "a combination of": Eisner, *The Contract with God Trilogy*, p. xviii.

200   "a story built around": Ibid., p. xvii.

200 "in a wine-soaked" and "With this book": Ibid., p. xvi.

200 "a Park Avenue publisher" and "No offense, Denis": Interview with Denis Kitchen.

200 "I looked at it": "Will Eisner," *The Onion (A.V. Club)*, September 27, 2000.

200 "It's a graphic novel": Jon B. Cooke, "Will Eisner: The Creative Life of a Master," *Comic Book Artist* 2, no. 6 (November 2005). All other direct quotations from this conversation are from this source.

201 "I thought I had invented": Will Eisner, "Keynote Address from the 2002 'Will Eisner Symposium.'"

201 "limited term," "graphic literature," and "graphic story": Andrew D. Arnold, "The Graphic Novel Silver Anniversary," *Time*, November 14, 2003.

202 "The drawings without": Harvey, *The Art of the Comic Book*, p. 106.

203 "Whatever the graphic novel": Ibid., p. 109.

203 "Graphic novels": Stephen Weiner, *Faster Than a Speeding Bullet: The Rise of the Graphic Novel* (New York: Nantier, Beall, Minoustchine, 2003), p. xi.

203 "Eisner is credited": Interview with Michael T. Gilbert.

204 "Eisner was one": N. C. Christopher Couch, "Will Eisner and the Graphic Novel: The Semiotics of Publishing," unpublished essay.

205 "When Eisner turned": Ibid.

205 "a near masterpiece": Dennis O'Neil, "Winners & Losers: Harsh Memories from Will Eisner," *Comics Journal #46*.

205 "What did you do": R. C. Harvey, "Will Eisner on the Future of Comics," *Comic Book Artist* 2, no. 6 (November 2005). All direct quotations in this passage are from this source.

CHAPTER TWELVE: OUTER SPACE, THE CITY—NO LIMITS

207 Epigraph: Maggie Thompson, "Will Eisner," *Golden Age of Comics #2*.

208 I'm gonna let it happen": Cat Yronwode, "Will Eisner Interview (Part Two)," *Comics Journal #47*.

208 "There has been": Letter from Denis Kitchen to Will Eisner, May 11, 1979.

208 "In view of information": Letter from Will Eisner to Denis Kitchen, May 16, 1979.

208 "I knew instinctively": Interview with Denis Kitchen.

209 Dave Schreiner: Interviews with Denis Kitchen, Lesleigh Luttrell, N. C. Christopher Couch.

209 "You get to know": Schreiner, *Kitchen Sink Press*, p. 6.

210 "equal parts" and "It gave me": Ibid.

211 "When I was reprinting": Interview with Denis Kitchen.

211 "He often referred": Interview with James Vance.

212 He did it": Interview with Denis Kitchen.

212 "Don't tell me": Ibid.

212 "Dave would say": Ibid.

213 "Just call me": Paul E. Fitzgerald, "Every Picture Tells a Story," *Washington Post*, June 3, 2004.

214 "worm's-eye view": Mike Barson, Ted White, and Mitch Berger. ". . . And I Threw In a Hat . . . ," *Heavy Metal*, November 1983.

214 "We're used to seeing": Cat Yronwode and Maggie Thompson, "Will Eisner, Part II," *Golden Age of Comics #2* (1982).

214 "Once you get": Dave Schreiner, "Stage Settings: Some 'What If . . .' stories," *The Spirit #28*.

215 "Will Eisner never threw": Yronwode and Thompson, "Will Eisner, Part II."

217 "He was an amazing": Interview with Tom Heitjes.

217 "What was interesting": Ibid.

217 "I saw him": Interview with Robert Pizzo.

218 "We were surprised": Ibid.

218 "I have a house": Interview with Ann Eisner. All other citations in this passage are from this source.

218 "He'd say": Interview with John Walker.

219 "I'm not using": Ibid. All other quotations in this passage are from this source.

220 "It's the bear": Ibid. All other quotations in this passage are from this source.

220 "stingy boss": Jules Feiffer, introduction to Eisner *The Art of Will Eisner*, p. 6.

220 "Oh, that's true": Interview with Denis Kitchen.

220 "His brother must have": Ibid.

221 "Despite being newly wed": Interview with Eliot Gordon.

221 "I'm still offended": Interview with Robert Weil.

221 "I wouldn't say": Interview with John Walker.

CHAPTER THIRTEEN: *A LIFE FORCE*

223 Epigraph: Eisner and Miller, *Eisner/Miller*, p. 88.

223 "sands of the hourglass": Interview with John Walker.

223 "The debate over": Eisner, *The Contract with God Trilogy*, p. xviii.

224 "You, being only": Will Eisner, *A Life Force* (Princeton, WI: Kitchen Sink Press, 1988), pp. 17–18.

224 "When Jacob talked": Dave Schreiner, "Notes from the Perimeter," *Will Eisner's Quarterly #6*.

227 "We have two": Ibid.

227 "Robert told me": Interview with Denis Kitchen.

227 "It's really an uplifting": Postcard from R. Crumb to Denis Kitchen, undated (postmarked August 4, 1988), as reprinted in Schreiner, *Kitchen Sink Press*, p. 86.

227 "Look at those gams": Interview with Denis Kitchen.

227 "He knew that Crumb": Ibid.

228 *Signal from Space*: Eisner would use this title only once, for the color version of the book. He was never satisfied with the color version, and after signing on with DC, he reprinted it in black and white, restoring its original *Life on Another Planet* title.

229 "Eisner's work": Untitled press release, *Ohio State University News*, December 6, 1984.

229 "After all": Will Eisner, "A Sunset in Sunshine City," *Will Eisner Reader* (Princeton, WI: Kitchen Sink Press, 1991), unpaginated.

230 "That was his": Interview with Ann Eisner.

230 "There was a silence": Interview with Denis Kitchen.

230 "Will, that's not": Ibid.

230 "He wanted her opinion": Ibid.

231 "one more year": Interview with Ann Eisner.

231 "To me, they were": Interview with Denis Kitchen.

231 "It was so funny": Interview with Jackie Estrada.

231 "carbon monoxide fix": Interview with Ann Eisner.

232 "Dave Schreiner and I": Interview with Denis Kitchen.

232 "At the end": Barry Wolborsky, "An Interview with Will Eisner," *Gray Haven,* n.d., online.

233 "We were so frustrated": Interview with Denis Kitchen. Kitchen eventually wrote a lengthy annotative appendix to *The Dreamer*, providing the real names and stories behind Eisner's novella, for *Life, in Pictures*, the posthumously published gathering of Eisner's autobiographical works.

234 "I couldn't find": Jon B. Cooke, "Will Eisner: The Creative Life of a Master," *Comic Book Artist* 2, no. 6 (November 2005).

235 "While each of": Eisner, *Comics and Sequential Art*, p. xi. Eisner updated this book from the time of its publication until, finally, a posthumous edition was issued by W. W. Norton in 2008. The Norton edition was used for this book.

235 "I said": Interview with Dennis O'Neil.

237 "*The Spirit* was": Andrew D. Arnold, "The Graphic Novel Silver Anniversary," *Time*, November 14, 2003.

237 "This represents an example": Eisner, *Comics and Sequential Art*, p. 114.

237 "That was his art": Interview with Dennis O'Neil.

238 "a turning point" and "From then on": Weiner, *Faster Than a Speeding Bullet*, p. xi.

239 "When I began": "V.A. Club: Art Spiegelman," *The Onion*, December 29, 2004.

240 "The superhero largely": Arie Kaplan, "Looking Back," *Comics Journal #267*.

241 "I wanted to write": Interview with Neil Gaiman.

242 "I became obsessed": Henrik Andreassen, "Timeless Insights: An Interview

with Will Eisner," *Seriejournalen #19* (spring 1995); reprinted in *Comic-Con International*, 2005.

243   "thought provoking" and "You've stressed": Letter from Dave Schreiner to Will Eisner, November 20, 1986.

243   "somehow absorb[s] the radiation": Will Eisner, introduction to *The Building* (Princeton, WI: Kitchen Sink Press), p. 4.

244   Eisner/Groth feud: Gary Groth, "Will Eisner: Chairman of the Board," *Comics Journal #267*; interviews with Ann Eisner and Denis Kitchen.

244   "frivolous and tepid": Groth, "Chairman of the Board."

244   "The review was harsh": Ibid.

CHAPTER FOURTEEN: WINNERS AND LOSERS

246   Epigraph: Mike Jozic, "Will Eisner: The Godfather of Comics," *Meanwhile* (online), interview conducted March 7, 2000.

246   "it was also": Denis Kitchen, "Origins of the Comic Book Legal Defense Fund," unpublished manuscript.

248   "I got up": Interview with Neal Adams. All other citations in this passage are from this source.

248   Siegel and Shuster: Jones, *Men of Tomorrow*, pp. 319–323; *The Comic Book Makers*, pp. 108–109; interviews with Neal Adams and Jerry Robinson.

250   "The first *Superman* movie": Interview with Jerry Robinson. All other direct quotations in this passage are from this source.

252   "This matter has gone": Will Eisner, "An Open Letter to Marvel Comics," *Comics Journal #110*.

252   Jack Kirby's legal struggles: Ro, *Tales to Astonish*, pp. 217–241; interview with Mark Evanier.

253   "A whole new generation": Eisner, "Open Letter to Marvel."

254   "I asked him": Tom Heintjes, "Stage Settings: The beginning of the end," *The Spirit #84* (CB).

255   "I will be interested": Dana Jennings, "Will Eisner in France," *Comics Journal #89*.

256   "It made my toes curl": Interview with Denis Kitchen.

256   "They have about": Letter from Will Eisner to Denis Kitchen, June 19, 1986.

256   *Spirit* movie: In 2008, a theatrical motion picture directed by Frank Miller was released. Although stylish, visually interesting, and filled with homages to Eisner and inside jokes about comics history, it was an unqualified critical and box office disaster. The difficulties in bringing the Spirit to the big screen, Eisner hinted in an interview with Tom Heintjes seventeen years earlier, might have stemmed more from the character's unique makeup than from others' efforts to bring him to the screen: "There's always been a great disparity between what I felt made *The Spirit* work and what other people thought,

with a couple of exceptions like Jules Feiffer, who was able to understand my approach almost intuitively . . . We've talked about many recent stories where the writers—and the artists, too—were not able to get inside the head of the characters and write stories that seemed plausible, given the characters' personalities. That same disparity also existed when people outside comics tried to handle *The Spirit*" (Heintjes, "The Beginning of the End").

256   Miller, in an interview for this book, though clearly in disagreement with the movie's harshest critics about *The Spirit*'s merits, seemed to agree with Eisner that the many complexities of the Spirit's character, as well as Eisner's personal investment in the character, made the Spirit difficult to translate to the screen. "He lived through *The Spirit* when he did it," Miller said. "One of the challenges of adapting his work was trying to capture all those different aspects, which is kind of like trying to catch a church of flying glass, the stained glass windows, because there was so much dimension to it."

257   "At first": Interview with Ann Eisner.

257   "I felt that": Ibid.

258   "Dave and Will": Interview with Jackie Estrada.

258   "It is to me": Eisner, *Will Eisner's Shop Talk*, p. 284.

258   "We mail out": Interview with Jackie Estrada.

260   "We've got to get": Ibid.

260   "You know, you get": Sarah Boxer, "Will Eisner, a Pioneer of Comic Books, Dies at 87," *New York Times*, January 5, 2005.

260   "the most influential": Will Eisner, introduction to *City People Notebook* (Princeton, WI: Kitchen Sink Press, 1989), p. 4.

261   "While it is true": Letter from Will Eisner to Dave Schreiner, June 29, 1988.

CHAPTER FIFTEEN: THE HEART OF THE MATTER

262   Epigraph: "AV Club: Will Eisner," *The Onion*, September 27, 2000.

262   "standing naked": Shawna Ervin-Gore, "Will Eisner," *Darkhorse News*, n.d., online.

262   "When I was younger": Ibid.

263   "To write about": Henrik Andreassen, "Timeless Insights: An Interview with Will Eisner," *Seriejournalen #19* (spring 1995); reprinted in *Comic-Con International*, 2005.

263   "When I showed": Ervin-Gore, "Will Eisner."

264   "I think it's": Letter from Dave Schreiner to Will Eisner, July 19, 1989.

264   "on the whole": Ibid.

264   "Would you consider": Ibid.

265   "Ambiguity and ambivalence": Letter from Dave Schreiner to Will Eisner, August 1, 1989.

265   "Enclosed": Letter from Will Eisner to Dave Schreiner, September 4, 1990.

265   "In 1942": Letter from Dave Schreiner to Will Eisner, September 10, 1990.

265   "My major misgiving": Ibid.

265   "This is your strongest": Ibid.

266   "My gratitude": Eisner, *To the Heart of the Storm*, p. 2.

266   "schmaltzy," "melodramatic," and "a vivid": "To the Heart of the Storm," *Publishers Weekly*, March 22, 1991.

266   "This is an outstanding": Don Thompson, "Graphic-Album Autobiography Catches Era's Spirit," *Comics Buyer's Guide*, March 29, 1991.

267   "is a major skill": Will Eisner, *Invisible People* (Princeton, WI: Kitchen Sink Press, 1993), p. 10.

267   "I grew up": Ibid., p. 9.

268   "In relating": Ibid., p. 85.

268   "I expect I'll be": Letter from Will Eisner to Dave Schreiner, November 5, 1991.

268   "You have to let": Letter from Dave Schreiner to Will Eisner, January 31, 1992.

268   "Still flailing": Letter from Will Eisner to Dave Schreiner, December 26, 1991.

271   "I developed": "AV Club: Will Eisner."

271   "After I finish": Tom Heintjes, "Interview with Will Eisner," *HA* (*Hogan's Alley*). n.d.

272   "mausoleum": Christopher Irving, "A Whole Lotta Spirit," *Richmond Comix* (online), n.d.

273   "to be sure": Ibid.

273   "It was a little": Tom Heintjes, "Interview with Will Eisner."

273   "I did not": Interview with Neil Gaiman.

274   "He was determined": Ibid.

274   "I had this": Ibid.

275   "I'm coming to": R. C. Harvey, "Will Eisner on the Future of Comics," *Comic Book Artist* 2, no. 6 (November 2005).

276   "It was pure, unadulterated": Interview with Frank Miller.

276   "I didn't know": Interview with Denis Kitchen.

277   "As you know": Letter from Will Eisner to Dave Schreiner, May 12, 1999.

277   "I see no": Letter from Will Eisner to Dave Schreiner, August 26, 1999.

279   "The stories in this work": Will Eisner, *Minor Miracles* (New York: DC Comics, 2000), p. 1.

279   "These orders guide": Interview with Diana Schutz.

280   "It's an innovation": Ervin-Gore, "Will Eisner."

280   "It only works": Harvey, "Will Eisner on the Future of Comics."

280   "I wanted to keep": Ervin-Gore, "Will Eisner."

282   "'A Purple Heart for George'": Eisner, *Last Day in Vietnam*, p. 1.

283   Eisner and Miller: Interviews with Frank Miller, Charles Brownstein, Diana Schutz, and Mike Richardson.

283 "It didn't go": Interview with Mike Richardson.

283 "It was mild": Interview with Frank Miller.

284 "I've been concerned": Letter from Will Eisner to Dave Schreiner, June 30, 1998.

284 "I know this will lead": Letter from Dave Schreiner to Will Eisner, July 18, 1998.

285 "strong book": Letter from Dave Schreiner to Will Eisner, October 13, 2000.

286 "crude and noisy" and "intelligent, resourceful": Will Eisner, *The Name of the Game* (New York: DC Comics, 2001), p. 4.

286 "There were bad marriages": Ibid, p. 2.

287 "We'll pretend": Ibid., p. 165.

287 "You show": Letter from Dave Schreiner to Will Eisner, October 13, 2000.

287 "If Aron cheats": Ibid.

CHAPTER SIXTEEN: POLEMICS

289 Epigraph: David Hajdu, "Good Will," *Comic Book Artist* 2, no. 6 (November 2005).

289 "proudest possessions": Letter from Michael Chabon to Will Eisner, October 19, 1995.

290 "I want to understand": Ibid.

290 "I interviewed": Michael Chabon, from "Paying Homage," *Comic Book Artist* 2, no. 6 (November 2005).

290 "I gave him": Scott Tobias, "AV Club: Michael Chabon," *The Onion*, November 22, 2000.

292 "Everybody needs validation": Interview with Jules Feiffer.

292 "Writing with images": Will Eisner, *Dropsie Avenue: The Neighborhood* (Northampton, MA: Kitchen Sink Press, 1995), unpaginated.

293 "Neighborhoods have life spans": Eisner, *Dropsie Avenue*.

293 "We're in a visual": "Will Eisner," *The Onion* (*A.V. Club*), September 27, 2000.

295 "Upon examining": Will Eisner, foreword to *Fagin the Jew* (New York: Doubleday, 2003), p. 3.

295 "Actually I am not": Letter from Will Eisner to Dave Schreiner, March 12, 2002.

296 "'Tarry a bit'": Eisner, *Fagin the Jew*, p. 5.

296 "A Jew is not": Ibid., p. 114.

297 "This book was intended": "The Grand Daddy of the Graphic Novel—A Talk with Will Eisner," *Bookselling This Week*, October 22, 2003.

297 "One man": Paul E. Fitzgerald, "Every Picture Tells a Story," *Washington Post*, June 3, 2004.

299 "He was immediately": Interview with Jon B. Cooke.

299 "He was incredibly gracious": Interview with Andrew Cooke.

300 "This is an industry": Interview with Jon B. Cooke.

300 "I was amazed": Steven Lee Beeber, "Wrath of a Pulp Patriarch: Will Eisner Draws a Rebuttal to the Notorious 'Protocols,'" *New York Times*, February 23, 2004.

302 "I remember being angry": Will Eisner, preface to *The Plot* (New York: W. W. Norton, 2005), p. 1.

303 "Am I trespassing": David Hajdu, "Good Will."

304 "I submitted his book's": Interview with Judith Hansen.

304 "We worked": Interview with Robert Weil.

305 "I need your opinion": Letter from Will Eisner to Dave Schreiner, August 21, 2008.

306 "Will's quest": Interview with Paul Levitz.

308 "We discussed": Interview with Robert Weil.

308 "He was tired": Ibid.

308 "Will be sending": E-mail from Robert Weil to Denis Kitchen, January 3, 2005.

308 "It was about": Interview with Ann Eisner.

309 "His seriousness": Sarah Boxer, "Will Eisner, a Pioneer of Comic Books, Dies at 87," *New York Times*, January 5, 2005.

309 "His final book": Andrew D. Arnold, "A 'Plot' to Change the World," *Time*, May 14, 2005.

310 "It is a testament": Jonathan Dorfman, "Poison, Penned," *Boston Globe*, June 26, 2005.

310 "an unprecedented, pioneering": R. C. Harvey, "The Plot Uncovered," *Comic Book Artist* 2, no. 6 (November 2005).

310 "In this whole process": Will Eisner, *Expressive Anatomy for Comics and Narrative* (New York: W. W. Norton, 2008), p. xi.

311 "I wish I had": Interview with Peter Poplaski.

312 "I never felt": Interview with Neil Gaiman.

312 "The wonder of Eisner": Interview with Frank Miller.

BIBLIOGRAPHY

BOOKS

Andelman, Bob. *Will Eisner: A Spirited Life*. Milwaukie, OR: M Press, 2005.

Beaty, Bart. *Fredric Wertham and the Critique of Mass Culture*. Jackson, MS: University Press of Mississippi, 2005.

Bell, Blake. *"I Have to Live with This Guy."* Raleigh, NC: TwoMorrows Publishing, 2002.

Buhle, Paul. *Comics in Wisconsin*. Madison, WI: Borderland Books, 2009.

Cabarga, Leslie. *The Fleischer Story*. New York: Da Capo Press, 1976; updated 1988.

Cardy, Nick, with John Coates. *The Art of Nick Cardy*. Vanguard Productions, 2001.

Cassell, Dewey, Aaron Sultan, and Mike Gartland, eds. *The Art of George Tuska*. Raleigh, NC: TwoMorrows Publishing, 2005.

Chabon, Michael. *The Amazing Adventures of Kavalier & Clay*. New York: Random House, 2000.

Couch, N. C. Christopher, and Stephen Weiner. *The Will Eisner Companion*. New York: DC Comics, 2004.

Diehl, Digby. *Tales from the Crypt*. New York: St. Martin's Press, 1996.

Eisner, Will. *The Art of Will Eisner*. Edited by Cat Yronwode (Princeton, WI: Kitchen Sink Press, 1982).

———. *Bringing Up Your Parents*. New York: Scholastic, 1980.

———. *The Building*. Princeton, WI: Kitchen Sink Press, 1986.

———. *The Christmas Spirit*. Northampton, MA: Kitchen Sink Press, 1994.

———. *City People Notebook*. Princeton, WI: Kitchen Sink Press, 1989.

———. *Comics and Sequential Art*. Tamarac, FL: Poorhouse Press, 1985.

———. *A Contract with God*. New York: Baronet Press, 1978.

———. *The Contract with God Trilogy*. New York: W. W. Norton, 2006.

———. *Dating and Hanging Out*. With Wade Hampton and Keith Diazun. New York: Scholastic Books, 1986.

———. *The Dreamer*. Princeton, WI: Kitchen Sink Press, 1986; reprinted by DC Comics, New York, 2000.

———. *Dropsie Avenue: The Neighborhood*. Princeton, WI: Kitchen Sink Press, 1995.

———. *Edge of Genius*. New York: Pure Imagination Publishing, 2007.

———. *Expressive Anatomy for Comics and Narrative*. New York: W. W. Norton, 2008.

———. *Fagin the Jew*. New York: Doubleday, 2003.

———. *A Family Matter*. Northampton, MA: Kitchen Sink Press, 1998.

———. *Gleeful Guide to Communicating with Plants to Help Them Grow*. New York: Poorhouse Press, 1974.

———. *Gleeful Guide to Living with Astrology*. With Ivan Klapper. New York: Poorhouse Press, 1974.

———. *Gleeful Guide to Occult Cookery*. With Ivan Klapper. New York: Poorhouse Press, 1974.

———. *Graphic Storytelling and Visual Narrative*. Tamarac, FL: Poorhouse Press, 1996; reprinted in revised, updated edition by W. W. Norton (New York), 2008.

———. *Hawks of the Seas*. Princeton, WI: Kitchen Sink Press, 1986.

———. *How to Avoid Death & Taxes . . . and Live Forever*. New York: Poorhouse Press, 1975.

———. *Incredible Facts, Amazing Statistics, Monumental Trivia*. Edited by Ivan Klapper. Research by Jason Hanson. New York: Poorhouse Press, 1974.

———. *Invisible People*. Princeton, WI: Kitchen Sink Press, 1993.

———. *Last Day in Vietnam*. Milwaukie, OR: Dark Horse Comics, 2000.

———. *The Last Knight: An Introduction to Don Quixote by Miguel de Cervantes*. New York: Nantier, Beall, Minoustchine, 2000.

———. *A Life Force*. Princeton, WI: Kitchen Sink Press, 1988.

———. *Life, in Pictures*. New York: W. W. Norton, 2007.

———. *Minor Miracles*. New York: DC Comics, 2000.

———. *Moby Dick: By Herman Melville, Retold by Will Eisner*. New York: Nantier, Beall, Minoustchine, 1998.

———. *The Name of the Game*. New York: DC Comics, 2001.

———. *New York: The Big City*. Princeton, WI: Kitchen Sink Press, 1986.

———. *101 Outer Space Jokes*. New York: Baronet, 1979.

———. *The Outer Space Spirit*. With Jules Feiffer and Wallace Wood. Princeton, WI: Kitchen Sink Press, 1983.

———. *The Plot*. New York: W. W. Norton, 2005.

———. *The Princess and the Frog by the Grimm Brothers, Retold by Will Eisner*. New York: Nantier, Beall, Minoustchine, 1999.

———. *Robert's Rules of Order*. New York: Bantam Books, 1986.

———. *Signal from Space*. Princeton, WI: Kitchen Sink Press, 1983.

———. *The Spirit Archives*. New York: DC Comics, 2001.

———. *The Spirit Casebook*. Princeton, WI: Kitchen Sink Press, 1990.

———. *Spirit Jam*. Northampton, MA: Kitchen Sink Press, 1998.

———. *Star Jaws*. With Barry Caldwell and Keith Diazun. New York: Baronet, 1978.

———. *Sundiata: A Legend of Africa, Retold by Will Eisner*. New York: Nantier, Beall, Mincustchine, 2003.

———. *To the Heart of the Storm*. Princeton, WI: Kitchen Sink Press, 1991.

———. *Will Eisner Color Treasury*. With Cat Yronwode. Princeton, WI: Kitchen Sink Press, 1981.

———. *Will Eisner Reader*. Princeton, WI: Kitchen Sink Press, 1991.

———. *Will Eisner Sketchbook*. Northampton, MA: Kitchen Sink Press, 1995.

———. *Will Eisner's Shop Talk*. Milwaukie, OR: Dark Horse Comics, 2001.

———. *Will Eisner's Spirit Casebook of True Haunted Houses and Ghosts*. New York: Tempo, 1976.

Evanier, Mark. *Kirby: King of Comics*. New York: Abrams, 2008.

Eisner, Will, and Frank Miller. Interview conducted by Charles Brownstein. *Eisner/Miller*. Milwaukie, OR: Dark Horse Books, 2005.

Feiffer, Jules. *Backing into Forward*. New York: Doubleday, 2010.

———. *The Great Comic Book Heroes*. New York: Dial Press, 1965; updated 1977.

Fingeroth, Danny. *Disguised as Clark Kent: Jews, Comics, and the Creation of the Superhero*. New York: Continuum, 2007.

Fitzgerald, Paul E. *Will Eisner and PS Magazine*. Fincastle, VA: Fitzworld.US, 2009.

Goulart, Ron. *Ron Goulart's Great History of Comic Books*. Chicago: Contemporary Books, 1986.

———. *The Great Comic Book Artists*. New York: St. Martin's Press, 1986.

———. *The Great Comic Book Artists, Volume 2*. New York: St. Martin's Press, 1989.

Greenberger, Robert. *The Library of Graphic Novelists: Will Eisner*. New York: Rosen Publishing Group, 2005.

Groth, Gary, and Robert Fiore, eds. *The New Comics*. New York: Berkley Books, 1988.

Hajdu, David. *The Ten-Cent Plague: The Great Comic-Book Scare and How It Changed America*. New York: Farrar, Straus, & Giroux, 2008.

Harvey, Robert C. *The Art of the Comic Book: An Aesthetic History*. Jackson, MS: University Press of Mississippi, 1996.

Heer, Jeet, and Kent Worcester, eds. *Arguing Comics: Literary Masters on a Popular Medium*. Jackson, MS: University Press of Mississippi, 2004.

Inge, M. Thomas. *Comics as Culture*. Jackson: MS: University Press of Mississippi, 1990.

Jacobs, Frank. *The Mad World of William M. Gaines* Secaucus, NJ: Lyle Stuart, 1972.

Jones, Gerard. *Men of Tomorrow: Geeks, Gangsters, and the Birth of the Comic Book*. New York: Basic Books, 2004.

Kitchen, Denis. *The Oddly Compelling Art of Denis Kitchen*. Milwaukie, OR: Dark Horse Comics, 2010.

Lupoff, Dick, and Don Thompson, eds. *All in Color for a Dime*. New York: Ace Books, 1970.

———. *The Comic-Book Book*. New Rochelle, NY: Arlington House, 1973.

McCloud, Scott. *Making Comics*. New York: HarperCollins, 2006.

———. *Understanding Comics*. New York: Paradox Press, 2000.

Nyberg, Amy Kiste. *Seal of Approval: The History of the Comics Code*. Jackson, MS: University Press of Mississippi, 1998.

O'Sullivan, Judith. *The Great American Comic Strip*. Boston: Bulfinch Press, 1990.

Pustz, Matthew J. *Comic Book Culture: Fanboys and True Believers*. Jackson, MS: University Press of Mississippi, 1999.

Ro, Ronin. *Tales to Astonish: Jack Kirby, Stan Lee, and the American Comic Book Revolution*. New York: Bloomsbury, 2004.

Robbins, Trina. *The Great Women Cartoonists*. New York: Watson-Guptill Publications, 2001.

Rosenkranz, Patrick. *Rebel Visions: The Underground Comix Revolution 1963–1975*. Seattle, WA: Fantagraphics Books, 2002.

Schreiner, Dave. *Kitchen Sink Press: The First 25 Years*. Northampton, MA: Kitchen Sink Press, 1994.

Simon, Joe, with Jim Simon. *The Comic Book Makers*. Lebanon, NJ: Vanguard Productions (rev. ed.), 2003.

Steranko, James. *The Steranko History of Comics*, vol. 2. Reading, PA: Supergraphics, 1972.

Talon, Durwin S. *Panel Discussions*. Raleigh, NC: TwoMorrows Publishing, 2003.

Waugh, Coulton. *The Comics*. New York: Macmillan, 1947; reprinted by University Press of Mississippi.

Weiner, Stephen. *Faster Than a Speeding Bullet: The Rise of the Graphic Novel*. New York: Nantier, Beall, Minoustchine, 2003.

Wertham, Fredric. *Seduction of the Innocent*. New York: Rinehart, 1954.

Witek, Joseph. *Comic Books as History: The Narrative Art of Jack Jackson, Art Spiegelman, and Harvey Pekar*. Jackson, MS: University Press of Mississippi, 1989.

FILM, VIDEO, AND DVD

Stan Lee Presents: The Comic Book Greats: Will Eisner, vol. 11. Livonia, WI: Stabur Home Video, 1992.

Will Eisner: Portrait of a Sequential Artist. Produced and directed by Andrew D. Cooke and Jon B. Cooke. Montilla Pictures, *Comic Book Artist*, and Schackman Films, 2007.

Will Eisner: Profession: Cartoonist. Produced and directed by Marisa Furtado de Oliveira and Paulo Serran. Scriptorium, 1999.

ACKNOWLEDGMENTS

It seems to me that, as a biographer, the easiest thing on earth to do is to thank someone for his or her assistance; the most difficult is to adequately express that gratitude. We depend on so many people to give us information, verify facts, supply connections, offer advice and guidance, provide valuable research materials, and, in general, become collaborators in the biography. This was especially true with this book. Although I was aware of Will Eisner's work for decades prior to the beginning of my research, I never met the man and, sadly, I would never have the opportunity to do so.

First, I'd like to thank Ann Eisner for sharing her memories of her life with her husband. Some of my questions were difficult for me to ask, and for her to answer, and I am certain that there will be analysis in this book that she will not agree with; but it's my hope that at the very least, she will find it as fair and honest as she is. In the dedications and acknowledgments of his books, Eisner always made a point of mentioning her importance—and for good reason.

Carl Gropper, Eisner's nephew, a true Will Eisner believer and guardian of the Will Eisner Studio, was invaluable in the writing of this book, not only for the information and photographs he supplied, but also for his friendship. Meeting Carl and his wife, Nancy, was one of the highlights in the researching and writing of this book, and I will always be grateful for the day they spent with me, driving me around to the Will Eisner sites in White Plains and New York City and especially for taking me to visit Eisner's grave.

Denis Kitchen, Eisner's friend, publisher, and agent, provided me with a wealth of information about Eisner and his work, including essential correspondence that added texture to this book and much of the artwork you see herein. Denis and I had crossed paths, although briefly, many years prior to the writing of this book, when we were both young and, as Eisner would put it, dreamers. It was a pleasure reconnecting on this project. I also appreciate the hospitality of Denis's wife, Stacey, for her help with photographs and her hospitality during my stay in the Kitchens' Massachusetts home.

I am pleased and proud to call Judy Hansen my friend. Her work in marketing Will Eisner's literary properties has been nothing shy of re-markable, and her candid observations on the business side of placing and publishing Eisner's work have been extremely valuable to this book. She deserves more credit than she will ever receive for helping shape the later portion of his career and, on a grander scale, helping shape the direction of comics. Thanks also to her husband, Peter Spielmann, who was ini-tially responsible for connecting me with some of the others mentioned in these acknowledgments.

I owe an enormous debt of gratitude to the comic book artists, writers, editors, publishers, filmmakers, historians, and friends and relatives of Will Eisner for their assistance: Neal Adams, Jim Amash, Lee Ames, Mur-phy Anderson, John Benson, Charles Brownstein, Paul Buhle, Nick Cardy, Andrew Cooke, Jon B. Cooke, N. C. Christopher Couch, John Dilworth, Lila Eisner, Jackie Estrada, Mark Evanier, Jules Feiffer, Paul E. Fitzgerald, Bob Fujitani, Neil Gaiman, Michael T. Gilbert, Kenneth Ginniger, Eliot Gordon, Jerry Grandenetti, Allan Gropper, Irwin Hasen, Tom Heintjes, Robert C. Horvey, Carmine Infantino, M. Thomas Inge, Al Jaffee, Charlie Kochman, Joe Kubert, Adele Kurtzman, Batton Lash, Stan Lee, Paul Levitz, Jay Lynch, David Mandel, Fran Matera, Scott Mc-Cloud, Frank Miller, Dennis O'Neil, Robert Pizzo, Peter Poplaski, Ken Quattro, Mike Richardson, Jerry Robinson, Diana Schutz, Roy Thomas, Maggie Thompson, Michael Uslan, Jim Vance, John Walker, Bob Weil, and Stephen Weiner. Thanks also to those who assisted me in lining up interviews and for other logistical help: Spencer Newlin-Cushing, Amy Gall, Joanna Gallardo, Lorraine Garland, and David Hyde.

Danny Fingeroth and David Hajdu, authors of outstanding books on comics, went far beyond the call of duty in helping me with this book. I feel blessed to have been able to spend a few hours with them, talking about comics in general and Eisner in particular, and both were extremely generous in assisting me in connecting with other important people on this list.

I met Dave Schreiner on several occasions in what now seems like a former life, at a time when he was editing a weekly alternative newspaper in Milwaukee and I was publishing my first work in the paper; but I never had the opportunity to talk to him after he began his work as Eisner's editor. Eisner trusted Schreiner implicitly, and it would have been good to hear Schreiner talk about his experiences. I had to settle for Dave's "Stage Settings" column in *The Spirit* comic book, in which Eisner discussed each of his postwar *Spirit* entries—a column that was later picked up and beautifully produced by Tom Heintjes. Even though we didn't talk, I owe Schreiner a lot, as I do his widow, Lesleigh Luttrell, who listened to my nonstop talking and, when I came up for air, provided me with valuable information about her husband and the photo of Dave and Will in this book.

Lucy Caswell oversees the Eisner collection at Ohio State University, and she and her staff were very helpful in answering my questions about Eisner and the collection and in supplying me with many of the photos in this book.

My most sincere appreciation to my agent, David Black, his assistant, Antonella Iannarino, and the staff at the David Black Literary Agency. David, I hope this book finds a place among all those impressive books in your office. It would certainly be an honor.

Margaret Maloney, my editor on this book, had worked on previously published books by Will Eisner, and her enthusiasm for Eisner and this biography was absolutely infectious. Working with her was a pleasure. Additional thanks to Kathy Belden and the staff of Bloomsbury.

Thanks to friends and family, who offered support, encouragement, or a good ear when needed: Al and Diane Schumacher, Susan Schumacher, Ken and Karen Ade, the folks at Franks Diner (especially past, present, and honorary "Backroom Boys"): I'm honored to know Mike Gordon, who was extremely helpful in the making of this book.

Finally, I'd like to thank my children—Adam, Emily Joy, and Jack Henry—for teaching me what really counts in life. It really *is* a chocolate-coated habanero pepper.

—Michael Schumacher
March 1, 2010

INDEX

A NOTE ON THE AUTHOR

Michael Schumacher is the author of ten books, including *Dharma Lion*, *Crossroads*, *There but for Fortune*, *Mighty Fitz*, and, most recently, *The Wreck of the* Carl D. He lives in Wisconsin.